Operation Avalanche

The Salerno Landings, 1943

Also by
DES HICKEY and GUS SMITH:

Miracle
Seven Days to Disaster

OPERATION AVALANCHE

The Salerno Landings, 1943

Des Hickey and Gus Smith

HEINEMANN: LONDON

William Heinemann Ltd
10 Upper Grosvenor Street, London W1X 9PA
LONDON MELBOURNE TORONTO
JOHANNESBURG AUCKLAND

First published 1983

ISBN 434 39180 8

Photoset by Rowland Phototypesetting Ltd
Bury St Edmunds, Suffolk
Printed in Great Britain by
St Edmundsbury Press
Bury St Edmunds, Suffolk

Contents

ILLUSTRATIONS

(Unless otherwise stated, all photographs in this book are reproduced by permission of the trustees of the copyright holders, the trustees of the Imperial War Museum, London S.E.1.)

Surprise, violence, and speed are the essence of all amphibious landings.

Winston Churchill,
The Second World War, Vol. 5

The whole operation demonstrated, once again, the perils of amphibious warfare and the fact that, whatever the intelligence estimates said, the *Wehrmacht* was still the most efficient, mobile and battleworthy army in the world.

Anthony Cave Brown,
Bodyguard of Lies

Quod coelum, Vala, Salerni; quorum hominum regio, et qualis via? – What is the weather like at Salerno and what sort of people shall I meet there?

Horace,
Epistles, 20 B.C.

Salerno, September 1943: The Command Structure

ALLIED FORCES ('*OPERATION AVALANCHE*')
Commander in Chief: General Dwight D. Eisenhower
Deputy Commander in Chief: General Sir Harold R. L. G. Alexander
Service Commanders: Admiral of the Fleet Sir Andrew B. Cunningham/Air Chief Marshal Sir Arthur Tedder

Ground Support: Lieut. General Mark W. Clark, *US Fifth Army* – divided into two corps: *US Sixth Corps:* Major General Ernest J. Dawley (36th and 45th Infantry Divisions with the 3rd and 34th in reserve); *British Tenth Corps:* Lieut. General Sir Richard M. McCreery (46th and 56th Infantry Divisions)

Naval Support: Vice-Admiral H. Kent Hewitt, overlord of *Western Naval Task Force* (mainly British) commanded by Commodore G. N. Oliver, and *Southern Attack Force* (mainly American) commanded by Rear-Admiral John L. Hall

Air Support: Defence of Salerno beachhead controlled by Brigadier General Edward J. House; Seafires of the Fleet Air Arm, operating from Royal Navy Carriers, under command of Rear-Admiral Sir Philip Vian

AMERICAN
36th (Texas) Division: Major General Fred L. Walker
36th Cavalry Recce Regt
132 Field Artillery Bn
158 Field Artillery Bn
189 Field Artillery Bn
323 Glider Regt
191 Med. Tank Bn
141 Regimental Combat Team

142 Regimental Combat Team
143 Regimental Combat Team
157 Regimental Combat Team
82nd Airborne Division: Major General Matthew B. Ridgway
504th Parachute Regiment: Lieut. Colonel Reuben H. Tucker
505th Parachute Regiment: Colonel James M. Gavin
509th Parachute Regiment: Lieut. Colonel Doyle Yardley
45th Reserve Division: Major General Troy Middleton
3rd Reserve Division: General Lucien Truscott
34th Reserve Division: General Charles 'Doc' Ryder
US Rangers (operating with the British 46th Division): Lieut. Colonel William Darby

BRITISH
British 46th ('*Oak Tree*') *Division:* Major General John L. T. 'Ginger' Hawkesworth
16th Durham Light Infantry
1/4 Hampshires
1/5 Hampshires
2nd Hampshires
2/4 King's Own Yorkshire Light Infantry (KOYLIs)
2/5 Leicesters
6th Lincolns
5th Sherwood Foresters
6th Yorks and Lancs
46th Recce Regt
2nd Bn Royal Northumberland Fusiliers
Royal Artillery
Royal Engineers
British 56th (*London* '*Black Cat*') *Division:* Major General Douglas A. H. Graham
6th Ox and Bucks Light Infantry
2/5 Queen's
2/6 Queen's
2/7 Queen's
44th Recce Regt
Cheshire Regt
8th Royal Fusiliers
9th Royal Fusiliers
The Grenadier Guards
The Royal Scots Greys
2nd Scots Greys
3rd Coldstream Guards

Commandos (operating with the 46th Division):
138 Brigade: Brigadier Robert 'Lucky' Laycock
2 Commando: Lieut. Colonel J. M. T. F. (Jack) Churchill
41 (Royal Marine) Commando: Lieut. Colonel Bruce Lumsden

GERMAN FORCES
Chief of Operations Armed Forces High Command (OKW): Lieut. General Alfred Jodl
Commander in Chief South: Field Marshal Albert Kesselring
Chief of Staff South: General Siegfried Westphal
Commander in Chief North: General Erwin Rommel
Commander German Tenth Army: General Heinrich von Vietinghoff
Panzer Corps:
15th Panzergrenadiers: Major General Eberhard Rodt
16th Panzers: General Sieckenius
26th Panzers: General Traugott Herr
29th Panzergrenadiers: Lieut. General Walter Fries
Hermann Göring Panzers: Lieut. General Paul Conrath/Lieut. General Wilhelm Schmalz

ITALIAN FORCES
Chief of Armed Forces (Comando Supremo): General Vittorio Ambrosio
Commander in Chief Army: General Mario Roatta
Chief of General Staff Navy (Supermarina): Admiral Arturo Riccardi

Before Salerno . . .

From the outbreak of World War Two Benito Mussolini was haunted by the recurring nightmare that the Allies would one day turn their attention to the conquest of his country.

Such a prospect caused Italy's Fascist dictator to fret about the possible conflict long before it happened. Yet in July 1939, in a gesture of loyalty, he had promised Adolf Hitler he would side with Germany in the event of hostilities. When that threat became a grim possibility he warned the Führer that war with Poland could not be localized, that it would 'become European'. He did not consider it wise to start such a war and urged Hitler to 'settle your differences with Poland'.

Mussolini feared that Britain and France would side with Poland. Consequently, until the eleventh hour, he sought to persuade Hitler to change his mind. Arguments were futile. Darkness descended on Europe on 31 August 1939, as a million and a half German troops began moving forward to their positions on the Polish border. At daybreak on 1 September the armies poured across the Polish frontiers, converging on Warsaw from north, south and west.

Two days later Britain and France declared war on Germany. A troubled Mussolini telephoned his ambassador in Berlin, urging him to entreat Hitler to send a telegram releasing him from 'the obligations of the alliance with Germany'. The Führer replied: 'I am convinced that we can carry out the task imposed on us with the military forces of Germany. I do not, therefore, expect to need Italy's military support in these circumstances. I also thank you, Duce, for everything which you will do in the future for the common cause of Fascism and National Socialism'.

Hitler kept in touch with Mussolini, writing frequently to inform him of mounting German victories. He told the Duce he was attacking Belgium and Holland 'to ensure their neutrality'. To improve his position with the Führer, Mussolini declared war on the Allies on 10 July 1940. Ten days later his forces launched an offensive against the French on the Alpine front, with no success. Mussolini felt humiliated.

When France fell, Hitler and his commanders planned the conquest of England. General Jodl, chief of operations at OKW, declared: 'The final victory over England is now only a question of time. Enemy offensive operations on a large scale are no longer possible.' Yet the truth was that the

German Army was ill prepared to invade England. The troops had received no training for seaborne and landing operations, and some German commanders were 'very sceptical' about the success of such an invasion. Hitler decided to postpone the operation.

By June 1941, although Field Marshal Kesselring's Luftwaffe *had carried out heavy raids over Britain for months at great cost, Hitler's mind was on Russia rather than England. When tension boiled over on the Rumanian question Hitler ordered his armies to attack Russia on 22 June, the day before the anniversary of Napoleon's 1812 invasion. Within three weeks the German armies had penetrated twice as far as Napoleon's had done. But the Führer had not reckoned on the Russian winter. The Red Armies were crippled but not destroyed. Moscow was not taken, nor was Leningrad.*

On the morning of 7 December 1941, the world, weary of war, woke to learn of a surprise extension to the conflict. Without warning, Japanese forces had attacked the American bases at Pearl Harbor. Although the bombers had missed the US carriers, their prime target, the attack aroused the indignation of the Americans, who quickly united behind their President, Franklin D. Roosevelt. It gave Roosevelt the excuse he had long awaited to bring America's weight to bear on the side of the Allies.

By late 1942 Hitler's conquests were staggering. German troops stood guard from Norway to Egypt, and from the Atlantic at Brest to the southern reaches of the Volga on the borders of Central Asia. Then, gradually, the tide began to turn. The Russian armies mounted a counter-offensive and Hitler was to admit that the prospect of a total conquest of Russia was fading.

The names of Montgomery and Rommel began to appear in the news headlines. The success of Montgomery's Eighth Army over the combined German and Italian forces in North Africa led Prime Minister Winston Churchill to believe that the Allies would soon be in control of the entire Mediterranean theatre of war, a belief that was strengthened by events in Tunisia early in 1943. Rommel's army had arrived there after a 2,000 mile retreat from Alamein. The Desert Fox, as he was now known, wanted to withdraw his troops and the Italian troops from the bridgehead, but neither Hitler nor Mussolini would agree to such a move. As the Allied armies closed in for the kill, the Axis troops awaited the inevitable blow, forgoing the opportunity afforded by misty weather of a screened withdrawal. They checked the Allies' first attempt to crack their defences, then collapsed when their front was penetrated in a powerful attack on 6 May.

This collapse was to have serious repercussions for both the German and Italian armies. The capture of eight divisions in Tunisia, including Rommel's veterans and the élite of the Italian Army, left Italy and the Italian islands of Sicily and Sardinia almost bereft of defensive cover. These forces might have provided a powerful defence for the Italian gateway to Europe, and the Allied chances of a successful invasion would have been slim.

The Allies, however, were not prepared to take immediate advantage of this opportunity, even though they had decided in January that a landing in Sicily should be the next step. Hitler thought it more likely they would land in Sardinia and offered Mussolini five divisions. Without informing Kesselring, the German Commander-in-Chief in southern Italy, the Duce refused the offer. His reluctance was due to a mixture of fear and pride: he could not bear that the world and the Italian people should learn that he was almost totally dependent on German help. At the same time he closed his eyes to the inadequacies of his forces. Finally, General Roatta, his new chief of staff, persuaded him to accept Hitler's offer of reinforcements, and the Duce agreed to three divisions.

The Italians, nonetheless, were ill equipped for the invasion of Sicily on 10 July 1943. their garrison consisted only of field divisions and poorly equipped defence divisions. The troops had no stomach for fight, and they certainly did not share their Duce's 'belligerent enthusiasm'.

After three days Montgomery's Eighth Army opened the way into the plain of Catania, although their advance was to be slowed down by German reserves. By 15 August, however, Italian and German forces were retreating across the Straits of Messina to the mainland. The six-day withdrawal of 40,000 Germans and 60,000 Italians made nonsense of General Alexander's message to Churchill that 'it can be assumed that all Italian forces on the island on 10 July have been destroyed, though a few battered units may have escaped to the mainland'.

Montgomery was now ready for the attack across the Straits.

Orders for this landing in Calabria with the code name Operation Baytown *were issued on 16 August. Montgomery drew up his plans with customary painstaking precision. Under the command of the 30th Corps almost 600 guns were assembled to provide a massive bombardment from the Sicilian shore to cover the landings near Reggio. Intelligence reports revealed that the Germans had left only two infantry divisions in Calabria, which suggested they were withdrawing from the toe. And the Italian forces were in disarray. What puzzled Montgomery was that Calabria seemed an unsuitable location if he was 'to coordinate operations with Mark Clark's Fifth Army which was poised to invade Italy in the Naples area in less than a week'. Surely this was playing into the enemy's hands? Was not the toe 'the worst possible place for creating an effective distraction'?*

Churchill, however, was adamant. He regarded the attack Montgomery's forces were to make across the Straits of Messina as one further step towards the total conquest of the Mediterranean.

General Eisenhower, Commander-in-Chief of the Mediterranean area, saw Operation Baytown *as vital in reducing the risks that would be incurred later in the main invasion of the Italian mainland some three hundred miles away at Salerno, an invasion by a combined American and British force under the command of General Mark Clark. For this mission Allied troops had been training for weeks on the beaches of North Africa.*

Orders for the landing of the Eighth Army at Reggio were not issued until 16 August, by which time the German withdrawal from Sicily had begun. On 19 August General Alexander, Deputy Commander-in-Chief of Mediterranean operations, told Montgomery:

> *Your task is to secure a bridgehead on the toe of Italy, to enable our naval forces to operate through the Straits of Messina.*
>
> *In the event of the enemy withdrawing from the toe, you will follow him up with such force as you can make available, bearing in mind that the greater the extent to which you can engage enemy forces in the southern tip of Italy, the more assistance will you be giving to . . . the Salerno landing.*

Montgomery was irritated by the vagueness of Alexander's orders. It seemed to him that no attempt had been made 'to coordinate my operations with those of the Fifth Army planning the invasion of Salerno'.

The attack by the Eighth Army on the mainland would be two-pronged. Units of the 8th would also land some days later at the strategic port of Taranto on the heel of Italy in an operation codenamed Slapstick. *Subsequently it was envisaged that these units of the Eighth would also link up with the Fifth for the concerted drive on Rome.*

Neither Churchill nor Eisenhower could have foreseen the ironic twist to the Baytown *operation. At 4.30 a.m. on 3 September 1943, the two divisions employed in the assault across the straits, the 5th British and the 1st Canadian, landed on the Calabrian beaches to discover, much to their surprise and relief, that the area was devoid not only of Panzers, but also of mines and barbed wire entanglements.*

By evening the toe of the peninsula was occupied to a depth of more than five miles. Then German resistance stiffened. Demolitions blocked the Eighth's progress to such an extent that it became apparent that a swift link-up with the Fifth Army would be impossible. Indeed, by 6 September units of the Eighth were scarcely thirty miles beyond the beaches where they had landed, and it would be days before they could reach the 'joint of the toe' – the narrowest part of the peninsula – less than one-third the distance to Salerno.

Churchill, always inclined to pitch his expectations of a quick victory too high, was impatient. But Montgomery was now too preoccupied with the battle in hand to give any serious thought to supporting a vast invasion in the Gulf of Salerno. He admitted he did not feel part of such plans because he was far removed from the scene. . . .

Part One

ARMADA

If Avalanche ends in disaster I'll probably be out.
General Dwight D. Eisenhower

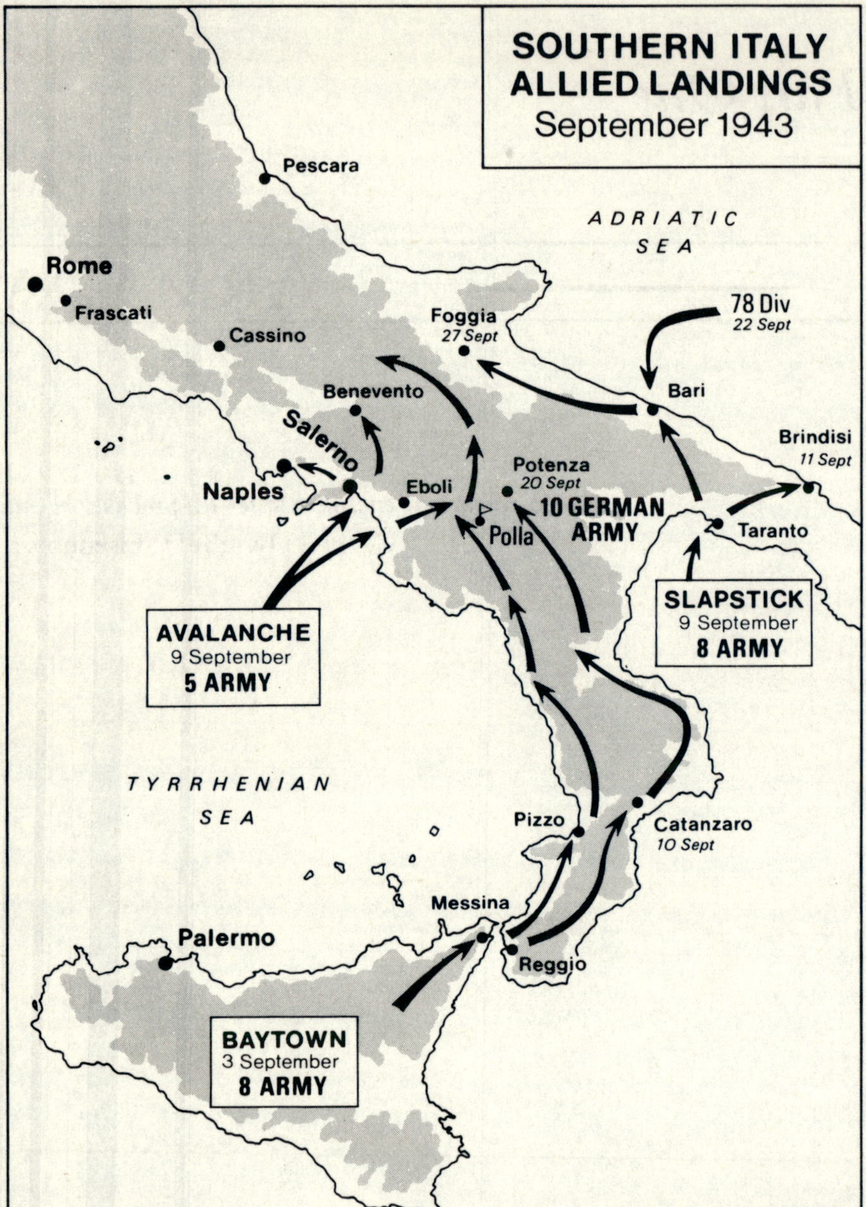

SOUTHERN ITALY
ALLIED LANDINGS
September 1943
Pescara
ADRIATIC
SEA
Rome
Frascati
Cassino
Foggia
27 Sept
78 Div
22 Sept
Bari
Benevento
Salerno
Naples
Eboli
Potenza
20 Sept
Polla
10 GERMAN
ARMY
Brindisi
11 Sept
Taranto
SLAPSTICK
9 September
8 ARMY
AVALANCHE
9 September
5 ARMY
TYRRHENIAN
SEA
Pizzo
Catanzaro
10 Sept
Messina
Palermo
Reggio
BAYTOWN
3 September
8 ARMY
Height over 1000 ft
0 miles 50
0 kilometres 100

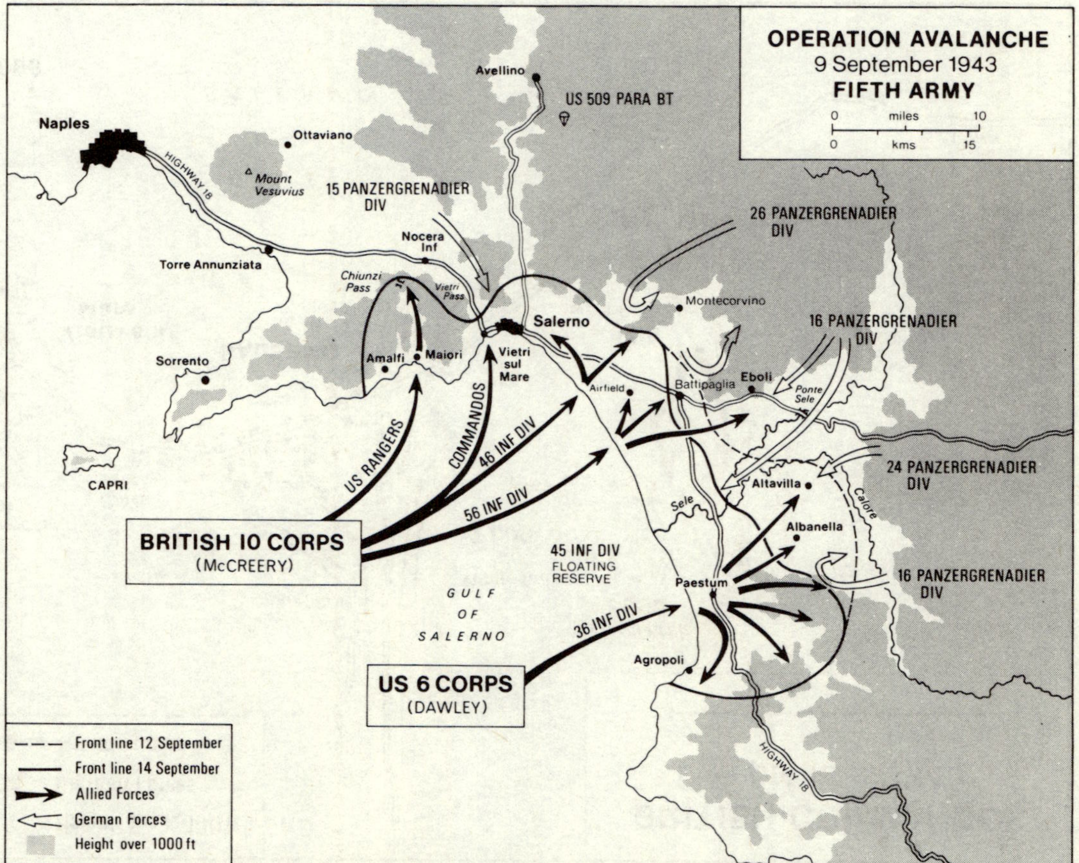

OPERATION AVALANCHE
9 September 1943
FIFTH ARMY
0 miles 10
0 kms 15
Avellino
US 509 PARA BT
Naples
HIGHWAY 18
Ottaviano
Mount Vesuvius
15 PANZERGRENADIER DIV
26 PANZERGRENADIER DIV
Nocera Inf
Torre Annunziata
Chiunzi Pass
Vietri Pass
Montecorvino
Salerno
16 PANZERGRENADIER DIV
Vietri sul Mare
Sorrento
Amalfi
Maiori
Airfield
Battipaglia
Eboli
Ponte Sele
CAPRI
US RANGERS
COMMANDOS
46 INF DIV
56 INF DIV
24 PANZERGRENADIER DIV
Altavilla
Sele
Calore
Albanella
BRITISH 10 CORPS
(McCREERY)
45 INF DIV
FLOATING RESERVE
GULF OF SALERNO
Paestum
16 PANZERGRENADIER DIV
36 INF DIV
Agropoli
US 6 CORPS
(DAWLEY)
Front line 12 September
Front line 14 September
Allied Forces
German Forces
Height over 1000 ft

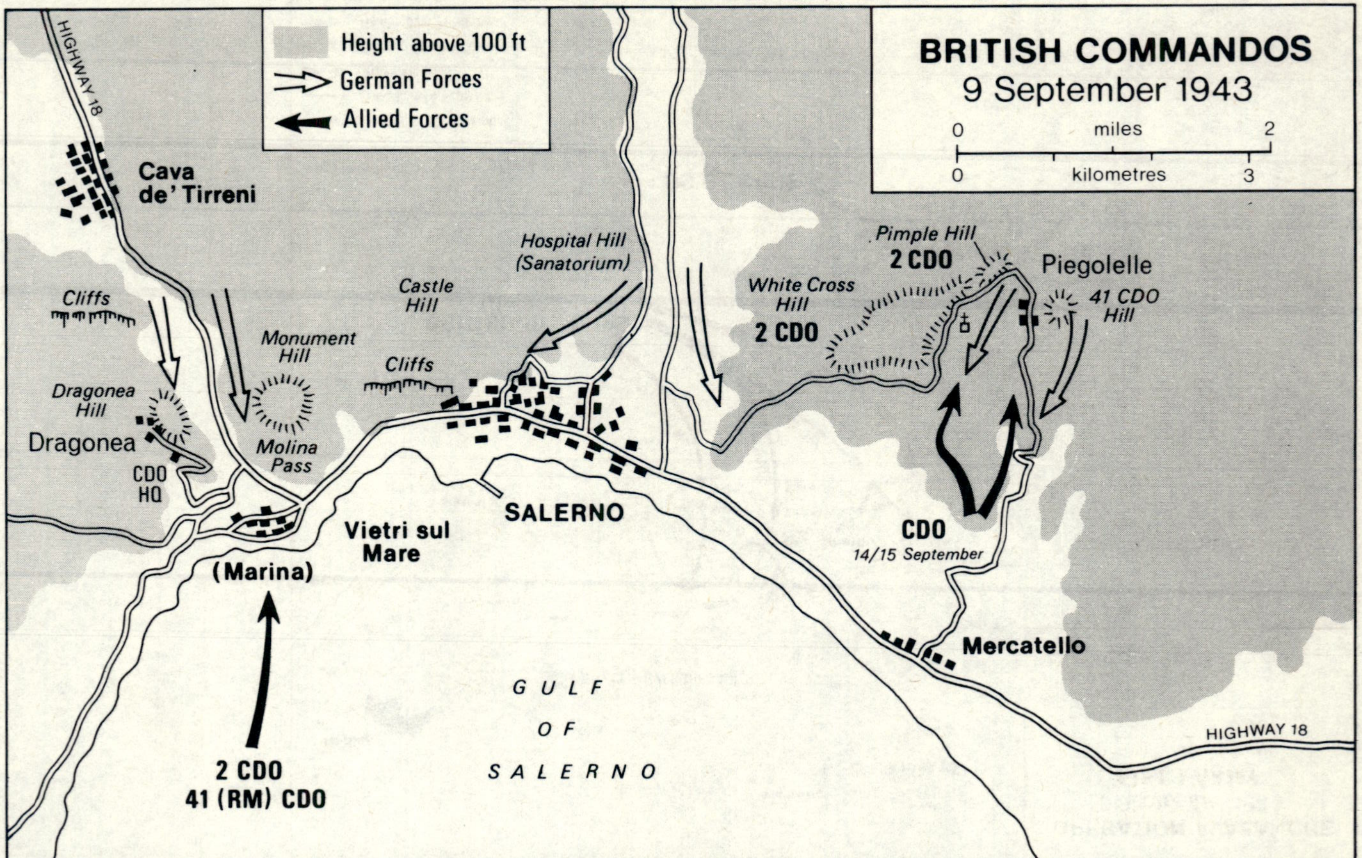

BRITISH COMMANDOS
9 September 1943
0
miles
2
0
kilometres
3
Height above 100 ft
German Forces
Allied Forces
HIGHWAY 18
Cava de' Tirreni
Cliffs
Dragonea Hill
Dragonea
CDO HQ
Monument Hill
Molina Pass
Castle Hill
Cliffs
Hospital Hill (Sanatorium)
White Cross Hill
2 CDO
Pimple Hill
2 CDO
Piegolelle
41 CDO Hill
CDO
14/15 September
Mercatello
HIGHWAY 18
SALERNO
Vietri sul Mare
(Marina)
2 CDO
41 (RM) CDO
GULF OF SALERNO

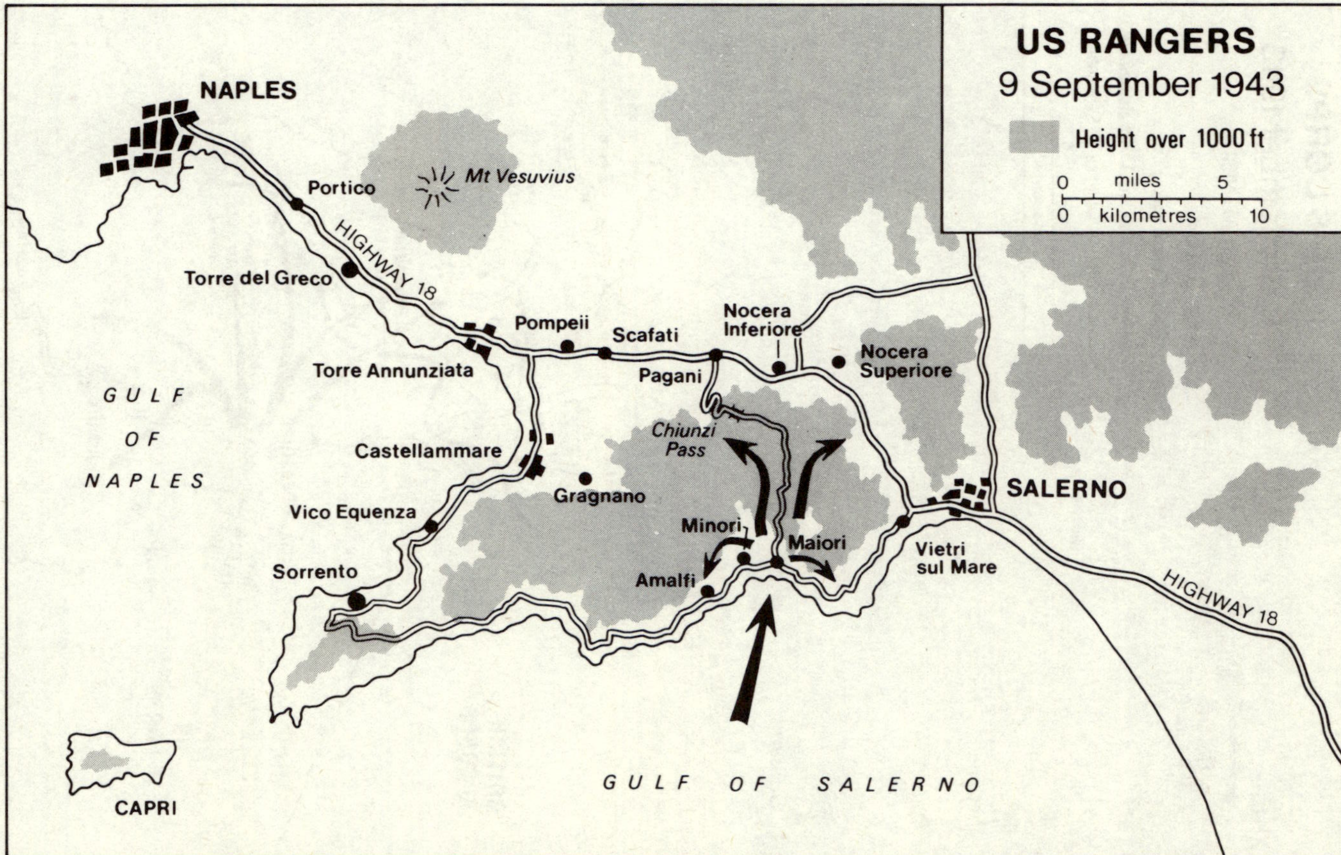
US RANGERS
9 September 1943
Height over 1000 ft
0 miles 5
0 kilometres 10
NAPLES
Portico
Mt Vesuvius
HIGHWAY 18
Torre del Greco
Pompeii
Scafati
Nocera
Inferiore
Nocera
Superiore
Pagani
Torre Annunziata
GULF
OF
NAPLES
Chiunzi
Pass
Castellammare
Gragnano
SALERNO
Vico Equenza
Minori
Maiori
Vietri
sul Mare
Sorrento
Amalfi
HIGHWAY 18
CAPRI
GULF OF SALERNO

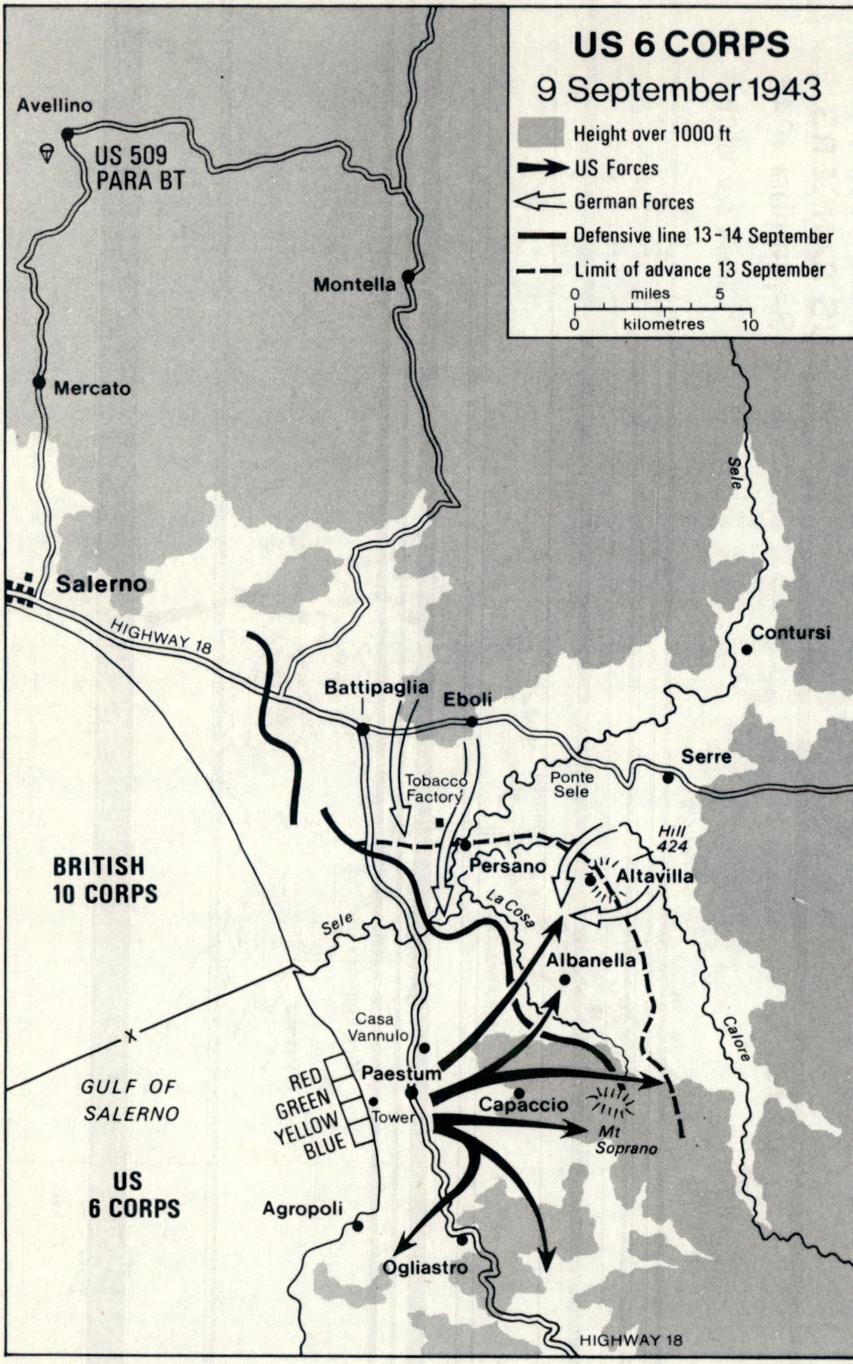

US 6 CORPS
9 September 1943
Height over 1000 ft
US Forces
German Forces
Defensive line 13-14 September
Limit of advance 13 September
0 miles 5
0 kilometres 10
Avellino
US 509
PARA BT
Montella
Mercato
Salerno
HIGHWAY 18
Battipaglia
Eboli
Contursi
Serre
Sele
Ponte
Sele
Tobacco
Factory
Hill
424
Persano
Altavilla
La Cosa
Albanella
Calore
BRITISH
10 CORPS
Casa
Vannulo
Paestum
RED
GREEN
YELLOW
BLUE
Tower
Capaccio
Mt
Soprano
GULF OF
SALERNO
US
6 CORPS
Agropoli
Ogliastro
HIGHWAY 18

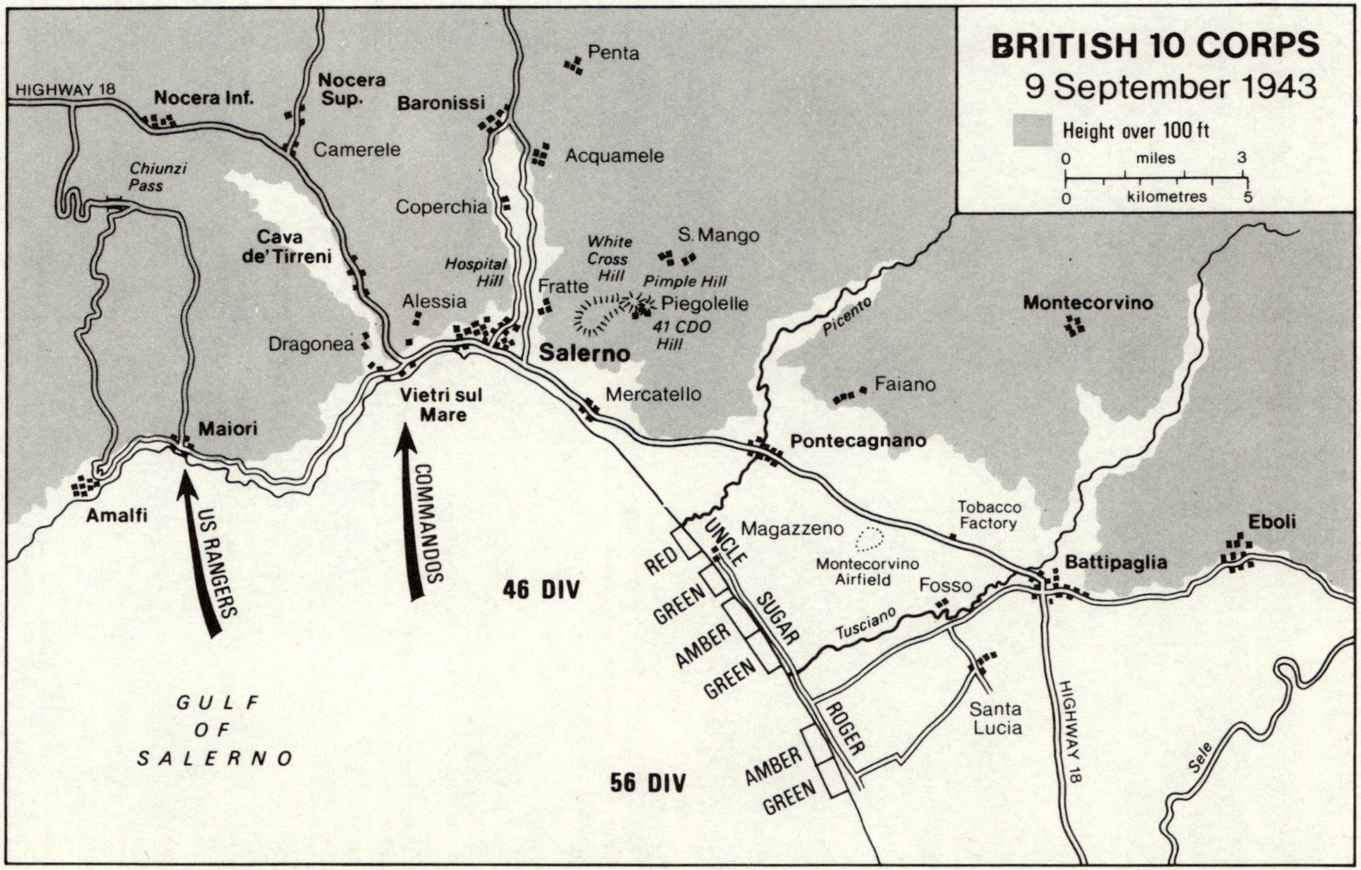
BRITISH 10 CORPS
9 September 1943
Height over 100 ft
0 miles 3
0 kilometres 5
HIGHWAY 18
Nocera Inf.
Nocera Sup.
Baronissi
Penta
Camerele
Acquamele
Chiunzi Pass
Coperchia
Cava de' Tirreni
Hospital Hill
White Cross Hill
S. Mango
Pimple Hill
Fratte
Piegolelle
Alessia
41 CDO Hill
Dragonea
Salerno
Picento
Montecorvino
Faiano
Mercatello
Vietri sul Mare
Maiori
Pontecagnano
Amalfi
US RANGERS
COMMANDOS
Magazzeno
Tobacco Factory
Eboli
Montecorvino Airfield
Battipaglia
Fosso
46 DIV
RED
UNCLE
GREEN
SUGAR
AMBER
GREEN
Tusciano
GULF OF SALERNO
ROGER
Santa Lucia
HIGHWAY 18
AMBER
GREEN
56 DIV
Sele

I
Invasion Fleet

Wednesday, 8 September, 1943. Early afternoon.

It was just twelve hours before the invasion.

A great armada steamed through the Mediterranean in the hot afternoon sun. On board the USS *Ancon*, a passenger liner in peacetime and now the flagship of the Task Force speeding off to the northern coast of Sicily, a tough, six-foot US officer with cropped, prematurely grey hair led three war correspondents briskly along narrow corridors and down a series of companionways into the bowels of the ship. 'Follow me, gentlemen,' called Commander Robert English.

Striding past a pair of stony-faced sentries guarding a bulkhead doorway he entered an area that reminded Lionel Shapiro, an enterprising young Canadian reporter, of the bustling floor of the New York Stock Exchange on a three million dollar share day.

It was the correspondents' first glimpse of the War Room.

Facing them, and covering the entire forward wall, was a map on which were flagged the estimated positions of Allied ships and aircraft in the Mediterranean on the sixth day of the fifth year of World War Two. To Shapiro the map was a complex network of criss-crossing lines converging on an area of Italy he identified as the Gulf of Salerno.

Intrigued, the correspondents followed the officer between banks of monitor screens at which Navy staff transcribed the flashing teletyped messages. English, a key naval planner, gestured them to a row of seats in front of a podium. Deftly untying a large map case he let the flap drop forward to reveal a detailed map of the Salerno area showing the city and its surrounding hills and villages. Directly through the centre ran the Sele River, snaking its way from the mountains across the central plain towards the sea, and dividing the long crescent of beach in half.

'This,' English declared, 'is the location for Operation Avalanche.'

Shapiro noticed that English's air of formality was now replaced by a boyish enthusiasm. With a rubber-tipped pointer the Commander indicated the assault points for Avalanche. It would be the biggest amphibious landing in history, a four-pronged invasion of the Italian mainland at Salerno, with the seizure of Naples, the port the Allies coveted more than any other, as the prime objective. The invasion would be undertaken by those British and American troops the correspondents had seen training in North Africa, men who wore identical 5A insignia on the sleeves of their khaki drill uniforms. These were the men of the Fifth Army, the first combined army of British and American troops since the Indian wars of the eighteenth century. On board the *Ancon*, which had sailed on Monday with its convoy from Algiers, they filled the decks and wardrooms with a babel of accents.

English paused in his briefing to let his words sink in. One of the correspondents, Reynolds Packard, asked: 'Commander, when do we attack?'

'At 0330 hours tomorrow.'

Packard looked surprised. The officer confirmed what the correspondents already knew: Lieut. General Mark Clark would spearhead the invasion as head of the Fifth Army. The Task Force was divided into three sections, Western, Southern and Northern, with support and covering forces including aircraft carriers and battleships. The main assault force was divided between Lieut. General Sir Richard McCreery's British Tenth Corps and the American Sixth Corps under Major-General Ernest Dawley.

Returning his pointer to the map English indicated the specific assault points. The Americans, comprising the 36th Texas Division commanded by Major General Fred Walker, with other divisions in reserve, would land south of the Sele River; the British, comprising the 46th and 56th Divisions, also with reserves, would land north of the river, just south of the city of Salerno. 'We expect the British to move quickly inland to capture Battipaglia.' He indicated the town on the map. 'As you will see, this is the most vital road junction on our beachhead. As for the Americans, we'll take Paestum further down the coast and clear the mountains dominating that section of the beach.'

The correspondents examined the map in silence, attempting to identify the locations. 'The initial success of Avalanche,' the Commander stressed, 'may well depend on the US Rangers and British Commandos. They'll make separate landings on the beaches further north at Maiori and Vietri to secure the mountain passes leading to the highway to Naples.'

He turned momentarily from the map. 'I guess, gentlemen, the toughest problem will be providing the air support from our bases in Sicily, 200 miles away. British Spitfires will have sufficient fuel for just twenty minutes over the battle area and our Lightnings for one hour. I must emphasize that we have never attempted to provide air cover at such a distance. You've got to understand the risks involved.'

From what they had heard the correspondents believed they were privy to one of the biggest operational secrets of the war.

'Our immediate objective is to capture the bridgehead and the neighbouring airfields.' But the officer reminded them, 'The final objective of Avalanche is the occupation of Naples and its port.' He looked directly at the correspondents. 'Any questions?'

'Any idea how long it will take?' Shapiro asked.

For the first time the American officer smiled. 'All I can tell you is that General Clark says we'll take Naples in three days.'

Shapiro was dubious. But English had shut his map case. The briefing was over.

Already the German units, spread out in position along the coast, were on defensive alert. Close to the coast at Paestum, thirty-one miles south-east of the city of Salerno, Major Herbert Duppenbecker, the greying Commander of the 1st Battalion of the 1/79 Panzer Grenadier Regiment, 16th Panzer Division, gripped the rail of his *Kettenrad*, the army's versatile motor cycle tractor, as he was driven along a dusty, bumpy road towards the pinewoods and sand dunes.

On the way down the dirt road he passed the Doric limestone columns of Greek temples, burnished with a golden patina. The anxious Duppenbecker had scarcely time to glance at these precious monuments to a colonization which had outlasted other wars and civilizations. It was here on the white beaches, close to these ancient temples dedicated by the Sybarites to Poseidon, god of the sea from whom the town of Paestum derived its name, that the enemy might land.

He tapped his driver on the shoulder, shouting to him to stop. Standing up in the rear seat he looked beyond the dark pinewoods to the dunes, bristling with low bushes, where his troops, stripped almost naked in the burning midday sun, were feverishly digging machine gun positions, laying minefields and preparing tank traps.

Duppenbecker stepped out of the *Kettenrad* and moved among the men, encouraging them in their work. His troops were thin on the ground; he had only 600 to hold a nine-mile front stretching north from Paestum to the mouth of the Sele River. The reinforcements he had demanded had not arrived, nor the ammunition, petrol or spare parts. In his diary this morning he had written: *I shall have to make do with what I have, and hope for the best.* If his men worked fast there might be just enough time to cut down trees, demolish bridges and tunnels, move in more tanks, and set up powerful 88 mm guns.

Among the sweating infantrymen he could distinguish the darker skins of the Italians from the 222nd Coastal Division. He wondered if the rumour was true that Marshal Badoglio, the elderly Prime Minister, was negotiating an armistice with the Allies. Were these Italians on the beach ready to capitulate? Perhaps so. If that happened he, like the other German commanders in Italy, had his secret orders. He would seize their weapons and vehicles. Any attempt at resistance would be ruthlessly crushed.

Boarding the *Ancon* at Algiers the previous weekend with his staff of thirty, the tall, gangling Lieut. General Mark Clark was met by Vice-Admiral Henry Kent Hewitt, Commander of the invasion armada. Hewitt escorted him to a specially equipped cabin which would also serve as his office.

On Monday the *Ancon*, flagship of the Western Naval Task Force, sailed from Algiers at the same time as other convoys, crammed with troops, equipment and supplies, left Oran, Bizerta, Tripoli, Termini and Palermo, the ports of departure for the Avalanche armada.

Shortly after dawn on Tuesday an Aldis lamp flashed on the *Ancon*'s bridge, to be quickly answered by another light some miles off. In the War Room Commander English looked up at the wall map. Positions were quickly re-marked, indicating that one of the convoys was steaming eastwards off their port side. The greatest invasion fleet in history was gathering.

By Wednesday convoy after convoy was steaming over the horizon in brilliant sunshine, a spectacular array of destroyers, corvettes, minesweepers, cruisers and landing craft, with the occasional battleship and aircraft carrier, stretching in formation as far as the eye could see, making a welded pattern as they moved eastwards. After two days' relaxation on board the flagship the restive Lieut. General Clark was at work in his cabin, pondering the remaining problems facing Avalanche. He looked up as Brigadier General Edward House, the air liaison officer for the invasion, arrived for a briefing. Clark wanted to raise with him again the problem of providing sufficient air cover for the convoys exposed to further attack. Two days ago there had been a blistering raid by enemy aircraft on one of the slow convoys anchored in the Bizerta roadsteads. Damage had been averted only by a rapidly laid smokescreen.

'Are you entirely satisfied about our air cover?' Clark pressed House.

'I can't say for sure,' House told him. 'That's still in the hands of Coastal Air Command.' House's invasion duties would not commence until the Fifth Army troops stormed onto the beaches of Salerno and needed the support of fighters and bombers from Sicily.

When Vice-Admiral Hewitt joined the men in the cabin he did not raise one of the most contentious issues of the operation, which was Clark's strategy to gain a tactical surprise. He considered this a grave mistake. The risk of heavy casualties was the fear of every experienced commander, yet Clark seemed to him prepared to send his assault troops ashore without a naval barrage. In spite of Hewitt's protests in the days leading up to the sailings Clark chose to ignore his advice; he wanted a silent approach to the beaches with no preliminary bombardment of the enemy's defences. Hewitt regarded such a tactic as absurd. Already the *Luftwaffe* had raided North African ports where the fleets were forming, killing twenty-two men, and they had bombed a convoy at Bizerta. Surely the Germans must know by now that Allied assaults would be made in the Naples area or nearby? Yet Clark insisted that a concentrated bombardment of German positions along the Salerno coastline could only result in the immediate summoning of reinforcements.

For weeks Clark's worry had been the shared command structure of Operation Avalanche. If the invasion was to go smoothly he believed it should have a single command structure; a shared structure was too unwieldy. To begin with, he had to accept Hewitt as head of naval operations until he could establish Fifth Army headquarters on the beach. Hewitt, in turn, had to depend on Air Chief Marshal Sir Arthur Tedder, whose bombers had been preparing the ground for the invasion by striking at targets in the Salerno area and along the coast. And Tedder was convinced that without air superiority Avalanche would not succeed.

Clark wanted complete authority over all services during the various phases of the battle. General Sir Harold Alexander, his immediate superior, had command of the 15th Army group, which included the Fifth Army and the Eighth Army, with his headquarters in Sicily. The air and naval commands were answerable to the Supreme Commander, General Dwight Eisenhower, who was at Allied Forces Headquarters in Algiers. Such a system could only lead to grave difficulties.

Clark had argued that Salerno was the wrong location for Avalanche, advocating instead an invasion in the Gulf of Gaeta, north of Naples, where there were no hazardous mountains and where airborne troops could be safely dropped. So convinced was he of the suitability of Gaeta that twice he flew to Allied Headquarters at the École Normale in the Algiers suburb of Bouzerea to seek approval for his plan from Eisenhower and Alexander. But Tedder threw cold water on his suggestions, insisting that Gaeta was too far distant from the airfields.

Now, as they went up to the bridge of the *Ancon*, Admiral Hewitt asked Clark, 'When can you take over?'

'Once you get us ashore,' Clark replied. Until his troops established a toehold on the beaches he was simply a passenger on board the flagship.

Standing on the bridge in the hot afternoon sun, surveying the ships of the gathering armada cutting white strips of foam on the glassy sea, Clark looked a superbly fit and eager commander. Within twelve hours he would lead an invasion by the world's first international army. A young forty-six, ten years younger than the seasoned Admiral standing beside him, Clark was the archetypal American commander: tough, pragmatic, a soldier's man. If he lacked the suavity of Alexander or the abrasiveness of Patton, he could move nonetheless with surprising ease between the military and diplomatic worlds. At six feet four inches he was so lean he looked as thin as a rake. His prominent nose was described as 'noble', his voice as 'deep and melodious', though one officer was heard to remark, 'Clark can bark as well as purr.'

This towering, enigmatic, military man was motivated by a powerful ambition. He hungered for a victory and saw Salerno as the campaign that must be won. Until now his entire career had been a preparation for Operation Avalanche, his first command. Critics held that so far he had won more battles at the negotiating table than in the field. They questioned his ability to lead the greatest amphibious invasion of the war. Yet his background was impressive.

Born into the army at Madison Barracks, New York, on 1 May 1896, Mark Wayne Clark had inherited a love of soldiering from his father, Colonel Charles Clark. On 17 April 1917, exactly two weeks after the United States entered the war, the young Clark graduated from the Military Academy at West Point. Wearing on his uniform the two bars of a captain, he sailed for France with the 11th Infantry on the 366th day of his army career. On Flag Day, 1918, he was wounded by shrapnel and on his recovery was assigned to G4 General Staff of the First Army. Determined to stay at the front, he returned to the battlefield at St Mihiel and the Meuse-Argonne and remained with the army of occupation in Europe until the summer of 1919. By now he was determined that the army would be his life. Between the wars his career was unexceptional. To his superiors Mark Clark was simply another officer. But when the Nazi armies swept across Europe promotion came swiftly. Soon he was Deputy and then Chief of Staff to Lieut. General McNair, reorganizing and expanding the American ground forces. Promoted to Lieut. Colonel, he flew 60,000 miles around the country, invariably introducing himself with a sudden thrust of the hand and a terse, 'My name's Clark. Don't think we've met?'

He began to enjoy the limelight. In August 1941, in the midst of this whirlwind assignment, he was promoted Brigadier General. By May 1942 he was a Major General, travelling to England with General Eisenhower to prepare for the build-up of American forces in the challenging new arena of war in Europe. Since West Point he and Eisenhower had been friends and now he was Ike's closest intimate in England. He became a familiar figure in London diplomatic circles, acquiring a new and easy charm. Prime Minister Winston Churchill enjoyed his company and called him 'the American Eagle'. Clark, in turn, was fascinated by Churchill's idiosyncrasies. During dinner one evening he watched with a mixture of awe and amusement as the PM noisily guzzled his soup, knocked over a wine glass with his elbow and, ignoring it, ordered a servant, 'Bring me a clean pair of socks.' Without missing a conversational stroke Churchill removed his shoes and changed his socks.

Clark was a man of little wit, yet he was good humoured, with no hesitation in telling a self-deflating story if he thought it amusing. But he drew a mixed response from newsmen. Some regarded him as vain, arrogant, self-seeking; others remarked on his thoughtfulness and attributed his meteoric rise to sheer hard work. As he drew closer to the centres of power Clark developed a self-confidence which could exasperate his contemporaries and superiors. Inevitably, he made enemies.

Eisenhower, whose main concern was to hold the Allies together and finish the war quickly, had unshakable faith in Clark. Without hesitation he appointed him Commander of the Fifth Army with control of 170,000 men from all branches of the services. It was accepted that Clark's friendship with Eisenhower could only benefit Avalanche; Clark would be able to call on greater supplies and reserves than any other general who might hold the command. Lieut. Colonel Robert Porter, an intelligence officer in the Sicily landings in July, shared Eisenhower's enthusiasm. Clark was 'a soldier, a leader, and a driver – and that's what you need at Salerno'.

Clark responded quickly to his new command. Although there could be no substitute for actual warfare he sought the closest approximation by putting his troops through an assault course to build an emotional armour against the shocks of real battle. By sending live bullets smacking into the ground around them and mortars bursting over their heads he provided his troops with some of the testing elements of Commando training. Officers and enlisted men alike were given the same preparation with 'discipline as its keynote and self-reliance as its ultimate aim'.

This nonstop general had no time for books. His attitude towards the fighting was simplistic: 'A young fellow with a war on is just praying to get into combat and do things.' Catapulted into high command, he claimed at first to be overwhelmed. Colonels were assigned to him who had been his seniors at West Point; now he was their general. 'I just made a hell of a lot of people mad,' he recalled.

Undeniably, he was Eisenhower's protégé. Their friendship had endured since West Point. They had always been close, although Clark was a couple of classes behind Eisenhower, and Clark's mother had asked, 'Ike, please keep an eye on my boy Wayne.' Eisenhower flew especially from Gibraltar to Algiers to pin the third star on Clark. He fought tooth and nail to have 'the complete military instrument' placed in the control of his friend who had been his little-known deputy in North Africa. Now the die was cast, and Clark was not to know of Eisenhower's significant remark at Supreme Headquarters to Captain Harry Butcher, his naval aide, before Operation Avalanche got under way, 'If Avalanche ends in disaster I'll probably be out.'

There was also a sensitive side to Clark. During his long absences from the States he wrote unfailingly to his wife Maurine in Washington. He felt their separation keenly. When he was promoted to General he wrote her, 'The more stars a man gets the more lonesome he becomes.' During the long evenings in North Africa he grew so miserable that he pleaded, 'I wish, Renie, you would send me Pal.' Pal was their black cocker spaniel, his wife's only link with the family and, when she travelled the country selling war bonds, a comfort for her mother in Washington. Once before when her husband had asked for Pal she had not taken his request literally and refused to have the dog sent out to him. His request from North Africa seemed genuine.

On board the *Ancon* he wrote Maurine a letter full of optimism, promising her Naples as 'a birthday gift'. As always, he signed himself, *Yours lovingly, Wayne.*

At precisely the same hour as the war correspondents were being briefed in the War Room of the *Ancon* Field Marshal Albert Kesselring, Commander-in-Chief South of the German forces in central and southern Italy, was hurrying down to the cellars of his headquarters in a villa at Frascati in the Alban hills, ten miles south east of Rome. He crouched for safety in a corner as 389 tons of Allied bombs rained down on the district.

Minutes before Kesselring had been having a telephone conversation with General Heinrich von Vietinghoff, Commander of the newly-created German Tenth Army, in Polla, a town on the edge of the Diano valley, some thirty-five miles south-east of the city of Salerno. As they spoke he heard the distant, muffled sound of anti-aircraft guns. He cut short the conversation just as the bombs came streaming from the thundering B-17s. For more than an hour the merciless attack on Frascati continued, demolishing sections of his headquarters and killing and wounding Germans and Italians in the town. Then, as suddenly as it began, it was over.

The beefy, pugnacious Kesselring was shaken but unhurt. Dazed, he emerged from the cellar of the stuccoed villa, his blue *Luftwaffe* uniform white with dust. Dusting himself down, he sought to preserve some outward calm. He knew he was lucky to be alive and was inwardly angry and distraught. For days his nerves had been frayed by worry and overwork. On Tuesday night he had learned of an Allied convoy sighted off the coast of Bizerta. He now believed they were plotting to kill him. Replacing his gold-braided cap on his balding head he climbed the steps from the cellar to inspect the damage to his headquarters as staff officers gathered grimly around him. Now he worried about an Italian betrayal. Had the Italians callously revealed the location of his headquarters? Had they known of the impending raid and deliberately kept it secret from him? Such behaviour was incomprehensible in view of his tolerance of the Italian leaders. Germany's military operations in Italy, he had to admit, were becoming 'isolated rocks surrounded by a quicksand of intrigue and uncertainty'. This bombing raid only deepened his pessimism.

The hard-pressed Commander-in-Chief South was less fortunate than General Mark Clark, who at least was assured of the loyalty of his political and military overlords. Churchill and Roosevelt supported Clark; Eisenhower and Alexander admired his professionalism. But Kesselring, convinced that a web of Italian intrigue had been woven around him, felt himself vulnerable. To make matters worse, he knew that not only was the self-seeking Field Marshal Erwin Rommel, the 'Desert Fox', plotting to undermine his position, but the autocratic General Alfred Jodl of the operational staff of *Oberkomman-*

do der Wehrmacht, the German High Command, known as *OKW*, was contemptuous of his judgments. Even his relationship with Adolf Hitler was strained as the diplomatic and military situation in Italy entered a dangerous phase. Perhaps if he were closer to the Führer at Rastenburg their relations might improve? He knew that men like Jodl were under Hitler's mesmeric spell at the field headquarters in East Prussia which Jodl had described as a 'mixture of cloister and concentration camp'. At the conspiratorial *OKW* little news of the outside world, apart from situation reports, ever penetrated; even the war news was unscrupulously censored before distribution. Such were Hitler's methods for maintaining power. By curtailing the knowledge of those around him he imagined he was enhancing his own.

Kesselring's achievements in the campaigns in Poland, the Netherlands and Belgium had impressed Hitler, but now he was simply 'a dupe among those born traitors' in Italy. The Führer provided him with the minimum of arms and supplies, although the persuasive Kesselring with his repeated demands occasionally extracted more resources than were intended. Hitler's concern was with the war on the Eastern Front where the Russians were pushing towards Kiev and it seemed as though the Sixth Army could not stop them. Jodl even suggested pulling divisions out of southern Italy as reinforcements. Yet Hitler, the acknowledged head of all the German armed forces, had shown sufficient faith in Kesselring to send him to Italy to 'restore order out of chaos'. While Kesselring needed his support, the Führer's idea of controlling the strategy on every front was to pester local commanders with niggling demands, an obsession which exasperated the Field Marshal and further strained their relations.

At Frascati, Kesselring's staff set to work to restore calm. The angry Commander-in-Chief inspected his damaged villa. When he learned that a map had been found in one of the bombers shot down indicating the exact position of his headquarters, his suspicions were confirmed. The Italians had been 'a party to the crime'.

Quickly he revised his timetable. Installations at Frascati were badly damaged. With the exception of one telephone line all communications were cut. He decided to remain at the villa and depute General Siegfried Westphal, his Chief of Staff, and General Rudolf Toussaint to drive to Italian army headquarters at Monterotondo, sixteen miles north-east of Rome, to keep an appointment with the Italian Chief of Staff, General Roatta. At the same time he ordered Westphal to strengthen the area around Rome. Through the smashed pillars of the veranda he could see the Via Tuscolana running down towards the capital. It was in Rome that enemy paratroopers would land; despite Hitler's views to the contrary, he was convinced of that.

At Rastenburg Jodl's intelligence agents had reported that General d'Armata Vittorio Ambrosio, the Chief of Italy's *Comando Supremo*, was finalizing secret peace proposals with the British and Americans. When this news reached Kesselring he faced the prospect of the final betrayal by his country's ally. He had trusted King Victor Emmanuel III and Marshal Badoglio, who had succeeded the deposed Mussolini as Prime Minister; now both these men must partly share the blame for the bombing that had claimed the lives of their own civilians that afternoon. Was it mere coincidence that before the bombs fell the fire brigades from Rome had reached the outskirts of the town? Surely this suggested foreknowledge of the tragedy? To Kesselring, a devout Catholic, deception was as despicable as betrayal. Though he frowned on Hitler's regard for Mussolini, 'the absolute dictator', he had accepted without question, when summoned to Rastenburg that August, the Führer's judgment that either Salerno or Naples, and not Sardinia or Rome, were the likeliest landing points for the Allied invasion.

Despite their conflicting opinions on strategy, he was ever-conscious of his debt to the Führer who had appointed him Chief of the *Luftwaffe* in the Thirties. That was the dramatic turning point of his career. At the age of forty-nine he learned to fly a plane and soon every moment was consumed with the momentous task of preparing the *Luftwaffe* for war. Though he proved a formidable technician and the master builder of a new concept of warfare, Kesselring had not calculated the risks involved. In those early months of the war he felt a creeping sense of helplessness as he counted the loss of almost 300 aircraft, more than 100 of them fighter planes. He remained unshaken, however, in his conviction that intensive bombings could bring a quick victory to Germany. He was wrong. The *Luftwaffe*'s blitz on Coventry brought not victory but reprisal attacks on German cities.

His detractors dismissed him as 'just an airman', lacking a soldier's talents, which was not quite true. At nineteen Albert Kesselring had joined an artillery regiment to begin his career, avoiding the cavalry because of the expense and the infantry because he hated walking. The winter of 1914–15 found him in Flanders, where his energy and organizing ability won him notice. It was said that he was 'extremely capable, with quick comprehension and great powers of decision'. His swift rise in promotion matched Mark Clark's in the American forces. In 1941 he was sent to Italy as Commander-in-Chief to share with Rommel the direction of the North African campaign. From his headquarters at Frascati he frequently lost touch with events at the front, and it was a measure of his stature that, when the lack of air cover hastened the withdrawal from North Africa, he remained in high command. Hitler made no serious attempt to replace him.

Since his arrival in Italy in November 1941, his German critics found his affection for the Italians 'diplomatically naive'. Such an attitude could be traced to his good breeding and Bavarian background. His professor father ensured that he received a liberal classical education at Bayreuth, and as a cadet in 1904 he was praised not only for his talent and hard work, but also for his charm. His good manners tended to alienate him from Hitler, whom he found lacking in social refinement.

As Commander-in-Chief South he had a considerable advantage in age and experience over Mark Clark. Twelve years Clark's senior, he had flown as a *Luftwaffe* pilot in hundreds of sorties in his favourite Föcke-Wulf 189 and been shot down five times. But at fifty-six he was a bachelor again, separated from the woman he had married at twenty-six. He had no faithful 'Renie' to whom he could pour out his heart in moments of loneliness. Officers close to him attributed his frenetic application to work as compensation for the absence of wife or mistress. Kesselring rarely relaxed, nor did he want his staff to relax. In appearance he was slightly portly, with a round, deceptively jolly, face that had earned him the nickname 'Smiling Albert'. Such looks belied his true character. He was fiercely determined and single-minded, and verbal barbs were his emotional armour.

Now, as rumours of Italy's imminent capitulation multiplied, Kesselring was assailed by doubts. Diplomacy had not worked with the 'treacherous Italians'. Despondent, he sat at his desk which had been dusted and tidied for him after the bombings. The realization that the enemy approaching the Italian coast was superior in air and sea power only increased his anxiety about the inadequacy of his ground forces. Since his meeting with Hitler in August supplies and replacements of personnel, equipment and arms, which he considered vital, had been almost completely cut off. His repeated demands to *OKW* were brushed aside with the excuse, 'We'll see – later on.' He believed he could master the enemy only in certain circumstances, and the further south the invasion took place the better his chances would be. But what if the enemy were to land in Rome?

Impatiently he drummed his fingers on the desk and waited for news from Monterotondo.

Because of her wealth of fittings and equipment the *Ancon* was known in Navy circles as the 'Hotel Ancon'. She was also the 'Pied Piper' of the convoy steaming eastwards off Palermo. Enemy planes making reconnaissance swoops might assume the ships were heading towards the toe of Italy in support of Montgomery's Eighth Army. This was the deliberate ploy of Allied HQ.

The tough, decisive Vice-Admiral Hewitt had become an expert in amphibious landings. He had put General Patton's troops ashore in three separate landings in North Africa in November and succeeded in landing troops on Sicily in July despite a dangerous and unpleasant swell. When the enquiring Lionel Shapiro went up to the bridge of the *Ancon* this afternoon, he found the Admiral, binoculars raised, scanning the massive fleet that fanned out in formation across the wide expanse of sunlit sea.

'Would you say, sir,' Shapiro asked him, 'that the enemy has spotted us?'

Hewitt smiled grimly. 'If they haven't,' he replied, 'they must be blind.'

At two p.m. a call came through to the 16th Reconnaissance Unit of the 16th Panzer Division in the Sorrento area west of Salerno where Colonel Dörnemann was in command. It was a preliminary alarm, signalling the threat of an enemy landing. Gottfried Rocholl, a slim, dark-haired, young lieutenant, had heard similar alarms often enough. He did not think it worthwhile to interrupt his men's afternoon siesta, or his own. The 16th Panzers had suffered terrible casualties in November at Stalingrad. By March they had regrouped in France and were now the best-armed of the Panzer divisions. Rocholl had continued to serve with the 16th, first in the south of Italy at Taranto, and now in the Salerno area under the leadership of Dörnemann.

At 3.40 p.m. he was awakened by a second call. '*Achtung! Operation Orkan!*'

Orkan, the Hurricane, was the code word announcing an imminent enemy landing. It made Rocholl reach quickly for his glasses. He buttoned the tunic of his olive green summer uniform and donned his cloth-peaked cap with its silver woven German eagle. Defensive measures must be taken immediately. Five days ago Montgomery's Eighth Army had crossed the Straits of Messina and landed on the beaches near Reggio. They were less than 250 miles from Salerno. If the Allies wished to avoid a long winter campaign they must soon attempt a major landing on the mainland. Where, he wondered, would they try to land? If a landing was attempted along the Salerno beaches the 16th Reconnaissance Unit would be ready. Three patrols of the unit had orders to take up positions along the coast at Salerno, Vietri and Castellammare. Rocholl's patrol was to head for Salerno.

Alerting his men, he ordered them to get the armoured cars ready.

Then he hurried across to the office of his commanding officer for his instructions. A quick telephone call to the signals officer for his radio ciphers and he would be ready to move.

Major Duppenbecker was driven back from the dunes to his command post at Paestum. Even in his light summer uniform he sweated in the heat. As the *Kettenrad* bumped over the dirt road he clung to the passenger rail and worried about the days ahead.

Riding past the ruined temples where the roses grew wild in the grassy meadows he thought of how the Carthaginian general Hannibal had been crushed in defeat in the shadow of these great Doric pillars. If the Allies attempted to land on these beaches he was determined they would meet the same fate at the hands of his fast-moving and devastating Panzer formations.

He had hoped to snatch a siesta that afternoon, but on walking into his farmhouse headquarters he was handed a message with the cryptic word, *Orkan*. The days of waiting were over. The invasion was on. He raised his field glasses and scanned the horizon for signs of the enemy fleet. Anxiously he swept the entire gulf from Agropoli, crowning the hill on his left, to Salerno and the Amalfi coast fading into the horizon in the north west. He saw only the gentle waves of the Tyrrhenian Sea shimmering in the afternoon haze.

II
The Betrayal

Wednesday, 8 September. Early evening.

At 6.30 p.m. there was an expectant air in Mark Clark's cabin. The Fifth Army chief, his aides and Vice-Admiral Hewitt tuned in to Radio Algiers. Clark recognized the voice of his former West Point colleague introducing himself in measured tones: 'This is General Dwight D. Eisenhower, Commander-in-Chief of the Allied Forces . . .'

Both Clark and Hewitt had anticipated this moment. What was crucial was the timing, nine hours before the scheduled invasion.

Reading slowly from a prepared text, the Allied Supreme Commander continued: 'The Italian Government has surrendered its armed forces unconditionally. As Allied Commander-in-Chief I have granted a military armistice, the terms of which have been approved by the Governments of the United Kingdom and the United States and the Union of Soviet Socialist Republics. Thus I am acting in the interest of the United Nations.' He emphasized that the Italian Government had bound itself to abide by these terms without reservations. 'The armistice was signed by my representative and the representative of Marshal Badoglio, and it becomes effective this instant.' Hostilities between the armed forces of the United Nations and those of Italy would terminate at once. 'All Italians,' he concluded, 'who will now act to help eject the German aggressor from Italian soil will have the assistance and support of the United Nations.'

Clark seemed reassured by Eisenhower's words. He remarked to Hewitt and his aides that he was certain the Italians would prevent the Germans from taking over the coastal defences and would refuse to run the road and rail traffic for them. If all went well the Fifth Army could reach Naples unopposed. 'At the worst,' he said, 'we could have a hell of a fight.'

On hearing the broadcast over the ship's loudspeakers the war correspondents were perplexed. Would the news mean a dramatic change in plans? Would they sail directly into Naples harbour instead of the Gulf of Salerno?

To the troops on board the *Ancon* who had rehearsed the invasion on the dusty beaches of North Africa, the news was a reprieve from the prospect of a long, hard war. As Lionel Shapiro hurried down the companionway he saw men who a few moments before had been sprawled about the decks, yarning and playing cards, shouting and cheering. At the War Room, he asked for Clark's G3, a former West Point footballer. 'Operation Avalanche?' the aide echoed. 'Sure, it goes ahead as scheduled.'

'But the armistice,' Shapiro pressed him. 'Isn't it good news?'

'For the purpose of our operation it may be bad news. We might have counted on having Italian opposition on the beaches. Now we may have to fight the Germans from the word go.'

In the wardroom of HMS *Hilary*, flagship of the Northern Task Force, conspicuous as a communications ship with her bristling array of aerial masts, Commander Anthony Kimmins swopped stories with a boisterous group of British and American officers. He paused briefly on hearing the loudspeakers crackle with *Heart of Oak*, the signature tune which preceded the BBC Overseas News. The news would probably be no different from earlier bulletins, he thought; the real drama would break next morning when the men on board the convoys would be the heroes. Through the atmospherics he heard the clipped English tones of the announcer: 'The Italian armed forces have accepted unconditional surrender . . .'

Abruptly he ended his storytelling. Officers jumped up from their chairs at the word 'surrender', and stood listening in silence to the details. In the excited conversation that followed questions were asked: 'Is the party over?' 'Do we go straight to Naples?' 'Will there be free ice cream?'

Kimmins heard a second voice over the loudspeaker, that of Sir Andrew Cunningham, Admiral of the Fleet, and overall commander of the Northern, Southern, and Western Task Forces comprising the Avalanche armada. Cunningham's patient voice struck a note of caution: 'With regard to the BBC announcement, I must state that there will be no relaxation whatsoever in our present preparations and no change in our plans. There is a very considerable force of Germans ashore. They will do everything possible to resist our landing . . .'

But the cheering drowned his words. Excited troops on the ships of the invasion fleet were flinging their helmets in the air and banging them on the steel decks, pounding each other on the back, and shouting, 'The Eyeties have jacked it in!' Launches were darting from the transport ships in the evening sun, circling the smaller vessels, as men yelled the news to each other. The sudden carnival mood was infectious. Wildly enthusiastic troops supposed, as one observer put it, that 'they would dock in Naples with an olive branch in one hand and an opera ticket in the other.' On British ships officers who should have known better opened hoarded bottles of Scotch and gin, while other ranks uncorked the last of their Algerian beer and wine. On American ships, where Navy rules banned alcoholic drinks, the men made do with paper cups of strong coffee.

Was Eisenhower's announcement ill-timed? Badoglio had begged him to postpone the broadcast when he learned that the Allied invasion envisaged an airborne drop on Rome. He was certain the drop was to go ahead, not knowing that at the last moment Eisenhower had cancelled his plans, swayed by reports that German forces in the capital were numerically too strong.

At least the broadcast left Admiral Hewitt in no doubt about his next move. Signals were flashed between the ships. Suddenly, the convoy steaming eastwards north of Sicily picked up speed and in a spectacular manoeuvre veered north towards the Gulf of Salerno.

H-Hour was less than nine hours away.

That late afternoon Adolf Hitler had flown back from Zaporozhe in the Ukraine in his Condor aircraft, arriving at the Wolf's Lair in Rastenburg with a 'strange feeling of unrest'. He went straight to his room.

Though he slept fitfully after the four-hour flight he was startled when his adjutant awoke him with news of the Italian surrender.

To the Führer it was the final betrayal. Except for Mussolini, he had never trusted the Italian leaders; they were 'rabble', 'riff-raff', 'a bunch of swine'. Their abject surrender had pre-empted by just twelve hours the ultimatum he was due to sign the next morning. In doubt from conflicting intelligence reports where the Allies planned to strike – Rome, Naples, Salerno, Sardinia, even the Balkans, were all suggested – he had determined to end the uncertainty by insisting that the Italians submit to a number of blunt demands to strengthen the German positions in the event of an enemy invasion. The Government and *Comando Supremo* would agree to complete freedom of movement by German units, the withdrawal of Italian troops from Alpine areas, and the creation of an Italian force in the south to free the Tenth Army for a counter-attack against invasion. In effect, the ultimatum demanded that the Italians acknowledge the supremacy of the German leadership over the Axis forces in Italy.

The papers were drafted and copies typed. He would have signed them and ordered their despatch next morning. Now, the shattering news changed everything. He demanded that Jodl call a full-scale war conference. Even Joseph Goebbels, Minister of Propaganda, was summoned from Berlin.

Meanwhile at Frascati Field Marshal Kesselring cancelled all engagements for the evening. With Westphal and Toussaint still at Monterotondo, he contacted his commanders at the front and ordered them to stand by. Then he authorized the switching of naval headquarters from Rome to Frascati. By now he was weary after the day's painful events, but his problems were to continue. Just after 6.30 p.m. Jodl rang from OKW to ask in an imperious voice if the radio news of Italy's surrender was correct. Kesselring was caught off guard. He muttered, 'I've heard nothing of this.' All he could do was promise to call back.

With only one telephone line available, enquiries were not easy. His staff could ascertain only that the news was 'a deliberate red herring' and that the Italians would continue to fight.

'Listen!' Captain William Rankin pleaded over the loudspeakers, 'I want you all to understand that the Germans are waiting in strength. We must be prepared for the worst.'

The young Glasgow medical officer with the 18th Durham Light Infantry in the Northern Task Force was dismayed by the wild scenes of enthusiasm on board his crowded transport carrying men of the 46th Division. To have given the assault troops false hopes at this stage was a grave mistake. He repeated his warning that they must worry about the Germans, not the Italians.

The cool-headed doctor was surprised at the tardiness of the British Command in informing the men that they were bound for the Italian mainland. Such was the over-emphasis on security during the planning stages of Avalanche in North Africa that, inevitably, it led to gossip and speculation. In Bizerta an American cook had supplied him with the names of the probable Allied invasion points in Italy. Security wasn't the Americans' strong point. The extreme efforts made to stop such information leaks had, he knew, far-reaching effects. Just two weeks before the planned invasion Major General H. A. Freeman-Attwood, Commander of the 46th Division, had written to his wife in England, 'I hope to be drinking a bottle of champagne in Italy on our wedding anniversary.' A vigilant censor spotted the reference and

Freeman-Attwood was removed from his command, some thought unjustly and with indecent haste, and sent home as an example to others. He was replaced by Major General John Hawkesworth.

In the heavy raid on Bizerta Rankin was among the doctors who attended the severely wounded Lieut. General Sir Brian Horrocks. He remembered the sky above the port that night, lit like a brightly coloured curtain. How absurd, he reflected, to imagine that the invasion could now be carried through with any element of tactical surprise.

At exactly 7.55 p.m. General Jodl was on the telephone again from Rastenburg. The German High Command had picked up a broadcast from Rome by Marshal Badoglio. Had the Field Marshal not heard it?

Calmer now, Kesselring explained that communications at Frascati were still disrupted. Jodl told him drily that Badoglio had broadcast to the Italians the details of an armistice granted by Eisenhower. The Italian armed forces were to cease all acts of hostility against the forces of the United Nations and to oppose attacks from any other quarter.

Listening to Jodl's distant voice a growing sense of isolation from *OKW* seized Kesselring. The General informed him that he was issuing the code word *Achse*, or Axis, authorizing the takeover of Italy. Kesselring was to occupy the central and southern ports, Rommel the north of the country. Sardinia would be evacuated and its divisions transferred to the mainland. The fleet would be seized and all Italian units disarmed.

Having given his news, Jodl hung up abruptly.

Stunned by the rapidity of these events, Kesselring called Westphal in Rome and asked him to enquire urgently of Roatta what he knew of a capitulation. At first the Commander of the Italian forces dismissed the news as 'a hoax'. Then, at 8.30 p.m., Roatta telephoned Kesselring personally to apologize. The news was true, he admitted, and had taken him by surprise. 'I had no intention,' he assured the Field Marshal, 'of hoodwinking you.'

Although prepared to accept Roatta's words, Kesselring had no doubt that Badoglio and Ambrosio had deliberately kept him in the dark to prevent him from taking swift counter-measures. On Jodl's instructions he ordered the signal *Achse* to be sent to all units. He was now prepared for the worst.

At Polla, the tetchy General von Vietinghoff, whose Hitler moustache made him instantly recognizable to his troops, was experiencing his own difficulties. When his staff picked up the BBC Overseas broadcast he contacted the Commander of the Italian 12th Battalion

Army Corps. General Arisio's comment on the armistice report was, 'A crude propaganda manoeuvre.'

Vietinghoff was about to issue a warning to his troops denying the truth of the surrender when Kesselring's confirmation came through. The Field Marshal asked him to issue a message to all units of the Tenth Army: 'The Italian Government has committed the basest treachery by concluding an armistice with the enemy behind our backs. We Germans must continue to fight against the external enemy for the salvation of Europe and Italy.' He urged them to maintain their battle spirit. If Italian troops refused to fight on their side, they were to be ruthlessly disarmed. 'No mercy must be shown to traitors. *Heil Hitler!*'

In ordering the 26th Panzer Division, fighting off Montgomery's advance in Calabria, to 'break contact and hurry north', Vietinghoff was acting from a powerful conviction that the invasion of Salerno was the main threat to the entire German strength in southern Italy. 'German forces available in this area', he had told Kesselring a few hours previously, 'are sufficient to repel a strong enemy landing attempt. I will need reinforcements urgently in the Naples–Salerno area.' But already events were overtaking the commanders. Ten miles from Frascati the jubilant Romans were pouring onto the streets, marching along the Corso Vittorio Emanuele, singing and dancing in the Piazza di Spagna, intoning prayers of thanksgiving in the Piazza San Pietro. Vengeful and bitter, Kesselring telephoned Westphal and ordered the arrest of the King and Badoglio. He was too late. In the midst of the celebrations the Royal Family and the Government had fled.

As news of the armistice spread throughout Italy that evening the few thousand remnants of Salerno's pre-war population of 90,000 emerged warily from their homes and shelters to venture into the empty streets. Some made directly for the Duomo in the old quarter of the city to ask the cathedral clergy to sing a *Te Deum* in thanksgiving. On great feast days the church bells were rung as a symbol of rejoicing; now the people wanted their priests to join with them in celebrating the good news. But the priests advised them: 'You should go back to the shelters. This armistice does not mean peace.'

The elderly Archbishop Monterisi, the shepherd who had remained with his flock, shuffled into the atrium of the eleventh-century cathedral and stood beneath the ancient arcades to explain that Marshal Badoglio's speech meant only that events had changed. 'It is not the end of the war,' he said in a frail voice.

But the Salernitani were weary of war and wanted to celebrate. Momentarily fear had relaxed its grip on the city. They walked about the streets again, among the ruined buildings, the legacy of the air bombardment that had begun on the night of 20 June with the bombing of the railway station, threatening their city with total destruction from the sky.

Until that fateful June night the horror of war had been remote from Salerno. Since the thirties the city, with impressive motor roads and a fine sandy stretch of Lido, had been a favourite resort. It nestled below mountains which enclosed a plain, stretching like a quarter moon south to Paestum and the fishing village of Agropoli, and was sheltered by the blue waters of the Gulf.

In this idyllic setting bathers crowding the white beaches and visitors strolling the promenades between the avenues of palm trees on the following sultry afternoon looked up in surprise as an enemy aircraft, its fuselage dazzling in the sun, swept in from the sea with a monotonous drone of engines. Incredulously they watched as bombs began falling between the busy railway station and the sanatorium. Hastily families gathered up their beach effects, shouting frantically to their children, as the blue sky was obliterated by an ugly cloud of black smoke and the air filled with the rumble of collapsing buildings.

For months the bombing of Salerno continued. Barracks, sports arena, railway crossings, churches, factories, offices, apartments, all were bombed relentlessly. On the fashionable Corso Vittorio Emanuele the staff of the German Command evacuated the eighty-six-room Montestalla Hotel when the bombers scored a direct hit. Municipal workers abandoned their desks, shopkeepers rolled down their shutters, and the splendid nineteenth century Teatro Verdi closed its doors to opera-lovers. For the first time since the turbulent Middle Ages Salerno became again a tormented city under siege. Carrying what belongings they could, Salernitani fled into the countryside, making their way across modern streets and leafy squares and along medieval lanes through which handcarts could scarcely squeeze. They were joined by those who lived in tiny, secret piazzas and tall, jostling houses that stared into each other's windows. All were fleeing into the hill country, to what they hoped was safety. Those who remained searched desperately through carts piled with dead and wounded for their lost ones. It was a cruel time for those who had prayed fervently to the Madonna for peace.

All that summer the beaches were deserted. As the bombs went on falling during the months of July and August the townspeople converted cellars and railway tunnels into fetid, overcrowded dormitories. When bombs destroyed the plant of the electricity company the city was without power and light. The air raid sirens were replaced by a cannon; three cannon shots signalled an alarm and one shot the 'all clear'. Even the huge red cross painted on the flat white roof of the sanatorium on the steep slopes of a hill above the uneasy city did not save the building from the raiders. The tubercular patients were moved with the nursing staff to dank tunnels and cold passageways beneath the hill, and already this atmosphere had precipitated the deaths of a number of the patients. On the lawn behind the sanatorium of Giovanni di Procida, simple white crosses were mounted in mounds of fresh earth.

At eleven a.m. on 8 September the tall, raw-boned young hospital chaplain Arturo Carucci climbed the central terrazzo staircase and stepped onto one of the empty ward verandas. He had caught the faint drone of an approaching aircraft. From his third-storey vantage point he spotted a single-engined Spitfire circling the city. It came towards the sanatorium, circling so low he could see distinctly the red, white and blue rondels of the Royal Air Force emblazoned beneath its silver wings. Instinctively he retreated into the shadows of the veranda as the Spitfire made wider sweeps over the area. Then the aircraft headed out to sea and was lost to view. How strange, Carucci thought. What did such a reconnaissance mean? Only when the aircraft had vanished over the horizon did the cannon sound a warning. No one could explain why the bombers had reduced the eastern sector of the city to ruins and spared the most strategic target, the port. What were they planning now?

Carucci was near despair. Realizing that the relentless raids had tormented his patients he wondered how many more nights these feverish men and women could survive the tunnels. When news of the armistice came through he was tempted to share their enthusiasm, but he knew better. Who could say what the night would bring? Badoglio's impassioned words did not mean the war was over. Had he not seen for himself the Germans moving their gun emplacements from the city to the hills and beaches? They were waiting for the enemy.

That night the bells of Salerno were silent.

Lieutenant Rocholl heard about the surrender from his commanding officer. He was taken aback, though not unduly surprised at Dörnemann's words. He hurried from the headquarters, his mapcase tucked under his arm, to the three armoured cars parked in front of a church. Calling his crews together, he told them he understood the Italians had signed an armistice with the Allies. 'It seems,' he said defiantly, 'that we Germans must fight alone.' Handing the men their radio ciphers, he ordered, 'Take your positions.'

Fixing his mapcase into place in the turret of the leading car, Rocholl decided on an impulse to loosen the automatic in his holster. He couldn't be certain how these Italians might react. Glancing quickly around, he satisfied himself that his men were ready to move. Waving an arm forward as a signal to the other two cars he called, 'Start your engines. Let's go!'

As the cars sped down the road in a swirl of dust he saw people in small groups, talking excitedly. Obviously they had heard of their country's surrender. He ordered his driver to go faster. The armoured cars could travel at 55 mph. 'See if you can make it 65,' Rocholl called. He wanted to reach his observation post before nightfall.

Meanwhile, at his farmhouse headquarters near Paestum, Major Duppenbecker was not surprised at the reaction of the Italian rank and file to the news of the surrender. Soldiers were already abandoning their own posts, changing quickly into civilian clothes and 'melting into the countryside'. When he was handed the final coded message of Operation *Achse*, '*Ernte einbringen* – Bring in the harvest,' he immediately ordered his gun crews to surround the Italian artillery before they could take offensive action and dispatched a platoon of Panzers to man the bridges along the coast to ensure they would not be sabotaged.

As no definite orders had reached the Italians from the *Comando Supremo* they were still in confusion. While many threw away their guns, others, especially the officers, were angry and prepared to resist. General Don Ferrante Gonzaga, the proud commander of the 222nd Italian Coastal Division, whose barracks had been destroyed in the raids on Salerno, had listened intently to Badoglio's emotional broadcast at his temporary command in the hills at Capaccio, a few miles east of Paestum. As evening wore on, he was dismayed by reports reaching him that his troops were being disarmed by the Germans or were throwing down their guns. Such cowardice appalled him. Born into a family steeped in military tradition, Gonzaga had fought in the First World War and been decorated for valour. Now he felt ashamed. In response to the armistice broadcast he ordered his officers to oppose any efforts to disarm them and sent a blunt message to Major General Sieckenius, Commander of the 16th Panzer Division, advising him that all collaboration between his Coastal Division and the Germans had ceased.

Sieckenius' reaction was swift. Within an hour of Badoglio's broadcast the oak door of Gonzaga's office burst open and a platoon of Panzers led by Major von Alvensleben stormed into the room brandishing sub-machine guns and stick grenades. Gonzaga, who had been briefing two of his officers, rose from his chair, startled by this intrusion.

'Do not attempt to resist,' Alvensleben warned him. 'We have thrown a cordon of tanks around your headquarters. Please hand over your arms, General.'

Gonzaga stood defiant. His lean face had paled. 'I have no orders to surrender.'

Alvensleben was insistent. 'Hand me your pistol, General.'

One of Gonzaga's officers made a move to hand his carbine to the German officer, but the General suddenly reached out as though to snatch it away. At once he was grabbed by two of the German platoon who wrested the gun from him. Gonzaga tore himself from their grasp, pulling desperately at the strap of his holster to release his Beretta. Enraged, he shouted at Alvensleben, 'A Gonzaga never surrenders! *Viva Italia!*'

Before he could fire they riddled him with Schmeisser bullets. He slumped across his desk, mortally wounded in the chest and head.

Alvensleben's face remained impassive. He reached across the body which was lying in a pool of blood and removed the Beretta still grasped in the General's right hand.

Except for the insignia of a war correspondent on the shoulders of his khaki drill uniform, there was little to distinguish Quentin Reynolds of *Collier's* from the men around him on the *Ancon*. He had enjoyed his supper of cream of celery soup, steak and onions and mashed potatoes, followed by apple pie. With no Scotch and soda to follow, the jowlish correspondent settled for a cup of coffee. At least it was real American coffee, an improvement on the 'godawful imitation French coffee' in North Africa.

Ignoring the grumbles of men who wanted to know why they hadn't been given two scoops of ice cream, as on the night before the Sicily landings, he read again the mimeographed sheet, signed by the *Ancon*'s executive officer Commander Swinson, which outlined plans for the next day:

> During Thursday 9 September it is expected that the *Ancon* will be in a transport area, operating its landing boats as directed, to debark certain army personnel and equipment.

The crew would be at General Quarters to repel enemy attacks by air or sea. The ship would lie at anchor, with the anchor at short stay, ready to slip at a moment's notice, and with full steam at the throttle.

Swinson ordered all men to keep their helmets and gasmasks by them constantly. Breakfast would be served at one a.m. to the troops going ashore. Reynolds wondered how men could eat a hearty breakfast before facing the enemy's guns. He had his own orders. Admiral Hewitt had asked him to brief the troops over the tannoy that evening. He would speak from the bridge and loudspeakers would carry his words round the ship.

'Give them the works,' the Admiral said. 'Tell them where we'll land and how many divisions. And you might stress the fact that our air cover will be excellent.'

'I hope you're right, sir,' Reynolds remarked.

'So do I,' Hewitt replied grimly.

At the Villa Angrisani, dominating the entrance to Vietri, the hilly crossroads town just outside Salerno, Fernando Dentoni-Litta, a sergeant with the Marine Command, decoded a telegraphed message from Admiral Arturo Riccardi, head of the *Supermarina*, the Italian Naval Staff: ARMISTICE SIGNED + RESIST THE GERMANS + DO NOT OPPOSE ALLIED LANDINGS.

Only three members of the staff at the villa, which was serving as a temporary headquarters for the command, were at their posts: a staff sergeant, a signaller and Dentoni-Litta. Convinced the Allied landings were imminent, the others had taken refuge in the railway tunnels.

Dentoni-Litta realized the books of code would have to be destroyed before either Germans or Allies arrived at their door. Gathering the eighteen books, he took them to a bathroom on the first floor. Tearing out handfuls of pages at a time, he set fire to them with a match and dropped them in the bathtub. It was dark at the villa when the last pages finally burned to ashes.

III
WALKER'S MEN

Wednesday, 8 September. Evening.

GENERAL CLARK'S BOYISH face showed visible signs of strain. To the experienced newsman Quentin Reynolds, the big man looked gaunt and anxious.

It was nine p.m. and the war correspondents had been summoned to a final briefing in Clark's stateroom. Although he knew the General enjoyed the company of accredited correspondents, and listened to their views, Reynolds was not deceived by the polite smile that crossed Clark's drawn features as he greeted them. He was aware that it masked the personality of a tough, shrewd soldier who sought publicity and was always curious to know what others were thinking. At the same time he respected him as a man of decision who would probably stay cool in a battle crisis.

The sinewy Clark rested his elbows awkwardly on the desk and sprawled his long legs that seemed part of somebody else's body beneath it. Eagerly, he asked, 'So what do you think of my plan, gentlemen?'

There was a brief silence in the room.

'Daring,' ventured Reynolds.

Clark warmed instantly to his subject. 'My God, it is, isn't it! I guess it's the most daring plan of the war. We're spitting into the lion's mouth and we know it.'

Lionel Shapiro looked hard at him. 'Is it, in your opinion, perhaps too daring, sir? Are you certain there has been enough time to prepare for this operation?'

'We were ready September 1.'

'I mean,' Shapiro probed, 'that hardly seems to me time enough to shift all these divisions and equipment from North Africa and still expect to run a split-second operation.'

Clark's smile faded. 'You've got to remember we've been working on invasion plans for months. I can assure you the Fifth Army is ready.'

To Quentin Reynolds' relief, a messboy brought coffee to the stateroom. Clark's aides, in keeping with the deliberate air of informality, handed round the paper cups. Reynolds Packard asked, 'So you hope to achieve surprise, sir, by the sheer daring of the plan?'

'We can't expect a strategic surprise,' Clark said calmly. 'Ours will be a flanking manoeuvre which the enemy will expect after the Eighth Army's frontal attack across the Straits of Messina. The Germans have studied the map as carefully as we have. They know we need a port and they have probably figured out that we need Naples.' Unwinding his long legs he elaborated, 'But I still hope to achieve a degree of tactical surprise. You see, there are two beaches favourable to a landing in the Naples area. One is Gaeta, just above Naples. The other is Salerno. The Germans must know we're going to attack in the Naples area. What they don't know is which of these two beaches we're going to attack, or when. So there will be some tactical surprise.' He paused. 'We may get hurt, but you can't play with fire without the risk of burning your fingers.'

The correspondents realized that it was already too late to question Clark's tactical plan: Shapiro asked him if he felt confident.

Clark's optimism was unmistakable. 'With a few breaks we'll pull it off.'

Was he apprehensive about the striking power of the *Luftwaffe*?

'Apprehensive? I'm scared stiff. But we hope to have two or three airfields by D-Day plus 2. Then our fighters won't have that long haul from Sicily.'

How soon did he expect to establish his headquarters ashore?

The General was emphatic. 'By D-Day plus 2, if everything goes according to plan. I want to get this ship out of the Gulf as soon as possible. It's far too vulnerable.'

Reynolds and Shapiro had stood up to leave when Packard asked, almost as an afterthought, 'Have you any serious reservations, sir?'

'None,' declared the General.

As the aides ushered the correspondents from 'the Boss's' cabin, Clark must have known he had concealed one personal reservation from them. Perhaps he felt it concerned only Eisenhower and himself. On the recommendation of General McNair he had accepted Major General Ernest Dawley as head of the Sixth Corps, although he was not acquainted with him. Later, when he talked to Eisenhower about Dawley, he found the Supreme Commander far from enthusiastic. But what could he do now? It was McNair's word against Eisenhower's.

While Clark tied up the loose ends of Avalanche, Major General Fred Walker, his seasoned onetime instructor at the Army War College, was among his own troops on board the USS *Samuel Chase*, flagship of the Southern Attack Force, with Major General Dawley and half his headquarters staff; the remaining staff were on the USS *Funston*.

The stocky Ohio veteran, whose heavy features gave him the appearance of an amiable mastiff, was returning to the European battleground for the second time in his career. In the battle of the Marne he had won the Distinguished Service Cross and the Purple Heart. Now, a quarter of a century later, at the age of fifty-six, the 'Old Man' was preparing to lead another generation of young Americans into battle.

Walker had his own misgivings about the mission ahead. Long before leaving the States he was convinced that his 36th Infantry Division, the Texas Army, was 'being shoved around'. Instead of war service his men were sent on summer manoeuvres, and when they reached North Africa they were given no combat duties. The strain of waiting and the endless spit-and-polish frustrated them. One bored GI wrote home, 'I wish we could get on with this dirty business, get it over with, and get home.' Even the rehearsals allowed for the landings were inadequate, little more than a repetition of the exercises his men had experienced during training. Walker had built his 36th Division from a bunch of raw recruits into a fighting-fit army. But these men didn't yet know what it was like to storm ashore on a hostile beach.

On the morning of August 31 at Fifth Army headquarters at Mostaganem each commander had presented his plans to Eisenhower. As an enthusiastic, pipe-smoking Air Chief Marshal Tedder promised air support General Patton leaned across to Walker and said in a voice loud enough to be overheard, 'Don't believe a damn word he says. If you see any friendly planes before Day 3 you'll be doing well.'

At least when General Omar Bradley visited division headquarters he offered Walker helpful suggestions based on his experiences in the Sicily invasion. Walker had been Bradley's student at the Army War College and regarded him as an able soldier. Bradley told him, 'There's bound to be confusion in the landing schedules. Just make sure that each man knows where he is to go as soon as he hits the beach.'

Walker's task was to capture the beachhead from Agropoli to the Sele River, a distance of some ten miles. His success, he reckoned, depended on gaining possession of the 3,000-foot Monte Soprano, which overlooked the beach, and of the key inland towns from Ogliastro to Altavilla. Whatever Clark might say, Walker expected to encounter at least one formidable armoured division in the area. He knew the 16th Panzer Division was there. Another division would probably arrive from the north before they hit the beaches. And, indeed, the attack on the toe of Italy by the Eighth Army would draw more enemy troops into reserve positions around Salerno. The communications centre on board the *Chase* had received a news communiqué from Zurich predicting a landing by Allied troops in the area of Naples and Salerno. Walker wasn't surprised. Enemy agents in Oran and Bizerta must have seen the preparations of the Fifth Army and known its intentions.

Although Walker had some doubts about Clark's assessment of the invasion he had established friendly relations with the tall and weather-beaten Admiral John Hall on the *Chase*. Hall always looked immaculate. His spotless white Navy uniform contrasted with Walker's unpressed, dusty khaki. 'Even in wartime,' Walker mused, 'the Navy never misses a bath or a good meal.' Hall was responsible for getting Walker's men onto the beaches, yet even the Admiral's assurances that he would put the 36th Division ashore on schedule had to be questioned.

When supervising the loading of the ships with troops and vehicles and equipment Walker had found the higher Army staff officers 'appallingly stupid'. Some were 'unreasonable', others 'just plain ignorant and incompetent'. They wanted him to remove combat equipment to make room for reporters and photographers with their vehicles. They suggested he alter his troop lists after he had made up his boat waves and landing plans. They asked him to take along heavy bridge equipment and grappling hooks to remove barbed wire, which he was convinced would never be needed. They even ordered demolition bombs to be stowed on craft already overloaded with personnel. He resisted their 'crackpot demands' with greater stubbornness than usual.

The Old Man had a reputation of never giving an inch.

On 4 September, the evening before the convoy sailed, Walker and General Dawley called to Fifth Army headquarters at Mostaganem for a conference with Clark and Alexander. Walker found Clark optimistic. 'These Italians will surrender when approached,' he assured them. American paratroopers would be dropped on Rome. The Italian defences along the coast would not oppose the landings. It sounded convincing, but it remained to be seen if his assessment was correct.

At noon next day they sailed from Oran and by evening they had joined the other convoys off Bizerta.

Walker's troops slept on the decks or played endless card games. He sat in on their instruction classes and talked to the men and their unit commanders. He was reassured that they knew exactly what to do and where to go when they hit the beaches. Each evening volunteer performers improvised an entertainment for which the men crowded every corner of deck space, perching on landing craft and hanging onto ropes and superstructure. They cheered the makeshift band and the amateur singers. When Technical Sergeant Sam Kaiser sang 'When Irish Eyes Are Smiling' and the national song of Texas, 'The Eyes of Texas Are Upon You, All the Live Long Day', Walker and his staff officers joined in the choruses, and with the news of the armistice the singing gave way to enthusiastic whoops and yells.

Just after nine p.m. Walker went on deck to inspect the craft assigned to him for disembarkation. Around him in the growing darkness he could make out the shadowy forms of sister ships as they steamed on together, their bows ploughing through the sea with a rhythmic swish. Near the prow of the *Chase*, on the starboard side, he located his craft. Peering over the rail he realized that when it was lowered into the water a man would have to climb forty-five feet straight down a rope ladder the height of a four-storey building to reach it. No problem for fit young Texas soldiers. But some of the older men in his team might find themselves and their weapons and equipment entangled in the ropes and become early casualties. He conveyed his misgivings to the commanding officer of troops and was promised another craft.

Gingerly he went down the gangways, stepping over sleeping bodies in the well decks, to check that his cot and blankets and toilet articles and four days' emergency rations of bitter chocolate had been placed in the jeep which was due to go ashore to coincide with his arrival. Satisfied that there were few outstanding problems for his soldiers, he went back to his stateroom and lay down fully clothed on the bed. For days he had fought the battle of Salerno over and over in his mind. As he tried to catnap, he rehearsed again the coming battles.

For the 'Old Man', Salerno was a new challenge.

'Where are my eggs?' Winston Churchill would ask, meaning his latest box of ULTRA intercepts.

To the Prime Minister the staff at Bletchley Park, headquarters of a highly complex intelligence system, were 'the geese who laid the golden eggs, but never cackled'. Through Bletchley he had daily access to the German secret signals, and even when overseas he was kept informed.

Neither Clark nor Eisenhower shared his undisguised faith in ULTRA material. In their estimation it was not paramount to the ultimate success of Avalanche. They agreed that, once battle was joined, the outcome largely depended on the quality of the commanders and troops in the field.

Yet Churchill saw ULTRA as one of the most effective means in wartime of reading the enemy's mind. At Bletchley Park, a Buckinghamshire mansion surrounded by Nissen huts, the secret war against the enemy was waged. Here was the source of ULTRA, an intelligence system which intercepted mechanically enciphered enemy signals, made them intelligible, and then distributed the translated text to the commanders at the front.

ULTRA was reading into the *Luftwaffe*'s enciphered Enigma messages: Enigma was the Germans' highly secret and complex coding machine system which had been broken before the war by the Polish Secret Service with the help of ULTRA. Now ULTRA was intercepting and reading messages from the German Air Ministry, gleaning vital information about enemy strength and movements; sometimes the contents of secret messages between Hitler and his commanders were in Allied hands even before reaching the German generals.

General Clark knew that the Deputy Supreme Commander, General Alexander, shared Churchill's extraordinary enthusiasm for ULTRA. Victory at Salerno, Alexander told him, depended partly on ULTRA for its success. It had already revealed useful information about the German forces in Italy. It was known that on September 6 the 16th Panzer Division was sent to the Salerno plain and was setting up 88 mm and other guns, cutting down trees and building strong coastal defences. It was the only German division in the area. From messages received at Bletchley it appeared that the Hermann Göring Panzer Division was dispersed through the plain of Naples from Caserta south and the 15th Panzergrenadier Division was northwest of this force in the Gaeta area. Both units were reorganizing after their losses in Sicily. It was also learned that some elements of the Third Panzergrenadier Division were at Frascati, evidently to guard the headquarters of Field Marshal Kesselring. The 26th Panzer Division was located halfway up the toe of Italy, while other German divisions were at Potenza and Reggio.

If Clark and Eisenhower were dubious about the value of ULTRA, Alexander had no doubts. 'We have broken the code,' he told the Americans enthusiastically. 'We can read the messages of Hitler.' Churchill's faith in ULTRA, he was convinced, was not exaggerated.

At fifty-two, General Sir Harold Alexander was at the height of his powers. Occupying a unique position in the Allied High Command, he was the only British Army Group commander, and since July had shown unusual ability in North Africa in fusing the efforts of two Allied armies into a 'single cohesive campaign'. More patient than

Montgomery and less autocratic, he fitted the American concept of a British general: he was fearless, courteous and immaculately turned out. And he shared Clark's view that the Allied victory would be swift and decisive.

Like Clark, Alexander's rise as a soldier was meteoric. During the First World War he was promoted Major at the age of twenty-five, and a year later became a Lieut. Colonel commanding a battalion.

Twice wounded during his four years in the trenches, he was decorated for valour. After Hitler's invasion of Poland he led the First Division of the British Expeditionary Force to France, commanding the First Corps in Flanders. As his troops prepared to evacuate the beaches at Dunkirk an aide remarked, 'Sir, it looks as if we'll have to surrender.'

Alexander replied, 'So it does. But I don't know the form of surrender. So it seems we can't.'

What endeared this handsome man with the trim moustache and piercing blue eyes to Eisenhower was his modesty and flexibility. General Omar Bradley described him as 'a General's General'. For a complex operation like *Avalanche*, which involved single-minded personalities, his 'blend of soldier and statesman' seemed an asset.

While it was still daylight, Lieutenant Rocholl and his patrol of armoured cars of the 16th Reconnaissance Unit of the 16th Panzers drove east along Highway 18, making a sharp turn right on the outskirts of Pontecagnano and climbed into the hills above the village of Faiano. From this vantage point they had a view across the Faiano plain northwest towards Salerno and Vietri and along the entire coastline.

Rocholl discovered that an Italian machine gun section had taken up a position close to the observation post; together they would form a small combat unit. He approached the sergeant in charge and discussed defensive plans with him. His final duty that evening was the positioning of the armoured cars. He would not leave them on the open road which ran along the forward slope of the hill; this would expose them to enemy fire. On the other hand, he did not want them too far away. He decided to place them round the bend in the road and in front of the observation post. In this position the radio car, which he parked facing back along the road, would have a good radio reception.

Soon it was dark. Except for the noisy Italian machine gun nest, the night was so still he thought it safe to let the men fry potatoes for their supper on the Esbit cooker. As they were peeling the potatoes his sergeant came running excitedly up from the radio car. 'Lieutenant!

Orders from Regiment HQ to take over the Italian positions.'

This was the final code message, '*Ernte Einbringen* – Bring in the Harvest.'

Rocholl acted instantly. Ordering one half of his unit to give him cover and open fire if he signalled with a white tracer, he led the others to the nearby machine gun nest.

'Your country has capitulated,' he informed the personnel. 'You must hand your weapons over to me. I will then allow you to make your way home.'

The men were laughing. Without a protest they threw down their guns, relieved that the war was over for them. Rocholl was surprised to find it was so easy.

When he crossed over to the Italian artillery position a second lieutenant handed him his revolver. But the battery commanding officer declared bluntly that he knew nothing of an unconditional surrender. He asked for permission to contact a superior officer.

'I cannot give you such permission,' Rocholl told him.

'Then I will not comply with your order,' the Italian retorted.

Rocholl knew what had to be done. 'You must hand over your arms to me, Lieutenant, and surrender your battery. Otherwise you will be shot.'

The officer stared at him in disbelief.

'Disarm them!' Rocholl ordered his men who quickly surrounded the officer and fetched out the Italian personnel. Rocholl took the man's revolver and emptied the chamber of its bullets. He handed him back the empty weapon. 'Now,' he said curtly, 'you may go home.'

His men gathered up the weapons and ammunition and took them back to the observation post. Now they could cook their supper.

Sixty miles from Salerno, as the Allied armada ploughed through the Tyrrhenian Sea, a continuous rasping buzzer sounded on the *Ancon*. Over the loudspeakers came the flat accents of the boatswain, 'General Quarters, General Quarters. Report to battle stations, report to battle stations.'

It was just thirty minutes since Clark had talked to the war correspondents.

Crews ran along the decks to their positions under a quarter moon that illuminated the convoys steaming towards the outer reaches of the Gulf on this balmy night. Suddenly the moonlight burned crimson gold as an enormous flare burst in the sky. One by one other flares, dropped by swift Föcke-Wulfs as beacons for the bombers that followed them, multiplied. Flare followed flare until the entire armada of some five hundred ships was silhouetted against a lurid backdrop. Then the sky was torn apart with red tracers as the ships' Oerlikon guns and machine guns opened up, shooting desperately at the bombers. As the flak rose the Junkers roared in, sweeping low with their heavy calibre loads.

Watching from the *Ancon*, Lionel Shapiro realized that the bombers were not penetrating to the centre of the convoy or flagship. Their bombs were falling about a mile off the *Ancon*'s port side where a flotilla of landing craft was moving in single file. It was on these vulnerable craft that the *Luftwaffe* was concentrating its attack.

On board an LCI, Landing Craft Infantry, crowded with British troops, Corporal David Hughes, 579 Army Field Company, Royal Engineers, wondered if his luck would hold. In North Africa he had been knocked unconscious and two soldiers beside him blown to pieces when clearing a minefield. Even his commanding officer had died in a desert minefield.

Crossing from Sicily on the LCI, which was no bigger than a trawler, Hughes and the other men had spent most of their time sitting or sleeping on deck. Now, as bombs and torpedoes began falling, they were ordered below and the hatches battened down. Crouched in his steel prison, Hughes thought, 'If this LCI is hit, we're all trapped.'

For forty minutes the Junkers swooped over the small ships. The rattle of machine guns and the menacing whistle of the bombs reverberated in the steel hull of the LCI as the men waited tensely in the darkness. One ship, HMS *Ledbury*, scored a direct hit and sent a bomber plunging into the sea, but only one landing craft was damaged.

Listening to the bombardment, Quentin Reynolds on the *Ancon* thought grimly, 'This is hardly an auspicious start to an invasion.'

IV
THE EARTH SHOOK

Wednesday, 8 September. Night.

THE SLIM HANDS of the eight-storey tower clock on the Lungomare Trieste pointed to 10.15 p.m. At the same time those huddled in their candlelit shelters or in the few occupied apartments of Salerno heard an explosion that shook the earth beneath them. Their first thought was that the bombers had returned. But there had been no warning shots from the cannon, no ominous drone of aircraft. Terrified, they crouched in chilling silence.

Then, in swift succession, further massive explosions echoed from the port area in the west of the city, the sector of Salerno that had been spared by the bombers. Old people hiding in the tunnels cried, 'They've come again!' On a corner of the Via Roma women ran into the street shaking their fists at the night sky and screaming, '*Basta! Basta!*'

But the orange flames leaping skywards and drifting across the water from the port installations were not the work of Allied bombers. The Germans had placed their deadly demolition charges in chunky brown boxes in the harbour mole, aboard ships, on cranes and in the stores, ammunition dumps, oil tanks and administration buildings. All were now melting in a roaring inferno, a defiant gesture to the enemy forces, a calculated act to ensure that the harbour would not be used for Allied shipping. The enemy would not have Salerno port, nor would they have Naples.

The demolition squads had done their work expertly. A pall of thick smoke billowed skywards as buildings collapsed in flames. Frightened inhabitants, who had been given no warning, fled from the intense heat. Others lay trapped in debris and would die before rescuers could reach them.

In the hilltop sanatorium of Giovanni da Procida Father Carucci had heard a crash 'like thunder'. Looking down towards the city he saw the sky lit by a brilliant red glow. Silently he prayed for those he feared were dead.

As he stood by his open window he was filled with sadness and foreboding by this further wanton destruction of his city. On hearing the sound of distant aircraft he looked up, not knowing whether they were German or Allied. All he knew was that the patients would be sleepless and fearful.

Lieutenant Rocholl and his men had just sat down to their supper of *Kartoffeln* when the first explosions made them spring to their feet. As flames soared into the night sky Rocholl raised his field glasses to his eyes. He could make out buildings and warehouses blazing and collapsing. One large vessel looked as though she would burn all night. This inferno, he surmised, was the work of the Panzers making the port of Salerno inoperable for the enemy.

The morale of his men was high. The 16th Panzer Division was the best equipped in Italy, with a full complement of officers and men totalling 17,000. The Division could muster more than 100 operational tanks and 230 armoured cars, a couple of thousand trucks and personnel carriers, and 600 machine guns and anti-tank guns. There were weaknesses, however. The Panzers were an armoured division, unsuited to coastal defence. They had no heavy artillery in the Salerno area and not enough coastal batteries. Rocholl feared that while his unit, under General Dörnemann, was staffed with many new faces after the losses at Stalingrad, the enemy convoys on their way to the coast were probably filled with troops hardened in the North African campaign.

Those Panzers who had been assigned to coastal defences were already in their foxholes or beside their machine guns. Crews sat in Tiger tanks, hidden in tree lines along the beaches, waiting to roll at a given signal. The men's earlier edginess was replaced by a growing awareness of danger as they watched the flames rising from the port area.

At his farmhouse headquarters Major Duppenbecker viewed the devastation through his field glasses. When he saw the sky burst into a spectacular fireworks display he knew the ammunition dump had gone up. Turning to an aide, he remarked, 'They're making mincemeat of Salerno.'

It was a perfect Mediterranean night. As he walked along the deck of HMS *Hilary* Commander Anthony Kimmins reflected that 'a honeymoon couple would pay one hundred pounds for such a setting'. Just then, in the direction of Salerno, he saw a vast oil tank lifted into the air 'like a child's toy'. The Germans had begun their demolition. Soon the sky was so bright he could see buildings above the harbour illuminated 'as though in a stage set'.

On the bridge of the *Hilary* General Sir Richard McCreery, so slender he seemed fragile, realized it was now too late to change plans. Against the crimson sheet of sky, he saw the dim outlines of the beach and the dark of the surrounding hills. He worried that the extent of the beachhead was too ambitious. He would have preferred a shorter bridgehead concentrated around Salerno itself. His Tenth Corps represented the Northern Attack Force in the invasion and Dawley's Sixth Corps the Southern. On the extreme left of the Northern Force the Rangers and Commandos would attack Maiori and Vietri. McCreery's main assault troops, the 46th Division on the left and the 56th on a wider front on the right, would establish a beachhead to include Salerno as far south and inland as Battipaglia, the hills overlooking Highway 18 to Naples, and the airfield at Montecorvino.

McCreery had always had misgivings about the Gulf of Salerno as a location for a major amphibious assault. The mountains enclosing the beachhead could prove a major obstacle; enemy artillery trained from those mountains on his troops could cause heavy casualties. In addition, the valleys of the Rivers Sele and Calore formed a low corridor dividing the Salerno Plain into two sectors, so that Fifth Army troops landing on either side of this corridor would be separated by about eight miles.

The General needed a successful campaign. He had served with the British Expeditionary Force in the disastrous campaign in France in 1940. Following a stormy working relationship with Field Marshal Auchinleck in North Africa, he was sacked as Chief of Staff. It was Alexander who drew him into the final stages of the Battle of El Alamein and, when Horrocks was wounded, recommended that he take over the Tenth Corps at short notice.

The men of the 46th Division were trained in combined operations, an intricate form of warfare that was still at an experimental stage; the ill-fated raid on Dieppe in August 1942 had been the first costly experiment. In a corner of Tunisia the final rehearsal of the assault landing took place; the entire intricate operation, including the making of a beachhead and the off-loading of vehicles, tanks, guns and supplies, was carried out. Yet even in these final preparations fifteen men of the Fifth Hampshires were killed and thirty injured when a mine exploded during the loading of a truck.

McCreery worried, too, about the degree of co-operation between the British and American commanders. Eisenhower had asked for 'a mood of partnership'. But during the planning of Avalanche Montgomery argued that the main assault should be made on the toe of Italy, and Clark contradicted him by saying this was impractical; the main attack must be made further up the coast to give the Allies possession of Naples and the nearby airfields. A compromise was reached whereby Clark's Fifth Army would be used as the main operational force at Salerno and Montgomery's Eighth would land at Reggio in a diversionary assault and join up with the Fifth at Salerno.

By now, McCreery hoped, the personality problems had been overcome for the major operation of the war.

Field Marshal Kesselring was unaware of the demolition of the port of Salerno. At his villa at Frascati he reflected bitterly on the behaviour of Hitler and Jodl at *OKW*, convinced they had written off his forces in the south and abandoned him to his fate. At least he would not have to listen for a while to the Führer's persistent interference.

While the Field Marshal was confused and made hasty decisions, General von Vietinghoff at Polla wisely allowed matters to take their own course as the Italian forces disintegrated. During the past few weeks his Tenth Army had assumed command over the 14th and 26th Panzers as the divisions reorganized and those which had fought in North Africa made up their losses in men and equipment.

In theory, the Italian army, confronted by an Allied invasion, ought to have taken over the coastal defences while the Germans launched their counter attack, but Kesselring had given little thought as to how to meet an invasion without Italian assistance. Neither he nor Vietinghoff had worked out detailed plans for combating the landings. The surrender and news of the approaching armada only revived strong fears in Kesselring that a landing would be attempted close to Rome. At 9.45 p.m. he wired the Tenth Army to alert the Panzergrenadier Division to be ready at a moment's notice to withdraw to the area around Rome. With the breakdown of communications and deliberate delays by the Italians in repairing faults, his message did not reach Vietinghoff that evening. Nor did his order that one of two divisions of the 14th Panzer Corps should be ready to assist the *Luftwaffe* in what he believed would be a decisive battle against Allied invaders and Italian troops near Rome.

Kesselring was convinced that a landing would be made on Rome from the air, or near Naples from the sea. It was clear that the overwrought Field Marshal was even now unable to comprehend that

Field Marshal Albert Kesselring. From his headquarters at Frascati, outside Rome, he masterminded the defence strategy against the Allied invasion forces

(*above*) 'Amber Beach' in the British 46th Division sector at dawn during the Allied landings at Salerno on September 9

(*below*) British troops run from a landing craft onto the beach at Salerno

the greatest invasion of the war was about to take place on the beaches of Salerno.

In his stateroom on the *Ancon* General Clark was informed at 10.45 p.m. that the Germans had destroyed the harbour installations at Salerno. His first comment to Hewitt was that the Germans 'had tightened their grip on Salerno.' Accompanied by the Admiral, he went up to the bridge and together they looked towards the distant fiery sky.

To Clark the fires brought H-hour nearer. His remaining worry was the availability of the 82nd Airborne Division which he still believed was necessary, even essential, for the success of Avalanche. During the planning stages of the operation he had been assured that the 82nd would be available to him for a strategic drop northwest of Naples. But Eisenhower had other ideas. Clark remembered his conversation with the Supreme Commander:

Eisenhower: It will be a shock to you, Wayne, but it has been decided that we'll make the drop on Rome.

Clark: Where are you going to get an airborne division to do it?

Eisenhower: The 82nd.

Clark: No, that's my division.

However, the plan for the 82nd Airborne Division to land at Rome was suddenly cancelled. Then Clark's own plan for dropping the 82nd further inland northwest of Naples on the Volturno River, some forty miles from the nearest beach landing at Salerno, was also cancelled. The reason given was that Tedder felt the advantages of an airborne attack on the Volturno would not be worth the probable losses.

Though discouraged, Clark had not given up hope. The 82nd Airborne was a vital emergency force. Eisenhower would hardly refuse his request again.

V
Trained to Kill

Wednesday, 8 September. Late night.

At 10.57 p.m. the moon set off Salerno.

By its fading light the grey ships of the armada, escorted by cruisers, destroyers and minesweepers, dropped anchor on reaching the rendezvous area some twelve miles off the beaches. The last enemy flares to hit the water had been snuffed out by the waves. Only the embers of the fires were burning in the harbour. Before midnight the blacked-out Task Force was in battle formation. Troop transports swung on their moorings as the outer lines of landing craft, hovering close to the larger vessels, waited for the invasion signal. In the warm night breeze the waves slapped lightly against the flat bottoms of the craft.

Save for the low throb of engines the Gulf was quiet. Crammed into hundreds of silent ships were 100,000 British and 75,000 American troops, the biggest Anglo-American force of the war to date, with every conceivable necessity for amphibious invasion, including 20,000 vehicles and guns and ammunition. The restive men knew that at last they had reached their destination. It was a curious sensation. In their narrow confines some wondered if they would be attacked from the shore. Would their arrival off the beachhead be met by a burst of fire from hidden coastal batteries? Others had seen searchlights sweeping the beaches and were convinced they had been picked up in the probing beams. Would screaming shells suddenly transform the stillness of the Gulf into a living hell?

From the bridge of the destroyer HMS *Blackmore*, in the Northern Task Force, her captain Lieutenant Terence Harrel peered through his night-glasses. The moon had set and under a starlit sky the sea was calm. An ideal night for a landing, he thought. Earlier, as they were running towards the rendezvous point, he had seen on the port bow the red glare of Mount Vesuvius, which could be mistaken at that distance for a lighthouse. When he said, 'That's Vesuvius!' one young officer thought he was joking, and simply laughed. 'You don't believe me?' Harrel asked. 'Then take a bearing.'

The captain was right. They were on course for Vietri.

During his briefing for Avalanche, aboard Brigadier Robert 'Lucky' Laycock's headquarters ship in Palermo, Harrel had been told that his mission was to lead a convoy of Commandos into Vietri. The troops would land on the beach in front of the village while he engaged a battery of guns reported to be sited to the east just above the beach. At three a.m. they had steamed from Palermo and joined the headquarters ship USS *Biscayne*, the destroyer HMS *Ledbury* and two minesweepers. Four hours later they met up with twenty LSTs.

Approaching the point at which the Commandos' assault craft were to line up astern, Harrel was surprised, as he scanned the coastline, at the stillness. No lights, and not a sound. Yet, as he warned his officers and men, the armistice would make little difference to the assault.

'Make no mistake,' he said, 'it will be a very tough proposition.'

Three fighting Churchills drank a battle toast on board the LSI, Landing Ship Infantry, *Prince Albert*.

'What curious names they give these operations,' Lieut. Colonel Tom Churchill remarked. 'Why in heaven's name, for this time of year and in such glorious weather, have they chosen the name Avalanche?'

Major Randolph Churchill, the Prime Minister's son and the most dapper of officers even in battle, smiled. 'Perhaps,' he suggested, 'because there's an avalanche of Churchills?'

During daylight they had sailed within sight of the shoreline and were now close to the lowering position. To Lieut. Colonel Jack Churchill, the most daring of Commando leaders, it was folly to approach a bridgehead in daytime. 'Damned ludicrous affair!' he snorted. 'The Hun must have seen this entire bloody great convoy!'

John Malcolm Thorpe Fleming Churchill was the leader of 388 officers and men of 2 Commando on board the *Prince Albert*. Strongly built and handsome, his blue eyes, fair hair and moustache gave him the swashbuckling appearance of an Errol Flynn. Indeed, discovering, as a reserve officer, that film studio work paid better than the army in peacetime, he had spent some years as a film extra. At the outbreak of war he was spurred to return to the Army by a sense of patriotism. Hurrying home from Oslo, where he had been competing in the world archery championships, he joined his Manchester Regiment. At Dunkirk in 1940, he fought off the Germans with his crossbow and arrow and was awarded a Military Cross for his bravery.

One morning in June 1940, on a week's leave after Dunkirk, Churchill sat with a group of BEF officers in the front row of a cinema in York to hear a young officer address them earnestly from the stage. 'My name is Stephen Patrick Wood. I'm in the Tank Corps. But I shall be taking over 5 Commando in the Special Services. I'm going to tell you about this new force, and if you wish to volunteer you may do so . . .'

Britain was edgy. German forces stretched menacingly all the way from Narvik to the Pyrenees and were expected to land at some point along the English coast by the North Sea. To counter this growing threat a special force had been formed to operate against them. Lightly equipped, they would be raiding parties capable of surviving for days without extra supplies of food or ammunition. They would need no transport other than the craft that got them ashore.

Winston Churchill wrote to Chief of Staff General Hastings Ismay at the time of Dunkirk: 'Enterprises must be prepared, with specially trained troops of the hunter class who can develop a reign of terror down these coasts, first of all on the "butcher and boot" policy; but later on, or perhaps as soon as we are organized, we should surprise Calais or Boulogne, kill and capture the Hun garrison, and hold the place until all the preparations to reduce it by siege or heavy storm have been made, and then away.'

In response to the Prime Minister's urgings the War Office, with understandable reluctance, agreed to the creation of a special force to be named after the companies of fierce Boer horsemen that had mauled British units in South Africa at the turn of the century – Commandos.

Despite open opposition from the regular army to the formation of the new force Churchill stood firm. Having discussed the idea over dinner one evening with Secretary of State for War Anthony Eden he went home to write a determined letter deploring the very questioning of such a force. 'The Germans,' he reminded Eden, 'have been right both in the last war and in this in the use they made of storm troops. The defeat of France was accomplished by an incredibly small number of highly-equipped elite, while the full mass of the German army came on behind, made good the conquest, and occupied it.' If there was to be a successful campaign in the coming months it must be of an amphibious nature, allowing opportunities for minor operations which depended on surprise landings by lightly-equipped forces accustomed to working 'like packs of hounds' instead of being moved about in ponderous army formations.

On 8 June the special force was approved on two conditions: no unit was to be diverted from the essential defence of Britain and the new force must make do with a minimum of arms. The 'pack of hounds' would mount a raid across the Channel 'at the earliest possible moment'.

To Jack Churchill, then thirty-three, the Prime Minister's plan meant simply raising a raiding force to 'give the Germans hell'. That morning in York he heard Major Wood tell his audience that he would interview the officers in alphabetical order and speak to each in turn for three minutes.

When Captain Churchill's turn came he was surprised by Wood's youthfulness.

'Now,' said the Major, 'name, rank, regiment.'

Churchill told briefly of his army career, his service with the advance party of the BEF at Dunkirk, and of his MC, one of the first in the war. Wood seemed impressed.

Over dinner details of the Special Services were explained. A Commando troop would consist of 50 men: a captain, two subalterns and 47 rank and file. Officers would earn £2-10 a week and soldiers 30 shillings, and they would be billeted in private houses along the coast. 'Go back to your regiments,' Wood told the officers, 'and tell the men about this new force.'

By the time Churchill sailed for Salerno he was a Lieut. Colonel and had led a number of Commando missions. At Christmas 1941 he led the raid on the Norwegian island of Vaägso, playing the 'March of the Cameron Men' on his bagpipes as the landing craft approached the shore. Injured in a demolition explosion, he added a bar to his MC. In Sicily, towards the end of July 1943, his 2 Commando was prevented from capturing Messina. According to Churchill, this was because Brigadier Curry of the 4th Armoured Brigade warned him that it was too dangerous. To Churchill's chagrin the Americans took the town.

Now the warrior Churchill was sailing into battle again, equipped with his claymore, crossbow and quiverful of arrows, and bagpipes. Nobody had yet objected to such impedimenta, although when General Alexander inspected the Commandos in Scotland before the Vaägso raid he remarked to Churchill, 'Oh, I see you're wearing a sword.'

'Sir!'

'I wore a sword in the first war,' the General recalled. 'We all wore swords in those days. But nobody's wearing a sword in this war, so why do you have one?'

'My family has gone to war for hundreds of years with swords,' said

Churchill unapologetically, 'so I don't intend to be the first Churchill not to carry one. What's more, Sir, I consider an officer who goes to war without his sword to be improperly dressed.'

'Quite right,' the General had to concede.

It was Churchill's batman, Guardsman Albert Stretton, however, who would carry much of this equipment, including an inflatable rubber bed, onto the beach at Vietri. Churchill had hung his razor-sharp, double-edged claymore in its scabbard from his webbing belt. He had a lightweight Beretta and two haversacks with his emergency rations.

For eighteen months young Joe Nicholl had sought a transfer from what he regarded as the intolerable boredom of anti-aircraft duties at Banbury. He enquired about the Special Service organization and was given the name of a Major J. M. T. F. Churchill with an address at Largs on the west coast of Scotland. Churchill had taken command of 2 Commando after most of the unit had been wiped out in the raid on St Nazaire in the spring of 1942.

Ordered to London, Nicholl arrived, as instructed, at Apsley House at the top of Piccadilly to discover the mansion was the home of the Duke of Wellington. He was not to know that Jack Churchill, seeking suitable candidates for the new force, had recruited the Duke of Wellington into the Commandos and promoted him to troop commander. The young Duke had returned home from the war in Abyssinia to succeed to his father's title. Reluctant to serve again in the Duke of Wellington's Regiment, he became a Commando captain and joined Captain Harold Blissett in a recruiting drive for the Special Services throughout England.

Disappointed, Nicholl returned to his unit to find a telegram waiting for him: IF STILL INTERESTED PHONE AYR 4242. Catching the overnight train to Glasgow he travelled on to Largs to be interviewed by Blissett and Wellington in a bare, carpetless room with photographs on the wall of Commando officers who had died in the raid on St Nazaire. At twenty-two the eager Nicholl was not going to be frightened off. Interviewed by Churchill, he was asked if he could paddle a canoe or use a bow and arrow. Walking to the window the Colonel pointed to a target he could hit with his crossbow. Turning to the tall, gangling young man he said disparagingly, 'We don't usually take people with glasses. Better see the MO.'

Nicholl suspected his chances of acceptance into the Commandos were slim. Yet within weeks he was at Achnacarry, the training centre in a lonely glen in Inverness-shire.

His preparation for battle began with an assault course. First, he had to cross a toggle bridge made from three ropes slung over a raging river. Then he climbed a tree to a height of forty feet. Balancing on a branch, he threw his toggle over a wire hawser, slipped it through his wrists, gripped firmly, and then pushed off, sliding down, hanging by his arms, to the opposite bank of the river. This was the Death Slide. 'It's all in the mind and the heart,' his instructors chanted.

Nicholl saw one volunteer fall from the hawser and land spread-eagled across the toggle bridge. A sergeant instructor yelled, 'Go up and do it again!' He saw a man slip when fording the river and drown, his steel helmet caught around his neck, in the mill race. Another man died in a burst of live machine gun fire during a simulated landing.

Now, as the *Prince Albert* moved towards the lowering position, Captain Joe Nicholl guessed where he was headed. Captain Frank Mason had shown him an aerial reconnaissance photograph of the beachhead, and he himself had been issued with a map of the terrain from which the name of the main town had been naively removed.

Nicholl was more curious than apprehensive.

A voice over the loudspeaker on LST (Landing Ship Tank) 163 in the Northern Attack Force, carrying British troops of the 56th Division, summoned 'all men in charge of special parties' to the bridge. Petty Officer Telegraphist James Sharkey climbed the companionway to report to the commanding officer.

With the group mustered and lining the rails the Captain addressed them. Pointing into the darkness, he said, 'That smudge ahead is the area of Salerno. Study it well. Compare it with your maps – because in a little while you'll be scrambling all over the place.'

Sharkey peered ahead. He could make out only a vague landscape. Then, looking through his night glasses, he saw the dim shape of a beach. But that was all.

Leaving Bizerta he had been handed an envelope containing a map of the beachhead with crosses to indicate machine gun nests. Clearly marked was a tobacco farm where he was expected to set up his radio communications. The accompanying instructions were brief: 'Take over tobacco farm. Set up radio link. Inform HQ ship when ready.'

'Each of you,' the Captain continued, 'has been allotted a particular task. Our job is to take you to the beach. Our gunners will provide you with covering fire while you make a beeline for your objective. After that, the rest is up to you and to your support troops who will land shortly afterwards.' He directed them to study their maps. 'Our section of the beach is marked Roger Green.'

On his map Sharkey saw that his objective, the tobacco farm, was close to Roger Green.

He went down from the bridge, passing a young infantryman stricken with nausea. Soldiers made poor sailors and he had seen other men sick on board the uncomfortable LST during the crossing from Bizerta. Sailing with the 56th Infantry, among a division of Black Cats, popularly known as 'Hell's Kittens', Sharkey found that he was much older than most of the men around him. He was in his middle thirties and had left behind him in Glasgow a wife and four young children. Before joining the naval reserve he had eked out a living, working occasionally on the docks or selling coal briquettes.

On board his landing ship men had shaken hands and slapped one another on the back at the news of Italy's surrender. He could not totally share their enthusiasm. It would not be an easy landing, he knew. He was not afraid, but he was tense.

To American Colonel Bill Darby commanding his Rangers was 'like driving a team of high-spirited horses'. Darby's middle name was Orlando; some officers suggested it might well have been Achilles. Save for a scar down the left side of his face, he was a strikingly handsome, muscular, slim-waisted soldier; even in battle he dressed smartly.

Darby claimed he knew each one of his men by name. Many of them were aboard the transport ship *Royal Ulsterman* in the Northern Task Force off Salerno. In a few hours they would make a landing on the beach at Maiori, the fishing village ten miles west of Salerno and the furthest point left of the invasion area.

Raised in 1942, the US Rangers were named after the buckskinned fighters of the American wars of the mid-eighteenth century. Although lacking the battle experience of the Commandos, they had been blooded in North Africa and were keen to fight. Among the eager troops was Don Earwood who had left school in Nebraska in 1941 to join the National Guard. Stationed with the 133rd Infantry in Northern Ireland, he heard that a Colonel Darby was looking for volunteers 'not averse to dangerous action' for a 'special combat force'. Bored with making beds and shining shoes, Earwood volunteered.

At the Rangers' camp at Carrickfergus, on the coast outside Belfast, he was interviewed by Captain Roy Murray, a small, cheerful man. Earwood saluted and handed him his papers. 'Private Earwood reporting, sir.'

'Fine,' Murray answered. 'I've got just the job for you, soldier. You can shine my shoes and make my bed.'

Earwood was stung. 'I ain't gonna do that, sir.'

'Why not? Are you refusing to obey orders?'

'I ain't shining no shoes, sir, and I ain't making no beds.'

Bluntly, the Captain informed him, 'Then it's the guardhouse for you, soldier.'

Earwood's cell was a small canvas tent protected by barbed wire. He sat there smarting at his treatment. Next morning he was ordered to stand to attention for the Colonel. To Earwood, the Rangers' commander looked fit enough to run a marathon.

'Godammit,' Darby said to him gruffly, 'are you giving trouble already?'

'No, sir,' replied the private. 'All I want to do, sir, is get into a fighting outfit.' He tried to explain his boredom with regular army life. 'I'll be damned, sir, if I'll shine any more shoes.'

Darby's steel blue eyes looked searchingly at the sturdy, dark haired youngster. 'Okay, soldier,' he said abruptly. 'I'll speak to Captain Murray.'

When Earwood was escorted to the Captain's tent Murray gave him a wry smile. 'I'll make a soldier out of you, Private Earwood – or else.'

Earwood was accepted for Ranger training with the warning, 'If you can't keep up, or if you make trouble, you'll be sent back to your outfit – at once. In this war we can't waste time on foul-ups.'

Gruelling days followed, days of relentless speed marches and mountain climbs, which left him totally exhausted. Murray gave the trainees no respite. Although he was in his thirties he moved like a twenty-year-old. One volunteer, James Altieri, would clench his fists until his palms bled from his fingernails in his struggle to keep pace with the other volunteers. The men's pale, drawn, sweating faces reflected their agony. By the end of the initiation course 1,500 of the original 2,000 volunteers had been rejected.

Darby's battalions were organized into sections, platoons and companies, and the young British Commando Brigade leader, Brigadier Laycock, was invited to address them. Slight and dapper, 'Lucky' Laycock stepped briskly from an olive touring car and strode across the parade ground, rhythmically striking his leg with his riding crop.

'You are pioneers,' he told the Rangers, 'in a daring field of warfare. At this critical time our fighting forces are reeling from earlier defeats. They must rebound and assume the offensive. The Commandos have provided the spark for that offensive spirit in the British army. You men are destined to provide that spark for the American forces in Europe.'

Earwood sailed with the selected trainees to Achnacarry, a battlemented, ivy-covered Scottish castle towering over squalid rows of Nissen huts. Driving into the camp they halted beside a small graveyard with freshly dug mounds of earth in which neat white tombstones had been planted. 'We've had a few accidents unfortunately,' a Commando officer explained casually. 'Some men were lost through carelessness, some through circumstances which were nobody's fault.' One stone read, 'He showed himself on the skyline'; another, 'He failed to take cover in an assault landing'.

Earwood knew that all his courage and resourcefulness would be needed to survive the course. At least he was athletic. He had competed during his schooldays in baseball and basketball and track events. He had learned to shoot and fish on the banks of the Missouri. But he couldn't swim. At Achnacarry he learned to swim in a week. 'You swam – or you went back to your unit.' One man who lied that he could swim was drowned.

The demands were extreme. Carrying his equipment and rifle, Earwood jumped from logs placed at a height of twenty-four feet. Fully kitted, he swam the fast-flowing river and climbed mountains so steep that when he slipped his feet slid uncontrollably from the bank. He learned to cook rats and eat them. He learned to cross a cat rope. And he learned to kill silently.

The tireless Darby was with his men every day, training as they did, never flinching. He swam the river with them, climbed the cliffs, went down the Death Slide. He asked them to do nothing he would not do himself. To Captain Herman Dammer, a tall, taciturn soldier appointed as his executive officer, Darby combined 'rare qualities of leadership with an instant appeal to his men.' Dammer had joined the Rangers from an anti-aircraft unit. Unused to the stress of combat training, he came to understand the close relationship between physical and mental well-being and how such well-being contributes to the ability to withstand the trauma of warfare. At Achnacarry he learned to treat himself for minor injuries and illnesses. Rangers were told, 'Only the half-dead will be accepted for sick call.'

As they rowed collapsible boats ashore in a simulated amphibious landing machine gun fire smashed their paddles to splinters. As they ran for cover bullets kicked up the dust around their boots and dynamite charges exploded in front of them. During one landing a Commando tossed a live grenade into a boat packed with Rangers. Cursing the man, a Ranger caught the grenade on the bounce and flung it into the lake where it exploded.

'Godammit, we're training you to destroy the Germans,' Darby swore at them, 'not to help them!'

By the time he sailed for North Africa Don Earwood was prepared for any assault landing. 'It was just as familiar as walking to your back door or down to the cellar or across to the corner store.'

For most of the Rangers Africa provided the first taste of battle. Stumbling into a slit trench James Altieri came face to face with the enemy. Startled, he almost forgot his Commando knife sheathed by his right leg. One swift thrust killed the man. As blood spurted over his hand Altieri wanted to vomit. 'It was sickening. It was brutal. But that was our job.'

Dammer led the 3rd Rangers in a landing in Sicily as the spearhead for the US 3rd Division. At Gela Earwood positioned himself in an upper storey of a house as Italian tanks came rumbling through the narrow streets. He saw Darby, sleeves rolled up, swinging a .50 machine gun on its tripod at an approaching light tank. One shot, aimed through the peephole, caught the driver clean through the forehead.

As the Italians flung back the hatch to dump the body, Earwood leaped instinctively from his first floor window onto the roof of the tank, lobbed a grenade through the open hatch, slammed it shut, and stood on it. The tremor of the explosion was 'just a pinprick'. He was more worried knowing that across the street his Ranger comrade, Wilbur Gallup, was aiming a bazooka at the tank.

By the time he sailed for Salerno on the *Royal Ulsterman* Earwood had been promoted Sergeant. At Maiori he would lead his own squad ashore.

VI
'Afraid of Being Afraid'

Thursday, 9 September. After midnight.

It was past midnight.

Crowded in their living darkness the invasion troops were more aware than at any other time of the relentless compulsion of the military machine which had recruited and moulded them and was now about to set them down on the shores of continental Europe. Across the entire width of the Gulf of Salerno the leading ships lay at anchor at the 100-fathom line. Intelligence reports had warned the Navy about the presence of minefields; troopships dared come no closer than twelve miles to the beaches. The darkness lent a ghostly air to the floating ships as on board loudspeakers began calling the troops to their stations. Bells rang and lights flashed. Scrambling nets were flung over the ships' sides. Assault boats were lowered from the davits.

With the troopships far from the beaches the men would have to remain in the assault craft for longer than was planned. Furthermore, with the time needed by the boats to reach the beaches and return to the troopships extended, the unloading operations would be slowed down.

Correspondent Quentin Reynolds saw General Clark in the War Room of the *Ancon*, walking with his aides among Navy staff who sat with earphones listening and talking to the other ships. At any moment Clark might have to change plans if the landing did not go according to schedule. The General looked calm and unruffled, though he must have known there was no precedent for an operation of this magnitude. If his flagship were seriously damaged by enemy fire the entire complex operation would be jeopardized.

The combat soldiers were edgy. As each moment brought them nearer to H-hour their tension increased. Some men of the 36th Division on board the *Ancon* secretly worried that they might fail at the decisive moment in their first battle. 'They were all afraid of being afraid, not knowing that fear is as universal as hunger.'

Lionel Shapiro was also quick to notice the tension which had 'mounted to excruciating levels'. For at least six hours, perhaps for longer, the enemy had been alerted to their approach. Surprise and deception were essential elements of this invasion, yet both had been lost. The success of Clark's tactic was 'gravely in doubt'.

The complacent mood induced by the news of the armistice was now broken. The troops knew the dangerous moment was at hand when they would have to wade ashore. Yet even before the armistice the men on James Daniel's LCI, Landing Craft Infantry, in the British sector had been assured of an easy landing. They had been shown an aerial reconnaissance photograph of the road they were to take from the beach. 'It's not mined,' an officer assured them. 'Look – you can see people walking around.'

After the surrender the officer told them, 'You may unload your guns.'

'Why, sir?' Daniel asked.

'Because now that the Italians have surrendered we'll most likely go straight to Naples.'

'Excuse me, sir,' Daniel's sergeant interjected. 'What about the Jerries?'

'Dash it,' the officer exclaimed, 'I clean forgot about the Germans!'

Whatever faced him on the beaches, Private Daniel, of the British 188th Pioneer Corps, 78th Division, was glad he would not have to spend another night trying to snatch some sleep, sitting upright on the wooden seats of the narrow, shallow-draught landing craft. Even though the sea was calm the craft pitched and rolled, and many of the men were sick.

On another LCI a tall Scots Guardsman with dark, spiky hair had also endured a miserable crossing. For two nights John Weir had tried to sleep sitting on a bench. It was 'like being afloat on a cork'. Until now, the cheerful Weir had to admit he had played at soldiers. He joined the Guards after working as a cement mixer in Glasgow. At nineteen, the Army seemed an adventure. He guarded the Palace, the Mint and 10 Downing Street. Fascinated, he watched Churchill come and go under heavy security, and he saw the storybook princesses Elizabeth and Margaret. Now he was nearing the end of a journey to a beachhead called Salerno, a spot on the map of which he had never heard.

It was accepted that in time of war Guardsmen went where they were most needed and Weir took heart from the battle-hardened soldiers he had joined for assault training in Bizerta. They had fought through the desert campaign and now, instead of going home on leave, were ready to fight again. The prospect angered them. Sometimes he wanted to ask how they had felt in their first battle, but he could not bring himself to form the question.

When he heard of the Italian surrender he was sure he was on his way to make love to Italian girls. Only as they neared Salerno did the officers reveal that a force of Germans was holding out. The brightly coloured kerchief he had tied around his neck seemed an irrelevancy. Instinctively, he gripped his rifle and felt for the small pouch with 500 rounds of ammunition slung around his neck and the grenades at his belt. He was among strangers, in a battalion of which he was the youngest member, sailing into the unknown. He had been bandsman, bugler, toy soldier. Now he was to learn what real war was like. Strangely, he didn't feel afraid.

Only when the loudspeakers called the troops to their assault stations did the men on Private Oswald Edwards's troopship abandon their gambling game of 'housey-housey'. Most of them were so engrossed in the outcome of the game that the battle ahead was forgotten. Though heavily equipped, they made the fifty feet climb down the nets from the ship's sides with ease. This was what they had trained for at Largs. Edwards, with the 4th Commando Beach Group in the 56th Division, clambered down the side in FSMO – Full Service Marching Order, wearing a steel helmet, carrying a loaded Sten gun, with a valise on his back and another at his side containing forty-eight hours' rations of powdered food, meat extract, chocolate bars, a tin of blended tea and sugar, and a mess tin for cooking over a portable 'Tommy stove'. Someone said he was to land on a beach in Italy. Where the beach was nobody told him.

'Throw away that garbage, Wally,' advised an American lieutenant. 'We'll look after you.'

Bombardier Walter Harvey, bound for the 46th Division beaches, dumped his British rations and accepted an invitation to eat in the galley of his American LST. Invariably, Harvey was surprised when officers called him by his first name. Such familiarity underlined the difference between British and American discipline. It was strange to the Tommy, second nature to the GI. During the voyage from Bizerta, Harvey had slept on the top deck of the two-tiered craft. Twenty-three and single, he was within hours of the most critical moment of his life. During his days in Bizerta the Americans had been so free with their information that he believed the landings must be common knowledge to the enemy. His kitbag had been taken from him and he was carrying only a small haversack with six spare magazines for his Thompson sub-machine gun packed in webbing pouches; he was promised more ammo on the beaches. The Americans gave him an expendable Mae West which he was to inflate before going ashore. 'When you hit the beach,' the lieutenant told him, 'pull the cord and get rid of it.'

In his khaki drill uniform Medical Officer William Rankin was indistinguishable from the other officers and men around him in the darkness. While he could not read the men's minds, he himself had no illusions. The Germans were waiting for them and it would be a bloody battle. He checked his 'monkey bag' which held the basic necessities for treating the wounded on the beaches. A few instruments, dressings, sulphonamide drugs and morphine tablets. Everything in order. His only concern was that he had no plasma. It would be available later, they told him, in the field hospitals.

By 1.50 a.m. six Fleet minesweepers of the Royal Navy, their paravanes out, had cleared two channels through the treacherous fields north of the Sele River in the area where the 46th and 56th Divisions of the British Tenth Corps were to make their assault.

Just after two a.m. in this sector the German bombardment of the armada began. The first three salvoes from the shore killed and wounded twenty-five soldiers and crew of an LST. Standing across the inshore boundary of transport area, the USS *Biscayne* shook as the shells landed perilously close.

Anticipating this enemy bombardment, US Rear-Admiral Richard Conolly had placed three supporting destroyers, *Brecon*, *Blankney* and *Mendip*, in firing positions as soon as the minefields were cleared. The onus was on him to protect the fifteen American LSTs carrying British troops to the lowering area. In accordance with Hewitt's instructions, he ordered the destroyers to return fire, and to protect his own flagship he directed his crew to lay down a smokescreen. Firing from 5,000 yards *Brecon*, *Blankney* and *Mendip* engaged the batteries, hoping to silence them. From the hills the enemy's powerful 88 mm guns responded with a massive barrage, raining shells on the convoy. Only the screen of darkness saved the ships from destruction.

By 2.25 a.m., as the firing slackened off, Conolly, his glasses slung about his neck, was still on the bridge of the *Biscayne* with General 'Ginger' Hawkesworth, British Commander of the British 46th Division. Acrid smoke drifted about them. It was time, Conolly remarked to the General, to get the landings going.

On the Hunt class destroyer *Blackmore* off Vietri, Lieutenant Harrel signalled one of the minesweepers to move ahead. Within minutes an explosion from the minefield shattered the silence.

Minutes passed. There was no further sound. Lining up astern of the destroyer, Harrel reckoned, were about half a dozen assault craft; in the darkness he could distinguish their shapes and the shadowy figures of Commandos.

At 2.15 a.m. the *Prince Albert*, further off Vietri, had begun lowering its six LCAs, Landing Craft Assault. One of the boats, carrying Brigade headquarters, moved off to join the LCIs carrying the men of 41 Royal Marine Commando. The remaining five boats, with 210 of all ranks of 2 Commando under Lieut. Colonel Jack Churchill, lined up astern of the *Blackmore*. Their first task was 'to secure the beach-head, strike and move off'. 41 Commando and Brigade HQ would follow and move inland to seize the pass at La Molina outside Vietri on the highway to Naples. A third wave, consisting of the rest of 2 Commando, would go ashore using the same assault craft that had put the first wave on the beach. The fourth and last wave, a back-up force, would consist of anti-tank gun troops and an American mortar company.

All three Churchills were in this Commando assault force, Major Randolph, Lieut. Colonel Tom, who was Laycock's Chief of Staff, and his brother Jack. Guardsman Stretton carried Jack Churchill's crossbow and arrows and bagpipes, and a cloth bag with a selection of the guns favoured by his Colonel, including an American .45 carbine and a Garand MI rifle, which Patton declared was 'the best battle implement ever devised.' Churchill would go ashore with his claymore and his favourite lightweight Beretta.

From his observation post at Faiano, Lieutenant Rocholl heard the boom of naval guns in the northern sector of the gulf. Hearing the mortars whistling inland, the reverberations as they exploded, and the 88 mm batteries and machine guns from the shore opening up, he knew the British and Americans in their landing barges were coming closer.

Using 8 kilowatts, with a tall, 'star' aerial hoisted on the radio car, his radio operator was transmitting reports so continuously to the regiment that he had not stopped for a moment encoding and despatching. Rocholl only worried that, with the strength of an MW transmitter like Cologne, their position might be easily detected. But then, he reckoned, the enemy forces would be too busy with their landings to intercept his station.

At his farm headquarters near Paestum, Major Duppenbecker heard the distant gunfire. Confident that he could depend on his Panzers to meet the threat on the beaches, he nonetheless worried about the lack of ammunition, especially for the 88 mm guns.

Only now were Field Marshal Kesselring's orders of the previous evening reaching General Vietinghoff at Polla. Faced with the need to make a decision, the General found himself studying conflicting orders. He was expected to hold the Salerno–Gaeta area and at the same time arrange for the withdrawal of the Panzers to the area around Rome. With a landing imminent at Salerno, his tactical and political reasoning indicated that he must first repel the invaders. Impatiently, he waited for news of the arrival of the 26th Panzers from Calabria.

At Frascati, Kesselring was hopelessly frustrated. After the flight of the King and Badoglio he rushed the 2nd Parachute Division to the southern periphery of Rome. One unit made a lightning swoop on the Italian headquarters at Monterotondo. But General Roatta and his staff had bolted.

With a start, General Walker, Commander of the US 36th Division, woke from his catnap on board the *Samuel Chase*. From outside his stateroom he could hear the echoing sounds of naval gunfire from the British sector. 'Softening up the enemy defences,' he guessed. Hopefully, such a barrage might mislead the Germans into assuming that the main assault was being launched on the northern beaches. He did not believe that German troops would be massed in strength on the beaches in the American sector. To comply with Clark's wishes, he had decided not to ask for fire support for his Texas Army.

At 2.30 a.m. in the American sector small armoured scout boats, their engines muffled with silencers, headed towards the shore to station themselves within 400 yards of the surf line. As they drifted in the darkness the young ensigns in the boats could hear from the roads near the shore the sounds of tanks and armoured cars rolling into position and the distant voices of German soldiers.

Minesweepers followed the scout boats, the same minesweepers from the Sicily operation. Watching from the *Ancon*, Admiral Hewitt wondered if the minefields could possibly be cleared by H-hour. He was astonished that Clark was sticking to his decision to commence the great assault in the American sector without a preliminary bombardment. It seemed that the prearranged plan to clear the boat channels and the adjoining fire support area of mines by 3.30 a.m. was too optimistic. Unlike the troops in the British sector, those in the American sector would have no support fire as they headed for the beaches. He had asked for gunboats, but Clark and the army would have none of it.

Off Red Beach a scout boat flashed an infra-red light towards the waiting assault craft. Another boat, opposite Torre di Paestum, the stone medieval watch tower, blinked a green light to show the way to Green Beach. Other boats blinked yellow and blue lights for their respective beaches. From the *Ancon*, General Clark could see the red tail lights of the wave leaders' boats and in the far distance the coloured lights of the scout boats. Wave after wave of assault craft pulled away from the transports, moving towards the rendezvous area three to four miles offshore. Behind the assault craft larger craft followed with supplies of *Dukw*s, tanks, and heavy weapons. Many of these landing craft, welded on American assembly lines, would be tested on the beaches of Salerno. All of them would run in to the water's edge where their ramps or retractable causeways would facilitate the rapid disembarkation of men, vehicles and supplies.

Shortly after midnight Clark had snatched an hour's sleep to prepare for the momentous dawn ahead. Now, watching the lights of the leading craft fade into the darkness, he was assailed for a fleeting moment by a feeling of helplessness. It stemmed from his passive role as observer on the *Ancon*. It was the Navy's job, not his, to ferry his troops to the beaches and get them ashore.

Hewitt joined him. 'You'll be in total command by tonight.'

'I will,' Clark said, 'if we establish that beachhead. I can't help thinking that casualties may be high. Pray God they won't.'

The same fear flashed through the mind of the aloof Lieut. General McCreery in *Hilary*. How was he to obviate the risk of a high casualty rate in his sector around the tobacco factory and Montecorvino airfield? Though he knew it would be difficult, at least he was heartened by the knowledge that the enemy would not know the precise landing points of the assault. Since the planning of Avalanche began he had argued with Clark on matters of strategy, but he was aware that Clark was as anxious as he was to keep casualties down. A deeply religious man, McCreery had a habit of rounding off exhortations to his troops with the words, 'We will go forward and attack with Divine assistance.' Tonight he felt pangs of concern for his men. The worst aspect of warfare was the waste of human life. 'I hate it, I hate it,' he would say with passion.

He had more confidence in the ability of Alexander. They were trusted friends who had fought alongside each other at Dunkirk. He shared Alexander's view that Allied superiority in the air and on the sea might, despite the disadvantages of a beachhead which left the troops vulnerable, swing the battle in their favour. In his dealings with

Clark he was on his guard lest the Commander of the Fifth Army 'inadvertently undermine Alexander's express objectives in overall strategy'. Yet, he wondered, why had Alexander accepted Clark's decision not to allow a preliminary bombardment of the coastal defences in the Paestum area? He was unaware that, since the start of Avalanche, Alexander had given no orders to Clark.

'We always talked things over,' Clark would say. 'Alex would take my view into account and we would more or less agree on a course of action. But actual orders – never.'

Nine miles west of Vietri, like an amphitheatre at the mouth of the Tramonti Valley, lies the fishing village of Maiori. So steep is the half-mile beach of soft sand that cruising yachts anchor close to the shore. Directly from the beach a road runs into the mountains to the Chiunzi Pass and the highway to Naples. It was on this beach that Colonel Bill Darby was to land his force of US Rangers.

Three battalions of his men climbed into their landing craft at the same lowering point as the Commandos. Once ashore on the shelving beach they would operate independently on the flank of the British sector. So keen were they for battle that they scrambled into the British landing craft while they were still hanging from the davits over the side of the *Royal Ulsterman*.

From the leading boat as it came alongside the destroyer that was to guide them in, Darby yelled up to the captain on the bridge, 'We're here! Let's go!'

In the steel assault boat, standing in the tight group of thirty-five men with rifles and steel helmets, his compass swung wildly. Unable to find direction or see through the darkness, he knew he would have to rely on the destroyer to guide him to the beach.

About one mile offshore the captain shouted down, 'Continue on your course!' Engines muffled, Darby's lead boat ran ahead. At 3.20 a.m. by his luminous watch dial, they reached the surf line. 'Maybe, Bill,' an aide quipped, 'Mussolini ran the trains on time. But we sure run our invasion on the button.'

Ten minutes ahead of the other assault troops in Operation Avalanche, the Rangers were ready to go ashore.

At Palermo, Brigadier Laycock had advised Lieutenant Harrel, 'If you can do it, put a few shells into the houses and keep their heads down.'

While the Commandos' assault craft were running towards the beach at Vietri the *Blackmore* swung to starboard, and Harrel ordered a couple of salvoes to be fired at the houses immediately overlooking the beach. Bursting in vivid explosions of orange fire, the destroyers' shells sent up spurts of rock and sand and battered the nearby buildings. There was no response from the shore.

Harrel ordered his officer in the gun control tower to aim the twin, four-inch anti-aircraft guns in the direction of the German batteries above the village. Working from a map reference which gave him what he hoped was an accurate position, he fired almost 100 shells. But 'it was like shooting heads on a parapet'. With no answer from the shore he could only hope that his diversion would help the Commandos. The greatest fear of any landing party in an assault is of deadly marksmen 'looking down their sights, calmly waiting for the opportune moment to pick you off'.

With each thrump of the *Blackmore*'s guns the assault boats trembled. Jack Churchill could see the houses of the hillside village illuminated by shell flashes. Save for the solitary bark of a dog there was no answering sound. Was the enemy lying low, preparing to give them 'a sticky welcome'? Then, just as the boats came close to the beach, two white Verey lights soared into the sky from the German battery position. It was 3.20 a.m.

Churchill grabbed his claymore. *Look out for it now*, he thought.

On board HMS *Hilary* Commodore Geoffrey Oliver, commander of the Northern Attack Force, wrote in his log, 'Any prospect of even local surprise has been lost.'

Wireless signals on naval channels from the communications ship were now resumed. Hewitt, in charge of all amphibious landings, decided it was pointless to preserve further silence. Yet Clark, listening to the distant gunfire, made no move to order a bombardment of the enemy's coastal defences in the Paestum area. He remained unshakeable in his decision to hold off the Navy gunners.

In the southern sector the German guns were silent. Avalanche had reached its most critical hour and the determined Mark Clark faced the most testing operation of his military career.

Was his gamble about to come unstuck?

Part Two

ASSAULT

'The invading army in the area Naples–Salerno and southwards must be completely annihilated and, in addition, thrown into the sea.'

Field Marshal Albert Kesselring, 9 September 1943

VII
Not Glory, but Survival

Thursday, 9 September. H-Hour.

For the men crowding the landing craft their nightmare of fear and pain was about to begin. Ahead lay the unseen shore, dark, mysterious and silent. From the British invasion sector on the northern beaches near Salerno came the cracking sound of the enemy's 88 mm guns and the thundering echo from the fleet. But along the southern coast in the American sector at Paestum only the faint echo of gunfire was audible. Here, the enemy, like the invader, was silent. General Mark Clark's strategy of 'tactical surprise' seemed, after all, to be a wise decision.

As General Walker's men of the 36th Army rode closer in their assault craft they strained to catch above the muffled motors any sounds from the shore. Did the enemy know they were coming? Or when? Or in what numbers? Walker's tough, but untried, troops had trained assiduously for this moment on the beaches of North Africa. Now this short, hazardous last run-in became a nightmare – the longest run they had ever made.

Scores of assault craft carrying US Regimental Combat Teams 141 and 142, part of Walker's US 36th Division, rode to the surfline and bumped the four areas of beach at Paestum selected for the American landings. Ramps banged down. Men went storming out, wading through the warm water, their weapons held high, onto the beach.

For the enemy it was the moment for which they had waited. As the combat troops of the Texas Army threw themselves in the sand, among dunes and scattered patches of scrub, or into shallow irrigation ditches, the terrifying shells from the Germans' 88 mm guns erupted without warning. Red killer tracers from machine guns crisscrossed the beach. The savagery of their reception shocked the troops. They were face to face with death.

The men following in the second wave of assault craft saw their comrades crawling and stumbling, falling and dying, beneath shells and bullets. War correspondent John Steinbeck reported, 'It didn't seem like men getting killed, more like a picture, a moving picture.'

One GI summed it up for him, 'If we thought we were going to sneak ashore we were nuts.'

A tornado of fire had swept over the men of the 3rd Battalion of 141 Regimental Combat Team, the first to hit the beaches. Three battalions of the 141st were landed on Beaches Yellow and Blue, the southern beaches in the American sector. They were ruthlessly pinned down.

Lieut. Colonel Edward McCall, their battalion commanding officer, instantly realized the risks. Enemy tanks were hidden behind the medieval Torre di Paestum, snipers in the tower were spraying the beach. Seeing his GIs frozen with fear and indecision at the water's edge, he yelled at them, 'Get up, you bastards! Get up and go!' Singly, and then in groups, his men found courage. Officers and NCOs took up McCall's cry and his troops charged into the inferno. It was an incredible transformation.

On another beach Private John Jones of the 2nd Battalion, 142 RCT, lost his platoon. Wandering among the dunes he stumbled on some fifty GIs cowering with fear, some of them crying.

'Come on, you guys!' he shouted at them. 'You'll never get home to Texas lying around here!'

Leading them off the beach, he urged them as they advanced to toss grenades into enemy machine gun nests among the dunes.

On Yellow Beach Private Harry Keefer of 141 RCT destroyed a machine gun nest with his Browning automatic rifle, falling at the same time from bullets from a German automatic weapon. When they found Keefer's body his finger was still pressed against the trigger.

Even before his assault craft grounded in the second wave Staff Sergeant Quillian McMichen of 142 RCT was hit in the chest and shoulder by tracer bullets. When the boat's ramp jammed, McMichen, though injured and in obvious pain, kicked and pounded the ramp until it fell down. Running onto the beach, leading his men to a firing position, he was mortally wounded.

Technical Sergeant Manuel Gonzales of the 142nd, searching for the other men in his platoon, saw a machine gun among the dunes peppering the GIs on the assault crafts. He ran, then crawled, until he was within grenade-throwing distance of the emplacement. He was spotted by the machine gunner who loosed a burst of tracer bullets, setting Gonzales' pack on fire. The sergeant wriggled out of his burning pack and flung two 'pineapple' grenades, wrecking the gun and killing the crew.

Not realizing he was alone Private James Logan of the 141st went sprinting across the beach, utterly heedless of shells and tracers. About eight hundred yards from the water's edge he saw in the darkness an irrigation ditch flanked by a crumbling stone wall. Jumping into the ditch he continued his run as three Germans rushed him from behind the wall. Without breaking his stride, Logan swung his carbine towards them, killing all three with a single burst. Further on, an enemy machine gun was firing at the GIs on the beach. He shot the gunner and, as the other men in the emplacement fled, rushed the gun and turned the weapon on the retreating Germans.

While disorganized companies fought the enemy in small groups on the beaches, one company of the 141st pressed inland from Yellow Beach. Like Private Logan, Captain Edgar Ford found an empty ditch along which he crawled for several hundred yards, his men following him, to reach an assembly area.

While Ford worked his way inland, the 1st Battalion of 141 RCT landed 500 yards south of the designated southernmost Blue Beach under Lieut. Colonel Carlos Smith and were cut off. The next wave of the battalion fared even worse. The beleaguered men ashore needed the howitzers of the US 141st Cannon Company, but as the first boat carrying the cannon was pounded by shells it turned away out of range. At the same time a second boat struck a mine that killed and disabled every man on board. As the burning boat drifted across the path of incoming craft the chaos in the landing area increased.

A third boat, however, successfully ran the gauntlet under concerted mortar fire and shelling. The ramp was lowered and men valiantly hauled a 75 mm howitzer safely ashore. Within minutes the gun crew, under First Lieutenant Clair Carpenter, had the cannon in action. They had fired only a few rounds when the crew, save for Carpenter and Corporal Edgar Blackburn, fell dead from the barrage. The survivors went on firing, blasting a machine gun nest and destroying a tank, until an 88 mm shell fragment smashed the gunsight. Undeterred, Carpenter waded waist-deep to the wrecked and drifting landing craft, stripped the cannon on the craft of its sight, and returned to the beach. He and the corporal had hastily adjusted the new sight when a direct shot wounded him and killed Blackburn outright.

Meanwhile, not all waves of 142 RCT on the left flank of Walker's 36th Division were put ashore on their designated beaches, Red and Green. Some were landed on the nearest beach; others failed to get ashore when, to avoid the enemy bombardment, Navy steersmen swung their landing craft about and put to sea again, causing further confusion. Some Navy personnel attempted to return with their troops to the transports, upsetting the intricate landing schedules. From now on succeeding waves could not be landed in time or in the proper place.

Off Green Beach a landing craft specially rigged for rockets edged to within eighty yards of the shoreline and fired a vivid carpet of three-inch shells over the heads of the troops pinned down on the beach. The awesome sound induced terror and for a time all enemy fire ceased. During the lull the deafened infantrymen, smothered with dirt from the blast, were able to move inland to reach the shelter of shallow irrigation ditches and rock walls. Lieut. Colonel Samuel Graham, 2nd Battalion 142 RCT, who had arrived at the beachhead in advance of his troops, rounded up some disorganized GIs. Together they crossed dunes and small swamps, moved through ditches and among clumps of trees, as machine guns and mortars opened up again, finally reaching a railway line parallel to the beach a mile and a half inland. It was an easy landmark to find, a temporary refuge where men could rejoin their units and leaders regroup their troops.

'Monte Soprano is our objective,' Graham told his GIs. 'I want every man on that mountain by nightfall.'

In the half-light the men could see the towering shape of the 3,500 foot mountain directly ahead of them. 'Like a corps of army worms' they began to move forward in small groups, as though indifferent to the enemy fire.

Major Duppenbecker had not slept at his farmhouse headquarters near Paestum. News of the approaching enemy convoys had made him apprehensive. He had taken all possible precautions in the area for which he was responsible, from the Sele River down to Paestum. But where would they land? And when?

Just after 3.30 a.m. the major's field telephone jangled. On the line was the commander of the strongpoint near Torre di Paestum, one of eight strongpoints Major General Sieckenius had ordered the Panzers to construct between Salerno and Agropoli, each manned by a full company of Grenadiers, supported by mortars, heavy machine guns, anti-aircraft and anti-tank guns.

'A sound of heavy engine noise from the sea, Major,' the commander reported. 'But our men can't see anything.'

Duppenbecker wondered if Paestum was to be the danger point at which he must mount his counter-attack. Minutes later a message was radioed through that the strongpoint was under heavy machine gun fire. He tried to reach the commander by telephone, but now there was no response. Had the strongpoint fallen in the first assault? At once he ordered a reserve company to be sent up and a heavy barrage laid on the beaches. Assuming the defence at Paestum to have been captured, he also ordered the 2nd Battalion Panzergrenadiers to attack with tanks northwest from Agropoli towards Paestum and the 1st Battalion to attack southeast.

Shells had damaged the Germans' vital telephone lines. Wireless messages from the Allied convoys were jumbling the frequencies, producing a hopeless babel of languages. Dismayed, Duppenbecker tried again to make contact with his commander at Paestum. But he could not reach him.

The fearless Lieut. Colonel William Darby, the Rangers' commander, would boast, 'When I run out of that landing craft I'm moving so fast I don't want to look right or left'.

To the north, ten minutes ahead of schedule, Darby and his handpicked US Rangers volunteers, who had fought heroically in North Africa and Sicily, stormed ashore at Maiori, the seaside town at the mouth of the terraced valley, seven miles from Vietri, where the steep wall of coastal rock suddenly splits open. The Rangers were natural spearheaders of an invasion and eager for battle.

An astonished Darby looked ahead to see, lined along the beach wall, directly in front of his men, rows of marine mines with sinister perpendicular horns. By morning the Germans would have been laying them in the sea. He led his Rangers inland through the town, up the Corso Reginna, past the high palazzos, and onto the narrow, winding mountain road leading to the Chiunzi Pass and the Naples highway. By now these young men who had campaigned with Bill Darby knew him as a combat leader of exceptional ability and personal courage. They had seen him carry wounded men from the battlefield. They had heard him challenge the Allied generals with a defiant, 'If the tanks come, then God help the tanks.' Like his other officers Darby liked to merge with his men who were distinguishable from the other GIs in Italy only by their red-and-black shoulder patches and cut-down leggings which helped them march faster. He wore no colonel's insignia, though sometimes he and other officers pasted Band-aid strips on the backs of their helmets.

Major Roy Murray, promoted since his months in Carrickfergus, wore two strips of adhesive tape on the back of his helmet to distinguish his rank. It was just after 3.20 a.m. when he and his 4th US Ranger Battalion unit swung left off the beach. His mission was to seal off the roads in the hills above Minori, the coastal village tucked into a rocky cove beyond Maiori.

First he combed the houses for enemy troops. Forcing his way into a house on the main street he noticed the remains of a half-smoked cigar still burning. He lifted a small box from the table. Fine German cigars. But the smoker had vanished.

Sergeant Arthur Schrader's company had swept ashore at Maiori in the first Ranger wave. Heading up the mountain road, past the medieval tower of San Sebastiano, two scouts went forward and discovered a group of Germans stationed in an armoured radio scout car. Signalling to Schrader and his men to drop to the edge of the road, the scouts moved forward stealthily in their Vibram-soled boots greased with saddle soap until they were alongside the car. Inside, the Germans were asleep. Coolly, the scouts dropped a couple of 'pineapple' grenades into the vehicle. The explosion reverberated along the narrow road.

It was the only noise the platoon would make that morning.

Sergeant Don Earwood's objective was the lighthouse along the steep coast road to the right of Maiori beach. Bypassing the town he and his three Ranger squads headed up the hilly road in the darkness. They travelled light. Each man's back pack consisted of a shelter-half and his rations, mostly chocolate bars. Apart from guns and ammunition the Rangers carried no other equipment. For night raids, Earwood, like many of his men, preferred to wear a stocking cap with a protective liner instead of his helmet.

The camouflaged lighthouse was not lit. An Italian guard, suddenly seeing four Rangers creeping up the road, ran towards them, hands raised high, shouting words of surrender. In the machine gun nest the Germans were alerted. Before they could reach the trigger Earwood had knocked out the nest with a 'pineapple' grenade. Kicking open the lighthouse door, Sergeant Lloyd Prewett, his second in command, lobbed a grenade inside. The others followed him, storming up the narrow, winding stairway. The interior of the lighthouse was an open area with a circular catwalk running around the inner wall. Earwood could see no doorway at the top of the tower. The enemy, he hoped, had no way out. But as the Rangers swarmed up the stairs they were machine-gunned from above. Two of them fell, one dying, in a hail of bullets. A third Ranger threw a grenade into the upper section of the tower. The lighthouse was theirs.

Sergeant Wilbur Gallup came ashore in one of the last Ranger waves with his mortar section of two gunners and two carriers. His orders were to clear the immediate beach road of the enemy.

He found a group of eleven Germans asleep, engineers who had mined the nearby cliffs at Minori and were waiting until daybreak before returning to Salerno. As the men of Gallup's section disarmed them, a motor cycle rider came roaring down the Salerno road onto the seafront to warn the engineers that the Allied landings had begun. He was too late. By now Maiori was in the hands of Darby's Rangers.

Off the beach at Vietri, a dozen miles away, the gun's crew of HMS *Blackmore* had run short of flashless charges. Now, with no choice but to switch to non-flashless ammunition, Lieutenant Harrel realized the Germans would pinpoint their position.

A high explosive burst in the water beside the destroyer, peppering the bow and damaging the vessel close to the anchor. Harrel knew his ship was 'a sitting duck'. The next salvo might score a direct hit.

His task had been to assist the Commandos in landing on the correct beach at Vietri and ensuring they were not fired on. No guns had replied from the battery above the beach, and that had been his main concern. A landing craft gun, which had provided covering fire, was now silent.

He ordered, 'Full astern'. Turning on her heel, the *Blackmore* headed out from the beach. Harrel was in a minefield, and he must return through the same waters through which he had come. He hoped the minesweeper had done its work.

Claymore in hand, Beretta snug at his hip, Lieut. Colonel Jack Churchill led his men of 2 Commando onto the empty beach at Vietri. It was precisely 3.30 a.m. One troop immediately formed a beach-head. Mortars were set in position as the remainder of the force formed up to assault the battery on high ground overlooking the beach. Churchill decided to approach the battery from the northeast, the inland side, under cover of fire from the mortars.

Progress was tedious as the Commandos felt their way through steep vineyards among rows of vines that grew about four feet high. At the end of each row there were narrow stone steps, but as these were difficult to locate in the dark the Commandos hoisted one another up until all the members of the force had reached the foot of the battery. Even to Jack Churchill, the hero of Vaägso, 'it was a sweat'.

Nobody had fired a shot at them. Contemptuously, Churchill kicked open the door of the battery. Empty. Inside, the guns lay silent and undefended. No Germans to be seen. Drawing his Beretta he explored the interior. The guns had been dismantled and smashed by hammer blows.

On the town side of the battery was a large building, a well-equipped school which had served as headquarters for the Germans. Each officer had had his own bedside telephone. Now it showed signs of hurried evacuation. A perfect headquarters, Churchill thought, for the Commando Brigade.

The boyish Captain Tom Gordon-Hemming had landed dryshod. He could not believe he had run onto the beach without even getting his feet wet. This was so different to what Jack Churchill had led him to expect when he made them plunge up to their waists in the sea on winter days in Scotland. Gordon-Hemming's job was to form the bridgehead, to hang on while the others went through.

When the adjutant, Captain Harold Blissett, came ashore he moved behind Gordon-Hemming to establish his headquarters under the side of the tall old buildings on the beach. Knowing that Churchill had set off with his forces up the hillside to the battery, he ordered his beachhead troop to clear the houses. Then he waited for the pistol shot that would signal the success of the Colonel's mission.

When Gunner Charles Dettmer, one of the youngest members of 2 Commando, ran off his landing craft at Vietri he was pushed aside in the scramble and fell into deep water. Though wearing his equipment and carrying his Sten gun and a breech for a heavy weapon he 'came up like a cork'. Soaked, he waded determinedly ashore. His troop was to form the perimeter just beyond the beachhead through which 41 Royal Marine Commando would pass. Dettmer knew he would remain cold and wet until the sun came up and dried him out.

Led by Lieut. Colonel Bruce Lumsden, the men of the 41 Royal Marine Commando landed on the beach and moved off quickly according to plan. Their object was twofold: to clear Vietri of the enemy and to seize and hold the narrow defile north of the town through which ran the road and railway from Salerno to Naples, the vital, steep-sided pass of La Molina.

By now the Germans were alerted. Moving into the upper part of the town towards the battery, Lieut. Colonel Tom Churchill, Laycock's Chief of Staff, came face to face with a giant German soldier. Before he could raise his gun his batman, Sapper Baldwin, had dropped the man with a couple of bullets in the belly. Brigadier Laycock, who came ashore with Brigade Headquarters, turned a corner to be confronted by a German levelling a rifle at his head. Laycock fired at him and missed. A Marine at his rear pushed him heavily to the ground and, lying across his body, shot and killed the German.

Soon the bulk of the Marine Commandos, under Lumsden, were heading off in the darkness towards the La Molina Pass. Sweating under their equipment, they were determined to reach their position before dawn. Rounding a bend in the road at the mouth of the defile a handful of Marines found a stationary Mark 4 tank. Instinctively, the men leaped into the ditch and opened fire, killing the tank crew as they slept by the roadside. Then, clambering onto the Mark 4, they threw an anti-personnel 36 grenade into the open hatch and ran clear as the tank's ammunition exploded. Minutes later these Marines were digging in on the thickly-wooded high ground to the right of the road and the railway.

Down on the beach Captain Blissett heard the success signal fired from the battery. The Colonel was in occupation. It was time for him to move 2 Commando headquarters up to Vietri town.

In the darkness a Marine Commando shouted, 'Come out with your hands up!'

In the town's Villa Angrisani Sergeant Dentoni-Litta didn't understand the words. But his fellow-sergeant, Mario Barone, could speak English and called to the troops as they emerged from the building, '*Noi siamo Italiani, non Tedeschi!*' – We're Italians, not Germans!'

Two troops of Royal Marine Commandos under Major John Edwards were clearing the town. Seven Germans captured near the battery had been sent down to Captain Gordon-Hemming on the beach. An elusive machine gun had been located and knocked out. Now, as the Marines hustled Dentoni-Litta and Barone out of the villa, a motor cyclist came racing up the hill road from Salerno. Marines who had mounted a gun at the crossroads fired a fusillade as the bike came into close range, smashing the headlight, but missing the rider, who escaped. A German staff car followed. They shot the driver dead and took the officer beside him prisoner.

Other Italian naval staff, some of them hiding in the railway tunnel, were rounded up. As they were marched with them down to the beach, Dentoni-Litta and Barone were convinced they would be ferried to the ships in the gulf. Descending the steep, cobblestoned Via Perla Marina, Dentoni-Litta noticed a woman watching them from a top window. Quickly he moved to the doorway of the house and scribbled in pencil on the wall, 'Tell my family I am prisoner of English,' and signed his name.

The woman had seen him. He hoped to God she would pass on the message.

'Follow the rockets, not the plan.'

In the British 46th Division sector the crews of the assault boats had been passed this order from General 'Ginger' Hawkesworth and Admiral Conolly. They were to put troops ashore on beaches neutralized by Allied rockets.

Two battalions of Hampshires were due to land on the two 'Uncle' beaches in the 46th Division area, Red Beach and Green Beach. The key objectives of these men of McCreery's British 46th Division were to capture the city of Salerno, the surrounding high ground around Salerno, and the Cava defile leading to the Naples highway.

Just before 3.30 a.m. a rocket ship had discharged 790 rockets directly onto Red Beach. The 1/4 Hampshires followed and landed on schedule. But the men of the 2nd Hampshires found themselves put ashore on the wrong side of the Asa River, 500 yards from their scheduled Green Beach, and were raked by machine gun fire. In the darkness officers and NCOs searched in vain for the landmarks they had studied on aerial reconnaissance photographs. The blame for this mishap lay with the rocket ship which had directed its fearful barrage almost half a mile off course, the rockets falling on Amber Beach in the 'Sugar' sector where men of the British 46th Division were now crowding those of the 56th off the beach.

In spite of the confusion Lieut. Colonel S. J. Martin, commanding officer of the 2nd Battalion Royal Hampshires, gave the order to push ahead. He hoped to reach his correct side of the river, but progress was difficult. Enemy gunners lurked in ditches and behind walls, waiting to pick off the advancing columns. Casualties were high, yet one company managed to fight its way into the town of Pontecagnano, the town across the railway line and astride Highway 18, where Martin ordered the men to dig in.

Meanwhile, on Red Beach in the 46th Division's 'Uncle' sector, the progress of the 1/4 Battalion of Hampshires was slow. Curiously, they had not heard the news of the Italian armistice and were prepared for the worst. Fighting strongly to get beyond the beaches, they came under unceasing fire from mortars and machine guns.

Approaching Amber Beach in the darkness Corporal David Hughes, 579 Army Field Infantry, Royal Engineers, passed his rum ration among the men. Everybody had taken a comforting swig. Now, as he ran down the ramp of the LCI, carrying full kit, a Bren gun, ammunition, and a mine detector, he had lost for the moment his fear. It was 3.50 a.m.

Some twenty men went running in front of him. As he reached

(*above*) British troops manhandle an anti-tank gun onto the beach at Salerno

(*below*) A barrage balloon hovers above Allied landing craft heading towards the Salerno beaches

British Bren gun carriers are driven ashore from a landing craft onto a beach at Salerno

Some of the first German troops taken prisoner by Fifth Army forces at Salerno are used to help unload Allied landing craft

the end of the ramp he saw the first man, already dead, floating in the water. Waist-deep, his Bren gun held above his head, Hughes waded onto the beach in the 56th Division's 'Roger' sector, under fire from machine guns and shells, and dived for cover among the dunes. Around him he saw men from the 56th's first 'Black Cat' wave, dead and dying.

He lay there, digging in as best he could, until the Navy guns had silenced the opposition on the beach. Then he and the six men in his section clambered to their feet and fanned out along the stretch of sand, searching for anti-personnel mines. Even in the darkness that was imperceptibly lightening he could make out the trip wires of four rows of 'S' mines, killer mines which, triggered off, would shoot four feet into the air and explode.

A landing craft had dropped its ramp and was putting Bren gun carriers and infantrymen ashore. 'Keep your heads down!' Hughes shouted at them.

The corporal and his sappers traversed the beach, dismantling the mines, first taking the tension off the wire, then unscrewing the igniter on top of the mine. Just beyond the dunes were Tellermines, as big as dinner plates, safe for a man to walk on, but lethal for a tank or vehicle to cross. When these mines were disarmed Hughes ordered two sappers to mark off the safe stretch of beach with white tapes. Then the carriers rolled in.

Minutes later an officer with wireless equipment set up a tripod on the beach and flashed a light out to sea, calling in more landing craft.

On the lower deck of his LST, Landing Ship Tank, Petty Officer James Sharkey, a telegraphist with the 'Black Cats' of the 56th Division, kept the engine running in his waterproofed Bedford truck. As soon as the ramp went down he would drive off.

The Division's objective was to land on 'Sugar' and 'Roger' Beaches, south of 'Uncle', capture the airfield at Montecorvino, then drive south towards Ponte Sele, the river bridge apex of the desired beachhead line.

Sharkey's orders were to drive with his leading signalman and orderly telegraphist as quickly as possible to the tobacco farm marked on his map, less than a mile from the beach. Here he was to set up his radio signals. In the three-ton Bedford he carried wireless equipment and a generator, and in the trailer twenty wireless sets.

Four *Dukw*s were parked ahead of him on the lower deck of the landing craft. When the ramp was dropped the first *Dukw* rolled off into the water and 'sank like a stone'. The second *Dukw* reached the water and was blown to pieces by enemy guns. As the third and fourth *Dukw*s slid into the water Sharkey pressed the accelerator pedal and shouted to the leading signalman beside him, 'Keep your gun at the ready!' He himself carried a .45 revolver. Ammunition was slung around his waist and medical supplies were stowed in the pockets of his khaki drill shirt and trousers.

As the Bedford hit the water the towbar of its trailer snapped. Sharkey was angry and scared. Jumping out of the truck, he saw that the trailer was lying partly on the ramp, partly in the water, obstructing the exit for the waiting armoured cars behind. He shouted to the men in the LST, 'Help me shift this bloody trailer!'

Sailors and troops ran forward to help, but they were strafed by a screaming Stuka. Sharkey and the signalman dived beneath the trailer, watching the bullets spurt through the water.

'Let's get the hell out of here,' urged the signalman.

'Stay where you are,' Sharkey warned him. 'There's only the sea on one side of us and Jerry on the other.'

As suddenly as it began, the raid was over. The trailer was lifted onto the beach; later it could be transported to the tobacco farm. Pointing the Bedford towards the road behind the beach Sharkey began to sing 'The Wheel of the Wagon is Broken' to keep his spirits up. Suddenly in the truck's headlights he saw the notice, *Minefeld! Verboten!* Assuming the lane for the Bedford was clear and that the rocket ship and the sappers had done their work, he drove defiantly on.

He reckoned he was lucky to have arrived this far without being killed.

The deadly fire of the German guns had taken its toll. By 4.15 a.m. the beaches, barely discernible in the hour before dawn, were littered with dead and wounded men and wrecked vehicles. Ammunition boxes, crates of medical supplies, cases of rations and spare parts, which had been unloaded from landing craft and tossed ashore, had mounted in unwieldy piles extending into the water.

So great was the log-jam off the beaches that approaching assault craft were unable to lower their ramps and wallowed in the water as frustrated captains searched for a place to land. Colonel Richard Warner, commanding officer of the 141st Regimental Combat Team, realized that unless he was given extra firepower he could not hope to overcome the German opposition. His men were outclassed, hopelessly outclassed, fighting the enemy with machine guns, rifles and grenades.

The frustrated colonel tried to set up essential communications between the beaches and the Navy. But radios had been lost in the sea or soaked when brought ashore. Warner was now completely cut off from the ships in the armada.

Despite this bloody reception accorded their men on the beaches and the high loss of life in the American sector the cautious Allied commanders found the general view of the massive invasion before dawn encouraging. For them, Operation Avalanche was proceeding as smoothly as could be expected. The US Rangers and the British Commandos had gained useful footholds and seemed in no danger of being dislodged. The concentrated naval bombardment against the German coastal batteries would have a telling effect as the morning advanced. Yet, despite Clark's optimism in his race against the clock, his commanders could not predict when a bridgehead might be established.

VIII
'Plain, Unadulterated Hell'

Thursday, 9 September. Before dawn.

General Fred Walker was angry and impatient. He watched with dismay as landing craft and *Dukw*s circled aimlessly a mile or so off Red Beach. He knew they were carrying vital artillery and tanks that should have been on shore to assist the infantry of his 36th Texas Division. Because these operations were under the control of the Navy and not subject to his orders he was powerless to act. What were the Navy personnel waiting for? Did they imagine the Germans were going to run away and leave the beaches free? In frustration he snapped at an aide, 'Why the hell didn't they take their chance and unload on schedule?'

But it was for his own men, his Texas Army, that he felt so helpless. They needed him, and he could not reach them.

Shortly after four a.m. the restive Walker and members of his staff, comprising eighteen officers and ten enlisted men, each 'carrying enough equipment for a pack mule', had been lowered in an LCVP, Landing Craft Vehicle Personnel, from the top deck of the USS *Samuel Chase* into the calm Mediterranean. As the LCVP was winched down the General saw men, burdened with weapons, ammunition and equipment, negotiating the swaying scrambling nets into waiting assault craft. His steersmen guided the LCVP towards a flotilla of other landing craft circling nearby, waiting for its full complement.

At 5.30 a.m. the circle straightened out and the boats headed for Red Beach some twelve miles away. Ahead and to the right Walker saw waves of LCVPs, each wave in column, moving at full speed towards the beach. Raising his field glasses, he scanned the shoreline in vain for troops or equipment. But training his glasses on the most southern beaches he saw troops landing under fire, strafed by enemy planes. He was satisfied the beaches were ideal for a major amphibious assault. Yet, he wondered, why was there so little activity on Red Beach? Where was the vital equipment? And where was the air support? Probably Patton was right when he had warned him at Eisenhower's meeting in Algiers not to expect air cover before the third day.

While Walker was heading for Red Beach, officers of 141 RCT on Yellow and Blue Beaches frantically endeavoured to reorganize their forces against a background of continuous explosions and enemy gunfire. By now the fourth, fifth and sixth waves should have been ashore, with bulldozers, jeeps, tanks, and field and anti-aircraft artillery. But they had not landed.

Bitterly, Lieut. Colonel Andrew Price, an executive officer with 141 RCT, watched his men dying among booby traps and trip wires. His troops were under fire from hillside coastal batteries at Agropoli on the right; ahead of them the enemy was entrenched behind menacing steel concrete emplacements. To Price, it was incomprehensible that there had been no naval bombardment of these coastal defences before the landing. The scene on Yellow and Blue Beaches was 'just plain unadulterated hell'.

Dismayed, he watched the German Mark 4 tanks rolling towards them, equipped with long, high velocity 88 mm guns and 50 mm armour. Some of them were fitted with canopies of 100 mm armour and even extra plates of 30 mm armour welded to the nose. How could his men knock them out with the weapons they carried in their hands? Vainly, they fired at them with rifles and bazookas, but it was 'like fighting barehanded'.

Under Captain Hersel Adams one company of 141 of the 36th Division was reformed. Against the marauding tanks Adams led his men forward through a barrage of mortar and machine gun fire. As the company advanced on the tanks, he was hit at close range in the right leg. Laying him beside an irrigation ditch his men gave him medical aid as the Mark 4s regrouped for another assault. In spite of his agony Adams shouted directions to his men in their attack. In the fierce skirmish that followed he was hit again by a machine gunner and died by the side of the ditch.

The tanks halted the men of the 2nd Battalion 141 who landed fifty minutes late. As they battled to press inland, the combat troops were harassed by tanks moving backwards and forwards across their exposed front until they were pinned down. Breaking from his unit, Private Raymond Guttierez ran forward, firing his Browning automatic rifle. Two bullets pierced his helmet, but he felt nothing. A third ripped his arm, yet he ran on until he located the enemy machine gun. Closing in from behind, he jumped into the nest and knifed the gunner to death. So swift and sudden was the attack that the German died without even a moan.

With reckless courage, Private Alfred Ruiz of the same battalion attacked a tank single-handed, exchanging fire with one of the crew who was armed with a machine pistol. So close did Ruiz approach the moving tank that he became entangled with its brush camouflage and was dragged helplessly for ten yards before he could break free.

The plans of the 141 and 142 Regimental Combat Teams were running into trouble. Concentrated enemy firing from strategic points, particularly from Monte Soprano, played havoc with landing schedules. The promised tanks and artillery, needed desperately on the beaches before dawn, were still at sea, pinned down in the boat lanes by enemy fire. Mortar squads came ashore without their ammunition. Wrecked landing craft drifted aimlessly or burned near the shore. Bodies and equipment floated in the water.

As fifty *Dukw*s carrying artillery pieces, ammunition and troops stood out of range of gunfire off Green Beach, support boats laid a smokescreen. Thirty *Dukw*s tried to reach the beach, but the smoke obscured the landmarks for the steersmen. Another sixty scheduled to land on Yellow and Blue Beaches in the 141 area were diverted by one of the beachmasters to Red Beach in the 142 area. Incredibly, by 5.50 a.m. almost 125 *Dukw*s were lying off Red Beach, some of them out of fuel and immobilized.

At least one important advantage had been gained. Major Duppenbecker's Panzer strongpoint on Yellow Beach at Paestum, too close for the Navy's guns, had been knocked out by the 531 Shore Engineers. The men laid steel matting and cleared the beach with bulldozers under appalling conditions. Many died in the crossfire, but by dawn they had killed or captured all the Germans in the tower.

Off the beaches, the cat-and-mouse game against the Mark 4 tanks continued. Corporal Royce Davis of 142 RCT found a spot from which he could aim his rocket launcher effectively. When his shots pierced the Mark 4 armour he crept up to the disabled vehicle and tossed a grenade into the turret. Nearby, Sergeant John McGill of 141 RCT leapt onto a tank and dropped a grenade into the open turret.

By 5.30 a.m. the 36th Division, despite many dead and wounded, was slowly gaining a foothold. However, the Texas Army had paid a heavy price.

Precisely at 4.17 a.m. on board the USS *Ancon*, riding at anchor among an array of warships, troopships and freighters, the bugle sounded its shrill note through the loudspeakers. It was another 'General Quarters', the seventh since midnight. Enemy planes were approaching the exposed fleet. The alert was the cue for weary staff officers to don helmets and lifebelts and hasten to the decks and their assigned stations while the crews of the anti-aircraft guns prepared for action.

On deck war correspondent Quentin Reynolds strained to hear the sound of the bombers. But there was none. Suddenly four vivid chandelier flares hung in the dawn sky less than 2,000 feet above the flagship. For the first time that morning Reynolds felt afraid. The *Ancon* was a prime target for the *Luftwaffe*. The Germans must know she was the nerve centre of this unique enterprise. Would this one-time passenger ship on the New York to Cristobal run escape the bombers?

Unable to sleep because of the alerts, Lionel Shapiro went on deck to see the fighter-bombers sweeping in from the sea to drop their loads on the ships in the gulf. Two bombs fell and exploded within seventy yards of the *Ancon*. As more bombs hit the water the flagship shook beneath his feet. Why the *Luftwaffe* failed to score a direct hit was beyond him.

As the *Ancon* shuddered again under the impact of two near misses, her anti-aircraft guns and those of nearby ships kept up a constant barrage. He watched the flak rise in brilliant red arcs. Parallel to the *Ancon*, a line of ships fired tracers until there seemed to be a million red and gold shafts lighting up the sky. Shapiro was reassured by the knowledge that Spitfires were on their way from Sicily to provide air cover. But the delay worried him. Why should the Germans have the skies to themselves?

When the fighter-bombers had finished with the fleet they flew on towards the shoreline, losing altitude and gaining speed as they dropped fragmentation bombs on landing craft unloading vital artillery supplies on the beaches. Then they swept inland, strafing the assault troops, until they disappeared over the mountain peaks. At 5.37 a.m. the Navy men discarded their helmets and Mae Wests. The raid was over. But the war correspondents feared it was only a respite.

General Clark had spent the time in the War Room of the *Ancon* studying reports of the progress of the invasion. Tense and unsmiling, he looked relieved only when the teletypes clicked out the news that the Rangers and Commandos had met with little opposition. The British 46th and 56th Divisions also reported some progress. But the reports were sketchy and he would not be pushed by the war correspondents into making predictions. Rarely, if ever, had they seen him in such cautious mood. The commander of the Fifth Army was concerned about the welfare of Walker's 36th Division.

'No news yet,' he was told by his aides. He asked the reason, but no one could explain the silence on the teletypes.

Cascading sea water drenched Captain Joe Nicholl and his troop of 2 Commando as their assault craft approached Vietri beach. At first Nicholl throught these were from the *Blackmore*'s shells dropping short. But he was mistaken. They were enemy shells.

For almost an hour the last wave of Commandos had waited on board the *Prince Albert* for the assault craft to return. On the decks, they had strained their eyes searching the darkness, wondering about the fate of Jack Churchill's Commando troops on shore. But the *Albert* was so far out in the gulf they could catch only the distant sound of bombardment.

Just before 4.30 a.m. they heard the slow rumble of returning LCAs. Within minutes they had scrambled into the empty assault craft and were headed for the shore. The dark cliffs of Vietri were forbidding in the early dawn. To avoid the enemy shells dropping around them the coxwains put on extra speed and went hard into the Marina. Unharmed, Nicholl and his men ran onto the sands.

Confused by the shelling, the coxswains mistook the beach parties working under mortar fire for Germans. Instead of unloading their vital supplies of stores and personnel kits for the Commando Brigade, the Navy men hurriedly closed the doors of the landing craft, turned about, and headed back to the *Prince Albert*. To men on other landing craft, they shouted the news that the Special Services Brigade had been driven out of Vietri and the Germans had retaken the beachhead.

Screened from enemy guns by tall pink and white houses on either side, Nicholl's men dashed up the cobblestoned road from the beach. When they reached the elementary school in the town Colonel Jack Churchill greeted them.

'The battery is captured, Joe,' the ebullient Churchill exclaimed. 'We're just mopping up pockets of Germans. Your troop will be in reserve.'

Nicholl led his men to a billet he was told was free of the enemy. Inside, he surprised the stout Italian naval commander of the port of Salerno hastily struggling into civilian clothes. 'Search every room,' Nicholl ordered his men. In a drawer he found the commander's naval ribbons.

From the Vietri beach Captain Gordon-Hemming and his troop made quick forays into the area on the left of the town. A German soldier was captured coming down a mule track. Two others were killed in a brief, savage skirmish.

On a road running up from the beach Gordon-Hemming met a black-robed priest hurrying to the church on the Via Mazzini. Now that the Commandos had landed safely and Brigade HQ was established, Gordon-Hemming thought it an opportune time for a Mass. The priest, he discovered, spoke neither English nor French. He himself could speak no Italian. Instead, he repeated the Latin words *Dominus vobiscum*, until the priest grasped what he meant. By five a.m. news of the landings had spread through the town and the church of San Giovanni was crowded with local people. To the congregation's astonishment a tall, young Commando officer in khaki drill battledress accompanied the priest from the sacristy to the altar to serve the Mass. In the body of the church were other Commandos.

The Mass over, the priest blessed the congregation. Gordon-Hemming turned to lead the way back to the sacristy, but the priest laid a restraining hand on his shoulder. He wished to say a few words to the congregation. As Gordon-Hemming listened the only words he understood were, '*Grazie, Capitano!*'

By now the position in Vietri was becoming stabilized, with 2 Commando organized around the battery position. Their casualties were an officer killed when a tank shell burst in the branches of a tree above his head and some men slightly wounded. Among these was Jack Churchill's batman, Guardsman Stretton. After treatment by Captain Brian Lees, the Commandos' medical officer, Stretton returned to duty.

Two troops of 41 Royal Marine Commando, who had cleared Vietri, rejoined their unit south of La Molina, and were now positioned defensively in the hills above the pass, overlooking the road on either side.

Communication was already established between Commando Brigade HQ and the 46th Division on the Salerno beaches. In the front room of the Vietri HQ Brigadier 'Lucky' Laycock was handed a message from Major-General Hawkesworth: 'Retake Vietri beach at all costs.'

Fuming, Laycock sent a reply: 'Impossible. Have never lost it.'

Not only had the Germans been driven from the Commando beachhead, but Colonel Jack Churchill had added another prized weapon to his select armoury – a Panzer officer's grey and silver dagger.

Meanwhile, rounding a bend before dawn on the coast road from Maiori leading east to Vietri, Staff Sergeant James Altieri and his US Ranger platoon were suddenly confronted by an enemy roadblock. Rows of jagged, foot-high, triangular concrete blocks extended across the narrow road and beyond them was a fortified blockhouse.

A burst of rifle and machine gun fire spattered the Rangers. Instinctively, they fell into attack positions. Sprinting ahead, First Sergeant Edwin Baccus deftly lobbed a grenade onto the roof of the blockhouse. Two Germans died and two were taken prisoner. Altieri's platoon pushed on towards Vietri. It was just after 4.50 a.m.

Other Rangers had been ordered to hold the Chiunzi Pass north of Maiori until the main forces came up from Salerno. With the town of Maiori secured, Sergeant Wilbur Gallup's company was now among the battalions climbing the hillsides on the left of the town towards the pass. A 240 mm gun began pounding their position from an enemy strongpoint they could not hope to reach with their mortars. Two British observers were accompanying them, one carrying a heavy wireless set. It was obvious to them that only the Navy could silence the enemy's big gun.

Nonetheless, for six exhausting miles companies of Rangers climbed the precipitous hills. By daylight they had dug in along the high ridges overlooking the Naples plain, dominating the enemy's main line of communication. Entrenched above the Chiunzi Pass, they formed 'the hub of the wheel'. Darby's executive officer Herman Dammer was confident that if they held the pass Clark's Fifth Army could pass safely through from Salerno to reach its objective at Naples within the scheduled three days.

A triumphant Colonel Darby radioed Clark on the *Ancon*, 'We have taken up a position on the enemy's rear. We'll stay here until hell freezes over.'

Father Arturo Carucci had slept fitfully. He worried about the remaining patients in the sanatorium of Giovanni da Procida above Salerno and those evacuated to the safety of the nearby tunnel. Dawn was breaking as he stood reflectively by the window of his sparsely furnished bedroom. Yet for hours the sky had been artificially lit by German and Allied shells and rockets. If the landings had begun, Carucci wondered, why had not the ships in the gulf attacked the city?

Some Panzers were in the streets stationed on the Via Independenza which leads west to Vietri. A unit of German tanks had established itself in the Piazza Luciani, in front of the deserted Teatro Verdi. Soon after daylight Italian snipers began shooting at the tanks from rooftops on the nearby Via Spinosa above the Annunziata church. The Germans responded with tank fire, killing two civilians and injuring a dozen others. They took twenty civilians prisoner as well as a group of Italian soldiers who had become separated from their units. Townspeople sheltering in arcades near the Via Spinosa were terrified that the Panzers would start reprisals.

Hearing the gunfire, Father Aniello Vicinanza, priest of the Annunziata, hurried down to the Via Independenza which the Germans had sealed off. Fearing the prisoners would be executed, he pleaded with the commander of the tank unit, '*Pietà, pietà!*' After a lengthy parley the Germans agreed to free the civilians. But the Italian soldiers would be held as prisoners of war.

In nearby Vietri Italian Marine Sergeant Fernando Dentoni-Litta was a prisoner of the Marine Commandos. No landing craft had come to take him and the other Italians off the beach which was under mortar fire. Instead, they were handed spades and shovels and ordered to bury the dead. As they worked in shirtsleeves in the dawn light a woman leaning out of the top window of a house with peeling yellow stucco offered up loud *Ave Marias*.

The prisoners digging the graves in front of the shuttered bars and wine shops did not stop until the burials were completed. Afterwards they were marched up to the elementary school where the Commandos had their headquarters. Dentoni-Litta noticed that some of the troops guarding them wore crucifixes and other religious emblems tattooed on their forearms. It was not an Italian custom.

On reaching the pink and ochre school with its tall windows he was escorted into a large room on the ground floor to face a fair-haired British officer with a clipped moustache and a colonel's insignia.

It was almost twelve hours since he had eaten. On the table he saw bread and the remains of a half-finished meal. The officer did not offer him any food, and Dentoni-Litta was too proud to ask. He was not to know that he was being questioned by Colonel Jack Churchill.

Scenes of growing chaos met the men of the 5th Battalion Hampshires, a reserve battalion, as they scrambled out of their landing craft on to Green Beach in the British 'Uncle' sector. It was just 4.35 a.m. The beach was raked by machine gun fire as 88 mm shells, directed at the fleet, screamed over their heads. Like the 2nd Hampshires, the 5th had been landed on the wrong beach. Digging in, the men waited for the forward battalions to mop up the remaining machine gun nests. On all sides lay mountains of vehicles and equipment.

Lieut. Colonel J. H. Robinson then ordered the 5th Hampshires to move inland and cross the Asa River to their correct side. Once there, B Company was ordered to advance inland up a narrow, walled lane towards the coastal village of Magazzeno. As they edged their way in single file on either side of the lane enemy tanks came rumbling down the stone-walled track. Ill-equipped with hand weapons, the Hampshires were quickly overwhelmed, some falling dead or wounded as the tanks fired furiously from close range, others crushed as they sought cover by the rolling steel tracks. 'Terrible carnage' was how one survivor described the scene. Yet a score of men, some of them badly mauled, escaped and worked their way back to Magazzeno.

For an hour the destroyers *Mendip* and *Brecon* and three gunboats pounded the enemy's coastal defences. They were hampered by the German gun crews in the hills, who kept shifting their 88s from one position to another. So well camouflaged were the German positions that their gun flashes and smoke could scarcely be detected by the Navy. To protect the assault troops landing on the beaches the destroyers threw up thick smoke screens.

Meanwhile, the 1/4 Hampshires had moved inland from Red Beach in the 'Uncle' sector and were feeling their way through thick vines and low trees. Progress was slow as enemy snipers kept up bursts of fire and half-tracks made occasional surprise forays. Yet some detachments managed to cross the main road to occupy positions in the low hills beyond.

Early this morning an urgent appeal from the beachmaster on Green Beach brought companies of the King's Own Yorkshire Light Infantry (the KOYLIs) and Lincolns ashore. Soon the sun was up and the enemy, with a panoramic view of the beach, began to shell discharging LCTs, destroying at least one. Failing to find a suitable assembly area for vehicles the beachmaster suspended disembarkation. Green Beach now presented a grim picture of a battlefield, with blazing jeeps and stranded, burning LCTs.

Ahead, the main body of 2 and 5 Hampshires had crossed the Asa without resistance and were half a mile inland with 5 Hampshires on the right, back on their correct side. Contact had been lost with one company detached to deal with enemy gunners. These troops, who met with scant resistance, reached the airfield south of Pontecagnano. On the other flank the company of 2 Hampshires which advanced on Pontecagnano surprised several German officers driving down the road in their staff cars.

Following the mix-up with the Hampshires on Green and Amber beaches the destroyers *Loyal* and *Lafore* steamed precariously close to the shoreline to silence enemy batteries. *Loyal* had a boiler disabled by a shell; *Lafore* was hit, but her crew carried out repairs and resumed firing.

Operating off Amber and Green beaches in the 'Roger' sector, through which the troops of the 56th had passed, the destroyer *Lookout* crippled a number of German batteries, one in particular which had sunk an LCT off Green Beach. *Nubian* fired at every target in sight, her guns beating off a strong attack by enemy tanks on the 'Black Cats' driving inland.

For two hours the LCT in which Private John Thomas, a driver with the Royal Engineers in the 46th Division, waited in his 15 cwt truck, lay off the beaches as Tiger tanks spat venomously into the mouth of the landing craft. Thomas hated to think what would happen if his truck, loaded with mines and explosives, were hit. When eventually they landed on Red Beach in the 'Uncle' area Thomas saw tin hats floating in the water. Following a guide car, he edged his way from the shambles on the beach along a narrow track to the assembly area of 271 Field Company, and parked his truck among the trees. The infantry were just ahead of them, pinned down and unable to move further inland.

From the shelter of the trees he could hear the crack of the 88 mm guns in the distant hills and would count five seconds to the crump of the shells landing on the beach. Around him were two scout cars, a compressor truck, a workshop vehicle, and a couple of jeeps. Halted a mile and a half inland from the beach it was clear that neither men nor vehicles could move on.

'Let's get the hell out of here!' a rugged American naval officer bellowed. 'This sure is no place for us!'

His LST heading towards the British beaches had been cracked by a couple of 88s which struck the top deck and the rail at the stern behind the crew quarters. On board was Bombardier Walter Harvey, with the 46th Division, who wasn't surprised when the ship turned around and headed into the gulf to wait for a safer opportunity to land.

Fifteen minutes later, as the LST ploughed its way towards the shore again, Harvey saw two stricken LSTs derelict at the water's edge, their crews lying dead. In the growing daylight the Salerno landscape was sharply etched: a narrow coast road, a level plain on the far side of the road, and then the hills. The Germans, he thought, must have an equally perfect view of the fleet.

As the LST rode into the shore he saw enemy tanks on the treeline beyond the dunes. Then the ship's jawlike doors, stretching from top to bottom, opened. The ramp went down, and Harvey ran onto the beach, getting only his feet wet. Discarding his Mae West, he sprinted, head down, as swiftly as the others, through the smoke and dust towards the dunes, and dug in.

At that moment all hell broke loose around him. Tanks, using the trees as cover, fired point blank at the assault troops coming ashore. He saw men stagger, fall and lie motionless. Swooping low, JU-87s strafed them. From somewhere in the distance a 210 mm gun pumped round after round onto the beach. In this living hell no troops could attempt to haul vital fieldpieces ashore. Instead, landing vessels' crews waved Sherman tanks down the ramps and watched hopefully as they trundled towards the treeline.

Tracers whipped around his assault craft as seaman Jim Docherty steered his complement of 35 tense and silent 'Black Cats' towards 'Roger' Green in the British sector. It had taken him half an hour to make the journey from the transport ship *Princess Beatrix*. In the darkness he used his compass to steer to the correct section of the dim white shore. Other boats were running alongside him and the first wave hit the 'Roger' beaches almost simultaneously.

Docherty throttled back the engines of his assault craft at the surfline. The bowman dropped the ramp and the men, lined up in three rows, ran out, those in the middle row first, followed by those on the left. When the deck was cleared, the ramp was raised, and Docherty reversed his craft off the beach, turned her round and headed back to the *Beatrix*.

By the time he had made his third journey to the beaches dawn was breaking and the beachmasters were frantically trying to move men, transport and supplies inland to clear the way for the next wave of troops and equipment. To the young Glaswegian the situation 'looked hopeless'. Back on the *Beatrix* he sensed a growing fear among the crew that they might lose the beachhead. He remembered that Dieppe had been chaotic, too. But this invasion was worse; it might be well-planned, but it was turning into a shambles.

Soon after six a.m. Lieutenant Rocholl ordered his three armoured cars of the 16th reconnaissance unit down from his command post in Faiano into the plain, keeping with him only a sergeant and three men as messengers. He decided to move to the battery position from which earlier he had cleared the Italians.

From here he looked down towards the gulf at the astounding spectacle of hundreds of ships spread over the Tyrrhenian waters between Agropoli and Amalfi. On the coast directly below him, landing craft, in spite of artillery fire, were unloading tanks, usually the last weaponry in an amphibious invasion. He feared the enemy was gaining ground. At the same time the dawn had revealed the enemy fleet 'as though laid out on a plate'. The ships presented the perfect target for the *Luftwaffe* and the Panzers' guns.

From where they stood spellbound Rocholl and his sergeant made a count of the numbers in the fleet. They reckoned the total was close to 360 vessels. Had the Panzer gunners enough shells for the 88s to do their job? That would be the biggest worry.

As the sun came up and the early mist lifted, Major Duppenbecker viewed the invasion fleet from his farmhouse headquarters close to Paestum. He had seen nothing like it before. His reinforcements of Grenadier tanks were at Paestum, a thousand yards from the strongpoint. A message came through that the strongpoint had fallen and that the Americans were digging in. The position was serious. His Panzers would have to take up new positions between Paestum and Monte Soprano.

At Polla General von Vietinghoff, commander of the Tenth Army, waited for news of the 26th Panzer Division he had ordered north from Calabria to strengthen the thinly-spread 16th Panzers. When news of the landings came through he sent immediate orders to General Wilhelm Schmalz, commander of the Hermann Göring Division at Caserta, north of Naples, to hurry south to Salerno to intercept the invasion forces. The units of the 26th would travel along Highway 18, through the dangerous Molina gap, to the gulf. It was more than thirty miles to Salerno. Vietinghoff could only hope that by nightfall his men would be driving the invaders back to the sea.

In the busy War Room of the *Ancon* General Clark sat tight-lipped. Although his optimism was invariably catching, this morning his mood was sullen. To the war correspondents, the General looked increasingly concerned as the minutes slipped by. The early news on the teletypes reported that the Rangers had taken Maiori and the Commandos nearby Vietri. But where was the artillery support they had been promised? Messages from the main British beaches reported casualties and slow progress.

Most reports reaching the operations rooms on the *Ancon* and the communications ship *Hilary*, where the tense General McCreery also awaited news, carried the disturbing postscript, 'Opposition strong'. It was going to be no walk-over, the correspondents agreed.

So far, Clark had had to rely on the officers and crews of the landing craft for news of the 36th Division. All of them spoke of death and confusion on the beaches at Paestum. Did Clark realize, Reynolds wondered, that the troops he had sent ashore under General Walker were 'a bewildered bunch of youngsters' who had 'never heard a gun fired in anger'? Only when the necessary heavy artillery and supplies reached the Texans could they hope to become a mature army. How they were reacting under the horror of combat he could not guess.

Messages from the British sector were reaching the communications' ships: LST 386 STRUCK MINE + BEACHED + LST 375 HIT BY SHELLING WHILE BEACHING + TEN WOUNDED + LST 357 HIT BY SHELLING WHILE BEACHING + FOUR DEAD FORTY-EIGHT WOUNDED + MINOR STRUCTURAL DAMAGE.

After what seemed an interminable wait the teletype began to click out the reports from the American beaches at Paestum. Reynolds, standing beside Clark, thought: *Is this to be another Dieppe? Another Gallipoli?*

The General, his boyish face now grim, read in silence the statistics of death and destruction clicking out on the machine.

The message ended: ON WHAT BEACH SHALL WE PUT OUR DEAD?

IX
'Shall I Live, Sir?'

Thursday, 9 September. Morning.

The Mediterranean dawn brightened imperceptibly into morning. A sullen red glow burning behind the peaks of the jagged mountains turned to brilliant blue. It was a Salerno sunrise unseen by the isolated crews in the wide hangars of the aircraft carriers. For hours they sweated over rows of fighter planes, working feverishly on engines, loading ammunition and bombs, filling petrol tanks. They had a deadline to meet.

Some thirty miles to seaward of Salerno, beyond the perimeter of the main armada, the British carriers *Attacker*, *Battler*, *Unicorn*, *Hunter* and *Stalker* were operating together. Supported by cruisers and destroyers, they had sailed from Malta's Grand Harbour at Valetta where hundreds of flags flying from battered buildings marked not the ships' departure but an old victory over the Turks.

Admiral Sir Philip Vian controlled this support Task Force from the cruiser *Euryalus*. He had won agreement on the experimental choice of the cruiser as his flagship only because the small carriers had limited space for operations' rooms. On board the *Euryalus*, removed from the noise of aircraft, Vian could give his total attention to manoeuvring the squadron assigned to protect the landing area and canopy the troops. From the bigger carriers, *Illustrious* and *Formidable*, under Rear Admiral Moody, he could rely on a covering force of fighters to provide protection for the Seafires over the beaches.

The Seafires, carrier-based versions of the Spitfire, were fitted with four 20 mm guns and operated best at low altitudes. But they were not robust and were easily damaged by any except a perfect deck landing. So confined were the flight decks of the five small carriers that getting the Seafires into the air and back on the deck was hazardous.

Even before dawn crews were warming up the motors of the aircraft. At 6.15 a.m. Vian gave the order that sent the first Seafires hurtling off the decks towards the beaches. With no *Luftwaffe* in sight, they had the sky to themselves.

Vian was aware that the battle was going badly ashore. From the American sector scanty reports were filtering through that the GIs were pinned down and suffering heavy casualties. Even in the British sector, where there had been an early bombardment before the landings, progress was sluggish. Aware that his Seafires were urgently needed, he ordered sorties to be sent up at hourly intervals from the Royal Navy carriers. His aircraft could remain over the beaches for eighty minutes, but he expected his force of carriers would need to operate in the area for some time. Climbing up to the bridge, he saw a further problem for his Seafires: the dead calm of the early morning. The carriers' maximum speed was 17 knots, insufficient for aircraft requiring a minimum wind speed of 25 knots for a safe landing. Because of the flying distance of 200 miles from the Sicilian airfields to Salerno, the Seafires would have to provide the assault troops with initial support until the Spitfires and Lightnings arrived. It meant a more crucial role for the Fleet Air Arm than was originally intended.

Admiral Vian stood on the bridge to watch his Seafires take off. A daring and experienced commander, he still relished being in the thick of battle. He had rescued British prisoners from the German vessel *Altmark* and commanded the flotilla that helped sink the *Bismarck*. What worried him this morning was the risk of losing his aircraft not in combat but in landing accidents.

A lone Italian plane was spotted flying south. Vian watched intently as a Seafire dogged its tail, firing an interrogatory burst. The Italian pilot lowered his landing wheels, a token of surrender. The Seafire pulled away and let him go.

At six a.m. the landing craft carrying the first Shermans of 'A' Squadron Royal Scots Greys approached the beach south of the Tusciano river. As the craft, loaded with half a dozen tanks and eight lorries, neared the surfline, a battery of 88s fired low over the water at close range.

Major Douglas Stewart ducked as a shell struck the turret of his Sherman tank. Five times his landing craft, still 100 yards from the water's edge, was hit.

Stewart heard the American captain shouting in desperation that they might make the beach if he could start the engines up again. He wanted to help, but he knew nothing of marine engines. Suddenly the landing craft burst into sheets of flame and soldiers and crew began jumping into the water. Stewart was wearing his Mae West as he plunged overboard. Floating on his back in the calm sea, he saw 88 mm shells turning over in the air. He had lost his kit and best camera, still in his tank.

The crew of a small assault craft pulled him on board. Transferred soon afterwards to a second, larger craft, he stripped off his wet clothes and was given a blanket to wear. When he finally reached the command ship his clothes were returned and the blanket taken from him. 'We'll get you back into the pipeline,' he was told. He knew this meant a return to North Africa where he would be kitted out and have to wait for a ship to take him back to Salerno. 'No,' he said stubbornly. 'I'm going back to the beaches – now.'

It was only after a destroyer had run dangerously close to the shoreline and silenced the battery of 88s at close range that the other landing craft carrying the Greys were able to land their tanks and heavy vehicles. A depleted squadron of tanks under the command of Captain Sir M. O. Williams took up battle positions facing south. Within ten minutes of moving off eight tanks had bellied down in fields waterlogged from the drained dykes and canals.

Radioing Brigade Headquarters with news of his plight, Williams caused alarm. With each passing moment, HQ knew, enemy tanks were moving closer. Bulldozers were hastily brought up from the beaches. But it took almost two hours to free the Shermans from the morass.

As the LCVP carrying General Walker and his staff closed on the beach, artillery shells rained down on the water in front of the craft.

As though from nowhere a Stuka streaked out of the sky shooting at an anti-aircraft balloon floating 100 feet up and anchored some 50 feet from the waterline. Startled, the General watched the balloon falling in flames and collapsing into the sea. Momentarily distracted, he did not notice the steersman dropping the ramp. The men on the craft waded into the water. Walker was astonished to find himself waist deep, some 75 feet from the shore. So impatient was the steersman that, before the General could wade onto dry land, he had turned the LCVP around and was gone.

Crossing the wide beach under intermittent artillery fire, Walker noticed that no mesh matting for vehicles to cross was laid. Nor were the sands disturbed, which meant that German land mines had not been removed. He looked for troops of 142 RCT, but none was in sight. He glanced at his watch. The time was 7.55 a.m. Leading his small party inland, he moved along the north side of the Greek ruins of Paestum with an uneasy feeling that he was desecrating sacred ground.

He passed two abandoned enemy radios still receiving messages in German. Wondering if he could pick up some useful information, he asked if anybody in his party spoke German. Nobody did. Disappointed, he pushed on, crossing the railway line which had been designated as the point at which the infantry was to be reformed. No GIs were in sight. Doors and windows of houses were tightly shut, curtains drawn and shutters closed. The area looked abandoned.

As he led the group alongside a stone wall towards a section house on the railway, artillery gunners in the hills to the east and on the railway to the south began shooting at them. He had just reached the house when a burst of shellfire sent two of his party diving to the ground. 'Come over here!' he yelled at them. The stone building would give them protection. They had run only a few feet when another shell burst on the exact spot where they had been lying.

From the section house he surveyed the surrounding area. Although he heard small arms fire from the direction where the 36th should be, he looked in vain for his Texans. About two miles away to the southeast the sun was flashing off a number of vehicles. Peering through his field glasses, he saw they were German tanks.

When the shelling stopped Walker led his men along the railway line just east of Paestum towards a large quadrangle of buildings which he had selected from aerial photographs during the planning of Operation Avalanche as his command post. As they approached them he was surprised to see a family dressed in their best clothes step out to greet them. The owner smiled and extended a friendly hand, introducing himself, 'Cesare Vannulo.' He gesticulated towards the little group around him, '*Mia famiglia*'. Then, pointing to a large tobacco warehouse, he told the Americans, '*Per vostri, signori!*'

Among the racks of drying tobacco leaves General Walker set up his command post. Each man in his party was armed and prepared to take care of himself if attacked by a German patrol. It was just before midday. He decided to make contact with the command ship. But communication proved impossible. All their radio equipment had been waterlogged in the landing.

Standing with members of the 36th HQ Intelligence Section at the rail of the USS *Samuel Chase*, Technical Sergeant Sam Kaiser watched the landing craft ferrying assault troops to the beaches and returning with the wounded. Then the craft began circling for almost an hour as though they could not get back to the beaches. He saw General Walker in one of the craft. 'Why in hell are they circling?' somebody asked.

'Why don't they take off?' He was puzzled that nobody on the *Chase* seemed to know how the battle was going on the beachhead.

It was late in the morning when Kaiser clambered down the rope nets with his kit, a .45 and a portable typewriter. The Texan following him, a clerk in G2 section, had one foot on the ropes and another on the landing craft when he asked, 'Is it too late to become a conscientious objector?' Everybody laughed, and for a few moments the tension eased.

Hitting the beach, Kaiser threw his typewriter in front of him among the dunes and tried to crawl under his helmet. 'I was so scared,' he remarked, 'my teeth were chattering!' What would the Germans think if they saw him landing with his typewriter? Around him were dead bodies, some of them blown apart, that had not been removed.

Under the shelling of the 88s in the mountains to their right they moved on through vegetation for about a hundred yards, then through an empty irrigation canal. Finally, they took to a gravel road leading to the tobacco warehouse. General Crowther was there and directed Kaiser and Master Sergeant Fred McFadden to set up their G3 section at a portable field desk. In a corner of the warehouse Kaiser saw bodies folded in mattresses, their feet sticking out, boots still on. For the first time the young Texan, whose parents had arrived in America speaking only German, was seeing death. Inwardly, he recoiled. He thought: *Will this happen to me?*

Sergeant Sam Stein was told, 'If you see any dead or wounded on the beach, forget it. Just keep going.' With other men of 143 RCT Stein was dropped 30 feet from the beach. So intense was the shelling from the 88s that the crew of the LCI refused to take them further. Although soaking wet, the diminutive Stein hardly felt the cold with the strain of battle. Then he saw his first dead body, a mere boy. The soldier lay in the sand with his rifle reversed and his helmet on it. The dead boy's mouth was open.

As they pushed on towards the tobacco warehouse Stein was astonished to see a two-star General squatting in the middle of the roadway, 'his pants down, taking a crap'. They passed a house outside which dead GIs had been laid against the wall, KIA tags on their toes.

When they arrived at the warehouse an Italian woman was on her knees, 'praying as fast as she could'.

The men of 167 Brigade, 56th Division, could thank the vagaries of the tide for preventing serious loss of life. Fortunately for these forward elements of 8th and 9th Fusiliers and the 7th Ox and Bucks, the current had borne them slightly off course. They had overshot the point at which they were meant to land and which the Germans had heavily mined.

As the men prepared to move inland during a lull in the shelling the Germans began a barrage of psychological warfare. A beach loudspeaker blared: 'Englishmen! Don't throw away your lives! This is another Dunkirk. See all the ships behind you? They've come to save as many as possible. But you will never make it. Throw down your weapons. Surrender before it's too late.' Within minutes the Fusiliers overran the warfare unit, taking the loudspeaker crew prisoner. As the crestfallen Germans were hustled towards the beach, one Fusilier shouted, 'It's your Dunkirk now, not ours.'

Enemy gunfire resumed as the men pushed inland. Their target was the key rail centre at Battipaglia. Progress was slow through the marshy land, with troops sometimes knee-deep in water. Near Santa Lucia, just east of Battipaglia, a reconnaissance patrol moved cautiously along a dirt road to discover three Mark 4s lumbering towards them. Finding themselves in danger of being trapped, the men retreated towards the company's section. 'Tanks!' they shouted to the other men in the company, who ran splashing into the marshes for cover. The Panzer tanks wheeled after them, crashing through the undergrowth, machine guns raking the retreating soldiers as they stumbled deep in the marshes. Within yards the tanks were trapped in the mud. Furiously, the drivers revved their engines until the motors screamed and the caterpillar tracks churned deeper. But the vehicles were stuck fast.

Now the Ox and Bucks returned and flung grenades at the Mark 4s until the hatches were thrown back and the Germans crept out, their hands held high above their heads in surrender.

Meanwhile, the final elements of 9th Fusiliers coming ashore were strafed by the *Luftwaffe*. Some of the craft received direct hits, others blazed fiercely in the water before they sank. Then the *Luftwaffe* turned tail as a squadron of Seafires swooped in from the sea.

To the left of the Fusiliers Brigadier Lewis Lyne's 169th (Queen's) Brigade had landed. Lyne was determined that his two battalions would capture Montecorvino, the important airstrip, by nightfall. He ordered his men in the face of concentrated enemy fire to move inland as quickly as possible. He was confident that by midday he could achieve his objective.

Corporal David Hughes and his six sappers of 6th Division had cleared the beach of mines and moved from the dunes across the road to dig in at the back of a house facing the beach. All seven had come through unscathed. They lay there, listening to the sound of 88s roaring from the hills and the shells from the Navy in the bay screaming overhead like express trains.

After an hour an officer rounded the men up into a platoon and they moved towards a tobacco plantation where the canes grew as tall as the men themselves. Beyond the plantation was a red-bricked building with a tall tower which the Germans used as a superb observation post. It made a perfect target for the infantrymen.

Wading ashore with the men from his landing craft, Private Oliver Edwards had used his Sten gun, not knowing what he was firing at, simply shooting wildly in the enemy's direction. 'We were firing like a lot of hooligans.' In a maize field they dug down, sweltering in full battle kit, shaken by the strafing. They were still wearing the blue shoulder flash of the Eighth Army. No one had told them they were now in a new army – the Fifth.

At midday Scots Guardsman John Weir waded ashore waist deep in water. Running past the dead and wounded and the abandoned vehicles, Weir and the other men in his company moved quickly inland through tomato fields into thick undergrowth. Above the vegetation he recognized the rooftops of the buildings comprising the tobacco factory, their objective. At that moment the Germans opened up with bursts of mortar fire. Weir and the men around him fanned out, moving cautiously. As the firing intensified, they were pinned down.

For the first time in his life Weir was in a real battle.

Driving his unmarked Bedford truck from the beach towards the tobacco farm, telegraphist James Sharkey wondered if the red-painted notice *Minefeld! Verboten!* in the field was a dodge by the Germans to lure the British vehicles onto the road so that they could pick them off. Sharkey decided to take to the fields.

Halfway across the first field a sudden bang lifted his truck a couple of feet off the ground. A caterpillar track went sailing over his head. Turning briefly, he saw an armoured truck following him burst into flames. The Germans had not lied. The field, after all, was mined.

He drove onto the roadway, passing a curious pair of dirty tramps sitting by the ditch, and into an open yard fronting a two-storey building with adjoining low sheds. He recognized his objective, the tobacco farm.

Parking the Bedford close to the side of the house, he and the warrant telegraphist immediately began hooking up four aerials to the wall. From the opposite side of the house firing started and he dived beneath the Bedford. Had the Germans seen him? He couldn't be sure.

'Are you there, Sharkey?' his warrant telegraphist shouted.

'Yes,' he called back. 'But don't stand up, Nobby, or you're a dead duck.'

Gingerly, the warrant telegraphist showed the top of his tin helmet. It brought a sudden burst of firing in his direction. But within minutes he had arrived safely beside Sharkey. Joined by the signalman, they climbed through the trapdoor beneath the Bedford into the interior of the truck. Sharkey was about to send his first signal to the *Hilary* when he glimpsed a naked man, his clothes ripped off by a bomb, staggering across the yard. Blood was pouring from the man's body which was peppered with shrapnel marks. At the sight of this grotesque figure Sharkey jumped blindly from the Bedford and ran from cover across the open yard. At that moment the German firing suddenly ceased.

Slipping one arm under the wounded man's shoulder he guided him with his other arm towards the shelter of one of the low buildings. He half-carried him through the low doorway and laid him on a bundle of straw. Injecting a shot of morphine he heard the man mumble some words he could not understand. 'Don't worry,' Sharkey told him. 'You'll be all right.'

The man smiled weakly and closed his eyes.

Sharkey dashed across the yard to the Bedford and contacted the *Hilary*. 'Ready for transmission.' By a prearranged signal he confirmed that it was opportune for the HQ staff to come ashore. Then he and the others ran wires to the beach points where the LSTs and LCAs were coming in. Now the beachmaster would be able to communicate by telephone with the wireless truck.

By the time the wires had been laid the beach was under heavy fire. Sharkey had to crawl back almost a mile to the farm. Now he waited for the signals officer and staff from *Hilary* to arrive.

To his dismay, Brigadier 'Lucky' Laycock learned that all was not well on the beaches. The plan had been for the Commandos to take control of the batteries, after which the divisions could land without being shot up by the enemy. Now, it seemed, there was to be no early relief for his men.

At midday a couple of Commando troops under Captain the Duke of Wellington were dispatched along the coast road towards Salerno. As a Tiger tank came lumbering up the hilly road towards Vietri one section under Captain Joe Bare took cover in a house built into the cliffside. Instantly, the tank crew began firing below the windows.

At that moment Captain Arthur Brunswick and Gunner Charles Dettmer were driving towards Salerno in a five-ton truck, loaded with explosives and bombs for a Piat, the lightweight replacement for the anti-tank rifle. Standing in the roadway, Bare frantically waved them back. 'Don't come any nearer!' he shouted. 'You're driving straight into the jaws of a tank!'

Parking the truck on a corner of the road, the Commandos managed to transfer a supply of 3-pound bombs before they were alerted by the sudden sound of heavy caterpillar tracks rumbling over the cobblestones. As a Tiger nosed around the corner Brunswick leaped into the truck and grabbed the wheel. Dettmer dived into the back as Brunswick reversed noisily, crunching quickly through the gears. Shells spattered the road around them as they headed for Vietri. One shell glanced off the side of the truck. Brunswick spun the wheel, tacking across the steep roadway. They knew that if the truck was hit they would be blown to bits. Dettmer was 'sweating like a bull'.

Learning that a Tiger was shelling the house in which Bare's men had taken cover, Wellington led a sub-section forward to deal with the tank. The Tiger opened fire, wounding three of his Commandos seriously. Wellington gave the men shots of morphine, signing their foreheads with an 'M' in marker pencil. In the beleaguered house he found four injured Commandos in charge of one man. Bare had been able to push on.

At the same time Colonel Jack Churchill ordered Captain Joe Nicholl to protect a troop positioned with two 6-pound anti-tank guns on a terrace between Vietri and Salerno. Arriving at the site, Nicholl was told that one tank had been knocked out and that the Panzers were retreating into the city. Sighting his Brens to cover the maximum amount of road, he spotted another Tiger emerging from the direction of Salerno. To the left of him, on high ground just above the road, he noticed Commandos under Captain Pat Henderson moving into position.

Two direct hits at 900 yards from the 6-pounders caught the tank. A second Tiger appeared, firing back. Two shots exploded just behind Nicholl. Turning to inspect the damage, he found that most of his Bren gun crew had been injured.

By now Henderson's Commandos had moved forward of the second Tiger and the Captain had positioned himself with a Piat behind a low brick wall in front of a house. Fitting the bombs into the cradle, he looked through the sights. The Tiger was about a hundred yards away, the Piat's battle range. Tucking the gun into his shoulder, Henderson squeezed the trigger. The shot fell short. Quickly he reloaded. The second bomb hit the side of the tank but failed to explode.

Unable to depress their gun low enough to reach the Piat, the

Tiger's crew battered away at the wall of the house. Shrapnel and masonry fell around him as Henderson went on firing until he scored a direct hit on the Tiger's turret. Its turret jammed, the tank retreated into Salerno.

Meanwhile in the Pass of La Molina Captain John Parsons' men from 41 Royal Marine Commando, who had blown up the Tiger soon after dawn, laid anti-tank mines, which they carried slung around their necks 'like cow pats', across the road and in the ground beyond it in the form of a necklace. Then they set up their Piat and rifle positions to cover this critical bend in the road.

As the day grew warmer and the sun rose in the sky enemy tanks came trundling around the corner from La Molina. The drivers, catching sight of the lethal necklace, rumbled to a halt. As they tried to reverse, Parsons' men caught them in their rifle and mortar fire.

By now the Special Brigade casualties were mounting so swiftly that Captain Brian Lees sent a runner to contact a field ambulance to evacuate the more seriously wounded men. Brigadier Laycock was worried. A message had reached him from the 46th Division that no link-up with the Brigade would be possible before late afternoon.

Meanwhile, climbing the hills above Maiori, the Rangers took until noon to reach their positions. The men of Sergeant Robert Ehalt's platoon were resting after the long, hot climb when Germans crept up on them, moving stealthily through the vines in elaborately camouflaged uniforms that allowed them to melt into the landscape. They attacked with Lugers and light weapons, as though testing the Americans' strength. Ehalt and the other Rangers fought back with BARs and tommyguns, but the Germans drove them down the hillside.

On the coast road towards Salerno Sergeant Don Earwood and his squad waited by the lighthouse for orders. In the tower and beside the machine gun nests lay the bodies of the dead Germans. Six hours had passed since the shootout. In the hot sun the corpses would start to decompose. The Americans gritted their teeth and rolled the bodies over the landrock on which the lighthouse stood and watched them spiral 300 feet into the water churning among the rocks below.

Prisoners and seriously wounded men were often an encumbrance to shock troops. One Ranger was dead, another so badly injured they could not carry him with them. Earwood took another look at the wounded soldier. A machine gun bullet had penetrated the front of his left shoulder and imbedded itself.

Just before noon the squad received orders to reorganize with their unit and push inland towards Highway 18. They would cut through the hills, bypassing Vietri, and follow a compass point to a prearranged meeting place. Earwood called up the medics on his walkie-talkie to take care of his injured comrade. Then he and his squad obeyed orders to 'move up real fast'.

Realizing the Rangers would form a perimeter by fanning out left and right along the coast road and pushing into the hills, Darby's executive officer Major Herman Dammer had decided on a scheme whereby every Ranger going ashore carried extra ammunition, maybe a box of machine gun arms or shells for a mortar. His idea was that the Rangers would drop these extra supplies on the beach where he ordered men to place them in special supply dumps.

Even though he was now assured of supplies for a few days, Dammer worried whether he could expect any follow-up landings on the beach at Maiori by supply vessels. Would the Rangers have to depend on divisions on the right to send them supplies overland?

Regimental Medical Officer William Rankin feared it would be a day of tragedy. Just before noon he had come ashore in the 'Uncle' area of the 46th Division. The enemy reception was worse even than he anticipated. With relentless fury the *Luftwaffe* strafed the beach on which scores of dead and wounded lay strewn among the immobilized tanks and vehicles. Under machine gun fire stretcher-bearers from the Durhams tried to remove the dead to make room for more troops to land.

Rankin's first patients were three medical officers, one of them with an open leg wound. Kneeling beside them with his 'monkey bag', he administered sulphonamide to prevent infection. Then they brought him Hampshires who had been mangled in the laneway by the German tanks. They had suffered terribly. Some died on the beach where they were laid. He saw men with gaping chest and abdominal wounds, their faces twisted with pain. As he gave them morphine it struck him that many were incredibly brave, enduring their agony silently, more scared perhaps by the sight of their injuries than the pain itself. A few screamed when their wounds were dressed.

Doctors in war tended to be impatient with men who showed fear disproportionate to their wounds, but they respected those who made light of severe injuries. 'Shall I live, sir?' a young Hampshire whispered to him. Rankin scarcely heard the words above the continuous din of artillery and mortars and the deadly rain of metal from shells and bombs.

Ordering the stretcher-bearers to evacuate the severely wounded as swiftly as they could, he scanned the area around the beach for somewhere to set up the vital regimental aid post. He had hoped to be able to move a few miles inland, but realized this was now impossible. Quickly, he fixed on a nearby tomato field. Even when the aid post had been set up the enemy strafing and gunfire made his work almost impossible.

A platoon of men had gone out and were bringing back more wounded Durhams and Hampshires. The horrors of the aid post were soon apparent – maimed arms and legs, arteries spurting blood, torn chests and abdomens, empty eye sockets, burned skin in tatters, the moans of the wounded.

This was the horror of combat in which death was commonplace.

Seventeen-year-old Mario Marino had been evacuated to the village of Coperchia, five miles north of Salerno in the Fratte area with his parents, brothers and sisters. They were among fifty or so families who crowded into the village after the first bombings in the city on 21 June.

News arrived this morning from Cava of the invasion on the beaches. People called to each other in the village streets, 'The English have landed.' They believed the war was over. Overjoyed, some began walking towards Salerno to greet the invaders; they were soon caught in the crossfire of German and British guns or killed by landmines. Though most Italians wanted the war to end, small numbers continued to side with the Germans while others wanted to resist them. The bulk of the partisans were in Salerno. In Coperchia, however, resistance could not be translated into action; the men possessed no guns. A unit of Germans retreating through Fratte, just south of Coperchia, was confronted by a group of Italian teenagers. One boy called to them, 'Nazi dogs! I hope the English kill you all!' Infuriated by the taunts, a German pulled the pin from a grenade and tossed it into the group. The boy who shouted the abuse died, others were wounded.

In nearby Baronissi the previous evening the small dark-haired Mario and his brother Aurelio had heard people in the bars exclaiming, 'The war is over.' Now they knew that for them it was just beginning. Behind the hillside house in which the Marino family and their relatives were crowded a unit of Germans had excavated tunnels for their radio communications. It was not long that day before the British had intercepted their signals and begun shelling their positions.

In distant Frascati, near Rome, Field Marshal Kesselring studied every message reaching him from the Salerno area. Although the Panzers were mounting a tough resistance he had to concede that the Allies possessed superior air and sea power. He was, however, relieved that the enemy had not landed in Rome, as he had anticipated. That seemed an error on Eisenhower's part. Such an invasion would have left him helpless, for he could not have contained Montgomery's drive up the toe of the peninsula and at the same time warded off an attack on Rome. Furthermore, he wondered why the Allies had made no attempt to mobilize the Italian forces in conjunction with the landings. They showed 'an amazing lack of imagination'. Had not Field Marshal Wilhelm Keitel, Hitler's chief of *OKW*, said, 'An Italian army which is not capable of betrayal does not exist'? Kesselring had made a wise decision by ordering the removal of Italian troops from the area of Salerno. The 4th Parachute Division, which had been transferred to Salerno from Sicily on 5 September as a backup to the Hermann Göring Division, was disbanded. So, too, was the 222nd Coastal Division whose troops had been unable to make contact with their commander in the German lines at Buccoli.

Later that morning Rommel telephoned him from the north to demand that all Italian prisoners in his possession be sent to Germany.

Kesselring resented such interference. He knew that for months the 'Desert Fox' had been demanding that Hitler recall him so that he could take over complete command in Italy, south and north. This conspiracy angered Kesselring who felt Rommel would have been better employed demobilizing the Italians in the north instead of allowing them to desert to form partisan bands. He was disappointed by Hitler's attitude, convinced that the Führer was yielding to Rommel's demands and rejecting his own priority calls for reinforcements. This morning he telegraphed the Wolf's Lair. He told Hitler that with his back to the wall he could not accept Rommel's orders. 'Please spare me instructions, Führer, that I cannot carry out.' He refused to accept Rommel as his superior.

His immediate concern now was Salerno. But events in the area around Rome following the Italian surrender gave him little time to advise Vietinghoff or Sieckenius. He must depend on Vietinghoff, a general's son and a leader who would remain calm in a crisis, to carry out his defensive strategy.

However, at Polla, Vietinghoff was completely frustrated by inadequate communications. He had no signal regiment and his few signal personnel were badly trained, inexperienced, and overworked. All Kesselring's urgent signals were delayed. At eight a.m., realizing the extent of the Allied landings, he conceded that an invasion in the Rome area was now unlikely. Instead of transferring troops to Rome he ordered the 14th Panzers to make 'a ruthless concentration of all forces at Salerno'. Here again communications proved virtually non-existent.

General Hermann Balck, commander of the 14th Panzers, had no telephone contact with Vietinghoff's Tenth Army and his radio contact was inadequate. He had received no accurate reports of the Allied invasion. Hesitating to reduce his defences to reinforce the troops at Salerno, he sent a regimental combat team of 15th Panzers, with most of the division's tanks and an artillery battalion, to the Volturno River.

Kesselring also depended on the ability of General Rudolf Sieckenius, commander of the 16th Panzers, to hold off the invaders at Salerno. But at the same time that Vietinghoff was sending orders to the 14th, Sieckenius became concerned by reports of landings at Castellammare, on the north of the Sorrento peninsula. He sent an urgent call for help to General Balck, but the response by the hesitant Balck was to order a reconnaissance battalion of the Hermann Göring Division to Nocera, north of the Chiunzi Pass. To Sieckenius, it seemed unfair that his 16th Panzers, spread thinly over a large area, must take the full brunt of the Allied invasion.

Undaunted by the odds against him, the indomitable Kesselring issued a confident message to all divisions in the Salerno area:

> The invading enemy in the area of Naples–Salerno and southwards must be completely annihilated and, in addition, thrown into the sea. Only by so doing can we obtain a decisive change of the situation in the Italian area. I require ruthless employment of all the might of the three army units. Every commanding officer must be aware of his historical responsibility. British and Americans must realize that they are hopelessly lost against the concentrated German might.

From the bridge of the USS *Ancon*, Admiral Hewitt watched a British monitor ship moving slowly half a mile off his port side. In a blinding flash her stern suddenly lifted and smoke began billowing from her deck. Hewitt knew that she had been struck by a floating mine that had eluded the sweepers. Although her stern was sinking, he watched the monitor stagger away, her two 15-inch guns still pointing towards the beaches, her ack-ack guns angled upwards.

All morning messages had clicked out on the teletype machines in the *Ancon*'s War Room. Yet communication between the ship and the 36th Division on the beaches remained unsatisfactory. At 10 a.m.

Hewitt had sent a message to General Ernest Dawley on board the USS *Samuel Chase*, ordering him to take command of the American troops ashore. At noon, as the situation for the Texas army became more uncertain, he sent a second message to Dawley. He wanted him to confer with Major General Troy Middleton, Commander of the 45th reserve Division. It was now imperative to land one of Middleton's follow-up regiments on the beaches.

But General Dawley, frustrated because he could get no adequate reports from the 36th, had finally lost patience. Before either of Hewitt's messages reached the *Chase* he left the ship to make a personal inspection of the beaches.

X
Dawley Goes Ashore

Thursday, 9 September. Afternoon to midnight.

THE SEA WAS calm with a moderate ground swell as General Dawley commandeered an LCT loaded with tanks and heavy vehicles and at 12.15 p.m. went aboard with a number of his aides.

As they neared Red Beach in the American sector an 88 mm shell landed in the water 100 feet in front of them; another shell exploded on the beach opening a huge crater in the sand. The taut Dawley hardly noticed the danger. A shell dropping short of his craft was nothing, he felt, to what the men of the 36th must be enduring on the beachhead. Twenty-five years previously this Wisconsin soldier had been decorated by the governments of four countries for his services as a field artilleryman in World War One. A colonel on the permanent army promotion list, he was appointed temporary major-general at the outbreak of World War Two. In 1941 he was given command of the Sixth Corps.

Stepping ashore on Red Beach soon after one p.m. he saw the sand pockmarked with disabled vehicles and field pieces, and signs, too, of hastily dug graves. He directed the immediate unloading of the LCT, then commandeered a landing craft and sailed with his aides south to Paestum where he borrowed a jeep from 142 RCT and drove inland.

As he approached the tobacco warehouse a shell crashed into a field not 75 feet from his vehicle. Dawley glanced at Colonel Eddie O'Neill, one of his aides, and grinned.

General Walker greeted him with a warm handshake. He respected Dawley's capabilities and was glad to meet him again. The two men discussed the progress of the battle. Dawley listened to Walker's report, but was noncommittal. Earlier that morning, Walker informed him, German Mark 4s had moved down from the north. Gunners of 143 RCT had knocked out four oncoming tanks and sent the rest retreating. These brief, but fierce, skirmishes had gone on all day. Walker confided to Dawley that he hesitated to send armoured combat vehicles into the open, fearing that they would be easy targets. 'Let the enemy tanks come at them,' he argued. It was his reason for ordering his own tanks to remain concealed.

As they talked a message was handed to Dawley from Admiral Hewitt on the *Ancon* directing him to take command of the 36th Division on the beachhead. Dawley noticed the message was timed ten a.m. and it was now late afternoon. Communications, Walker explained, were proving difficult. His radio car had been sunk in the landings. Nobody knew what had become of the jeep assigned to Dawley. What about the two special radio-equipped jeeps? Dawley asked him. Walker, who had taken exception to their loading at Bizerta, only knew they had been unloaded on the beaches. They had not been seen again.

Dawley set off on a further inspection of the beaches before returning to the 36th command post at the warehouse. Quickly he scribbled a situation report to Clark, hoping it would be delivered to the *Ancon* without too much delay. He indicated that operations on Beaches Red, Green and Yellow were satisfactory. Hewitt's second message, which had been sent at noon, had now arrived, directing him to contact General Middleton on board LST 404 to make plans for employing the back-up 45th Division on the beachhead. And Clark wanted Dawley and Middleton to confer with him the next morning. Dawley left the command post of the 36th to return to Red Beach from where he set out in search of LST 404.

It came as a surprise to Walker that Dawley had made no specific suggestions about the deployment of his forces. He immediately gave orders to his officers, directing Colonel Martin of 143 RCT to push east to gain possession of the road along the west side of Monte Soprano, and Colonel Forsythe of 142 RCT to take the bridge over the River Sele. He expected Brigadier General Miles Cowles to set up anti-tank defences as fast as supplies came ashore. With more anti-tank weapons he was confident his troops could take care of enemy counter-attacks. By nightfall he believed his men would be on Monte Soprano and beyond Capaccio. Despite the heavy losses in the landings he shared Dawley's confidence that the men of the 36th would soon cross the Sele to bridge the gap between American and British positions.

Shortly after Dawley's departure from the beachhead the war correspondent Lionel Shapiro came ashore, accompanied by one of Clark's liaison officers from the *Ancon*. At Walker's HQ in the tobacco warehouse Shapiro found an atmosphere of 'uneasy satisfaction'. The real heroes of the day, he was told, were the beach engineers, many of whom, refusing to take shelter during the frequent enemy raids, had fallen mortally wounded as they hauled ammunition and field pieces from the landing craft. In a nearby green field the young Canadian was shown the first American cemetery on the Italian mainland. There were too many corpses for him to count.

In the early evening he left the beachhead to return to the *Ancon*. An American destroyer, steaming offshore, was firing steadily into the face of Monte Soprano from where a battery of 88s was lobbing shells onto the beaches. The battle of Salerno, he thought, is just beginning.

Since dawn the thunderous din of naval batteries had echoed across the gulf, pounding enemy positions behind the beaches and in the hills. On the dangerous right flank of Sixth Corps, less than a mile off Blue Beach, the destroyer *Ludlow* was silencing shore batteries and giving vital support to landing craft still carrying supplies ashore. *Ludlow* was taking her orders from Rear Admiral Lyal Davidson on board the light cruiser *Philadelphia*, directly facing the mouth of the Sele River.

From early morning Davidson, a lanky gunnery expert, had commanded naval gunfire support in the American section and by late afternoon was monitoring calls from fire patrol parties on the shore. Delays in negotiating minefields and establishing communications with shore parties had prevented other fire support vessels from moving in during the day. Admiral Hall, on board the flagship *Samuel Chase*, was disappointed that the ships were not performing as efficiently as on D-Day in Sicily. An exception was the *Philadelphia* and her four destroyers which had inched their way through the minefields in the afternoon. *Edison* and *Bristol* were 6,000 yards off shore, firing on enemy artillery, trucks and tanks; *Edison* was reported to have knocked out eleven tanks. Only *Woolsey*, straddled by enemy fire, had to retire for a time beyond range. The cruiser *Savannah* had a busy day firing on enemy infantry observation posts, artillery batteries, and the town of Capaccio. Her gunners knocked out three tanks.

Meanwhile the flagship *Philadelphia* launched her spotting planes. One of them, in conjunction with a plane from the light cruiser *Savannah*, flushed out a group of German tanks near Red Beach. Seven tanks were destroyed by salvoes from the *Philadelphia*. By late afternoon the flagship had fired almost 300 rounds of 6-inch shells.

Further out in the gulf, the *Ancon* flashed a message from air headquarters to Admiral Vian's flagship *Euryalus* that Montecorvino airfield had been taken by 2/6 Queen's. It was incorrect information, but it sent a lone Seafire into the air towards the airfield. As the plane came in to land it was destroyed by enemy shells. Another Seafire, returning to one of the carriers, failed to catch the arrester wire with its landing hook. Skimming over the crash barrier, the plane plunged helplessly into the sea and was lost.

Vian was worried not only about the strain on his pilots, who had each made three sorties that morning before the arrival of Spitfires and Lightnings from Sicily, but also about the risks they ran in attempting to land their aircraft. Flying at 70 mph in a dead calm towards a floating platform, of which they could see only the tip, was hazardous. One Seafire was now lost, others had pitched forward against the taut arrester wires, damaging the propellers.

A suggestion reached him from Captain Henry McWilliam, commanding the carrier *Hunter*, that nine inches be sawn off all propeller ends. Neither the Admiral nor his Chief Staff Officer Captain Guy Grantham knew if this idea was aerodynamically sound. However, trusting in the technical knowledge of McWilliam, Vian decided to authorize the operation.

As for the pilots, their only disappointment that day was that they had seen so little of the *Luftwaffe*.

The landing by the Rangers on the narrow Maiori beach and their thrust through the mountains to the Chiunzi Pass had surprised the Germans, most of whose divisions were concentrated south of Vietri. Darby's men were dug in on both sides of the strategic pass and had sealed off the coastal road left and right of the town, an area the Germans had left sparsely manned.

Darby urged his men on, and Sergeant Robert Ehalt's company received radio orders to counter the early attack on their position above the pass. Sweating up the mountain again, they drove the Panzers back.

General von Vietinghoff's commanders now had the task of fighting the Rangers in these precipitous hills and along the narrow, twisting road which runs up from Maiori to the pass and then drops into the plain of Naples. In effect, the Rangers had secured the left flank of the Fifth Army beachhead and were poised like a knife at the Germans' jugular vein. Vietinghoff ordered black-uniformed paratroopers and élite shock troops to storm the hills above the defile to break the Rangers' grip. At all costs he must regain control of the area.

Meanwhile, further to the east, German mortars were falling on Commando positions inland at La Molina, and on the coast at Vietri Colonel Jack Churchill sent 3 Troop to 'Monument Hill' on the right of the town. Recce patrols stumbled on a German patrol engaged on the same mission. With a burst from his tommygun a sergeant from 3 Troop killed every man in the patrol.

A squadron of the 44th Reconnaissance Regiment from 138 Brigade got through from the main beaches with the help of Wellington's 2 Troop, still hanging on grimly on the western outskirts of Salerno. Their progress was aided by Captain Pat Henderson's Piat which had helped clear the road of Tiger tanks. An Italian woman brought a message back to Wellington that the squadron had joined up successfully with Colonel Lumsden's 41 RM Commando in the narrow defile at La Molina.

However, both 41 Commando and 2 Commando were taking a heavy mortaring. On the Via Mazzini in Vietri, an 88 shell burst outside the school which served as Brigade HQ, grievously injuring an Italian family. Commandos ran out of the building and lifted the bodies of three teenage girls, their bright cotton frocks stained with blood, from the roadway. They carried them into Captain Lees' first aid post. But the girls' abdominal wounds were so appalling that Lees could not save them.

Alarmed at the chaos on Red Beach in the British 'Uncle' sector, where long lines of congested vehicles had piled up, General Hawkesworth, commander of the 46th Division, made a sudden decision. He decided at one p.m. to place all troops on the right under 128 Brigade.

Brigadier M. A. James now found himself holding a narrow stretch of dunes covering Green Beach in the 'Uncle' sector with the remnants of two Hampshire battalions and companies of the KOYLIs and Lincolns. Ahead were enemy tanks and gunners. Later in the afternoon James was relieved to discover that the enemy was withdrawing, a situation which allowed him to restore some order to the beachhead.

At the same time Hawkesworth ordered Brigadier E. P. Harding's 138 Brigade HQ to land and take command of the left sector. When Harding and his staff landed an hour later they found the Commandos and Rangers holding fast at Vietri and Maiori and 1/4 Hampshires in position in the low hills across the Salerno road. On and beyond Red Beach were the York and Lancasters, less one company and without transport. Harding ordered them to advance to take the high ground east of Salerno to block the San Severino road.

Meanwhile B Squadron 46th Recce Regiment, which had landed a limited number of vehicles, moved off at 4.30 p.m. from the beachhead. Finding the main streets of Salerno blocked by demolitions, they moved cautiously through the side streets. Few civilians were about. At the western exit of the city they made contact with men of 2

Commando who had had a tough day's fighting and were glad of this first junction with the 46th Division. The squadron then moved up the winding road through the Vietri defile and, surprisingly, entered Cava de' Tirreni, the town beyond the defile, where German positions were still manned. In a side street they captured a young German soldier who gave them vital information that 25 tanks and 500 infantry were assembled only a mile and a half away, ready to advance.

Dusk was falling, so the Recce decided it was safer to pull out of Cava and return to Vietri.

Late in the afternoon the 88 mm gun located on the rear slope of the mountain near Lieutenant Rocholl's observation post above Faiano was knocked out by the Navy. To Rocholl's surprise, 3 Company of the 16th Panzer Reconnaissance Unit was ordered to abandon position and move to a second line of defence at a road block near Coperchia, north of Fratte. With them went the machine gun section from Rocholl's OP.

The young lieutenant was now alone on the ridge with a handful of men armed only with Lugers. Lying back in the sun among the vines, he plucked and ate the grapes and sent an occasional message to the armoured cars on the road below. Just as he began to feel that such relaxation was dangerous, tracer bullets whipped past his ears. Rolling down the hill out of range, he shouted to the others to take cover. He could hardly believe what was happening. Had the enemy ventured so close? Again came the unpleasant spatter of machine gun fire as a handful of men from a British reconnaissance came to within a few yards of his OP.

Now that he was discovered, Rocholl realized that he must establish a new position. Although he had no orders to withdraw, he knew that if he remained on the ridge for the night he and his men would almost certainly be wiped out. Half running, half stumbling down the hill with his men towards the armoured cars, he climbed into the forward car and ordered the patrol to drive towards Salerno.

It was just six p.m. when they reached the devastated city. Rocholl had an uneasy feeling as they drove through the dead, deserted streets that AT guns were hidden around corners ready to shoot at them. Traversing the length of the city from Torrione to the centre, the patrol turned right and climbed the Via dei Principati into the suburban hills. Studying his map, Rocholl decided that the big sanatorium overlooking the city, the gulf and the valley beyond Fratte would make a perfect observation post from which he would have an open road of retreat.

Father Carucci had stayed at the sanatorium to comfort his patients, the majority of whom were in the tunnels in the care of Dr Gugliacci. Walking in the gardens at dusk he could still see the gigantic fleet of ships in the Gulf of Salerno and hear the awesome noise of their guns. As shells passed directly over the sanatorium the priest trembled for the safety of his patients.

Towards seven p.m. an excited Mother Irene Marchesi, the Mother Superior, came hurrying to him with the news that a patrol of German armoured cars was coming up the road. At once Carucci read the situation. A military occupation of the sanatorium could be disastrous for the patients. Dr Michele Izzo, the director, had not returned from a visit the previous afternoon to Baronissi. It was up to Carucci to confront the German commander and parley with him.

The tall, slightly stooped priest hastened down through the gardens beneath the palm trees to where the armoured cars were halted under the bridge by the hospital entrance. In faltering German he asked to speak to the officer in charge. A dark-haired young man with glasses wearing a Panzer officer's uniform stepped forward from the first car. Carucci introduced himself. The officer nodded stiffly and said, 'Lieutenant Rocholl.'

The German spoke a little Italian so the priest explained in a mixture of both languages that more than one hundred patients were under special care in the hospital and that a military occupation could cause the loss of lives.

The officer looked at him in silence. His apparent indifference made Carucci wonder if his words had carried any conviction.

'I, too, am a Catholic,' Rocholl explained politely. 'I am aware of your situation, Padre. But I'm sorry. Your hospital is essential to our military defence.'

Carucci pleaded forcefully for the lives of his patients. The officer's attitude changed. 'If we don't take over your hospital, then you can expect the English to take it over.'

Raising his voice, Carucci insisted, 'I assure you, Lieutenant, that I will protest against any army trying to occupy this hospital.'

The officer was clearly unimpressed. Desperately, Carucci begged him, 'If you agree to leave us alone, I am prepared to offer myself as a hostage.'

The NCOs standing around the officer smiled. Just then a sergeant from one of the armoured cars approached Rocholl and whispered to him. Turning back to Carucci, the officer extended his hand. 'In three minutes, Padre,' he assured him, 'we shall be gone. We have new orders to encounter the enemy elsewhere.'

Relieved, Carucci shook his hand and wished him, 'God bless you.'

Clicking his heels smartly, Rocholl raised an arm. '*Heil Hitler!*' The other men in the patrol echoed the salute.

The priest stepped into the shadows of the bridge as the armoured cars revved their engines and clattered down the road. Then he returned thoughtfully through the gardens to his patients.

Would this be his last encounter, he wondered, with the military?

Lieutenant Gunter Schmitz knew that at all costs Montecorvino airfield must not fall into enemy hands.

Spitfires had bombed the landing strip and destroyed two *Luftwaffe* planes. Intelligence informed him the enemy urgently required the airfield for the use of their aircraft flying from Sicily. With his 250 men of 2 Company 16 Panzer Pioneer Battalion, backed by armoured cars and half-tracks, Schmitz ringed the airfield and approach roads. Alerted that enemy troops, supported by tanks, were advancing, he set up his mortars and machine guns. As the Shermans rolled into view he ordered an immediate attack.

Hardly was the bloody battle with the Queen's begun than he was ordered to withdraw his men towards the tobacco factory outside Battipaglia. To the young Lieutenant, confident that he could drive the enemy from the airfield, this order was baffling. Pulling out, as instructed, they were strafed by enemy planes. His men hit two Lightnings, downing one of them, and even now his gunners were still mortaring the airfield, preventing enemy occupation. Satisfied that he had inflicted heavy casualties, he withdrew reluctantly to new positions.

It was later in the evening when he drove through the burning ruins of Battipaglia, south towards the banks of the Sele River on Highway 18. He had split his company into small groups, one of them occupying the tobacco factory south of the town, another clashing with the Fusiliers before halting near the village of Santa Lucia. On his orders, another patrol demolished a key bridge over the Sele. That action pleased him particularly.

Convinced that the airfield, the tobacco factory and Battipaglia could be held against naval, air and tank attacks, Schmitz found the news from other sectors of the front unsatisfactory.

Captain Spetzler of the 16th Tank Division had encountered tough resistance on the edge of La Picciola, close to the villages of Santa Mattia and Santa Lucia, though on the opposite bank of the Tusciano. Halted by heavy shelling and artillery fire, the division had finally broken through to the perimeter of the airfield. The 1/64 Battalion was outflanked, and only by a broad sweep towards the north had it succeeded in joining with other combat troops through Faiano and Montecorvino. All sections of 10 Tank Regiment 2 were cut off when encircling the airfield, but they, too, had finally broken through.

In the American sector the Panzers had retreated as the Texans pushed towards Capaccio below Monte Soprano. Now they were fighting to block the Allied entry into the mountains.

Schmitz reckoned that reinforcements of men, artillery and tanks were urgently needed if positions were to be held in the ensuing battle. He could certainly hold out for a time, but not indefinitely. Had his superiors underrated the strength of the invasion forces?

It was after eight p.m. when General Dawley left the beachhead in a landing craft commandeered from Green Beach. He directed the coxswain to sail in search of LST 404 on which he was to confer with General Middleton, but nobody on board his LCM, Landing Craft Mechanised, seemed to know of the whereabouts of 404.

So heavy was the blitz from the *Luftwaffe* and the 88s in the hills that the ships in the armada were constantly changing their positions and anchorages. Confused, Dawley decided that the only way to locate the elusive LST was to ride out to the *Ancon* for information.

An aide confided to him, 'I think we're on our way to Naples.' The General was not amused by the remark. The coxswain, who seemed to have lost his way, changed course. Now they were headed due west towards Sardinia. Dawley suggested he should hail other landing craft to ask about the whereabouts of the *Ancon*. After searching the gulf for some hours they eventually located the flagship. It was almost midnight.

Climbing the gangplank, one of Dawley's aides succeeded in rousing General Alfred Gruenther, an old friend of Eisenhower's, from his bed. A surprised Gruenther came to the foot of the gangplank where Dawley outlined the situation on the American beaches. He admitted he had been unable to locate LST 404 and asked what time General Clark wanted to meet him and Middleton the next morning. 'Forget about the meeting,' Gruenther told him. 'Clark has changed his mind.'

Impatiently, Dawley turned to the coxswain, 'Get us back to the *Funston*.' The weary General was determined to catch some sleep before organizing his staff to go ashore again next morning. Meanwhile, by the time Lionel Shapiro arrived back on the *Ancon* late that night, the *Luftwaffe* had made ten further raids on the flagship and the transports clustered around her. An officer told him the bombs were falling with improved accuracy.

Going below to the War Room he found exhausted staff officers still concentrated on the teletypes, apparently indifferent to the tremors of the ship and the incessant bark of her anti-aircraft guns.

Below decks the heat was stifling. All safety doors had been secured and the ventilation system cut off to prevent any intake of smoke into the ship. Shapiro's khaki drill shirt was so drenched with sweat that he sought the cool of the decks. Etched against the ghostly light of flares, he saw figures passing ammunition along a human chain.

Another bomb exploded, sending a wall of spray over the side of the ship. The *Luftwaffe*'s fighters and bombers were swooping in from the hills without respite, bent on sinking the Allied fleet. It seemed a miracle that the ships were still afloat. How long more could the *Ancon* escape a direct hit?

When General Walker received the disturbing news that the Germans had blown up the bridge over the Sele River on Highway 18 he was thankful at least that, despite heavy casualties, the greater number of Texans were ashore and had reached some important objectives. They had taken a hill two miles from Capaccio railway station, another hill to the south of it, and the town itself. One company had fought its way almost to the top of Monte Soprano.

Although 141 RCT were still pinned down on Blue Beach on the right flank, Walker convinced himself that his Texans would eventually move forward to beat off further counter-attacks. By the time he turned in he calculated that his beachhead stretched over a perimeter of twelve miles with a radius of almost five miles.

He and his staff sought safe corners in which to snatch some sleep. Technical Sergeant Sam Kaiser chose the back room of a concrete outbuilding open to the sky. Crawling with his bedroll beneath a row of storage casks resting on a concrete base a couple of feet off the floor, he tried to sleep despite the noise of shelling and a raging toothache.

While Walker and his men rested, German reinforcements were rolling in from the mountains, the Hermann Göring Division was hurrying south from Naples, and leading elements of the 29th Panzergrenadiers had already reached the beachhead less than 24 hours after they had been ordered north from Calabria.

All day the LST on which Charles Coffey was signalman had ferried British troops ashore. After dark his ship went in to evacuate the British wounded. Medics carried the injured up the ramps on simple stretchers secured with two poles on each side. Coffey and the crew made the men as comfortable as possible on deck. Many were so badly wounded it was too risky to take them below.

With only a pharmacist and a couple of medics on board, the Captain of the LCT decided to steer his craft in search of the hospital ship. Because of the shelling the ship had pulled out into deep water and he could not locate her. Unless medical help was found quickly he knew that many of the men lying in agony on his deck would not survive. He hailed passing LSTs until he found a craft with a doctor on board.

Coffey and the crewmen unloaded 'all those poor guys' onto the bigger craft and then returned to the beaches in search of more wounded.

On Green Beach in the 'Uncle' area Regimental Medical Officer William Rankin and the medical orderlies had worked all day treating the injured at the aid post. The badly wounded were taken to landing craft and ferried out to the hospital ship. Some of those who died were buried where they lay.

Rankin was exhausted. He saw friends carried into the post seriously wounded, some of them dying, and dared not betray emotion. But the experience hurt him. As darkness fell he sedated a young soldier, then amputated his leg, sewing up the vessels after the operation.

He had been promised a surgical team and sappers, but none had arrived. On his right the relentless 88s continued shelling. His orders had been to send the injured to medical teams inland, but no teams had been landed by nightfall. Now he had to negotiate with the beachmaster to have the wounded taken out by sea. He evacuated almost a hundred men.

Wounded Hampshires were still being carried in, many of them badly mauled by tanks. So preoccupied was he in tending their injuries that he had no idea how the battle was going. Neither medical staff nor supplies had reached him. Captain Rankin could only guess that something had gone seriously wrong with the invasion.

With orders to withdraw to the road block north of Fratte, Lieutenant Rocholl decided to drive first from the sanatorium into the city to establish that it was free of enemy forces.

On his return through the hills, heading towards Fratte, villagers ran into the roadway, throwing flowers at the armoured cars and shouting, '*Viva Inglesi!*' Yesterday, Rocholl thought bitterly, these people were our allies. Tonight they are presumptuous enough to imagine the British are on the march. Foolish people.

On reaching the road block he met the quartermaster who had

arrived with mail and rations and drove with him to Regimental HQ. By now it was almost eleven p.m. and the Commander had gone to bed.

'Don't worry,' the adjutant assured him. 'He received all your radio messages. He's pleased with the information you sent him.'

Dismissed, Rocholl returned to his patrol and called the crews together. Telling them he appreciated the work they had done, he complimented in particular the radio operator who had remained at his set without a break for thirty-two hours, even going to the latrine with his earphones on and carrying his message pad.

It was time for supper, he told them. After they had eaten he entered up his diary, describing his encounter with the priest at the hospital. 'What a strange conception these Italians have of war,' he wrote.

Then he turned in and 'slept like the dead'.

At the end of the crucial first day a feeling of guarded optimism prevailed among the Allied commanders. However, for most of the time General Clark had been frustrated by the vagueness of the situation reports reaching him. His aides had observed his changing moods. Serious early doubts gave way to gradual optimism, especially as reports filtered through that the beachhead was secured. He was reassured by General Walker's report that his men would not be shifted by enemy counter-attacks and would push on towards the Sele River. From the *Hilary* General McCreery reported that, although not all objectives had been achieved, the Tenth Corps had seized sufficient ground to make the beachhead tenable.

Clark had no real worry about the seven mile gap still yawning between the British and American Corps. Although this should have been closed by nightfall, he realised that with the intensity of the fighting neither Generals Walker nor Graham had been able to spare sufficient men to expand their fronts. He had to admit that progress had been disappointing, nowhere approaching the expectations of the plan for Avalanche. True, the 36th Division in its first taste of battle had won control of the plains south of the Sele River and had pushed on towards the high ground with an average penetration of five miles. Only on the extreme American right flank, in the direction of Agropoli, had they failed to make any real progress, although they had repulsed vicious enemy counter-attacks. But the Germans were still in control of the dominating heights. Discussing the situation with Admiral Hewitt, Clark would only say, 'The gap is not too serious.'

Later that night he signalled General Alexander that the beachhead had been established. He assured him he was now about to start the drive to take the dominating mountain heights covering the highway to Naples. It was a touch of the old Clark optimism reasserting itself even in crisis. Yet he had to admit it had been a trying day in the operations room of *Ancon*, piecing together the sketchy reports. The subdued General was to recall, 'By nightfall I felt we had achieved as much as could be expected.'

He repeated to Eisenhower that he did not regard the gap between the British Tenth Corps and the American Sixth as 'too serious'.

At his headquarters in Algiers Supreme Commander Eisenhower was concerned not only with Avalanche, but with General Montgomery's progress up the toe of Italy. Although that progress was slow, hinting perhaps at Monty's caution, he was confident that the Eighth Army would reach Salerno within a few days. Clark, he had no doubt, badly needed the assistance of the experienced Eighth. He learned that resistance by the Germans on all beaches was heavily concentrated, especially on the Sixth Corps front. He could appreciate Clark's request to send the 82nd Airborne Division into the area. But he would have to wait.

Avalanche, he felt, would be 'a matter of touch and go' for the next few days. With uncharacteristic pessimism, he confided to an aide, 'I feel we are in for a very bad time in the Avalanche area.'

At that moment the spectre of failure haunted the Supreme Commander.

XI
'The Feel of Battle'

Friday, 10 September. Morning till afternoon.

General Clark awakened on board the *Ancon* to a dawn tinted with crimson. It was eerily still after the noisy bombardment of the night before. No sound of gunfire was heard from the enemy's coastal batteries in the hills above Paestum. Clark assumed that the 16th Panzers were already moving their resources to the British sector.

At precisely 7.30 a.m., accompanied by his aides, Clark left the flagship and boarded a landing craft for the beachhead. Since the invasion began the restive General had found it almost impossible to determine the exact battle situation from the sweltering confines of the ship's War Room. He was more anxious than ever to go ashore to see for himself what was happening and get 'the feel of battle'.

Reports of setbacks tended to upset the optimist in Clark. Uncertain of what awaited him on the beaches, he had decided to travel without the press corps. A vain man, he was acutely aware of the value of publicity in a war campaign and had directed that all press despatches from the front carry the full designation, *With Lieut. General Mark. W. Clark's Fifth Army*. This had become something of a joke among the correspondents who would have no further opportunity of questioning the General until he set up his shore headquarters.

Clark was now aggressively determined that the Fifth Army, his first command, should do well. This morning he wanted to see the 179 RCT, the first combat team from the 45th Division, his floating reserves, on the beachhead.

As he stepped onto the dry, sandy beach in the bright morning sunshine a large German shepherd dog came bounding towards him, leaping joyously at the sight of his master, and almost bowling him over. Clark was obviously pleased to see his dog, yet relieved that the war correspondents were not around. Mike had caused problems in *Ancon*. Ignoring the rules forbidding dogs on transports, a sergeant had tied a label to the dog's collar and turned the animal over to a group of soldiers going ashore. The label read, *This is General Clark's dog. He is going to Salerno*.

In *Ancon* the crew's tolerance of the dog had reached breaking point. Now, on the beach, the dog was again behaving badly. Climbing into a jeep to drive with his aides to the 36th command post at the tobacco warehouse, Clark reluctantly directed that Mike be tied up.

An edgy General Dawley also arrived at the command post from the *Funston* at this time and Clark asked him to take command of all units of the 45th Division as part of the Sixth Corps to protect the left flank of the 36th. To a surprised General Walker this denoted a change in the command structure.

Before embarking in North Africa Walker had been assured that he would be in command of all troops south of the Sele River during the first three days of the invasion and responsible only to Clark. Now Dawley was being placed in charge.

The command structure had already caused obvious tension between Clark and Dawley. Since the start of the invasion Walker had reported directly to Clark, an arrangement which baffled Dawley. Was Clark, Dawley wondered, being devious? Clark's excuse to him was that this arrangement was 'more convenient' until Dawley was able to set up his headquarters ashore. In army circles, however, it was known that the two commanders were not on the friendliest terms. The sensitive Dawley was not an officer to conceal his displeasure easily, nor on this occasion did he try to do so.

The veteran Walker, on the other hand, was not interested in the politics of command structures. He was concerned only for the progress of the war and the welfare of his men. He preferred to fight battles, not personal feuds. This morning he merely reported to Clark the news of the campaign in his sector since the landings.

Dawley set up his command post with a small, and as yet inadequate, staff adjacent to that of the 36th. Now he could take over responsibility from Walker for tactical operations south of the Sele. When Colonel Robert Hutchins, commanding officer of 179 RCT, arrived he directed him to advance to the Sele to make contact with the British Tenth Corps.

Meanwhile Clark, accompanied by three MPs as tall as himself and husky enough to appear twice his size, took the wheel of a jeep and, followed by a second jeep with his aides, drove to the beach. Then he took a boat to the Tenth Corps sector to confer with General McCreery.

Mike stayed behind, howling and whining for his master.

Although during the night of the invasion they had reached the vital crossroads outside Battipaglia, where the highway divides into southern and eastern arteries, it was not until early light that British troops of the 9th Fusiliers began their advance on the town.

'We're on the move,' Lieut. Colonel Ted Hillersden called to his men. 'We're going straight into Battipaglia.'

The rugged six-footer, who had just returned from Brigade HQ with his orders, directed them to move towards the railway junction and the town. His batman, Fusilier Albert Fitzgerald, edged among twisted railway tracks that pointed steel fingers skywards. Wrecked rolling stock was smouldering in the marshalling yards. Engines and freight wagons lay upended after the summer-long bombardment by Allied aircraft. On his left he could hear moving vehicles. He drew his Colonel's attention to the sound. They could be lorries, but he felt certain they were enemy tanks.

Entering the town's broad main street the Fusiliers began selecting vantage points. Fitzgerald moved down a narrow alleyway and positioned himself on some steps. Tired after a night without sleep, he began dozing off. Suddenly bullets from a Spandau whistled past his head. The Germans were closing in.

At the same time RAF Mustangs and Spitfires from Sicily had arrived over the battle area, diving low, strafing enemy positions. Offshore, naval batteries aimed their shells at the inland roads, striking at the enemy's transport and communications. At one point a destroyer raced inshore at speed, firing salvoes at the German 88s. So close were the shells that one Fusilier recalled, 'We were bloody nearly shaved.'

Meanwhile, the Germans stubbornly defended Montecorvino airfield against strong attacks by the 3rd Coldstream Guards, determined to prevent Allied planes from landing there. Realizing its strategic importance, they fought off attacks on the tobacco factory, situated a few miles away, between the airfield and Battipaglia.

At 7.30 a.m. the 6th Grenadier Guards were ordered to take the factory buildings. Close to the barbed wire with which the enemy protected the main buildings and the adjoining outhouses, they began digging in. Suddenly armoured cars and tanks swept into view, supported by infantry. Under a merciless hail of mortars and tracers one platoon of guards fell dead and wounded. The survivors, fearing death was inevitable, began running in spontaneous panic in the direction of the beaches. This panic was evidently caused by the sudden annihilation of their comrades and the realization that they were clearly outnumbered. When the news reached General D. A. H. Graham, the Grenadiers' divisional commander, he was furious. He abhorred cowardice. Even though the Grenadiers were low in morale and clearly outclassed, he wanted no panic among his troops. Ordering his officers to seek out the scattered Grenadiers and regroup them, he began to plan another attack.

Men of the Scots Guards, who had been behind the Grenadiers, moved forward to take their place and attack the tobacco factory.

Dismayed at the volume of fire, Guardsman John Weir edged cautiously towards the buildings, firing his Bren wildly in the direction of the enemy. Bullets thudded into the earth around him. Grenades sent up smoke and débris in front of him. He winced as he saw his best friend, a young Guardsman from Glasgow, drop 'like a sack' when a mortar shell exploded beside him. Desperate to help, he crawled to where he lay. He could see blood trickling from where the mortar splinter had buried itself beneath his armpit. The young Guardsman muttered something. Weir caught only the words, 'a burning in my side'. Then his friend was dead.

Ahead he saw another Guardsman stumble and fall beneath a burst of machine gun fire. Around him lay dead comrades. *My God*, Weir thought, *we're dying like flies.*

With mortars and bullets raining on them from enemy positions in and around the factory, the Guardsmen were finally halted, no longer daring to move further. Against such counter-attacks further progress was impossible. They began to fall back, taking up new positions. As they retreated, Weir fired round after round from his Bren at the factory. But he knew they could not shift the Germans.

Late in the morning Lieutenant Günter Schmitz, whose 2nd Panzer Regiment had fought in the initial defence of Battipaglia and Montecorvino airfield, was surprised to receive a message that General Sieckenius wished to see him at divisional headquarters. Driving over to Eboli, three miles east of Battipaglia on Highway 18, Schmitz was in subdued mood. Normally cheerful, he was still smarting over the previous day's incident at Montecorvino when he was ordered to retire to new positions at the very moment he was convinced the enemy was in retreat. His men had been replaced by the 2nd Panzer Regiment under Major Freiherr von Falkenhausen.

At Eboli an aloof and unsmiling Sieckenius received him. The commander of the 16th Panzer Division came to the point at once. He asked Schmitz to give his version of the Montecorvino incident and explain why he had retired to new positions.

Taken aback by the General's peremptory tone, Schmitz replied that he was acting under orders and against his own judgement. He made as forceful a defence as he could of his action. Impressed by such frankness, Sieckenius said finally, 'I understand, Lieutenant. This was not your fault.'

They discussed the campaign briefly. Schmitz got the impression that Sieckenius was a worried commander. Too much, the General admitted, had been left to the 16th Panzers. 'The odds against us are immense,' he said. 'But we must carry on the fight.'

Since the invasion began Sieckenius had scrutinized reports from all fronts. Enemy naval batteries had proved more devastatingly accurate than he had believed possible and were providing immeasurable assistance to the invading forces. In the area around Battipaglia and Montecorvino he feared his men were in danger of being outflanked. Wisely, the Pioneers had blown up sections of the road between the airfield and the foothill village of Faiano to slow the enemy's advance. He was now hopeful the Hermann Göring Division and sections of the 15th Panzergrenadier Division were close enough to Salerno to be able to join the battle later in the day. But he was concerned by the news that reinforcements from the south, especially the 29th Panzergrenadier Division, were delayed by lack of fuel; only defiant counter-attacks by the 16th Panzers could gain precious time until reinforcements arrived. Unless help arrived quickly it would be impossible to drive the enemy back into the sea as Field Marshal Kesselring had ordered.

Driving back towards Battipaglia Lieutenant Schmitz joined up with a reconnaissance troop of his regiment. On a narrow road near the village of Santa Lucia he passed wrecked armoured cars and trucks, disabled tanks and scores of dead. To the young Lieutenant, it was a depressing sight.

Outside Santa Lucia machine guns unexpectedly opened up on the troops. Beside him a lieutenant groaned as he was hit in the face by tracers. Blood began spurting over his uniform. Schmitz suddenly felt the *Kübelwagen* collapse beneath him, destroyed by a shell. Feeling a sudden, sharp pain, he gripped his chest. He knew he was wounded by shrapnel. The *Kübelwagen* tumbled sideways and he remembered only being lifted out of the vehicle and placed on a stretcher in a field ambulance. A wounded British officer lay beside him as they were driven away to the hospital at Sant' Angelo.

So close had the enemy come to Vietri that by eleven a.m. a dozen Germans had climbed the 1,300-foot White Cross Hill overlooking the town and were firing with Spandaus on troops and civilians in the streets.

Lieutenant Colonel Jack Churchill went up on the roof of the school headquarters on the Via Mazzini with Brigadier 'Lucky' Laycock and Captain Harold Blissett. Peering through his telescope, Laycock spotted the Germans setting up machine gun positions. He estimated they were as close as a thousand yards.

Churchill shouted to Captain Arthur Brunswick, who had assembled his mortar crew nearby, 'See those buggers up there on the hill? Shoot your mortars at them. See if they'll clear off.' He called in his Brens, and guns and mortars were soon firing at the hilltop. A mortar shell landed among the Germans and he clearly saw one man hurled into the air, arms and legs spreadeagled as he turned a cartwheel before coming down.

'Best shooting I've come across in 2 Commando,' he called to Blissett.

The Brigade was now so insecure that it was imperative to occupy the heights around the town. Two troops of 2 Commando were sent forward, leaving only the heavy weapons troop.

Early in the morning the Recce Squadron of the 44th Reconnaissance Regiment, finding the enemy entrenched at La Molina at the start of the Cava gap and overlooking the 41 RM Commando positions from the hills above the valley, had withdrawn to rejoin the 138 Brigade at Salerno. At 7.15 a.m. the Commander of 138 had arrived at SS Brigade Headquarters to explain that he had been unable to extricate more than one battalion from the beaches. So worried was he about the increasing threat to his forces that he admitted there was nothing he could do to reinforce the Commandos or come to their immediate aid. He asked them to try to hold on.

Laycock demanded that he at least arrange naval support fire. It would be of help if the Germans at La Molina and Cava could be shelled. The Commandos also needed urgent supplies of 4.2 mortars, Piat ammunition and wireless batteries. The Commander promised to supply what he could. By ten o'clock the Germans had infiltrated positions south of La Molina. Creeping forward across the wooded slopes of the defile they began mortaring and machine gunning the positions of 41 RM Commando from less than 3,000 yards.

Scaling the almost sheer face at the rear of the hill from which the Germans had shelled Vietri 2 Troop of 2 Commando captured those Germans who had not been killed or wounded. Slowly, the men of 2 Commando began forming a perimeter in the hills around Vietri.

The precipitous and difficult terrain had not been sufficiently anticipated in the planning of the invasion. More infantrymen were needed, yet they were not available from 138 Brigade. Later in the morning, however, 138 sent up promised 4.2 inch mortars and machine guns, sufficient to thicken the fire support of the Commandos. Soon afterwards a Field Company of the Royal Engineers reported to SS Brigade HQ. They had been sent as infantry, but nobody had explained this to the officers at Brigade HQ who did not realize how serious was the situation on the beaches. They were not to know that engineers, service corps troops, ack-ack gunners, even the port control men that Charles Coffey had ferried ashore in his landing craft the previous night, were being thrown into the invasion as infantrymen. Lacking such knowledge, the Commando officers decided to hold the Royal Engineers' company in reserve. And they had no further reserves with which to influence the progress of the battle.

In the hills beyond Vietri the men of 41 RM Commando held out against repeated attempts by the Germans to break through south of La Molina. All morning their positions were shelled, mortared, machine gunned. Even the mortars which had been sent to reinforce their firepower could not halt the enemy troops who were moving closer with every moment.

At the harbour at Salerno Sergeant Dentoni-Litta, familiar with the port installations, conducted two British officers on a short tour. The sight that met them on the quayside was of destruction on a massive scale. Buildings were in ruins or burned to the ground. Ships were sunk or half-submerged in the water. Cranes were toppled or twisted.

The Allies had been hopeful that, from the start of the invasion, supplies could be ferried into the harbour. Since the landings the big, Texas-built rescue tug *Favorite* had stood close inshore to haul away damaged landing craft. During most of D-Day Roy Jensen, a South African seaman gunner, had stayed with the ships; other gunners closed up on the ack-ack guns and the Oerlikons, but only once did they open fire. In the forenoon the *Favorite* began towing a loaded pontoon into the damaged harbour, assuming the area to be free of the enemy.

As the tug moved into the débris-strewn port and alongside the quay, Jensen sighted a party of armed Germans. Before the enemy could open fire the tug's captain had put the diesel-electric engines full astern and backed pontoon and tug out of the harbour.

Yet no matter what forces came and went the immediate need of the inhabitants of Salerno was to survive. Dismissed by the British, Dentoni-Litta and Staff Sergeant Barone scoured the city in search of food. In a quayside warehouse destroyed by explosions they found an abandoned supply of *tubetielli*, a favourite Neapolitan pasta. It would stave off their hunger while they found a way out of the city.

Lieutenant Adrian Gallegos, waiting impatiently to go ashore on the American beaches from a landing ship which was slowly disgorging tanks and armoured vehicles, saw a jeep lifted into the air by an exploding land mine. In a cloud of sand the driver was thrown clear. Apparently unhurt, the man began to run along the beach 'as though he was temporarily out of his mind'.

Gallegos was with the Advance Naval Section of a special force which had the duty of developing resistance in enemy territory. With him was Lieutenant Malcolm Munthe, heading the military section of the same force. Together they had travelled from Sicily on a ship packed with combat troops of the 179 Infantry Division which since midnight on 8 September had remained off shore. Gallegos had been told that if the Germans did not oppose the landings in strength, as some commanders hoped, the ship and its men and supplies would be diverted to Anzio. But this morning the 179 RCT, part of General Middleton's 45th Division, was ordered ashore. He watched the men run across the beach as the sand was churned up in neat white lines by tracers and Messerschmitts screeched out of the sky like huge hawks. When his turn came he agreed with Munthe that they should walk coolly up the beach. 'Whatever happens,' the tall Highlander cautioned Gallegos, 'we mustn't run.'

The noise of the shelling from the shore and the boom of naval guns pounding the inland positions was deafening. As they passed between rows of white tapes marking off a laneway cleared of mines, Gallegos saw on either side groups of dead soldiers. They lay half covered by the sand just as they had fallen when shell or mine had killed them. It sickened him to think that at any moment he might die such a violent death with his chest smashed in or his head blown off.

Middleton had ordered the 179 to advance to an assembly area close to Highway 18 north of Paestum. The combat team would now pass from army reserve into the control of Dawley's Sixth Corps. In an effort to close the gap on the right of the Sele Clark had decided to shift the corps' boundary to the north of the river.

In a small square near Paestum Gallegos stood among the men of the 179 listening to an American Marines colonel read a list of instructions from a mimeographed sheet. As the troops gathered around him three Messerschmitts swooped out of the clear blue sky, machine gunning the group. Men dashed for cover. Gallegos crouched behind the shell of a burned-out German armoured car. Undeterred, the tall, grey-haired colonel continued reading his instructions as though nothing was happening.

Only by taking such a terrible risk, Gallegos realized, could the colonel hope to instil confidence in these troops who, until this morning, had never known the terror of warfare.

With the Germans cleared from the tobacco farm and the HQ staff from *Hilary* in control, communications between farm, beach and the ship were fully operational. Telegraphist James Sharkey, who had set up the operation at the farm on D-Day, decided to go in search of petrol. Unfolding his map, he ran his finger across the paper to find the letters POL (petrol, oil, light). He located a supply point only a few hundred yards up the road.

Borrowing a jeep from the beachmaster, he drove to the point and helped himself to some jerricans of petrol which he placed in the back of the vehicle. Stepping into the office to make out the necessary requisition chit for the fuel, he was surprised to find it empty. Something hard was pushed into the small of his back and a German voice ordered, 'March!'

Sharkey raised his arms. A young Panzer pushed him roughly out of the hut and towards the roadway. Approaching his jeep, Sharkey slowed down. The gun was stuck sharply into his back. 'March!' he was told. He quickened his pace. On the road he again slowed down. Again the sharp reminder. The German steered him towards the right, away from the British lines.

About fifty yards farther on Sharkey slowed again and the Panzer jammed the gun into his back. This time the telegraphist flung himself forward on his hands and, lifting one foot behind him, caught the German in the crotch with the sharp heel of his boot. The German gasped as Sharkey ran like hell, back towards his lines.

Pistol shots rang out as he jumped into the jeep and drove off. Speeding along the road he caught a glimpse of a Mark 4 behind him, a neat black Iron Cross outlined in white paint prominent in his rear mirror as it rounded a bend. As the tank's guns lined up to hit the jeep he pushed his foot to the floorboards. Driving down to the beach, he locked the wheel to steer the vehicle in a straight line. Then, rolling out of his seat, he flung himself into the ditch. Driverless, the jeep sped straight towards the beach while a bruised Sharkey crawled back, as he had done the previous day, to the tobacco farm.

When he reported to his officer, Lieutenant Lee, that he had been taken prisoner by a German soldier and had escaped, Lee told him, 'Wait a moment,' and went upstairs. Returning, he asked Sharkey to follow him to a room above the wireless centre. A sentry stood guarding the door. Lee told the telegraphist, 'Answer whatever questions you are asked.' Pushing him inside, he shut the door.

Coming from the bright morning sunlight it took Sharkey a few moments to adjust to the darkness of the room. There was an unpleasant smell. As his eyes focused in the dim light he recognized the two tramps, toes sticking out of their boots, he had almost run down with his Bedford on the morning of D-Day. One of them asked him, 'Tell me, did the German smell clean?'

'What the hell are you talking about?' asked the confused telegraphist, surprised at the Oxbridge accent. Impulsively, he turned to go, but Lee pushed him back into the room.

'Do what you're told. Answer their questions.'

Sharkey realized that the filthy pair were British Intelligence men. But, God, they stank.

They questioned him about the German who had captured him and the area from which he had escaped. Was the soldier wearing full boots or half boots? Was his uniform tidy? Were his hands clean? Was his hair neat? Sharkey knew they wanted to establish if enemy reinforcements had arrived and if a German command post was nearby.

He answered as best he could. When they told him he could go, Lee explained that if the Germans captured him again they were entitled to shoot him. Would he prefer to be shipped back to North Africa?

'No, sir,' Sharkey told him. 'If I'm going to die, I want to die among my mates.'

'Very well,' said Lee. 'Carry on.'

As the telegraphist went downstairs the Lieutenant remarked that the wounded man he had carried into the farm the previous morning was asking to see him.

Sharkey crossed to the outbuilding to find some twenty wounded lying there. The young man he had rescued waved to him. Grabbing Sharkey's hand, he shook it warmly. The telegraphist was astonished when the man said to him in broken English, 'I am German.'

Walking back to his Bedford he heard the sound of the naval guns firing in the direction of the supply point where he had been captured, probably working on information he had given the Intelligence men. He saw the tank that had followed him a smouldering wreck, knocked out by grenades. The smell of human bodies burning inside the vehicle made him want to retch.

It had been a trying morning for Father Carucci. British forces had arrived early at the sanatorium and were already in the gardens when he heard the news. Hurrying down, he was confronted by a young major who shook hands with him and assured him that the hospital would be treated with respect and that the patients need have no fears.

To Dr Soffietti, who also came down, the officer gave the same assurances. Later, Carucci learned that for some hours previously the major and his men had been patrolling the area, moving in single file towards the sanatorium, and pointing guns and pistols at civilians who approached them.

Beside the mortuary chapel he and the doctor found other British soldiers who looked at them suspiciously. When Soffietti suggested they should find a more suitable observation post, an officer stepped forward brandishing his pistol. Catching sight of the priest he replaced the pistol in his holster and offered cigarettes. Then he ordered his soldiers to position themselves elsewhere.

Late in the morning a British Colonel arrived with an interpreter, determined to find out all he could. Why was the city deserted? he asked Carucci. Where was his bishop, Monterisi? What was the state of public health? When the questioning was ended and the Colonel stood up to leave, Carucci was surprised to see his stern features break into a sudden smile.

Soon afterwards another officer arrived at the hospital entrance. Carucci met him at the swing doors of the porch and extended a hand in welcome. The officer looked at him contemptuously. 'One does not shake hands with a loser,' he snapped. Carucci struggled to retain his composure and led the officer into the first-floor reception room. It was to be a brief interview. The officer merely wanted to know about the common diseases of the area.

It was one o'clock in the afternoon when the chaplain heard that a group of senior officers had arrived. This time, he was told, one of the Allied generals was on the terrace.

Hurrying out, he found a number of officers standing beside a small convoy of jeeps. He recognized the young major who had visited him earlier in the morning. Standing with his back to them, surveying the hillsides with his field glasses, was an officer in battledress, taller than the others and wearing an American steel helmet.

'That,' the Major informed Carucci, 'is General Clark. He's the commander of this invasion.'

Carucci went forward to welcome the general and invited him into the sanatorium. Accepting a glass of Cinzano from Soffietti, Clark said, 'I give you my word that we shall protect your hospital.'

XII
'A Bloody Toll'

Friday, 10 September. Afternoon till midnight.

General McCreery, the stern commander of the British Tenth Corps, waited at his headquarters with growing anxiety for General Clark to arrive. The mounting list of casualties had made him despondent. Avalanche had already taken 'a bloody toll' of his men, particularly the Hampshires. In spite of these bitter setbacks he was determined that the troops of the 46th and 56th Divisions must ultimately succeed in the quest for victory.

General Hawkesworth's leadership of the 46th gave him renewed hope. 'Ginger' Hawkesworth was a skilful infantry tactician, a commander who understood the value of artillery support and could inspire his men on the beachhead. But studying reports of the 56th Division in the area of Battipaglia and Montecorvino he formed a disturbing picture of an intense conflict, the outcome of which seemed uncertain. Kesselring's counter-attack, he suspected, was imminent. The veteran Field Marshal was a master of defensive tactics and must not be underestimated.

It was with mixed feelings that he greeted Clark who loped into his headquarters like 'a film star who excels in Westerns'. Though both men shared the common goal of an overall success in the Italian campaign, McCreery disagreed with what he saw as Clark's over-eagerness to probe the enemy's defences over too wide an area to find his weak spots. Quietly, almost deferentially, the slim British commander warned Clark that in the British sector it was 'touch and go all the way'. He told him he expected a powerful enemy counter-attack within the next twenty-four hours and emphasized that German concentrations in the Northern sector of the beachhead made it doubtful whether his Corps, at its present strength, could advance the fourteen miles eastward through Battipaglia and Eboli towards the Ponte Sele, the projected meeting place with the American Sixth Corps.

He pinpointed two particularly sensitive areas: the extreme left flank on the Sorrento peninsula, where the Rangers were fighting to hold the Chiunzi Pass against increasing opposition, and the gap on the right flank of the Tenth Corps in the low ground between Battipaglia and the Sele River.

Clark, however, remained optimistic. He assured McCreery that considerable progress had been made in the American sector, where both Dawley and Walker were satisfied with the situation. Despite McCreery's disquiet at the fighting engulfing his divisions, Clark believed this was a temporary setback. If assistance were needed, he told him, it could come only at the expense of the Sixth Corps. Yet before their meeting ended he agreed that in view of the enemy's different strengths McCreery should have help. He sent an observer to Darby's headquarters at Maiori who assessed the situation and recommended that the Rangers be reinforced with motorized infantry to include artillery, tank and chemical battalions, combat engineers and a company of a tank destroyer battalion.

Gunner Charles Dettmer of 2 Commando saw Clark and McCreery in Vietri that afternoon on their tour of inspection of the Tenth Corps battle area. A gunner attached to the American mortar squad which was giving fire support to the Commandos suddenly threw his cigarette on the ground and worked his heel into it. 'That's the General,' he muttered. 'That's Clark.'

To Dettmer the General looked more like a professor than a soldier. The sallow-faced Clark and preoccupied McCreery passed without even noticing the two men.

Less than an hour after Clark had left the area and shortly after Hawkesworth had visited Brigade HQ to compliment the Commandos on their holding action, the Germans resumed their shelling. Forward troops of 41 RM Commando and the Brigade HQ in Vietri came under heavy fire.

Throughout the morning the Royal Marines had fought back repeated attempts to break through their positions in the defile at La Molina. Yet, though two troops of 2 Commando were in the hills above Vietri, the shelling intensified. To the officers at Brigade HQ it was obvious that the Germans were softening up the Commando defences for a large-scale attack.

A direct hit severely wounded Lieut. Colonel 'Bertie' Lumsden, commanding officer of 41 RM Commando, and his signals officer, and killed other signallers. Major John Edwards, Lumsden's second in command, took charge of the unit and replaced signals personnel from Brigade HQ.

By late afternoon one troop of 41 were in danger of being overrun as the Germans moved forward along front slopes of the hills west of the valley, passing above and below their positions. A new line of attack was established 200 yards to the rear of these positions, thus exposing the left flank of the Commandos. Unless the flank was secured before darkness nothing could stop Germans penetrating 2 Commando positions around Vietri during the night.

On his visit to Brigade HQ Hawkesworth had been unable to promise further relief. Colonel Jack Churchill was impatient. He had seen one of his men, Private Killeen, killed when a shell landed behind the battery as he was cooking a meal. He knew that the enemy would be in Vietri before evening. Now he needed help.

In response to his call the commanding officer of the 6th Lincolnshire Regiment arrived at the headquarters in the elementary school. He apologized to Churchill that he would not be able to mount an attack before dusk; he was unfamiliar with the terrain and his troops were unprepared. But he promised to send a company to strengthen the 2 Commando position north of Vietri and relieve the two troops on the western approaches to Salerno. These necessary reinforcements would free 3 Troop of 2 Commando for an attack on the ridge west of 41 RM Commandos' positions overlooking their left flank.

Within hours the positions held by 3 Troop were taken over by a company of Lincolns and a section of tanks arrived to give support and covering fire. Now, Churchill decided with relief, he could begin his assault before dusk to capture the ridge overlooking the Marines' leftward position.

On his way to the hill with his troop Lieutenant Joe Nicholl met Bren gun carriers from the Lincolns in the main piazza, the meeting place for the townspeople and the point from which three roads radiated to Salerno, Molina and Cava, and across the Roman viaduct towards Dragonea and Maiori.

'Going up the hill?' a driver asked him. 'We've been ordered to take you there.'

The Commandos piled into the carriers with their kit. With a roar of exhaust the vehicles swung out of the piazza and around the corner towards the bridge across the valley.

Nicholl's driver shouted, 'Bit unhealthy here. Keep your heads down!'

Nicholl ducked as the vehicle accelerated. A shot rang out as they sped across the bridge. Around the next bend the carriers halted. 'From here on,' Nicholl's driver said, 'you'll have to walk.'

Edging forward up the hill in the gathering dusk each tree and terrace loomed sinister. Whatever the dangers, Jack Churchill was convinced they could secure the positions they needed before dark.

On their way to hook up with the Commandos at Vietri Staff Sergeant James Altieri's Ranger platoon arrived at a fortified naval observation post close to Vietri on the coastal road. The two-storey building stood on a bluff at a hairpin bend. On the roof were guns and emplacements.

Altieri divided his men into small groups. He had orders to take the naval post and 'clean it out'. Bazooka teams and BAR gunners assaulted the post for almost an hour until Altieri was able to storm the building with his men in the teeth of tracer bullets. So determined was the Ranger platoon after this fire fight to take the post that all seven Italian troops in the station were killed and several Rangers wounded.

In the hills rising sharply above the vital Chiunzi Pass the fiercest fighting was taking place. Rangers had dug in on the forward slopes of the mountains as the Germans, working in patrols of company strength, attacked throughout the day in an effort to outflank them. The twisting road through the mountains leading to the plain of Naples and Highway 18 was becoming the stake in a series of furious battles to determine its control.

Inevitably enemy attacks were preceded by blistering mortar and artillery barrages on the thinly held Ranger front. From where Sergeant Arthur Schrader was positioned on the forward slopes Rangers scanned the area with binoculars, passing their observations to a British naval officer and a Royal Marines sergeant who made contact with the navy and directed the shelling of German guns east of the pass. Schrader found the procedure relatively simple. Pinpointing the area from where shelling was coming, they simply checked the position on the map and passed the co-ordinates to Ranger Three HQ, which in turn relayed the information to the gunners in the Gulf of Salerno.

From these mountain observation posts Rangers directed mortar and artillery fire on enemy troop and supply concentrations below, forcing the Germans to abandon traffic along the network of roads in the valley. To Darby's men it was the chance 'to pull another stunt of forward observing, as we had done in Sicily'.

This evening the Germans began shelling the Ranger positions and the Salerno area with *Nebelwerfer* smoke shell mortars. Schrader's men could not pinpoint them.

Major General Sieckenius, commanding the 16th Panzer Division, had sent a message to Field Marshal Kesselring at Frascati expressing his hope that with sufficient reinforcements the 16th Panzers could hold out against the enemy assault, perhaps even begin to drive the invading forces back towards the beaches. But as the battle raged around Battipaglia and the airfield at Montecorvino his doubts increased.

He was studying reports that the Americans had taken the mountains dominating Paestum where the 79th Panzergrenadiers were fighting to dislodge them; that the Pioneers had retreated from the village of Santa Lucia after the wounding of Schmitz and the other officers, and that the British had penetrated to Belvedere beside the Battipaglia crossroads. He worried for the crews of his tanks in the face of artillery fire and air bombardment. Almost all their counterattacks had to be made downhill from high ground in full view of the enemy. He wondered how many tanks would be operational by the end of the day. Waiting for reinforcements at his divisional headquarters at Eboli he became despondent. General Vietinghoff's plan to bring up the 29th Panzergrenadiers the previous evening to relieve the appalling strain on the 16th Panzers had come unstuck. Instead of the expected troops only their commander, General Walter Fries, had arrived at Vietinghoff's headquarters at Polla with bad news. The 29th Panzers had no fuel and were immobilized on Highway 19 between Polla and Sala Consilina.

Vietinghoff could hardly believe what Fries was telling him.

Nobody, Fries explained, had informed the 29th Panzers of the location of fuel and supply depots. Worse, a tanker and fuel depot at Sapri had been blown sky high by the depot's commander who imagined they were about to be attacked.

Vietinghoff could only attribute this appalling setback to the poor organization of fuel supplies and the lack of an army quartermaster. The 29th Panzers must get supplies as quickly as possible and he must spare the 26th Panzer Division a similar mishap. Immediately, he took steps to remedy the fuel shortage. General Arisio came to his aid with Italian fuel, which he arranged to rush to the 29th Panzers. Then he sent an urgent message to Kesselring to send fuel by air.

This setback had cost precious time. Instead of arriving as the powerful striking force he had anticipated, only straggling units of the 29th Panzers reached Salerno that afternoon. Vietinghoff ordered them to be committed at once to the area between Eboli and Battipaglia where, at all costs, he must prevent the Allies breaking though. He knew the 26th Panzers had few, if any, tanks. The Hermann Göring Panzers had no more than thirty operational tanks. The 15th Panzers had suffered heavily in Sicily and had only seven tanks in Salerno. The 26th Panzers were also without their Panzer Regiment, which was attached to Kesselring's headquarters at Frascati. So critical was the situation at Battipaglia for the 16th Panzers that Vietinghoff ordered them that afternoon to 'do everything possible' to hold the heights surrounding the gulf until sufficient numbers of the 26th Panzers arrived to reduce the pressure and mount a counter-attack.

At Frascati Kesselring, though still anxious about the defence of the Gulf of Gaeta, ordered one regiment of the 3rd Panzergrenadier Division to be shifted to the 14th Panzer Corps to boost the Hermann Göring Division. Urgent appeals had been made to him by the commanders of the 14th Panzer Corps to confront the Allied naval artillery, which was 'causing havoc'. That afternoon General Balck called the elimination of this devastating artillery 'the prime requisite' and begged Kesselring to muster all possible air strength against the Allied ships in the gulf.

As a result, Kesselring decided to give priority to air attacks on enemy ships. The field marshal, who had learned to fly in middle age, understood the need for air cover. Several weeks ago he had given *Luftflotte 2*, the Second Air Force headquarters in Italy, orders to attack Allied shipping while at the same time conserving resources for the battle to come.

This evening he was no longer in real doubt that Salerno was to be that battle.

He ordered *Luftflotte 2* to send up every available aircraft against the Allied Fifth Army. Although 625 aircraft were dispersed between France, Corsica and the Italian mainland, only 120 fighters and 50 fighter bombers were immediately available at bases in central and southern Italy. But he had at least one advantage over his adversary Clark: it was a short distance from the Italian airfields to the Allied beachhead. He wanted Field Marshal von Richthofen, commander of *Luftflotte 2*, to ensure every available pilot was flying sorties over the battlefield.

Late in the afternoon German batteries began shelling the area around the sanatorium of Giovanni da Procida. The young major from the Durhams who had stayed to lunch seemed surprised that the chaplain and staff were prepared to remain in the buildings. 'Aren't you afraid?' he asked them.

Aldo Gatti, an Italian army lieutenant, repeated the question in Italian. Carucci and Soffietti merely shrugged their shoulders in reply.

Carucci was surprised at the Allied optimism. He could scarcely believe their claims that Naples was in their hands, that Italian and Allied paratroopers were fighting side by side in Rome, that Italy had been occupied as far north as Turin. Why then such German resistance here at Salerno? Their answer was that the Germans were fighting back merely to cover the withdrawal of their troops from Calabria.

Electrical power was by now so reduced in Salerno that radio broadcasting had ceased. The staff at the sanatorium felt themselves isolated. Soffietti ordered the sisters, staff and patients to move into the tunnels for the night. Crossing the park with one of the sisters the Mother Superior came across a frightened German soldier who had strayed from his unit. The nuns brought him milk, which he refused, but he accepted some bread and meat. Mother Superior gave him a religious medal of the Virgin. The soldier took it, kissed it reverently, and then began to cry.

Mother Irene sought to comfort the young man with words of hope and encouragement, but she realized he did not understand Italian. The soldier placed the medal in his wallet which contained a snapshot of his wife and children. Then he was gone. She doubted if he would get very far. Allied troops were surrounding the sanatorium.

Quentin Reynolds had gone on deck on the *Ancon* to watch the naval guns destroying enemy tanks and silencing gun emplacements. The navy, he thought, was doing everything except marching into Salerno. If it had not been for these ships perhaps the troops would already have been driven off the beaches. So closely were American and British ships working together that it was almost impossible to tell where one left off and the other began.

About a mile beyond Yellow Beach in the American sector he noticed a sudden, brief, golden flash, followed by a burst of thick, black smoke; then, a moment later, a telltale puff of smoke appeared on the beach. At the same moment the cruiser *Philadelphia* in the fire support group, lying 300 yards on *Ancon*'s port side, opened up with her six-inch guns. One salvo after another thundered shorewards at the 88s. Reynolds reckoned by his watch that the *Philadelphia* kept up her barrage for at least fifteen minutes. Then the firing ceased. From the shore and the hills came no further flashes.

He was assured that any commander on the beachhead asking for gun support got it within fifteen minutes, occasionally more quickly. The destroyer *Nubian* had fired 341 rounds of 4.7 inch shells, battering a group of German tanks, demolishing an enemy battery, and blowing up an ammunition depot and a group of army vehicles. The cruiser

Mauritius had answered seventeen calls for fire and expended almost five hundred rounds on troops, artillery and tanks. Support was given by the cruisers *Uganda* and *Orion* and the monitor ship *Roberts* joined in. When the firing ceased the message signalled to the flagship was usually 'Target destroyed'.

If the invasion of Salerno was to succeed, then Reynolds reckoned it would be the Navy's success.

When the mortar shells exploded in the main street of Battipaglia troops of the 9th Fusiliers began setting up their AT guns to confront the enemy tanks. An impatient Colonel Ted Hillersden ran towards one of the guns, hoping to sight it more accurately.

From the alley where he had positioned himself, Hillersden's batman, Fusilier Albert Fitzgerald, watched in horror as a shell exploded among the gun crew. He saw his colonel falling in the roadway and ran into the open to help him. Blood was pouring from Hillersden's chest and arm as Fusilier Fitzgerald dragged him towards the shelter of the alleyway. 'Help me up,' Hillersden whispered to him.

But the six-foot colonel was such a heavy man that the small, wiry Fitzgerald was unable to get him on his feet. Clearly, Hillersden was losing a lot of blood. He asked Major Masters, at the gunners' OP, for morphine. Breaking open the packet he removed the tube, searched Hillersden's arm for a vein and pushed the needle into the skin.

Hillersden looked up at him thankfully. 'That worked. I feel a lot better.'

Fitzgerald called to a medical orderly and together they lifted the big man onto a stretcher. At the aid post they cut Hillersden's tunic off and applied a shell dressing to the gaping shoulder wound.

When he left the aid post to return to his position some hundred yards away, the tanks were shelling the troops relentlessly. About 5.30 p.m. he noticed the Tigers rolling slowly down the main street. The Fusiliers could not hope to beat back this attack. Hurrying over to the aid post he warned Hillersden, 'Tigers are coming, sir. You may be taken prisoner. Do you want me to stay with you?'

'No, no,' the Colonel said determinedly. 'Go without me.'

The orderlies had decided to evacuate the most badly wounded, including a Major Dalton, from the front line by field ambulance. Hillersden volunteered to wait for the enemy. He had an intense dislike of the Panzers and the prospect of spending the rest of the war in captivity dismayed him. But now there was nothing he could do but submit to his fate.

With Fusilier Reg Tiller and two other soldiers Fitzgerald stationed himself in an upper room in a house overlooking the main street. Fixing the sights of his Bren on the street he crouched in waiting as the Tigers came closer, battering the houses with their shells. Turning to Tiller he realized that he and the other Fusiliers had gone.

He hurried downstairs, making for the rear of the house, where he found the driver of a German rations truck they had taken prisoner earlier in the day waiting for him. It would have been convenient to shoot the man on his way out, but he could not bring himself to raise his gun.

'Go on. Get out,' he ordered him.

The German refused to move, indicating that he wanted to stay with Fitzgerald and the British.

'Come on, then,' Fitzgerald said impatiently, pushing him towards the courtyard at the rear of the house.

As they emerged into the open he realized the prisoner was wearing a German army steel helmet. He pulled it from the man's head and flung it away. Together they went in search of the other Fusiliers.

Late in the evening Fitzgerald found himself back at the crossroads outside Battipaglia, the point from which the attack had started. He reckoned that 500 Fusiliers had marched on the town; now there were about 50 of them. Dividing into two groups, they lined each side of the roadway and dug in for the night. Not even Major Delforce, who had taken over command, knew that one platoon had hidden in a loft above a room in the town now occupied by the Panzers.

Although they had landed on D-Day on the same beach as A Squadron of the Royal Scots Greys, the tanks of B Squadron were held in reserve with 201 Guards Brigade, in a lemon grove west of the airfield at Montecorvino, while the Shermans of C Squadron, with 169 Brigade, made for the airfield. The Shermans knocked out a handful of German tanks, suffered some casualties, and were shot at in mistake by their own infantry as they returned to their lines.

By this afternoon B Squadron had advanced towards the station at Montecorvino and had lost two tanks in enemy attacks. At 5.30 p.m., just as the Germans were driving the 9th Fusiliers out of Battipaglia, B Squadron received an urgent call for help.

Moving along the track which followed the west bank of the Tusciano River, the squadron reached the main road at the village of Belvedere.

Lieutenant Ted Robinson's troop advanced down the main road towards Battipaglia itself. Robinson's orders were to push as far inland

On board a landing craft Allied troops watch a monitor ship shelling German positions at Salerno

At the bridge at Fosso a British anti-tank gun crew prepares to fire at an approaching German half-track troop carrier

British Fusiliers set up an observation post in a ruined building at Battipaglia

A British Bren gun carrier advances through the ruined streets of Salerno

as possible to cut the road from Battipaglia to Salerno. Riding with his crew in the Sherman, his machine gunner seated beside the driver, he realized that his desert range of 1,000 yards was greatly reduced among the villages and fields, the hedges and ditches of the Salerno countryside. Three hundred yards north of the bridge he was ordered to halt and shoot up any enemy tanks approaching from the town. From this position he could see the river, the road to Salerno and the entrance to Battipaglia.

Before long a Mark 4 emerged onto the bridge and Robinson shattered it with his guns, knocking it out. Later, a second tank attempted to edge around the first tank to block the bridge; his sergeant shot it up.

Maintaining radio contact with his squadron leader, Robinson guessed from the messages over his wireless that the invasion was going badly. 'Hold your position for tonight,' he was ordered.

As the night wore on he suggested to his squadron leader that if they brewed some tea it would help keep them awake. 'All right,' he was told. 'But for God's sake don't get out of your vehicle.'

Meanwhile, Regimental Medical Officer Rankin prepared to spend his second night at the aid post. He and his team of medical orderlies and stretcher bearers had succeeded in conveying many wounded soldiers to the landing craft en route to the hospital ships. Now he was treating men from the front line who had cracked under the strain of the constant shelling; their condition stemmed from the noise, the fear and the exhaustion of continuous action. Some showed an almost phobic reaction to the shelling by the 88s, others were so broken by battle that they whimpered like children.

Unable to make allowances for this aspect of battle fatigue, the army could decide only whether or not a man was fit for combat. But to Captain Rankin the men arriving at his aid post were pathetic figures through no fault of their own.

Even on this, the second day, he had little idea of how the invasion was going. Soldiers recounted rumours and the BBC bulletins he heard through the wireless static were sketchy and inconclusive. He had been unable to transfer his aid post inland; he was short of supplies; the surgical teams had not arrived. Exhausted, he was preparing to snatch some sleep when one of the Durhams came to him with a report of a commotion on the beach. Americans from the landing craft, the man exclaimed, were looting the wounded, stealing watches and wallets, 'anything they can lay their hands on!'

Rankin was shocked. It was common for troops to loot the dead, but looting from the living was another matter. By late evening a platoon of Durhams had been placed to stand guard over the wounded with fixed bayonets. To the doctor, the men lying on the beach were 'dumb, wounded animals', and this was the only way they could be protected.

Major Edmund Ball, liaison officer with American ground forces, had gone ashore with a handful of Fifth Army officers in the morning and driven by truck on Highway 18, turning right onto the secondary road that led to the big tobacco warehouse at Casa Vannulo.

At the command post he learned that the left flank of the Sixth Corps was having a tough time attempting to capture the strategic hill town of Altavilla. Unable to locate either of his radio trucks, Ball decided in the late afternoon to ride out to the *Ancon* to locate Edward House of the United States Air Force, who was controlling the air defence of the beachhead from his fighter-director centre on Hewitt's flagship. Ball wanted to ask how at this stage he could help. Taking a command car from the motor pool at the warehouse he drove down to the beach, passing the historic ruins of Paestum where he noticed a medical clearing station and field hospital had been set up.

Just as he was leaving the beach in a *Dukw* a couple of stretcher-bearers carrying a wounded young GI flagged him down to ask if he could take the soldier to a hospital ship standing a few miles offshore. Willingly, Ball agreed. He and the *Dukw* driver loaded the young soldier on board and made him as comfortable as they could. The boy, badly wounded in the leg, told them he was eighteen and from Oklahoma.

They headed towards the white-painted hospital ship, a former passenger ferry that had plied between Dublin and Liverpool. As they came within hailing distance of the ship, which had a large Red Cross on its side, it started to move slowly away. They called to the crew on deck, 'We've got a wounded soldier.' But the ship was under way and a deck officer shouted down, 'Send him back to the beach. They'll pick him up later.'

The GI took it well. Ball hailed another *Dukw* heading towards the shore. The soldiers on board transferred the wounded man in the middle of the gulf and Ball set out again to find the *Ancon*.

They travelled for fifteen miles before spotting the flagship anchored far out in the gulf. Quickly Ball went on board. He reported to General House, told him all he could of the situation ashore and asked for instructions. As they talked, 'General Quarters' was sounded through the ship's loudspeakers. The *Ancon* would have to get underway again to try to elude the enemy bombers.

Ball hurried down the ladder and climbed into the *Dukw* to head back towards the shore. *If enemy planes come bombing and strafing*, he thought, *there's no way you can dig a foxhole in an iron deck.*

When General Clark returned to the *Ancon* that evening he discovered that during his absence a message had been received from AFHQ in Algiers requesting that landing craft carrying the floating reserve of the 45th Division be sent back to North Africa at once.

Unable to contact Clark on the beachhead, Admiral Hewitt had decided to comply with the order, and the craft were already on their way. Throughout the day ships were moved out of the gulf as soon as they were emptied. Already the last of the larger AKAs, Auxiliary Ship Cargo Attack, of the Southern Attack Force were unloaded and would shortly sail for North Africa. Lieutenant Harrel in *Blackmore*, which had guided the Commandos into Vietri, was senior officer of the escort of a convoy of assault ships which since the early afternoon was sailing towards Bône and Bizerta.

Clark had ordered two battalions of the 157th Infantry ashore on the British right flank north of the Sele River. He was furious to learn that these troops had been unloaded south of the Sele. Why were they landed far from the beach on which he had ordered them placed? General Gruenther gave the explanation that the British commander of the ships transporting the 157th was 'darned if he was going to stay out there any longer and take this shelling and the air attacks'. He had put the troops ashore, Gruenther suggested, through a misunderstanding.

Clark told Gruenther he had promised to reinforce the hard-pressed Tenth Corps. He sent written instructions to General Dawley to prepare a task force battalion to support the Rangers. He was specific as to the composition of the force: a battalion of infantry, supported by artillery engineers, tanks and 4.2 inch mortars. He wanted the force ready to embark from a Sixth Corps beach the next day.

By shifting the Sixth Corps boundary north of the river he hoped to close the Tenth Corps gap near the Sele. He had ordered Middleton to use the 179th and 157th Infantry, which was now ashore, even though on the wrong beach. But only the second and third battalions of the 157th had reached the beachhead. Because of a shortage of shipping the first battalion was not expected to arrive from Sicily for another five days.

There was another problem. Having been put ashore on the wrong side of the Sele, the troops of the 157th Infantry could not cross the river because the Germans had destroyed the vital bridge. Clark ordered engineers to work through the night to throw a pontoon bridge across the river.

Although the beaches were heavily congested Clark's aides reckoned that at least 80 per cent of the contents of the Avalanche convoys was now ashore. Unfortunately, troops were too busy fighting the enemy to clear the supplies. But to the General this seemed relatively unimportant. He sent an enthusiastic message to General Alexander, assuring him that he would soon be ready to attack north through the Vietri pass towards Naples.

His optimism was surely unfounded. The fact the convoys were unloaded and ships on their way back to North Africa did not mean the situation was favourable. Montecorvino and Salerno remained in German hands and the enemy was preparing to launch a full-scale offensive. Could Clark truly believe that within a day or two his Fifth Army would march north to Naples?

In the half darkness Scots Guardsman John Weir heard a voice say, 'That's deep enough.' He stopped digging, threw his shovel on the edge of the grave and climbed out. Dusk had fallen and the Scots Guards near the tobacco factory were burying their dead.

All his young life Weir had been interested in playing the bagpipes, having fun, seeing the world. He was so habitually cheerful that his mates referred to him as 'a bit of a Scots comic'. But nobody had prepared him for this moment. He stood silently watching as the bodies of his comrades were lowered into separate graves. He heard the padre say some brief prayers. Then fresh earth was spread over the graves and simple crosses with the soldiers' names placed in the mounds. In the gloom the faces of the hardened veterans around him betrayed nothing. He suspected they were grieved and angry at the loss of their comrades. To be surrounded by such men after the ferocity of the day's fighting gave him strength. Strangely, he had no idea how the invasion was progressing. All he knew was that the Guards' job was to clear the Germans from the tobacco factory. When the compo rations were brought out he felt suddenly ravenous. As they sat and ate to the sound of the distant 88s and the echoing navy guns the tension was suddenly broken. He even cracked a joke with another young Guardsman. Then, in the dark, he burrowed into the slit trench he had dug. He felt a real soldier, but to gain this knowledge he had lost two of his best friends.

Late that evening the unmistakable voice of Hitler was broadcast to the German people. Surrounded by his closest aides, the Führer had recorded the speech in the Wolf's Lair at Rastenburg. Himmler, Göring and Jodl had been with him as he broke what had been a long radio silence since the Italian surrender.

For the first time his speech was relayed without the customary Goebbels introduction, the '*Sieg Heils*', the cheers, the applause of a Nazi audience, all customary to whip his listeners into a mood of receptive enthusiasm. Hitler began speaking in a slow, almost melancholy voice, then he raced through the rest of his script at speed.

It was an angry speech, understandably the bitterest he had made, for Italy had been out of the war for hours before he knew about it. He praised his former ally Mussolini. 'I am grieved by the sight of the grave injustice inflicted on this man and the degrading treatment meted out to him, whose only care these past twenty years and more has been for his people, as though he were a common criminal. I was, and am, glad to call this great and loyal man my friend.'

For Badoglio and his backers he expressed only contempt. He had learned too late that they had secretly negotiated a surrender a week ago. 'The Italian Government,' he warned, 'may try to justify as it likes the decision to break the alliance, to leave the war, and by this decision to make Italy a battlefield. It may try to call it a necessity, but it will never find an excuse for the fact that this was done without as much as informing its ally beforehand.' He warned that 'very severe measures' had been ordered to protect German interests in Italy. In an obvious warning to his Balkan satellites, he added, 'May Italy's fate be a lesson to all of us to stand faithfully by our Allies in the hour of greatest distress and gravest emergency.'

He spoke for fifteen minutes. Then the broadcast ended abruptly, without the customary *Horst Wessel Lied*. Even the usual hysteria was missing. It seemed a hasty exercise prompted by the shattering events of the last two days. The King, the Crown Prince, Badoglio, Ambrosio, Roatta, all had fled. The Italian Fleet had sailed from Spezia to Allied ports under a pretext. Even the fuel depots at Naples had been set ablaze by the Italian Navy, 'possibly deciding the fate of every German soldier in Italy', declared one pessimistic observer.

Hitler at least was satisfied that *Operation Achse* had been put into effect. SS General Karl Wolfe had been appointed police adviser to a new Government and a Prime Minister, Alessandro Pavollini, appointed by Hitler, had broadcast from Germany, announcing that in the name of the Duce he was forming 'a Government with clean and decent aims, composed of men who have shed their blood for the Fatherland and are always ready to do so.'

At the same time that Hitler's broadcast was relayed to the Germans, Rome Radio broadcast an ultimatum, delivered in Italian by a German announcer with a strong accent, ordering all Italians still resisting to lay down their arms. The Italians were told to present themselves to the military authorities where they would be given food, issued with new uniforms, and sent to fight side by side with their German comrades. If these orders to disarm were not obeyed, then their commanders would be shot.

Hitler's broadcast contained no personal barbs directed at the Allied leaders, which was unusual, especially as the Führer's pride had been stung by what he had learned from an intercept of a telephone call by the Foreign Secretary Anthony Eden to Churchill in Washington during the day: Churchill was waiting for a military triumph in Italy before returning to the public acclaim of the British.

For Hitler this was too much. Even if Germany had to forgo some of her other conquests, the Allies at Salerno must at all costs be turned back.

Near Paestum the beaches were still under enemy attack. Colonel Eddie O'Neill, searching for General Dawley, had just turned off Red Beach when a low-level air attack killed six officers of 531 Engineers. Although the raids had continued all day on beaches where troops and supplies were pouring in, the engineers had worked bravely under fire. Dawley, who did not return to his command post until close on midnight, had inspected the beaches at a late hour and written in his diary, 'Strafed and bombed'.

At his CP in the warehouse, where he was still trying to get communications satisfactorily established, General Walker decided, 'Georgie was right.' At Mostaganem Patton had warned him to expect no air cover for days. But Walker was not to know that North West African Tactical Air Force HQ was attempting to reduce air cover over the assault area. Admiral Hewitt and General House protested that the aircraft allotted to Avalanche were meeting only the minimum requirements. No change, they pleaded, should be made until Allied aircraft were actually based on the beachhead.

With the 179 astride Highway 18 protecting his left flank to prevent the Germans crossing the Sele, the 142 in the vicinity of Albanella, and the 36th artillery, under General Miles Cowles, giving special attention to German troop concentrations beyond Monte Soprano, Altavilla and the Calore area, Walker calculated that he could hold onto his outpost until Montgomery's Eighth Army arrived from the south.

The town of Capaccio, on the slopes of Monte Soprano, had been taken by 143 without a fight. Troops had moved in past abandoned enemy artillery emplacements, yet within hours a German reconnaissance patrol of seven armoured cars and four four-wheeled armoured vehicles poured in on the highway from the south-west, unaware that the town was already in American hands.

Alerted by outposted riflemen, Captain Marion Bowden allowed the enemy to penetrate the American lines and drive down the main street. Then he ordered his men to chop the armoured convoy to pieces with every available weapon, including their anti-tank guns. Three armoured cars were destroyed outright, others captured. Eight Germans died, and 14, including an officer, all from the 16th Panzers, were taken prisoner. When Captain William Yates looked at the Germans' command car it reminded him of a 1925 Buick which had belonged to his grandfather.

Since 7.30 p.m., Walker knew, the 3rd Battalion of 143 had been in occupation of Albanella. A temporary airstrip was being laid near Paestum, the hold on Monte Soprano was strengthened, and contact had at last been made with the British on the left flank.

All along the British sector of the beachhead, troops prepared for a long and bitter encounter.

Pinned down in a field across the road from the beach Private James Daniel, with the Royal Engineers, had seen three of his comrades die on the beach and others wounded. Now, despite the shelling, the men had dug a latrine in a corner of the field, a deep trench with a plank of wood across it. But because of the continual bombardment they could not use it. Daniels saw one soldier cross to the latrine. He called to him, 'Hey, don't go over there!'

But the soldier walked on, muttering, 'Sod it!'

A shell burst beside him and took both his legs off.

Corporal David Hughes and his sappers made attempts to repair roads the Germans had blown up near the beach. In the afternoon he saw his first Tiger tank, compared to which the British tanks were 'just like Dinky toys'. Except for a neat hole which a navy shell had pierced in the casing the tank was unmarked. Peering inside he saw the burnt-out corpses of three Germans. 'All that was left was their guts.'

Hughes and his sappers dug in at the tobacco plantation, 300 yards from the beach where they had landed.

Still trapped in the clearing with his 15 cwt truck, loaded with mines and explosives, John Thomas sat among the array of other vehicles. He had no idea of how the fighting was going. He heard rumours that 'Monty's boys are on their way'. Not knowing what might happen next, he pulled the camouflage netting over his vehicle, drawing the ends out at each corner so that from the air it would look like a clump of trees or bushes.

Bombardier Walter Harvey had seen fifteen of his comrades killed and nine wounded. He had moved across the road from the beach, past a low wall over which dead Germans lay draped, into a villa with wrought-iron gates and a wide driveway. The house had been abandoned by its owners, who had made a run for it, leaving the beds 'as though they had just got out of them'.

British scout cars had parked in the driveway. But that afternoon the enemy's guns opened up, shelling the line of men queueing with their mess tins at an open-air cookhouse. The Germans did not need to look for the enemy in the hot September weather; they followed their movements simply by watching the dust rising from their vehicles. They knew the territory and could pick them off with predicted shooting.

So obvious a target was the villa that when night fell Harvey and the rest of the men moved to open ground. They were expected to force their way up the coast road to Salerno, but progress would be impossible until they had cleared the enemy from the dangerous high ground on their right.

Nearest to Salerno, Private Oliver Edwards remained in the field where maize grew several inches above their heads. They had dug latrines with spades and shovels. Now, as it neared midnight, there was little conversation among the men of the 4th Commando beach group of the Tenth Corps.

In the American sector Lieutenant Gallegos, the British Navy man who had landed with the combat troops of 179, dug a foxhole for the night as the Germans began a sustained aerial bombardment on the large concentration of men and materials crowded together in a small area without cover. The air was filled with the smell of phosphorus and the roar of explosions. Shrapnel fell thick and fast as Gallegos drew his blanket around himself and covered his face with his steel helmet. He prayed the night would not last long. Between one wave of bombers and the next there seemed to be only brief intervals. Huddled in his trench, he asked God to let him live until morning.

Major Edmund Ball, liaison officer with the Fifth Army, who was at Walker's CP, cursed the choice of Casa Vannulo as a headquarters. It was among the most prominent buildings on the American beachhead and too obvious a target. Wrapped in his bedroll in what had been a vegetable garden outside the warehouse, he tried to sleep as enemy planes dropped huge candelabra flares, lighting up the whole countryside as though it were day. 'A hell of an air raid tonight,' wrote one of

Dawley's aides in his diary, 'shaking this place to its foundations.'

Only Quentin Reynolds on board the *Ancon* found an answer to the terror of the night. He took a sleeping pill and slept through three 'General Quarters'.

XIII
'This Reminds Me of Gallipoli'

Saturday, 11 September. Morning till midnight.

THE DESTROYER *Rowan*, patrolling this morning off Salerno, was torn asunder by a tremendous explosion amidships. Struck by a 17.7 inch torpedo from one of three marauding E-boats, she sank in less than a minute, with most of her crew dead, or flung into the sea.

For twelve hours the *Luftwaffe* had come swooping again and again over the armada in the gulf. Lionel Shapiro had lain awake listening to the noise of aircraft and the barking of the ack-ack guns. Despite his sleeping pill, Quentin Reynolds had heard 'General Quarters' sounded so often during the night that, finally, soon after nine a.m., he put on his lifebelt and steel helmet and went up on deck. As he reached the main deck a bomb exploded close to the *Philadelphia*, a cruiser in Rear Admiral Davidson's fire support group for the Southern Attack Force. Slightly damaged, the *Philadelphia* continued steaming, but the attack was the cue for the cruiser *Savannah*, awaiting calls for gunfire support off the Paestum coastline, to increase her speed. Reynolds saw her, the sun glinting on her gun barrels, some two hundred yards off the *Ancon*'s starboard. He was at the rail now and above him he could see Clark and Hewitt in conversation on the bridge wing as the *Savannah* steamed past.

At 9.30 a.m., just as Clark was about to go ashore, those on the decks of the flagship heard a persistent screaming noise, increasing in intensity. Looking up through his long-range binoculars one of the crew saw the silver-painted wings of a bulbous-nosed Dornier 217 flashing about 12,000 feet above the flagship. Hearing the unusual sound, an AA gunner remarked that it must be the new German glider bomb the forces were talking about. 'Jerry has something hot,' he ventured. For days rumours had swept the flagship that the enemy was preparing to deploy radio-controlled glider bombs carried by fast aircraft. Fitted with fins and rocket boosters, giving them a maximum range of eight miles and speeds of up to 660 mph, the bombs were said to be guided visually from high-flying Dorniers which could release them at a safe distance from the target. Naval intelligence had warned the armada of this 'dangerous device', though experts were divided as to the merits of the missiles, which carried a warhead explosive charge weighing 660 pounds. Some asserted they had a limited destructive capacity, others doubted they could be deployed with accuracy. Glider bombs had, however, been used on a limited scale earlier in the war and the Allies had found no defence against them.

Hearing the noise grow louder, Hewitt and Clark were certain the bomb was about to hit the *Ancon*. There was nothing they could do. Seconds later the missile exploded harmlessly in the water. Then they heard the eerie noise again and were convinced that a second glider bomb was speeding towards the flagship. Quentin Reynolds found himself gripping the deck rail on the starboard side so tightly that his wrists ached. With a crash, deafening to those on the *Ancon*, the bomb exploded on target.

'It's the *Savannah* – she's hit!' a sailor on Reynolds's right yelled.

The bomb had hit the cruiser just forward of the bridge. Clark saw a sheet of orange flame sweep upwards from the No. 1 gun turret. He stood frozen as a gigantic flame roared eighty feet in the air, receding to reveal the bodies of men who had been blown skyward falling into the orange smoke that was turning oily black. Though billowing waves of smoke soon hid the forward part of the ship, the General was certain that the missile, which had struck the turret, had passed through the cruiser's deck and exploded below.

To Reynolds the scene was 'straight out of a movie'. He seemed to be watching miniature boats in a miniature sea, unable to convince himself that the figures that came tumbling from the sky with the flames were real men. He watched as the stricken *Savannah* continued steaming slowly, her bow low in the water. Then she turned across the *Ancon*'s bow and came past their port side. He ran to the other rail of the ship. The smoke had cleared sufficiently for him to be able to see flames clawing the gun turret 'like nervous fingers'. Peering through his field glasses he saw figures darting about the forward deck and, close to a blackened smoking hole, he could make out the crumpled barrel of a heavy gun. As the cruiser came parallel with the flagship another wall of flame and smoke suddenly soared into the sky as she rocked with another explosion.

'Christ!' shouted a crew man. 'That's her magazine. The loading room has got it!'

Motionless, Reynolds watched men frantically hosing the forward turrets. Small craft raced to the side of the stricken cruiser, some of them hauling injured men from the water. Salvage tugs came alongside and damage control parties began sealing off the flooded and burning compartments. Suddenly, Seafires were buzzing overhead. Too late now, Reynolds thought.

Clark realized the *Savannah* was moving bravely under her own power. Satisfied that she would make it out of the area, he decided to board a landing craft with his aides to go ashore. It was just ten a.m.

Hewitt saw the General off and then went to his cabin to be handed a message from Admiral Vian: 'My bolt will be shot this evening. Probably earlier.' Assuming this to mean that Vian would have to leave the area for refuelling, he worded a reply: 'Air conditions here critical. Can your carrier force remain on station to provide earlier morning coverage tomorrow?'

Vian sent him an affirmative: 'Will stay here if we have to row back to Sicily.'

Hewitt was not to know that Vian's carriers were down to emergency fuel. His preoccupation was with the mounting danger to the *Ancon*, the centre of naval, air and ground communications for the invasion. He must consider taking her out of the gulf, away from the attentions of the *Luftwaffe*. Even with smoke screens and ack-ack fire he could not hope to protect her from these alarming glider bombs. Deciding his luck could not hold out much longer, he sent a message to Admiral Cunningham, asking for extra destroyers.

From the White House the previous evening President Franklin D. Roosevelt and Prime Minister Winston Churchill had issued an appeal to Marshal Badoglio and the people of Italy, calling on them to 'take a decisive step to win back for your unfortunate country an honourable place in the civilization of Europe'.

Since his escape from Rome, Badoglio had moved headquarters with his Government to Brindisi, where King Victor Emmanuel had joined him. Badoglio's flight to the south was important to the Allies; they realized that while he was in their hands he would implement the terms of the armistice he had signed with Eisenhower. So long as he remained the head of a legally constituted Italian Government the Nazis would have difficulty in promoting their puppet Government of Pavollini.

The message from Roosevelt and Churchill broadcast to the Italians this morning informed them that Allied forces had entered Italy at many points and that the Germans would soon be driven out. 'In the hour of your country's agony, it has fallen on you to take the first decisive steps to win peace and freedom for the Italian people.' They must not trust the Germans, who had abandoned Italian troops on the battlefield, sacrificing them to cover their own retreat; they must realize that Hitler was threatening to subject them to the cruelties he was perpetrating in other lands. 'You have already freed your country from Fascist servitude. There now remains the more important task of cleansing Italian soil of the German invaders. Now is the time for every Italian to strike his blow.'

In a later broadcast, Badoglio and the King asked the Italian people to abide by the terms of the armistice and not to resist the Allied forces. Their appeal, which was broadcast over an unidentified station, declared that German armed forces had occupied Italian towns and ports and were carrying out acts of aggression against the population. 'The moment is very grave,' their statement continued, 'and only virile decisions can save Italy.'

Overseas, the mood of the Italians was perhaps exemplified by Arturo Toscanini who, on the previous evening, conducted a broadcast concert by the NBC Symphony Orchestra in New York. With no audience, save his wife, son, cook, and maid, the maestro, in shirt sleeves, announced the title of his concert as 'Victory, Act One'.

It was 11.30 a.m. on that warm, clammy morning when a procession of trucks, armoured cars, jeeps and tanks drove slowly through the bomb-scarred streets of Salerno, bumping over the rubble-strewn Via Roma towards Piazza Amendola and the town hall.

The broad street was deserted, the shutters firmly drawn on shop windows and balconies. Few Salernitani were there to see this cavalcade drive through the city, but by the time it reached the square a small, curious group of elderly, unshaven men, women with unkempt hair and children with wan faces, had gathered.

From the rear seat of the leading jeep a tall, impressive colonel in a neatly-pressed khaki uniform and steel helmet surveyed the scene with curiosity. Colonel Thomas Lane, an Irish American of the United States Army, was to be the city's governor. Beside him sat his aide-de-camp, Captain Riola, an Italian American whose mother was from Calabria and father from the Abruzzi region.

As the convoy drew up in the square beside the Fascist-built town hall Riola asked in Italian where he could find the mayor, the town clerk, or the chief of police.

'There's no one here,' said one woman. '*Nessuno, Capitano.*'

'Are you sure?' asked a puzzled Riola. 'Not even a priest?'

'*Ah, si, si!* The priests are here – and the Archbishop.'

'Can you fetch a priest, then?'

Some of the women crossed to the Annunziata Church and returned with Don Vicinanza. As the priest came hurrying into the square the colonel stepped down from the jeep and shook his hand warmly. Speaking in Italian, Riola said: 'The people look like hungry tramps. Are they short of food? Are there no well-off people here?'

Vicinanza explained that many of the people remaining in Salerno were elderly; the majority of Salernitani had fled to the neighbouring hill towns and villages. 'Because of the war everybody is poor.'

'What of the priests?'

Vicinanza told him the clergy had remained in the city, as had Archbishop Monterisi. 'We considered it our duty to stay.'

Accompanied by the priest, Lane and his aide-de-camp entered the town hall, above which were engraved the words *Potestatis Civium Sedes*, and went up to the mayor's office. The colonel gave orders that his staff of clerks, medical orderlies and security police who had travelled with the convoy were to instal themselves in the civic offices. While the troops garrisoned themselves in the square, he told Vicinanza he wished to call on the Archbishop.

They drove in the jeep across the leafy square and turned off the Via Roma up the hilly Via Duomo to the eleventh-century cathedral. Lane and his aide walked up the broad steps of the adjoining residence and seminary where the elderly Monterisi greeted them, surrounded by priests of the diocese. Lane, a devout Catholic, immediately knelt on one knee and kissed the Archbishop's ring. Monterisi gave him his blessing and motioned him to his study.

The frail primate came quickly to the point. He wished the Allied forces in Salerno to respect the promises of the armistice. 'You represent the civilized nations, Colonel. But we too are a civilized nation. So I would ask you to give precise orders that our women will be respected as well as our private property and our historic monuments.'

'These orders have already been given in effect,' Lane assured him.

As the Archbishop rose and crossed slowly to the door with him, the colonel expressed a wish to visit the tomb of Pope Gregory the Seventh in the cathedral.

Don Vicinanza led the colonel across the atrium into the south transept of the cathedral to the chapel where the Crusaders had laid their arms to be blessed. Beneath the altar was the tomb of Pope Gregory VII, originally known as Hildebrand, who died in Salerno in 1085 with the words, 'I have loved justice and hated iniquity, therefore I die in exile.' It seemed to Lane an apt place to pray in silence for a few moments. Leaving the cathedral, he remarked to the priest, 'Hildebrand disclaimed the German emperor. I hope, father, he will help us expel the German oppressor from Salerno.'

He drove with Riola back to the Town Hall. The Allied Government was now officially in possession of the city.

General Walker fumed when he learned that two Spitfires coming in to land on the improvised airstrip near Paestum had been shot down by mistake by anti-aircraft guns of the 36th. 'Our AA is lousy,' wrote one of the Sixth Corps aides in his diary. Walker blamed the 'trigger-happy gunners of our anti-aircraft units'. He ordered Colonel Wilson, who commanded the attached AA units, 'I want no more firing on friendly aircraft. Our guns must hold their fire until aircraft can be positively identified as German.'

From the moment he had set up his headquarters at the Vannulos' tobacco farm he had made no secret of his ambition to gain possession of the high ground in the area of the old town of Altavilla, a position that afforded the Germans a panoramic view of the Gulf of Salerno and the entire American sector. Now, soon after noon, he was heartened by reports that men of 142 RCT had just occupied the strategic hill town. Lieut. Colonel Gaines Barron's 1st Battalion had moved into Altavilla, meeting only slight opposition. Two other battalions were also in position south of the town, near Albanella. He also learned that two squadrons of P-38s, 31st Fighter Group, had landed safely on the improvised airstrip. This was good news. The airstrip would be vital to the progress of the invasion.

Just after two o'clock Generals Clark and Dawley came by the command post to explain the arrangements for bringing in more reinforcements. Under Colonel Charles Ankcorn, the 157 RCT was committed from army reserve to assist the 179 RCT of the 45th Division by moving up the west side of the Sele to seize the fords north-west of Persano. When Major Shields of the British Tenth Corps arrived with news of British troop movements north of the Sele Walker handed him a situation report for McCreery.

But the SITREP was never to reach the Tenth Corps General. Crossing the Sele on the return journey, Shields and his driver were captured by a German Panzer unit.

By now the sanatorium of Giovanni da Procida was occupied by the Durhams and Lincolns, and Father Carucci wondered if it would soon be a target for the Germans. From his window he could see the soldiers, more numerous than on the previous day, beyond the perimeter fence where they had dug slit trenches and set up mortar positions.

The young major had respected his request and that of the staff to prohibit his troops from entering the hospital without the permission of the authorities, although they were allowed to fetch water from a fountain near the main door. He watched the soldiers filling buckets and carrying them to outbuildings, which he assumed were in use as army kitchens. Telephone wires now ran between the lower branches of the trees and from wall to wall. On the main road below him, towards Fratte, he could see German troops in position behind the arches. The town was in their possession and the area between them and the sanatorium was a no-man's-land.

The crash of a shell near the sanatorium broke the afternoon stillness. Patients who had been standing by the windows hurriedly withdrew to the corridors. Carucci heard the boom of the fleet's guns as they renewed their firing on targets around Fratte. He and Soffietti decided to board up some of the windows for safety. Machine gun skirmishes in the woods were reaching as close as the hospital gardens. He thought it would not be long before the British and German patrols were fighting it out among the hospital buildings.

Meanwhile, at the northern exit to Fratte Lieutenant Rocholl placed his armoured cars close to the left hand side of the road to await further orders. This was the side nearest the gulf with a perpendicular slope which would give him cover from the ships' guns which were firing uninterruptedly. He reckoned the spotter was positioned on a hilltop about a mile away, probably close to the sanatorium, and could see his patrol clearly.

Shells were dropping closer and, as the shrapnel fell, Rocholl and his men crouched instinctively together in their vehicles.

With a sharp crack, followed by a violent explosion, a shell exploded on the edge of the slope, directly above the second armoured car. Earth and dirt showered into the turrets. It was no longer safe to stay in this position, so Rocholl ordered the patrol to withdraw beneath a bridge about two hundred yards to their rear. The young lieutenant was shaken by the power of the enemy's naval guns.

Major Edmund Ball had made a second trip out to the *Ancon* and returned with General William Wilbur and other Fifth Army HQ officers.

On their way to Walker's command post the *Luftwaffe* made a sudden raid. Jumping out of the command car, the officers crouched for safety in the doorway of a small stone house. As they sheltered from the falling flak, Ball noticed a group of Italians grouped around a fire over which they were cooking a meagre supper. Although obviously frightened, they were determined to go on with their meal. The incongruity of this domestic scene viewed through the window only accentuated the noise and violence of the war outside.

When the raid had spent itself they moved further up the road until a second wave of bombers, sparking off an outbreak of anti-aircraft fire, came droning over. The noise was deafening. Again the officers took shelter, this time in a ditch alongside the road. Ball suddenly noticed, when the bombers had passed over, that the driver of a nearby truck was still firing a 50 calibre machine gun wildly in the air.

General Wilbur went up to the man and asked, 'What the hell do you think you're doing?'

'Everybody else is shootin',' the soldier said. 'So I guess I'd better shoot too.'

Was this the motivation, Ball wondered, for the firing around them? Was it simply mob psychology?

When they arrived at the CP Wilbur handed Walker General Clark's instructions to send one combat battalion to reinforce Darby's Rangers. Walker decided to give the job to the 1st Battalion of 143 RCT. Later Sergeant Sam Stein and his men in the battalion were told by Captain Pete Peterson, 'Okay boys. Here we go.'

Moving down to Red Beach to board the landing craft, Stein noticed that much of the tangle of vehicles and supplies had been cleared away.

Clark sent a message to McCreery giving details of the reinforcements he was sending to be placed 'under Darby's command' in the Tenth Corps' sector. His message ended: CONTEMPLATE ABOVE SHOULD GUARANTEE YOUR DEBOUCHEMENT FROM THE VIETRI PASS WHEN YOU ARE READY TO MOUNT ATTACK NORTHWARD.

To McCreery such a guarantee seemed unduly optimistic.

Fearing that the tenuous line would break before the marauding enemy tanks, 167 Brigade HQ ordered every ablebodied man near Battipaglia to the front where Fusiliers and Ox and Bucks were fighting desperately to hold their positions. Clerks, cooks, truck drivers, all were moved up as every available soldier, irrespective of his duties, was pressed into service as an infantryman.

American Engineers, ordered to the British sector to help build an improvised airstrip, were approached by a regimental sergeant major who told them he urgently needed their help in stemming the German onslaught.

'No, sir,' retorted the Americans' sergeant. 'We're here to work, not to fight.'

Drawing his revolver, the RSM levelled it at the American's head.

'Take your choice,' he said quietly. 'Run the risk with Jerry, or I shoot you here and now.'

The American looked at him in astonishment.

'My advice,' the RSM went on, 'is to try your luck up front. You'll have a chance to be a hero and win a medal. All you'll get here is a bullet.'

'Okay,' the sergeant muttered, and moved with his men towards the lines.

Attacks by German tanks supported by infantry intensified during the afternoon and evening. Beneath the weight of this frightening assault men of the British 8th Fusiliers panicked. In total disorder, they began to retreat along the five-mile stretch towards the beaches, some flinging their guns away as they ran. Morale among the 8th was poor, ammunition was scarce, and against the tanks their weapons were inadequate. Even in North Africa, they had never seen anything so terrifying as the German Tiger tanks. The Tiger, with its 88 mm electrically fired gun, had earned a reputation for a frightening combination of armour, firepower and engineering sophistication. Rumbling towards the outclassed Fusiliers, these 72-ton tanks looked 'like bloody great battleships'. Lance Corporal Tom Whittaker, stationed at an observation post near a farmhouse, saw men running in panic, one group clinging to a motorcycle, some shouting hysterically, 'The tanks are coming behind us!' Many of the fleeing soldiers were confronted by officers and NCOs before they reached the beaches and ordered back to the front line. RSM George Hollings, thirty years in the Army, placed his burly, six-foot frame in front of the retreating Fusiliers and pointed his revolver at them. 'This,' he told them, 'is as far as you're going.'

Near him, a Guards officer, unable to believe that British soldiers were retreating, was crying with anger and frustration.

Major Douglas Stewart got himself another Sherman from the 'beach brick' ordnance staff. Once again he took command of A Squadron, supporting the attempt by 167 Brigade to reach Battipaglia. His men noticed he had suffered burns to his hands and face, but he made light of his injuries.

The squadron's task was to support the attack by 167 Brigade which was to be made along the track running north-east from the crossroads, about a thousand yards south of the town. Moving inland, the Shermans drove cautiously up the track, avoiding the waterlogged ground on either side. When they had advanced 500 yards the infantry laid mines on the tracks as a defence against the German tanks. Then the Shermans withdrew to the crossroads and in the evening were ordered to leaguer at Santa Lucia.

Riding back in the darkness, the crews of A Squadron heard reports that infantry and anti-tank gunners were retreating in panic, their numbers cut up by heavy tank and infantry attacks, closely pursued by German Tigers.

'Return immediately,' the tank crews were told. 'Hold the canal north-east of the crossroads – at all costs.' But they saw no sign of the enemy.

B Squadron had spent the day on the main road between Battipaglia and Belvedere, preventing attempts by the enemy to cross the Tusciano. Though harassed by snipers and mortars, Lieutenant Robinson had remained with his troop, sitting in his Sherman, just north of the bridge at the entrance to the town, for twenty-four hours.

Meanwhile, in a desperate attempt to break through enemy positions the Scots Guards attacked the tobacco factory again in the early evening. But the Germans were well dug in.

The undergrowth was thick, tobacco plants grew well above a man's head, and the maze of buildings within the area impeded the Guards' progress across the railway line. To allow the gunners an opportunity to shoot in such terrain without wounding their own men, the officers eventually ordered a partial withdrawal. Casualties were so high that the line now had to wait for further reinforcements.

Guardsman John Weir was assailed by a curious fatigue, due, he thought at first, to lack of sleep or the excitement of battle. As dusk gathered he knew there would be little chance of sleep. There were graves to be dug and water to be drawn from the wells. During the afternoon he had brought in a group of prisoners, dishevelled and unshaven, unlike the Guardsmen who were expected to wash and shave even in battle situations. He felt no hatred for these men, if anything, sympathy. Older than himself, they looked like family men who should be at home with their wives and children. Yet he had no compunction in shooting Germans. He had used his machine gun freely since the landing, although he couldn't be certain if he had actually killed a man.

As a lorry drove up and a quartermaster sergeant stepped down to distribute compo rations for the next day, Weir prepared to spend another night in a slit trench. Yesterday, lying in wait near the tobacco factory, he had heard one Guardsman call to another, 'Are you all right?' The answer came back, 'He's dead.' He had winced at these words. The futility of such a death bewildered him. He had learned much from the battle-hardened soldiers around him, but although he had practised spiritualism as a youngster, he had not learned to accept the death of friends. The burials of his comrades hurt him, and the noise of battle scared him.

That morning, on the road near the railway line, he had met two young Guardsmen trembling and mumbling incoherently. He could not understand what they were saying, but he saw that they had thrown their rifles away and did not want to go back to the front. He prayed that he would not, like them, become shell-shocked.

By late evening General von Vietinghoff was so heartened by the achievements of his troops that he decided to mount a large-scale counter-attack within twelve hours. Men of the 16th Panzers had fought a successful resistance at Battipaglia and Montecorvino and were harassing the Americans in the Chiunzi Pass. And reinforcements were at last arriving in the Salerno area.

His most serious problem was the continued shortage of fuel which had plagued the progress of the 26th and 29th Panzers. That afternoon one of his staff had flown to Frascati to discuss the fuel situation with Kesselring.

The Field Marshal, already planning further *Luftwaffe* forays over the Salerno beachhead, was fully in agreement with Vietinghoff's plan for a major counter-attack. He could not understand why Hitler would not accede to his demands for further reinforcements. He was convinced that this would be 'a bloody battle' before the enemy was driven back to the sea.

What infuriated him was to be handed by the staff officer from Polla the copies of most of the Tenth Army's radio messages sent during the previous day. Communications in Campania were less reliable even than he had suspected. None of these messages had yet been received, either by wireless or telephone, by his staff.

Exhausted, Major Ball lay down to get some sleep at Walker's HQ at the tobacco warehouse. Earlier in the day he had arranged his bedroll on the porch of a little house in the courtyard where he hoped to escape the worst of the bombardment during the night.

The evening's news was not reassuring. American troops near Altavilla were reported to be cut off and thrown back on their gains. The Germans had counter-attacked, driving them through the valley corridor to Persano as deep as the rear of the 3rd Battalion of 179 RCT, just a couple of miles up the road from where he now wrapped himself in his bedroll. The 179 was in trouble. Having made a thrust up the corridor of the Sele and Calore rivers they had been hit from the flanks and the rear by German infantry and tanks operating out of Eboli.

Clark had sought to help the British by shortening the line of the Tenth Corps and giving the 45th Division the job of guarding the left flank of the Sixth Corps. Thus the 45th had been thrust into the weak area between the 36th on the right and the 56th on the left.

Ordered to advance on the west side of the Sele to capture the fords north-west of Persano, 157 RCT had got bogged down. By nightfall the men of 179 RCT had been driven back from their objectives and on the left flank the British and a few supporting American units were locked in battle with the enemy. At its deepest the beachhead reached only ten miles inland and on the northern flank it tapered to about a mile.

Although the Commandos, 'visibly dwindling in numbers', and elements of the 46th were holding the pass from Vietri against mounting enemy opposition by infantry and tanks, 41 RM Commando had suffered 198 casualties out of a total force of 350.

In three days the Germans had taken 1,500 Allied prisoners.

A British colonel on board the *Ancon* remarked grimly, 'This reminds me of Gallipoli.' It was 'the same mess', he declared, with the enemy in the mountains pounding them to bits with their shells.

Watching the messages from the beachhead clicking over the teletypes, Quentin Reynolds was convinced that they were reaching a new and more dangerous stage in the campaign. Clearly, the messages revealed that on this, the third night of the invasion, Avalanche had reached stalemate. In the British sector Battipaglia was still to be taken and Montecorvino airfield could not be used. Only in the American sector had the beachhead been expanded. Clark's prediction of a short, three-day push to Naples was wide of the mark.

When Reynolds climbed the companionway to the deck it was dark and the *Ancon* had heaved anchor. Escorted by two destroyers, she was steaming out of the gulf. Hewitt had decided to move his flagship away from the dangerous battle area. For the time being he wanted nobody to know her whereabouts and, to this purpose, ordered strict radio silence.

With some reluctance, Clark admitted to his aides that it was not yet advisable to set up headquarters ashore. He was pondering a message from General Alexander: *You can use the 82nd Airborne Division in any manner you deem desirable. All combatant elements of the 82nd are now concentrated at Sicilian airports.* He decided to defer his decision on the 82nd for another twelve hours.

Towards midnight, when the *Ancon* was fifty miles out of Salerno, the clanging of alarm bells announced another 'General Quarters'. The noise awakened Lionel Shapiro, who dressed quickly and went on deck. He found the gunners at their posts and the human ammunition chain assembled in position in the moonlight. But there was no order to fire.

Overhead he heard the drone of aircraft. For the first time since the invasion began the *Ancon* was without the ack-ack protection of the naval units, her location a secret even from her own fighter cover. There was no communication between the flagship or any other naval vessel. The ship's detecting apparatus revealed enemy bombers on the port side.

XIV
'Fight to the Last Breath'

Sunday, 12 September. Morning till afternoon.

THE FEROCIOUS *Luftwaffe* blitz was over, leaving in its wake an unreal calm across the Gulf of Salerno. Now, in the early morning, a Royal Navy LCI was unlashed from the side of the *Ancon* and lowered into the water to ferry officers for General Clark's headquarters ashore, in addition to a 'prodigious amount of office signals and camp equipment.'

General Mark Clark could hardly wait to move his headquarters ashore. He had been assured that the beaches were working smoothly and that the task force, from which the *Ancon* had isolated herself, was scarcely damaged by the night-long bombardment. Yet, just as the landing ship pulled away from the flagship, a burst of ack-ack fire challenged a new wave of *Luftwaffe* fighter bombers.

'A 200-gun salute,' quipped one of the General's aides, 'to mark our departure.'

With the bridgehead embracing the city of Salerno and surrounding areas, the Sele plain inland as far as Battipaglia, though not the town itself, and the entire stretch of beach as far south as Agropoli, it seemed safe to establish Fifth Army headquarters on dry land. The Palazzo Bellelli, close to the Sele River, was selected as a headquarters, but when Clark saw the building he decided it 'stuck out like a sore thumb'. The nearest road ran through Battipaglia and the building lay directly in the path of a German attack. 'It's far too vulnerable,' he remarked dismissively to Captain Jack Beardwood, his senior aide.

Instead, he moved south, closer to Paestum, where the administrative staff were already bivouacking in pup tents and running Fifth Army affairs from a large 'calamity tent'. During his months in North Africa Clark had kept two headquarters, one a house for his own convenience, the other a trailer in which he gave interviews to the press corps. The trailer was intended to convey to reporters the image of a rugged army man. 'Clark,' recalled one aide, 'would never want to be caught by reporters in the Caserta Palace.' Near Paestum a bare, yellow stucco house was chosen as PRO headquarters and a special tent was raised for Clark's personal quarters.

While the tent was prepared Clark spent the day roving the beachhead in a jeep. Up and down the line he found the news depressing. The two fingers which the 45th Division had extended towards the Ponte Sele were bruised, and were even in danger of being cut off. North of the Sele the British were taking the brunt of the punishment near Battipaglia as Panzer units thrust inexorably in and out, determined not to allow the exhausted troops an opportunity to consolidate before thrusting forward again. At Altavilla the 142 RCT were in trouble as the enemy infiltrated around the battalion's position. General Dawley told him that Walker had called to his CP at 9.15 a.m. to express his anxiety about the 'worsening situation'. Clark realized that the German counter-attack was inevitable. If it were delayed by three or four days his army would have time to summon the necessary strength ashore to meet it; if it came quickly the situation would be difficult, perhaps more difficult than he cared to admit.

Unfortunately, his arrival on the beachhead this morning merely raised men's spirits. As word spread of his decision to set up headquarters ashore many troops in the American sector were prepared to believe that not only was the bridgehead battle almost over, but that it was virtually won.

Mass was over. In the chapel of the sanatorium of Giovanni da Procida Father Carucci crossed to the kitchens for breakfast. Looking out from the terrace he saw an armed German soldier at the entrance door, obviously standing guard. At that moment a group of German soldiers burst into the kitchen, searching for the British. Where was the hospital director? they demanded. Carucci called Aldo Gatti who donned a doctor's white coat and came down to confront them, introducing himself as the medical director.

'Are there any English in this building?' an officer asked.

Gatti remained unruffled. 'No,' he said firmly.

The officer snapped, 'We *know* there are English here.'

Gatti was adamant. Convinced at length, the officer asked for information about the city and the distance from the Giovi hills down to the beach.

At that moment Gatti saw, over the officer's shoulder, a woman orderly helping two Durhams carry buckets of water across the courtyard from the fountain. Two of the German soldiers had also seen the trio, and one raised his rifle to aim at the Durhams. 'Don't shoot,' the other soldier cautioned him. He moved onto the terrace, whistled, and called, '*Guten morgen, Signorina!*'

Gatti and Carucci realized the woman's presence had saved the Durhams' lives. But the officer warned them, 'If the English enter this building it will be bombed.'

For three nights Charles Dettmer of 2 Commando had gone without sleep. Last night the Commandos on Dragonea Hill had been relieved by the Lincolns and KOYLIs, pulled down to Vietri and billeted in houses close to the viaduct on the northern edge of the town, which carries the coast road to Maiori. Willingly the villagers had given up their beds to the dirty, sweat-stained soldiers, but few Commandos had an opportunity to sleep. Soon after dawn they were ordered up the line again. The enemy had kept up relentless pressure against the 138's positions and Vietri and Salerno. 'The position is lost,' the Commandos were told. 'Get back up there.'

At 9.30 a.m. Commando units moved forward to try to regain their former positions, troops of 41 RM Commando moving into the valley south of La Molina and the hills to the right of it, and those of 2 Commando occupying the hills to the left of the Marine Commandos and the high ground immediately north of Vietri. By now the front was narrowed and casualties were depleting their numbers. Out of the 400 of all ranks of 41 RM Commando only 310 remained, and of 2 Commando 304 out of 338. The Brigade had no additional reserves and further naval support at this point was not available.

With a small section from Vietri HQ Captain Harry Blissett, a former schoolteacher, moved to a forward headquarters in a monastery building 600 yards from the village of Dragonea, with the hills rising on either side. He surveyed the countryside sceptically. The steep hillsides were terraced, the trees grew thickly, and each small field was surrounded by a wall up to six feet in height. Nowhere could he see a field of fire longer than fifty yards.

Sweating up these slopes in the hot sunshine, Lieutenant Joe Nicholl regretted that the Brigade had no transport of its own. His men were doing the work of light infantry without infantry facilities. From the saddleback he scanned the valley below, deceptively silent. Suddenly he noticed distant figures, about a mile away, crossing an open field. 'Must be the Hun,' he decided. A Bren gunner asked permission to shoot. The first single shots gave no indication of a strike. Unconcernedly, the figures continued to move.

'Raise the sights,' Nicholl suggested. 'Maximum range.'

The gunner put 1760 on the drum. Now the shots began to register and soon the figures disappeared.

To Charles Dettmer, positioned in a vineyard on the slopes of Dragonea, the Commandos' situation was unusual. He understood they were to have made their initial attack and then withdrawn while the main force moved in. They were not trained for defensive fighting, yet here they were expected to retake infantry positions. A German soldier in Panzer uniform suddenly stepped out from a terrace. Surprised by the sudden movement, Dettmer instinctively swung about, raising his gun. But the man's hands were held high, palms open flat.

Dettmer, who spoke some German, asked, '*Was machen Sie hier?* – What are you doing here?'

'*Ich bin Ihr Gefangener,*' the soldier answered. – 'I am your prisoner.'

Dettmer took the man's rifle, surprised at its lightness, as a second soldier stepped out from the terrace. He, too, stood with his hands high, but carried no weapon. Dettmer marched both men down to Blissett's HQ. The first German told him he was a schoolteacher and could speak a little English. The second wore a tiny gold cross on his private's uniform. 'Catholic?' Dettmer asked him.

'*Ein Pfarrer,*' the soldier admitted. 'A priest.'

'Then why,' Dettmer pressed him, 'aren't you wearing an officer's insignia?'

The priest explained that he had refused to join the Nazi Party and was conscripted as a fighting private. 'When they tell you to fight, you fight.'

Dettmer learned they were members of the Hermann Göring Division. The Germans were throwing their reinforcements into the battle of Dragonea.

All morning the 1st Battalion of 142 RCT was harassed by incessant artillery bombardment. Communication lines were broken, radios destroyed. Before the battalion could organize its position on the vital hill, designated as 'Hill 424', which had been taken late on Saturday night, the Germans began their counter-attack.

Hill 424, with the small, medieval town of Altavilla perched on its lower slopes, was strategically vital to the Fifth Army; its possession denied the enemy a commanding view of the Salerno area and the movement of Allied troops. Yet to the Germans it was not simply a superlative observation point, it also gave them access to the routes of withdrawal in the event of a successful attack by the Fifth Army or by the Eighth moving up from the south. With steep slopes covered with scrub and olive groves, the hill was neither easy to attack nor defend.

Deep ravines cut through the vegetation and the terraces were covered with vines. Nowhere could the troops of 142 RCT find satisfactory defensive positions. Terraces and ravines reduced their field of fire to 150 yards and visibility was so restricted that the enemy could approach unobserved within striking distance.

This morning B Company of the 1st Battalion was occupying the high ground above the road north of the old town, A Company was north of the summit, and C Company on the south slope of the hill. Shortly after noon C Company reported that it was pinned down by a counter-attack on the forward slopes. Sergeant Roland McWilliams, leading a platoon of C Company down the hill against the enemy, heard enemy troops creeping through the vines to his left rear. Hearing machine gun fire from this direction, he sensed a trap. 'Fall back, you guys!' he ordered his platoon. Cautiously, he led his men behind another platoon's left flank where, on the edge of the hill, the Germans had set up a machine gun. Knocking out the gun with grenades, he yelled at the men in the other platoon to pull out in that direction. Then he heard a sergeant call in panic to the officer in command to 'show a white flag'.

But Lieutenant Paul Maywalt refused to surrender. He stood his ground until the men had pulled back and the unit moved up to join B Company on the battalion's left flank. In trying to disengage they were hit from the north-east by a fresh German assault. Noticing an enemy machine gun crew working its way up towards the extreme left of his company's position, Private Clayton Tallman at once set off alone to intercept them. As he ran alongside a stone wall the Germans spotted him and opened fire. Coolly, Tallman jumped onto the wall for a better view of his attackers. Taking deliberate aim, he fired three shots, hitting each of the enemy gunners in the head.

At one p.m. the battalion commander, Lieut. Colonel Gaines Barron, decided to go forward to direct operations in the area newly assigned to A Company. Unaware that the troops had been unable to reach their positions, Barron walked unwittingly into enemy lines, and was wounded and taken prisoner.

Now the Germans quickly broke through the original A Company area, cutting the battalion sector in half and knocking out all communications. Major William Mobley, the second in command, ordered the personnel of the battalion CP and the weapons company to withdraw from Altavilla. Under fire, the men pulled back. As B Company retreated under mortar fire one platoon leader found he had not enough men to carry the mortar down the hill. On an impulse he took a mule from a nearby house, loaded the mortar and ammunition onto the animal, and led it down the hillside.

Captain Jürgen Wöbbeking and the 600 men of his artillery battalion of the 29th Panzergrenadier Division had reached Auletta, north-west of Polla. Now with orders for action, the young Kassel-born commander moved ahead of his men in a *Kübelwagen*, a German type of jeep, to reconnoitre the enemy positions. Surprised at how poorly defended were the positions, he ordered his battalion to move in.

When the invasion began at Salerno his men had been resisting attacks by the Eighth Army in the south. Now, despite heavy losses in Sicily and an outbreak of malaria in Calabria, morale remained high. With three heavy batteries, two with 15 cm howitzers and one with 10 cm cannon, Wöbbeking was confident his men could help drive the enemy from the beaches into the sea.

Moving forward in a south-westerly direction, they arrived in the mountainous area between Serre and the Calore River, with Altavilla in the hills to the south. Raising his field glasses, Wöbbeking viewed the armada in the gulf. He had to admit it was an impressive sight. On the way across from Polla his battalion had been strafed by enemy aircraft; now, the battleships in the gulf were firing shells in their direction. Ordering his men to spread out, with forward observation officers accompanying the infantry, he prepared for action. Though surprised at the initial lack of enemy resistance in the area, he guessed he would not have long to wait before enemy tanks appeared.

Shermans were hidden among the trees on the edge of a wood covering a mountain slope on the southwest bank of the Calore. Soon they opened up on the advancing Panzers, forcing them to a halt. Wöbbeking ordered his batteries to fire on the tanks, which quickly took evasive action. Deciding to place one of the batteries in a narrow pass in the mountains through which the river twisted, he directed a second battery to fire on the tanks from the left, pushing them further to the right until, inevitably, they were forced onto the road running along the southern bank of the river towards the pass. There his second battery began firing a barrage of shells as the Shermans slowly negotiated the narrow, winding road.

Wöbbeking watched with satisfaction the result of his tactics. Three tanks destroyed, the rest abandoned by their crews.

At four p.m. General Walker went to see General Dawley at the Sixth Corps command post. During the early afternoon he had been visited by two officers from Fifth Army HQ with contingency plans for dropping units of the 82nd Airborne Division to reinforce the beachhead. Walker guessed that Clark was a worried man.

At the CP he found Generals Dawley and Middleton waiting, and the three commanders grouped themselves around the clipped-down situation map. Walker had a high regard for both men. Dawley he had first met on field manoeuvres in the Philippines in 1913; Middleton, a younger man, had been an instructor like himself at Infantry School.

Dawley indicated a front a mile and a half long which Walker reckoned was about a mile and a half east of Persano, the village wedged at the eastern and narrowest point of the junction of the Sele and the branching Calore rivers. Into this crucial corridor, the fork between the two rivers which divided the Allied and German forces, Dawley wanted Walker to send a battalion to cover the gap between the 45th Division on the left and the 36th on the right. 'The right flank of Troy's 45th,' Dawley explained, 'will be opposite the left flank of this battalion of yours, Fred, just across the Sele.'

Walker was puzzled. He felt certain that the right flank of Middleton's 45th was some two and a half miles south-east of the point Dawley indicated on the map. Middleton made no comment and Walker wondered if he realized what Dawley was saying.

He had to assume that Dawley's information was correct. When the meeting ended he passed the order to Colonel Joseph Martin, the CO of the 143 RCT, to send his 2nd battalion, which was the Division reserve, into the Sele–Calore corridor; even though his troops would have five miles to march, it was the nearest battalion. He asked him to warn Lieut. Colonel Charles Jones, the battalion commander, to conceal his men from enemy observation after they were in defensive positions.

The meeting between the generals was to prove crucial to the subsequent fortunes of the Sixth Corps. Yet it would seem that neither Walker nor Middleton noticed, as they stood around the map table on this clammy afternoon, that Dawley was unusually edgy. Officers had already remarked on the change in his behaviour. He was said to have turned away in horror at the sight of the dead GIs near Paestum, shouting, 'Take them away! I can't stand them!' It was a situation that prompted one of his own aides to write in his diary of 'lots of dead piling up' and 'beginning to get ripe'. A medic went to one of the Army chiefs with the complaint, 'General Dawley is just going wild.' In the opinion of some Fifth Army officers, the Sixth Corps commander was 'cracking' at this stage. 'He looked,' commented one of Clark's men, 'completely zonked.'

Clark cannot but have noticed Dawley's condition at Fifth Army HQ later that afternoon. Yet neither Clark nor Eisenhower had done much to bolster Dawley's self-confidence, and their lack of encouragement had set Dawley brooding. He wrote in his diary that day that Walker had reported to him that the 142 RCT on Altavilla had been 'heavily attacked'. For his part, Dawley had asked Walker to send a battalion into an area from which, whether or not he knew it, the troops of 179 RCT of the 45th Division had already been driven.

Later in the afternoon Dawley visited a forward CP where he reported 'mortar and MG fire on road'. Colonel Eddie O'Neill, who travelled with him, saw the General striding ahead while the rest of the Sixth Corps sought cover from the bombardment by 88s and tracer fire from machine guns in ditches or by the side of the road. 'The General insisted in walking right down the middle of the road and I finally had to actually order him to get into a ditch.'

Optimistically, Dawley sent an engineer battalion, supported by a cannon company, to clear the road above an irrigation canal near the Sele River in the hope of establishing physical contact between his GIs and the British Tenth Corps. He wrote in his diary of a 'considerable fight' at the Fiocche tobacco factory west of Persano. He spelled the name 'Persona', and was to refer to it as 'Persona' thereafter.

At the northernmost point of the invasion area, Lieut. Colonel Bill Darby set up headquarters in an old hotel on the sea front at Maiori. The town's solitary hotel, the San Francesco, had only eight rooms and two baths, but it was empty of guests and untouched by mortars, and it was sufficient for the Rangers.

Darby spent much of his time driving up the mountain road through the Chiunzi Pass or roving east and west of the town encouraging his men. The Rangers all knew their commander by sight. The broad-shouldered Darby wore no colonel's insignia; only his black and red shoulder patch and his cut-down leggings marked him out as a Ranger from the Fifth Army's regular GIs. 'There wasn't a day,' Sergeant Don Earwood recalled, 'when we didn't see Darby.'

The 1st and 3rd Ranger Battalions overlooked the Chiunzi Pass from mountains which rose abruptly to several thousand feet. The lower slopes were ridged with terracing like bales of corduroy, the upper slopes were wooded or rocky. By now the Navy had perfected their gunfire in support of the Rangers, responding to the instructions of observers with 15-inch shells which Darby heard bowling up the pass 'like a freight train with the caboose wobbling from side to side'. The naval fire was supported by the Rangers' 4.2 mortars and cannons. In the beach area the chemical warfare section had constructed small carts which neatly fitted the ramps of the LCIs. When loaded with ammunition, these carts were pulled ashore and towed into the pass by jeeps or captured German half-tracks. To reach the highest strongpoints on the steepest slopes mules were used, many collapsing from exhaustion before reaching the summit.

The scheme devised by Darby and his executive officer Herman Dammer whereby each Ranger had carried additional rounds of ammunition ashore which he then dropped on the beach, had proved invaluable. Yet even with this extra ammunition Darby reckoned they were 'scrambling' and with present supplies could hold out for only a few more days. Dammer realized the landings were 'not as happy as they might have been' and passed the word, 'We have to make damn sure we aren't moved'. He was concerned about the risks of bringing up further supplies of ammunition by road; future supplies would have to be landed on the Maiori beach.

During the morning Rangers at the Maiori HQ flagged down a motor torpedo boat racing past the shoreline. The MTB cut its engine and nosed into the beach. A Ranger supply officer went on board and borrowed a ride down to the main beaches where a beachmaster listened to his demands and agreed to load an LST with 4,000 rounds of 4.2 inch mortar ammunition. Within hours the ammunition was on the beach at Maiori and Dammer began to arrange its dispersal to Ranger strongpoints in the pass. Then, to his dismay, he discovered that the shells he had been sent were British and without rifling. They would be useless in his American mortars.

Yet Ranger confidence was riding high. This morning companies of the Fourth Battalion had seen Naples from a distance, the first troops of the Fifth Army to glimpse the great port that was Clark's objective in the invasion. They had seized Monte Pendolo, overlooking German positions at Gragnano, astride a secondary road running down to the Gulf of Naples. Other companies had pushed up the coast road to the plain, destroying a German roadblock and capturing a strategic mountain jutting into the Tyrrhenian Sea and blocking the Sorrento Peninsula. Wilbur Gallup, mortar section sergeant, headed with a platoon towards Amalfi reaching the outskirts of Castellammare, just below Vico Equenza. Across the gulf, in the centre of the horseshoe, he could see Naples.

It was evident that the Germans had made no strong thrust along this coast road for fear of exposing their troops to shelling from the Navy; they had not forgotten the destruction wrought on their columns by naval shell fire during the campaign in Sicily. But when Gallup's platoon reached the edge of Castellammare they were fired on and forced to turn back.

As the platoon marched south along the road towards Amalfi they heard the sound of a vehicle coming behind them. 'Scatter, you guys!' Gallup shouted. The Rangers ran for cover to the coastal edge of the road as a *Kübelwagen* with an officer and driver dropped into low gear and rounded the bend. At that moment the rear section of the platoon caught the staff car with bazooka fire, sending it plunging over the edge into the sea below.

Piloting a Ju-88, Kesselring flew down to Polla, some thirty-five miles south-east of Salerno, for a field conference with Vietinghoff, commander of the German Tenth Army. The delay in communications infuriated him and he was anxious to acquaint himself at first hand with the situation on the battlefield. Sitting down to study the maps with the Commander of the Tenth Corps the Field Marshal in his *Luftwaffe* uniform had the air of a leader confident of the outcome of the campaign, yet without illusions as to how success would be achieved. Kesselring's friendship with Vietinghoff was based on their mutual respect of each other's abilities and their shared dislike of Hitler's interference in decision making.

Though most of the 29th Panzergrenadier Division's forces had already arrived in the Salerno area, Vietinghoff admitted to the Field Marshal his concern that the division had not yet taken over the sector south of the 16th Panzer Division. Nonetheless, he planned a large-scale attack within hours. Kesselring listened as Vietinghoff outlined his plans. His final advice to him was to ensure that his troops were not outflanked by Montgomery's Eighth Army before the enemy was pushed off the beaches.

Vietinghoff saw him off, slightly perturbed that the pilot Field Marshal was determined to fly over the battlefield before returning to Polla. Kesselring, though anxious to 'feel the pulse of the situation,' admitted later that this hazardous flight was 'not necessarily so enjoyable'.

When he was gone Vietinghoff took a telephone call from General Traugott Herr, commander of the 26th Panzers, requesting permission to withdraw to a shorter line between Montecorvino and Eboli. Herr explained that he had received reports from air reconnaissance that a convoy of 300,000 tons was unloading in the gulf. 'My forces are too exposed,' complained Herr. 'We can't withstand an attack by such a massive force.'

Sceptical about such numbers, Vietinghoff replied that he doubted the accuracy of the report. It would not be the first time air reconnaissance had passed on incorrect information. Herr checked out the figures and called him back. The figures, he admitted, should have read 30,000 tons.

'You are wasting time, General,' Vietinghoff retorted, lecturing Herr on the importance of checking facts before contemplating such

A PIAT mortar team lying in wait for the Panzers

(*below*) British troops alongside a Sherman tank near Battipaglia

A tin-helmeted General Mark Clark nears the beaches at Salerno on his first trip ashore after the landings

General Mark Clark meets U.S. paratroopers after the first jump near Paestum during the Salerno beachhead crisis

drastic action as withdrawal to a shorter line. Nonetheless, he agreed that the 26th Panzers should withdraw to a more favourable position on the right flank. This would give the Tenth Corps an opportunity to regroup for the attack.

Vietinghoff at this moment had no complete knowledge of the strength or even the true identity of the enemy troops and divisions. He knew that the Fifth Army had made the landings, but he had received reports that the British First Army was also involved. He was soon to learn the true weakness of the enemy's position – the expanding gap in the Sele plain between the Sixth and Tenth Corps.

General Clark had driven back and forth across the beachhead all day, 'breathing dust and eating dust'. Some of the vehicle drivers had improvised a makeshift mask which they tied over their faces to protect themselves, and sometimes Clark found it necessary to cover his face with his handkerchief in order to breathe as they travelled about. He felt 'like a dirty Western bandit on the prowl'.

Yet the dust and the dirt were nothing compared to the disturbing reports filtering through from the front lines.

The 157 RCT under Colonel Charles Ankcorn, shifted to the British flank after landing in the wrong sector, had been ordered to advance along the north bank of the Sele to the Fiocche tobacco factory on high ground near Persano to protect the exposed flank of the northerly finger of the 45th Division. But Ankcorn learned the Germans were across the river, occupying the town, and had ringed the factory with tanks and machine guns. Seven American tanks fell into the trap and were caught in a devastating fire. The high ground around the town, which the 179 RCT in its move towards Ponte Sele had failed to capture, was also in German hands, serving as a spearthrust directly into the centre of Clark's beachhead. If the enemy were to push the spear deeper he would divide the Sixth from the Tenth Corps and gain valuable ground from which to attack both flanks. Clark wondered if Dawley had been fully aware of the strength of the enemy on his left flank. Why had he not taken steps, or been able to take steps, to protect himself in that sector after the failure of the 179 in its thrust towards Ponte Sele? With the German counter-attack developing, he found that all the troops had been committed to a cordon defence, leaving none in reserve to meet an enemy break-through. The British were out of Battipaglia and General Graham had shortened his line, which was now 3,000 yards south-west of the town. 'You must not yield another inch,' he urged his troops in an impassioned speech. 'I call on every man to fight to the last round and the last breath!' The Commandos were fighting to regain positions lost at Vietri in the north. The 142 RCT were out of Altavilla. But, worst of all, the gap between the British 56th and the Americans was beginning to yawn. The Fifth Army was 'getting into a very tight place'.

A commander must have an alternative plan. This afternoon, for the first time, the prospect of evacuation crossed Mark Clark's mind.

He went down to the beach at Paestum and looked at the mountain of supplies. Recalling the admonition at West Point to prevent supplies falling into the enemy's hands, he wondered if he must soon issue orders to destroy these stores and equipment. Faced with such a theoretical problem at the War College an instructor would give him hell if he failed to take the necessary steps. But Salerno was not theory. Could such an order do anything but destroy the morale of his troops?

XV
The 'Fitz Battalion'

Sunday, 12 September. Afternoon till midnight.

To the distant crack of 88s Major Edmund Ball crossed to the tiny chapel at the end of the courtyard of houses at the tobacco warehouse for Sunday service. Officers and men were waiting for a chaplain to arrive when a GI stepped from the congregation, seated himself at the small, foot-pedal organ and began to play familiar hymn tunes. A lieutenant colonel led the singing and the men's voices, gathering strength, filled the chapel. Then, one by one, soldiers stood up to express their thanks for being alive and for God's protection during three terrible days. To Ball the service had the comforting spontaneity of a Quaker meeting.

The ceremony over, he rode out to the *Ancon* again with Colonel Gale, complaining of his sense of helplessness on the beaches without his radio team. Aboard the flagship he told General House all he knew of events on the beachhead. The 142 RCT had lost Altavilla and his friend Colonel Gaines Barron had been captured. Although the 45th along the Sele River had been strengthened by reinforcements from the 36th they had met fierce opposition and were 'getting badly shot up'. The Ponte Sele, carrying Highway 18, and the only bridge north of Persano, some five miles to the south-west, crossing the wide, ten-foot deep river, was still in continuous use by the Germans to move troops, guns and supplies along Highway 18 into the Salerno area. Officers on the beachhead had pleaded with him to organize an air attack on the bridge. But his request was turned down. 'Not a suitable mission for the Air Force,' he was told.

Ball could only assume that the Air Force would not accept the bridge as a target because of the antipathy of Colonel Darcy. It seemed to him that Darcy, 'extremely jealous' of the autonomy of the Air Force, was convinced that the force should be 'a separate arm running its own affairs and fighting its own wars, as it thought best, and completely on its own.' He guessed the Colonel resented suggestions from a liaison officer with the ground forces. 'I personified to him attempted encroachments on the Air Force's prerogative.'

He rode back to the beaches in an LCT on board which a waterproofed jeep had been loaded for his use. At the surfline he climbed into the vehicle and drove down the ramp into the water. At once the jeep stalled. The landing craft pulled away and Ball was left sitting in the water with the waves of the Tyrrhenian Sea breaking over his back. As he tried to start the spluttering engine two ME-109s came screaming down the beach, bombing and strafing troops and landing craft. Ball abandoned the jeep, jumped into the water, and waded ashore soaking wet.

Sheltering in the uneasy atmosphere of the sanatorium in the Giovi hills above Salerno Father Carucci heard a furious battle erupt around the buildings. Thick smoke billowed up from the gardens as wounded young Durhams and KOYLIs were carried into the hospital by their comrades.

Mother Superior approached him to suggest that she and the sisters should venture into the grounds to evacuate the wounded. Carucci was at first reluctant to agree; finally he decided that he and one of the sisters would go together. Men's shouts and the spatter of machine gun fire filled the air as priest and sister, crawling on hands and knees and sheltering behind trees at every few yards, reached the first wounded soldier and pulled him to safety. Mother Irene and the other nuns carried the man into the hospital as Carucci and the sister returned to the battle area in search of more wounded.

It was after six p.m. when the battle subsided. Carucci and the sisters were calming a shellshocked young British soldier when the building shook around them. Clouds of acrid black smoke swept through the wards and corridors and the air was rent with explosions. The Germans had kept their promise to bomb the hospital. Debris and fragments of glass showered down on them as Carucci shouted, 'Move into the central wing – or get down to the boiler room!' Another storm of shelling began as staff and patients huddled together, some falling on their knees in prayer.

'It's suicidal to stay here,' Soffietti said. 'The building could collapse around us.' He wanted each person to make his own way to safety.

'Where will they go?' the priest asked.

'The tunnels, if they can get to them.'

To reach the tunnels meant crossing a no-man's-land where fighting flared spasmodically. 'Perhaps,' Carucci suggested, 'we should try to get down to the city?'

When Soffietti pointed out that the road was under German artillery fire and would be hazardous, they agreed to try for the tunnels. Gatti, Soffietti and Carucci would each accompany a small group of patients and sisters. Carucci took four patients, two men and two women, and during a lull in the shelling set off across the gardens. Gunfire resumed and they flung themselves on the ground, crawling to a ditch where they lay for almost an hour. When the shooting stopped they hurried down to the woods and made for the tunnels.

It was now dark. In the tunnels Carucci was welcomed by a group of refugees, most of them exhausted and hungry. There was little he could do for them. He knew the sanatorium had just enough food to last the patients a couple more days. Soffietti joined them and they debated what to do. Carucci decided it was time to approach the German commander to appeal for a ceasefire. They must be allowed to evacuate the tunnels and the sanatorium.

Before dark in Vietri Gunner Dettmer supervised the burial of Sergeant Philip Rubin. The tall, handsome Londoner had died when a Tiger tank fired a shell into a house that 2 Commando were occupying. The shell had ripped through a downstairs room before exploding, whipping the shirt from Rubin's back. His body was unmarked; he had died from total concussion.

As mortars fell around them Dettmer conscripted four prisoners, two of them the men he had captured in the vineyard, to dig the grave. Instead of a cross he placed a piece of paper with Rubin's name, rank and serial number in a bottle and pressed it into the earth above the grave. One of the Germans, a young, blond Panzer, saluted. The private who was a Catholic priest offered to say prayers, but Dettmer stopped him.

'*Jüdisch*,' he explained. '*Er war Jüdisch*.'

The stocky Major Josef Fitz, affectionately known to his men as 'Gustl', was determined to capture Dragonea just north of Vietri before dark. To the Germans the hill and its village of yellow stucco houses leaning into narrow streets was strategically vital.

The twenty-seven-year-old Austrian was renowned for his almost reckless courage. To his Panzers of the 2nd Parachute Battalion of the Hermann Göring Division, who would 'go through fire for him', he was as daring and exemplary a leader as Jack Churchill to his Commandos. Described as 'a soldier from head to foot', Fitz had joined the Austrian Federal Army in 1937 and transferred to the Wehrmacht a year later. During the campaigns in Poland and Russia he had cheated death on eight occasions and wore the *RitterKreuz*, Knight's Cross, among his decorations to prove his valour.

On recovering from severe wounds in the Russian campaign Fitz joined the Tank Division of the Hermann Göring Panzers during the summer of 1943 and was soon in command of the 2nd Parachute Battalion of the Hermann Göring Panzers. He trained them at Döberitz for battle, then brought them, kitted in tropical uniform, by train from Berlin, through France to the south of Italy. This morning they had reached Cava de' Tirreni. Though exhausted from lack of sleep, he was determined they should take Dragonea without delay.

General Hawkesworth meanwhile had sent the 138 Brigade into the Dragonea area to relieve the badly mauled Commandos. Men of the Lincolns, KOYLIs and Yorks and Lancs arrived to discover the charred bodies of British and German dead, still burning from the barrage of phosphorus bombs.

Fitz now roused the enthusiasm of his weary Panzers. Standing in the turret of his Tiger tank, he waved his Luger and urged them on with shouts of '*Sieg Heil!*' Soon the dusk was noisy with the crash of shells and the staccato bursts of machine gun fire. Oblivious to the mortars bursting around him, Fitz led his battalion of 600 men up the road from Cava and through the village of Dragonea, driving Lincolns and KOYLIs before him and taking scores of prisoners. Stitching their heels with vicious bursts of Spandau fire, he drove the British down the slopes, carrying his men forward with a fanatical show of courage.

The British abandoned the bullet-pocked village and staggered from their hillside dugouts in surrender. The village and hill of Dragonea were in German hands again and the 'Fitz Battalion' now threatened the vital pass of La Molina.

Swooping low over the gulf the *Luftwaffe* bombed the three hospital ships anchored there. Regimental Medical Officer Rankin watched as bombs fell close to the white-painted *Leinster*. One grazed her stern, slightly damaging the former Irish sea ferry. Though Rankin and his team had sent a constant flow of casualties to the hospital ships, they were still unable to move the aid post inland. As the air attacks and the shelling continued, food and medical supplies became scarce. Already they were surviving on hard rations.

As night fell Rankin heard rumours among the Durhams and Hampshires that the Germans were mounting 'a big push'. During the afternoon he had noticed a rise in the numbers of casualties. For the first time since the landings he was faced with the possibility that he and his medical team might have to evacuate the beachhead.

Men were drifting meanwhile in scattered groups from the battle lines at Altavilla.

A Fifth Army aide saw tanks retreating from the lines, driven 'in a wild, erratic manner suggesting panic'. One tank lurched to a stop near him and 'the crew clambered out and fell into each other's arms, weeping'. What the hell was going on at the front? It seemed as though morale was breaking down, not just because of the ferocious assault by the reinforced Panzers, but because most of these rookies were experiencing real warfare for the first time. Another observer saw troops of the 1st Battalion 142 RCT retreating towards the gun lines, 'some of them in panic'. It was not pleasant to see American soldiers running away.

With the 179th routed on the left from the high ground near Persano the gap was wide open for the Germans to pour in. On the right they swept through the troops at Altavilla, now placed in the most advanced positions along the entire 36th Division front. Amid growing panic and confusion Colonel John Forsythe, commander of the 142nd, tried to call up trucks from the 36th to rush more men into Altavilla. But no trucks were available. Dismayed by events, Forsythe went forward, hoping to direct the most hard-pressed of his companies, and was mown down by Spandau fire. Convinced they were cut off from the rest of the regiments, isolated companies of disheartened and demoralized soldiers abandoned Altavilla and Hill 424.

By now the strain between the generals was becoming apparent.

During the day Clark directed Dawley to extend his left, 'but not too much', and move the troops towards Battipaglia.

When Dawley complained of his 'paucity of reserves', Clark told him flatly, 'Do it just the same. Send two battalions and make it strong.'

Dawley told the hard-pressed Walker to send a battalion into the Sele–Calore corridor for 'a holding action'. Walker decided to send the 2nd Battalion of the 143rd, the division reserve. With his forces depleted the commander of the 36th Division had to devise the means of retaking Altavilla. The 1st Battalion of the 143rd had been sent to Darby at Maiori. He had only the 3rd Battalion with which to attempt the recapture of hill and town of Altavilla. He directed Colonel William Martin, regimental commander of the 143rd, to organize a two-pronged attack. One battalion was to climb the northern edge of the hill to take the town, the other to advance along the ridge line from Albanella to assault Hill 424. The attack must begin at six a.m. tomorrow morning. If extra troops were needed, he told Martin to use the depleted forces of the 1st Battalion of the 142nd.

By nine p.m. Martin and General Miles Cowles, the 36th Division artillery chief, were reorganizing a force from the scattered remnants of the 142nd. Eventually they collected 225 officers and men from three companies. Martin knew that bridges had to be repaired, trucks found, plans laid. And troops of the 3rd Battalion of the 143rd had many miles to walk northwards from their positions near Capaccio. By now it was too late for reconnaissance.

It was a pitch black night when another Ranger patrol crept down from the heights above Castellammare to test the German strength. Slipping past scattered enemy outposts the Rangers reached the outskirts of the town beyond Vico Equenza.

Castellammare was more strongly defended than they believed. Entrenched behind a barrier of 88s the Germans opened up with a range of firepower. For almost an hour the patrol battled with them in guerrilla fashion before withdrawing in the manner they had perfected for tight spots. First, they carried out their wounded; then the remainder of the patrol split up singly or in pairs and headed into the hills again as the Germans blasted at the darkness.

Three Rangers stayed behind, hidden in the roof of a farmhouse. They had decided to wait until daybreak to study the enemy positions and make sketches of the machine gun and mortar posts.

During the night it rained torrentially. Lieutenant Alfred Miller, who acted as an interpreter for Clark, wrote in his diary, 'Cold ground. Pup tents. Lousy washing facilities. Artillery firing all night. Rain all night.' Like other HQ staff in the wooded bivouac area near Paestum he had unrolled the pup tent from his pack, set it up, and piled sand around the edges. Nobody had told them to dig a trench around a tent so that when it rains the water runs into it. The hardened British knew what to do. Private James Daniel, like other men in his corps, had dug a square trench around his bivvy. The electric storm was so noisy that for a while he imagined it was the navy guns firing from the gulf.

Near the tobacco factory Scots Guardsman John Weir crept through the undergrowth in the darkness, pressing his ear to the earth. This was his first night on listening patrol. Ahead of him loomed the factory buildings from which sporadic firing came. He crawled along the wet ground, listening for enemy sounds, wondering if the Guards could break through the defences around the factory. How much longer would the fighting last? How many more dead would he bury?

In the forward CP of the 36th Division Sergeant Sam Kaiser was knocked off his mat by a lightning bolt which hit a telephone wire a quarter mile away and ran along the ground, killing two sleeping GIs in a pup tent.

Major Edmund Ball listened to the noise of heavy firing and air bombardment. The night sky was lit by flares and lightning. In a porch at the tobacco warehouse he turned in, hoping he would not wake up a prisoner of the Germans.

All day they had worked to make Clark's HQ tent habitable. They had hammered a floor together to keep him off the ground, laid drains, installed lighting, and provided him with a bed with a spring mattress and a generator to run his ice box and movie projector. By the standards of war it was comfort. Only the German shepherd dog was missing; Clark had decided 'Mike' was a nuisance and the HQ staff never saw the animal again.

'Let's admit it,' a dust-covered officer remarked to the General at the end of the tour of the beachhead, 'our troops are tired. Those goddamned 88s have played hell with them.' The German plan for smashing the Allied bridgehead was developing a recognizable, even predictable, pattern. The enemy made thrust after vicious thrust while preparing the inevitable counter-attack. Admitting that his Fifth Army troops were close to exhaustion, Clark asked Hewitt to order his naval units, the only effective artillery fire that could be mustered, to approach as close to the beaches as possible to blast the German concentrations. Clark knew, and his staff knew, that the crisis of Avalanche was fast approaching.

The greatest danger lay in the area between the Sixth and Tenth Corps, the Sele–Calore corridor, with a gap of five miles covered only by a perimeter defence of reconnaissance units. It was plain to Clark that the Germans would launch their major counter-attack in this area, and he began to question Dawley's strategy. The Sixth Corps commander was shifting forces into the gap, but when the 179th moved to join the 157th north of the river, Walker's 36th was exposed along its left flank, extended to a front of 35 miles, far too wide for a division under strength. Was Dawley, Clark wondered, fully aware of the German concentration on his left flank? Had he misinterpreted the failure of the 45th Division's thrust towards Ponte Sele and Eboli?

For his part, however, Dawley maintained that he had made the right decisions and done as Clark had told him. When Walker had come to his CP during the evening to report that his battalions on Altavilla had been driven off and his battalion south of the Calore attacked by tanks from three sides and 'cut to pieces', Dawley directed him to 'move everything he had' to build up a new line. Yesterday he had sent a force to Darby at Maiori on Clark's instructions, yet in trying to move the force away from Paestum the Navy complained to him that they 'knew nothing of the expedition'. When the last of the troops set off the landing craft lost their way and returned to the American beaches to be ordered to start out again. Dawley reported this shambles to Clark on the *Ancon*. But Clark, he wrote in his diary, 'claimed he never got any message'.

Clark arrived at his tent HQ with his early optimism evaporated. Privately, he agonized about the unexpected setbacks. This had been the day of the most intense German opposition and the prospect of victory was receding. Altavilla was lost. McCreery was concerned about the defeat at Battipaglia and the many prisoners taken. The airfield at Montecorvino could not be used because of continuous enemy shelling. The Commandos were pinned down in the Vietri defile. The 46th Division was barely holding on. Even the Rangers, astride the Chiunzi Pass and dominating Sorrento, were too weak to exploit their success. More than 3,000 men were dead, wounded or missing, almost seven per cent of his total force. He needed the assistance of Montgomery's experienced troops, yet the Eighth Army was making slow progress from the south through difficult terrain. Without such reinforcements he did not know how he could stem the German onslaught.

Although he knew he must now consider contingency plans for evacuation he sent a message to General Sir Harold Alexander which underplayed the true crisis at Salerno. 'The situation,' he reported laconically, 'is unfavourable.'

Part Three

CRISIS

I hope you are watching above all the battle of Avalanche, which dominates everything.

Prime Minister Winston Churchill to General Sir Harold Alexander, 14 September.

Everything possible is being done to make Avalanche a success. Its fate will be decided in the next few days.

General Sir Harold Alexander to Prime Minister Winston Churchill, 15 September.

XVI
Battle for Dragonea

Monday, 13 September. Dawn till early afternoon.

Somebody was hammering sharply and repeatedly at the door. Lieutenant Joe Nicholl shouted at them to come in, but there was no response. Nicholl of 2 Commando was dreaming. Through long avenues of sleep he drifted to consciousness, slowly realizing that what he heard was the sound of mortars on Dragonea.

The shelling broke the silence of the Salerno dawn. At Commando headquarters in Vietri soon after midnight a terse message had been received from the demoralized Lincolns and KOYLIs on Dragonea requesting relief. By now Major Josef Fitz's 2nd Parachute Battalion of the Hermann Göring Division was firmly in control. Before first light 2 Commando was attacked from the front and on both flanks. Two forward troops had lost touch with Commando HQ as enemy units sneaked south-east over the hill to fire on the rear of the Commandos' positions.

Commando Captain Tom Gordon-Hemming, also on Dragonea hill, timed the start of the enemy's 'enormous, concentrated barrage' at 5.58 a.m. Unable to cope with this fierce assault, he ordered his two Commando sections to withdraw. He left two wounded men behind, giving them morphia shots from the cyrettes he carried and marking an 'M' on their foreheads with a brown chinagraph. Casualties began streaming back to the forward HQ where the adjutant, Harold Blissett, found the mortar and artillery attack 'murderous.'

Deciding they should each sleep two hours on and two off throughout the night on the hillside, Nicholl had handed his wristwatch, a twenty-first birthday present from last year, to Sergeant Hill, instructing him to call him in two hours. Now it seemed as though scarcely half an hour had passed. He called out to Captain Frank Mason, 'You all right?'

'Shut up,' came the blunt reply.

The dawn mist was too thick to be real. Close by, he realized, troops were laying a smokescreen. From out ahead came the staccato of Spandaus, the crack of rifle shots, the occasional distant shout. Then men came crashing down the hill, through the trees, towards his position. Instinctively he knew there was no need to shout a password. These were Commandos. Sergeant Rudge burst into the clearing with the scattered remnants of his troop.

'We've had to fall back,' Rudge gasped. 'Broome has been killed.'

Captain Richard Broome had doggedly fired his rifle until he fell riddled with Spandau fire. Rudge had sprayed a full drum of MG bullets at the enemy, killing a handful before collecting his 15 Commando survivors. 'Three Brens were out . . . We've got to shorten the line . . .'

Nicholl passed the word to Captain Mason who would inform HQ. Rudge and his men had moved back when Nicholl heard the clink of weapons ahead. Through the smoke a crouching figure with a machine gun materialized at the end of a terrace. A *Fallschirmjäger* in distinctive rimless helmet and camouflaged paratrooper's smock. Taking aim, Nicholl fired a pistol shot and the para ducked behind a boulder.

He nudged Gunner 'Chick' Burns in the slit trench beside him. But the little Scot made no move. Nicholl turned quickly to see a neat bullet hole in the man's forehead. Grabbing Burns's rifle, he aimed at the lower left corner of the boulder. Unless he were left-handed the German would try to fire around his cover. Just then Mason shouted to him, 'Get your section together. We've got to move.'

Snatching as much of Burns's ammunition as he could, Nicholl, crouching low, doubled across to the slit trench where Private Davis had taken cover. The sides had caved in. He scratched at the soil to uncover all he needed to see: the charred remains of the big policeman he first met on the assault course at Achnacarry.

'Get back to the wall – about a hundred yards behind you!' Mason was yelling. 'We'll cover you.'

Calling his riflemen, Nicholl reached the shelter of the wall. It provided good cover and from here he could send messages quickly up and down the steps of the vineyard terraces. At the top of the steps was a small hut and, beyond the hut, an open stretch of a hundred yards leading to the summit of Dragonea. He ordered Fermoy and Shemons to cover the flank with the Bren. Scarcely had they taken up a position when Major Dick Lawrie, the second in command, called him back. 'Report from 4 Troop. There's a Tiger firing at them over the other side at Cava.' They would call up Lieutenant Brunswick's mortar section on the wireless to try to knock out the tank.

As they moved beneath a cluster of saplings for cover, Mason shouted at them, 'Don't bunch!' At that moment a shell erupted like a thunderclap in the leaves above them, sending shrapnel hissing through the branches. Sergeant Hill was badly wounded. Lawrie had fallen back, making hideous gurgling noises. Nicholl tried to lift him and saw with horror a great gaping wound in his throat. Frantically, he pulled out a field dressing, knowing, even as he did so, that it was pointless. Lawrie's life's blood was spurting out, a flow that no dressing could staunch. Fumbling in his breast pocket he pulled out a morphia cyrette. Gently pushing Lawrie's shirt sleeve up, the slight movement causing the officer evident agony, he pushed the needle into the bare skin and squeezed gently. *How easy it is*, he thought. Then, gingerly, he dipped a finger in Lawrie's blood and signed the letter 'M' on his forehead.

The clearing was deserted. He called to the top of the hill to summon help. But Mason was slumped over the wireless set, killed by fragments from the same shell. Nicholl was now in command of the troop. Mentally he worked out how many men he could get together to regroup. There were not many left.

At eight a.m. General von Vietinghoff held a breakfast conference with his aides. The commander of the Tenth Corps was now confident he could retake Salerno and was summoning all the reinforcements he could for what he believed would be the final push culminating in the ultimate destruction of the Allied beachhead.

Intercepted radio messages suggested the Americans were contemplating evacuation. Smokescreens near Battipaglia indicated a general retreat. More confident with every moment, Vietinghoff sensed another Dunkirk.

While he could draw no positive conclusions that the Allied withdrawal was imminent, he told his aides that he believed the enemy forces were no longer able to withstand the heavy and constant pressure of the German forces and were preparing their withdrawal. He had also discovered the surprising gap between the two Allied Corps. He could not credit that such a division was the result of poor planning; so far as Vietinghoff was concerned, the Allies had voluntarily split themselves into two sections as part of their evacuation procedures; the arrival of additional shipping in the Gulf of Salerno convinced him that this was, in fact, the position. Scenting victory, he steeled himself for the final attack, determined to add to the Allies' humiliation by sealing off their escape route. From early morning combat groups of the 16th Panzers had taken up attack positions in the

Sele–Calore corridor. He directed General Herr to attack with his 26th Panzers at noon along the hills north of Battipaglia and Altavilla.

Breakfast over, he arranged for a further conference with Herr in the evening. But within hours Herr was able to report that the attacks by the 26th Panzers were succeeding, with the 29th Panzer Grenadiers and the 16th Panzers joining in the battles.

During the morning an agitated General Dawley telephoned Clark. 'The Germans,' he exclaimed with alarm, 'have broken through the Persano sector. They're fanning out in our rear area.'

Clark was shocked. This was his first intimation that such a critical situation had developed in that area.

'What are you doing about it?' he shouted down the line. 'What the hell are you doing about it?'

There was a lengthy pause before Dawley, now oddly calm, replied, 'Nothing. I have no reserves. All I've got is prayer.'

Clark could not believe his ears. Had Ike been right? Was Dawley, after all, the wrong man in a crisis? There was no time to waste in speculation. Kesselring's offensive had begun in earnest. Reports confirmed that he had sent a strong force, led by tanks, against both flanks of the 1st Battalion 157th Infantry at Persano where the Allied line ran along the Sele River.

Clark pored over the map of the area with his aides. Clearly, the Germans had taken them by surprise. Their tanks had slipped through a defile, allowing the German infantry to cross the river. Kesselring was pushing forward his spear which he had thrust into the centre of the Allied beachhead, splitting the American and British sectors almost to the sea. Clark admitted that Kesselring had chosen the sector where the Allies were least able to resist such a powerful attack.

As the battle raged near Vietri in the British sector, Lieutenant Arthur Brunswick of 2 Commando was ordered up the hill. A Tiger tank was firing on the Commandos from Cava and he was directed to bring his six-inch mortars to Dragonea. On the way he and Gunner Charles Dettmer went into the forward HQ to collect a wireless set.

Even at this early hour Dettmer, the wireless slung in a canvas bag over his shoulder, found it a sweat climbing the steep hill. Just beyond the line Sergeant Burke, a six-foot Irishman, was holding a dugout with a lance corporal and a private.

'Where's this tank?' Brunswick asked them.

It was a question that Burke never answered. At that moment a mortar shell blinded them with dirt. Brunswick cried, 'They've given the position away! . . .' and started to run towards the summit. Dettmer wanted to warn his officer to stop. Before he could form the words another explosion flung him into the air. Spiralling down he knew he had lost his right arm. He thudded into the ground, his buttocks torn with shell fragments. He could hear Brunswick groping about nearby, groaning in pain. Instinctively, he got to his feet, determined to retrieve the wireless. Then he stopped and thought. *What's the use of a bloody radio now?* He headed down the hill 'like a chicken which still runs around with its neck off'.

Captain Dick Broome was asleep in his slit trench. Dettmer recognized his luxuriant black moustache and shook him by the shoulder to wake him. Broome's steel helmet fell off, his head lolled to one side.

Dettmer's actions became those of a man in a dream. Stumbling down the hill he passed Captain Guy Whitfield and a small group of Commandos from 5 Troop. As shells began striking around them Whitfield threw him to the ground to protect him. The officer applied a tourniquet to his shoulder, then gave him a shot of morphia. Dettmer noticed that he was marking his forehead with a blue pencil.

He heard Whitfield order Jock Cree, his Glaswegian batman, to help him down the hill. Cree gave him a hoist over a six-foot wall, one of the walls that Blissett had found such a nuisance. He fell heavily on the other side, then got to his feet and carried on. At the bottom of the hill, where Cree left him to rejoin his troop, Dettmer saw Charles Priest, his mortar sergeant. 'Give them some from me,' he whispered. Priest smiled grimly. Then, almost blindly, he staggered towards the viaduct leading from the foot of Dragonea into the town of Vietri.

A Spandau opened up as he crossed the defile, cutting chips from the parapet. Only when a field ambulance, a large red cross painted on its canvas top, drove towards him did the shooting stop. A medical orderly jumped out and helped the grievously wounded young gunner into the vehicle. 'Tiny' Burke was in the ambulance, tending a man lying face downwards. Dettmer saw it was Brunswick whose back had been torn away by the shell. Burke was trying to prevent him from turning, pleading, 'Please, sir. Please lie still.'

Brunswick suddenly cried out and with an almost superhuman effort wrenched himself from the sergeant's grasp and fell on his back. He lay very still. Dettmer was certain he was dead.

At the regimental aid post the gunner was placed on a palliasse alongside other wounded men. A darkhaired young woman bent over him. '*Bambino, bambino,*' she called him tenderly. To Dettmer she was the Dark Angel.

Reports meanwhile were reaching the Rangers at Darby's Maiori

HQ that the Commandos were 'getting badly shot up' on Dragonea. Two companies of the Fourth Battalion holding Monte Pendolo, above Gragnano and Castellammare, were pulled out and shunted south to Vietri.

During the night these Rangers, reinforced by elements of the 82nd Airborne Division landed at Maiori, had attacked the town of Gragnano, stealing down to enemy positions along a narrow goat track. But, just as at Castellammare, the Germans were waiting, concealed in machine gun positions covering the approaches to the town. The leading Rangers were sprayed with a deadly crisscross of tracer fire as the 88s, less than 200 yards away, opened up at point blank range.

With only rocket guns and tommy guns, the Americans were ill-prepared for such a merciless assault. Yet two rocket gunners stood their ground, concentrating their fire on the nearest 88 position. They scored direct hits, destroying the gun and wounding the crew. As they withdrew, a direct blast from another 88 mowed one of the gunners down, wounding the other. Convinced that the Americans were holding the sector with a large force, the Germans had reinforced their platoons along the foothills of the mountains from Castellammare on the Gulf of Naples across to the Nocera defile on the right of the Chiunzi Pass.

This morning the exhausted two Ranger companies were relieved by paratroopers of the 504th and moved south to Vietri. Staff Sergeant James Altieri remembered, 'Things were getting out of hand for the Commandos. It looked pretty rough.'

Shortly after the first shots were fired in the battle for Dragonea three battalions under the command of Colonel William Martin, code named Martin Force, assembled for another attack on Altavilla to the south-east.

The 3rd Battalion 142 RCT had marched from Albanella, while after midnight the 3rd Battalion 143 RCT had arrived below Altavilla from Capaccio. These two battalions, with the 1st Battalion 142 RCT in reserve, were to counter-attack the town, the towering Hill 424 and the unnumbered smaller hill.

Although there was no opportunity for daylight reconnaissance, the pincer attack was preceded by a violent fifteen-minute artillery barrage which pounded the German troops holding the town and the surrounding hills. Men of the 3rd Battalion 143 moved along the ridges towards the town, destroying enemy patrols and machine gun nests with grenades and bazooka fire. Within a few hours they were in command of the ridge line near the town. Two companies then made their way up the slope. At first they were met by sporadic fire which intensified as they edged towards the upper slopes of the hill, finally halting them. Meanwhile the attack by the 3rd Battalion 142 on the unnumbered hill ran into trouble and the men were unable to make further progress against the enemy's defences.

As the troops of 143 pushed forward again, approaching the higher ridges, Colonel Martin decided they needed more protection on their right flank. The reserve company under Lieutenant Harry Dragaw was ordered to take the town and establish a command post. At that moment Martin's men began to receive heavy mortar and artillery fire. It was just after 7.30 a.m. when the Panzers attacked en masse, driving the Americans slowly back towards the lower ridges of the hill. Alarmed, Martin called for help. Enemy fire was cutting his battalion to pieces.

Realizing that the assault battalion was in deep trouble, General Walker called on the depleted 1st Battalion of 142 RCT. By now the German artillery barrage was overwhelming and the relief battalion was practically wiped out on the slopes. At 1.15 p.m., in the face of superior enemy firepower the Americans withdrew, deciding to regroup for another assault late in the afternoon.

In a stone hut on the outskirts of Dragonea Captain Brian Lees, the Commandos' medical officer, had established his aid post. At 7.30 a.m. 3 Troop had reported to him that they were sending two casualties. That was Lees' last contact with HQ.

As mortars fell close he moved his twenty wounded men to the centre of the small building. It was stiflingly hot. He crossed to the doorway for a breath of air and saw two soldiers in field-grey standing with their backs to him, about twenty yards away. Quickly he shut the door. 'The Hun are outside,' he whispered to his orderlies. 'Say nothing to the men.'

The Commandos had been driven so far from their earlier lines that Lees' aid post was now in enemy territory. He could not leave his patients, two of whom were gravely injured. Within the hour his aid post would be mortared by his own troops.

Cautiously, an American LST approached the beachhead carrying troops of the 23rd Armoured Division, an independent brigade attached to the Fifth Army. Among them were two South Africans, Ordnance Officer Edd Cook and Recovery Officer Jimmy Martin. Even now, on the fourth day after the initial landings, the shelling by the enemy 88s was so heavy that Cook imagined the landing craft was the principal target of the German offensive. 'They got us coming in on D-Day,' the Captain told them, almost proudly. 'My cabin's still a mess.'

Rescue ships in the gulf were playing hoses on a doomed hospital ship. Though brightly lit like the other two hospital ships, *Newfoundland* had been attacked at dawn by a force of *JU-88*s. Bombs splashed harmlessly into the water around *Leinster* and *Somersetshire*, but *Newfoundland* was struck amidships and within minutes she was blazing from stem to stern. Crews rushed to evacuate the patients, but a group of American nurses were trapped by the blaze, and died.

Martin noticed the crew of his LST were edgy, perhaps because of the bombing in the gulf, perhaps because their craft had already been damaged. They were insistent that when they reached the beaches the troops should leave the landing craft as quickly as possible. Before the ramps went down Martin had unchained his jeep.

He and Cook and the others moved quickly into the shelter of an orchard. They dug foxholes and then got to work. Before noon Cook was driving inland, searching for spare parts. A voice yelled at him, 'What the hell are you doing? If you want to stay alive then get the hell out of here!'

Realizing he had strayed into a forward patrol area he quickly turned his jeep about and drove back towards the sea. He had not known how restricted the beachhead was; at this point it was just one mile deep. He was more surprised when ordered to make preparations to 'get our people away in the event of an overwhelming enemy attack'. To Cook it seemed incredible that, so soon after the landings, there should be talk of evacuation.

The outcome of the battle for Dragonea seemed now in doubt. On the steep, vine-clad slopes the Marine Commando positions were overrun. Germans streamed past the little village, firing on the rear of 2 Commandos' positions. It could not be long before the German thrust smashed the hold of the Commandos now clinging tenaciously to the hillside without hope of reinforcements.

To Colonel Jack Churchill it was 'a hell of an attack'. Brigadier Laycock had asked for help from 138 Brigade, but only fire support was available. Behind them lay Vietri and the sea, and unless the enemy was beaten back Vietri and Salerno would both be retaken. Faced with such a desperate situation Churchill boldly decided to launch a counter-attack with a troop of 2 Commando under the Duke of Wellington, replacing Major Lawrie, and a troop of Marine Commandos under Major Edwards. The jeep in which he had driven across the viaduct towards Dragonea hill had been knocked out by a shell. He had left his favourite Garand rifle, a gift from the Rangers in Sicily, on the seat, but he was reassured to have his Italian Beretta on his belt as he made for the HQ not a hundred yards from the village.

He met two soldiers coming down, carrying a wounded man. 'Where are you going?' he challenged them.

'We're taking this man down, sir. He's badly wounded.'

'I don't give a damn if he's dying!' the colonel shouted. 'Put him down! You should never have left the line. Get back up there!'

He had always advised his men, 'You may stop firing to tie up a wounded man with a field dressing. You may call an officer who carries morphia for a man in pain. You may give a drink to a wounded, thirsty man. But you must *not* leave the line.'

Lieutenant Nicholl was not surprised to see 'Colonel Jack' climbing the hill. 'Situation is tricky,' Churchill admitted to him. 'But Morny's coming up to take command of all troops on Dragonea.'

When Wellington arrived he arranged for Nicholl to reorganize his troop so that he could hold his position. Nicholl told him he needed a Bren team; Shemons and Fermoy had been hit by an 88.

'Any infantry can do our job,' Lieut. Colonel Peter Young, a Commando leader, had said. 'Only we, the Commandos, can do it in the time allotted.' But that time had almost run out. Fighting with his men to retrieve their positions, Captain Hemming heard the monotonous, deadly chatter of the German MG 42s. It made his Commandos' Brens sound antiquated.

General Alexander's message from Oran to General Montgomery was pressing. Could he not make an immediate junction to bolster the Salerno bridgehead?

Alexander was not to know that the commander of the Eighth Army was privately worried that he might be close to his first failure. Although the initial landing on the toe of Italy on 3 September had been unopposed, the trek towards Salerno was proving far tougher than even he expected. His army was separated from the Salerno beachhead by steep mountain passes and immense ravines. Retreating Germans had left a trail of wrecked bridges and railway tracks behind them. Clearly, Montgomery had insufficient resources for a march of such a hazardous nature. Meanwhile, a second force of 8,000 men had landed at Taranto on 9 September and moved fifty miles inland. His main force on the west coast were making only such progress as the terrain permitted. He had a total of only three divisions, and a scarcity of fuel made it impossible for any but the lightest of his vehicles to travel with speed.

His advantage was in being with his men. Every day he drove among them, encouraging them with his personal leadership. For their part his troops enjoyed this sense of intimacy with their general. Driving along the roads of Calabria British soldiers and Italian prisoners cheered him. A soldier would shout, 'Here comes Monty!' and the cheering would pass along the column. Responding to such enthusiasm the black-bereted little general would stop his jeep and distribute packs of cigarettes to the expectant troops. It was an atmosphere which could be sustained only in the vacuum that had been created for the Eighth Army by the situation in Italy. Montgomery's was an army marching through an empty desert of mountains. To Alan Moorehead, one of the war correspondents travelling with the Eighth, 'Monty was back in the sort of command he enjoyed best of all: a private expeditionary force fighting its battles utterly remote from the rest of the world. Locked away in the mountains, he treated his army as a kind of family.'

Even in the Western Desert the Eighth had never been so remote as they now were in the Calabrian fastnesses. Ahead of them the men knew only that the Allies had landed somewhere near Naples and that a vast country of mountains and ravines divided them.

Moorehead's despatches might not have been appreciated by the exhausted troops on the Salerno beachhead. They had been told the Eighth Army would arrive at any moment to reinforce them and push back the enemy; they had been assured that Montgomery was 'racing two armies at a spectacular rate' to link up with them. But to the troops of the Fifth the 'spectacular' progress was not evident. Correspondent Lionel Shapiro had spent the morning at Clark's Press HQ with other correspondents, including newcomer Herbert Matthews from the *New York Times*. He heard tired men asking, 'How far away is this Eighth?' and 'When are the other divisions coming ashore?'

Shapiro and his colleagues knew that the Eighth was at least a hundred miles from Salerno; it would be days yet before it arrived. Montgomery obviously underestimated the psychological influence of the Eighth's reputation and failed to understand the galvanic effect the appearance of even a handful of his troops would have on the beleaguered defenders of the beachhead. When critics later accused him of excessive caution he was quick to retort that the obstacles to his progress were immense. He could not hope to reach Salerno before the 15th or 16th, and even then he would be unable to buttress the manpower at the beachhead in the space of a day or two. It was also no secret that the single-minded, even autocratic Montgomery disliked the idea of a shared command and his heart was not in Operation Avalanche.

From a short reconnaissance on Sunday Captain Theodore Andrews, 2nd Battalion 142 RCT, had learned some of the risks involved in defending the Sele-Calore corridor.

This morning the Texan officer drove along the road to Persano, passing the crumpled bodies of 45th Division men and Panzers, a legacy of yesterday's desperate fighting. At nine a.m. he reported to Colonel Martin at 143 RCT regimental headquarters that enemy tanks were in force near Eboli and moving in his direction. 'Relay orders to Colonel Jones,' he was told. 'Tell him to hold his position in the corridor at all costs.'

Jones, commander of 143 RCT, took a small patrol on a short reconnaissance along the Sele. On the way back towards Persano he encountered a patrol sent across the river to contact the 45th Division on the left. The patrol leader informed him that the right company of the division was now south-west of Persano, but was expected to move up to a position roughly across the river from the battalion's lines.

This was the message Jones transmitted to his 2nd Battalion command post. It was logged at the battalion HQ at 12.50 a.m.

In his HQ tent among the olive groves near Paestum General Clark was irritated by a BBC broadcast suggesting that Montgomery's Eighth Army was 'dashing up the Italian boot' to his rescue. So far as Clark was concerned Montgomery's progress was not so much a dash as a crawl. The BBC's habit of weighting their wartime news bulletins in favour of the British forces irked him. He felt the Americans were not receiving due credit for their herculean efforts to make Avalanche a success.

From early morning reports were reaching him suggesting a heavy build-up of enemy pressure on all fronts. The rapidly deteriorating situation now warranted extreme action. The best way to stem the dangerous, mounting enemy tide, he decided, was to employ parachute reinforcements in the beachhead. Knowing that the 82nd Airborne Division was now, as Alexander had told him, 'concentrated at Sicilian airfields', he had arranged that some elements be dropped near the town of Avellino this evening to strike at the enemy's rear lines. Now he sent a message to Alexander cancelling the plans to drop the 82nd behind German lines. Instead, he scribbled what was perhaps the most hasty message of his career to General Matthew Ridgway, the 82nd's commanding officer:

> I want you to accept this letter as an order. I realize the time needed to prepare for a drop, but this is an exception. I want you to make a drop within our lines on the beachhead, and I want you to make it tonight. This is a must.

He emphasized that he had learned only yesterday that the 82nd had not been dropped on Rome and jotted down further details to ensure that Ridgway would understand why he was 'asking for the impossible – that he make a drop within a few hours after he received the letter.'

Clark asked an aide to find a pilot to deliver the letter personally to Ridgway at Licata in Sicily. By now a number of pilots had landed aircraft on the hastily prepared landing strip south of the Sele. One of them was Captain Jacob Hamilton, and he volunteered to carry the letter to Ridgway. At Clark's HQ he was provided with maps and briefed to explain to Ridgway exactly where the parachutists should be dropped.

Although surprised at Clark's decision, Alexander was aware of the German build-up along the Salerno front. Because of the confused and contradictory nature of the reports, however, he failed to grasp the extreme urgency of the situation. Yet he had never underestimated the wiles of Kesselring. Already he had acted to bolster the Allied forces. The first units of the 7th Armoured Division were scheduled to land before midday and he had pressed London to reassign 18 LSTs, which were docked at Oran en route to India, to ferry immediate reinforcements.

Meanwhile Kesselring's offensive strategy was becoming more apparent. In the British sector enemy 88 shells had battered the airstrip at Montecorvino, which was held by the Queen's Battalion, ruling out yet again any hopes the Allies entertained of using the tarmac for their Spitfires and Lightnings. Units of the 16th Panzer Division began probing the positions held by the 56th Division, whose line stretched from Battipaglia down to the American sector. By now the British troops were almost too exhausted for battle and during the morning made withdrawals in the area around Battipaglia. But officers ordered them 'not to give another inch of ground'. Scots Guards and Fusiliers came under attack, but held their positions.

By noon General McCreery, studying the situation map at his headquarters at Pontecagnano, was in no doubt that Kesselring and Vietinghoff were throwing everything into a final, desperate assault on the Allied lines. Acutely aware of the precarious position of the

American forces, he realized the British were 'very much on their own'. At least the Commandos were fighting for Dragonea and the Germans had not broken through at the tobacco factory. He regretted that Alexander was not on the mainland to direct the battle for himself. To McCreery, 'Alex' was too far from the beachhead to have a telling effect on the progress of the battle. So too, for that matter, was Eisenhower.

At Paestum Clark sensed that the most crucial hours of the campaign were approaching. He could not face the prospect of humiliation at the hands of Kesselring. This morning he was assailed by a strange sense of foreboding. It was absolutely imperative that he should have the 82nd Airborne on the beachhead. These hardened paras could cause havoc, disrupting enemy communications, blocking enemy supply routes, forcing the Germans to divert units that would otherwise be used in their main assault to anti-parachute missions.

For days Clark's mood had alternated between disappointment and frustration. Now, for the first time in 48 hours, he felt a sudden brief surge of his old optimism.

Through the village of Dragonea and across the surrounding slopes the din of battle could be heard. Charging with grenades and bayonets, the triumphant Panzers of Major Fitz's battalion drove back the élite Commandos with reckless courage. Spent cartridges, rifle clips, ammunition boxes, were strewn around the smoke-filled slopes. In the village a battered armoured vehicle blocked a narrow lane, a half-demolished house was in flames. Commandos and Panzers fought with ferocity on the hillsides and in the alleyways beneath a plaque commemorating Dragonea's dead in World War One.

Edwards and Wellington led the counter-attack as a storm of explosives, fired by the Field Regiment, struck the German lines. Indifferent to the fire, the black-uniformed commander, waving his Luger, led his men forward, shouting, '*Sturm, sturm!*' Then, stumbling, he fell as a red hot fragment of shell ripped his thigh into a mess of bloodied flesh. NCOs dragged him to safety. Cursing his bad luck, the battle-hardened young Panzer leader allowed himself to be bandaged by a medical orderly. He would play no further part in the battle for Dragonea.

The loss of their indomitable leader dented the morale of the Panzers. Skilfully they had shifted their positions during the battle, but they lacked emplacements, dugouts and shelters on the hillsides. Now they faced the relentless counter-attack of the Commandos who fought their way over the hill and into the village. Unable to withstand such a maelstrom of fire, the Panzers' resistance began to crack. Laying a smokescreen, they pulled back to secondary positions, leaving behind in the streets and on the slopes their dead and wounded. More than half the battalion had been wounded or taken prisoner during the murderous fighting of the morning. From his position on the upper slopes Lieutenant Nicholl caught a flash from a cruiser in the gulf just as the Tiger which had wrought such havoc on the Commandos trundled behind a house in the valley. He heard the whistle of the shell, saw a puff of smoke forming at the base of the wall, and then the wall crumbled outwards. As the Germans retreated down the hill towards Cava he moved forward with his men, recovering the ground for which they had fought since dawn. The earth was burned dry and pockmarked with shell holes; trees and bushes were charred black; the heavy foliage of the autumn vines lay flattened. Among these vineyards, whose wines the poet Horace had praised, many men had died. Colonel Churchill counted the losses: seventy-five men of 2 Commando had fallen, forty-five of 41 RM Commando. In one morning a quarter of 2 Commando had been lost and many of his best officers were dead: Broome, Lawrie, Mason and, probably, Brunswick by now. It had been a Bloody Monday.

By 1.30 p.m. all the Commando positions were retaken, the wounded were evacuated, and Captain Lees, cut off at his aid post for four hours, was relieved.

For the moment it was over. The pass of La Molina was safe. But at a terrible price.

XVII
A Message for Ridgway

Monday, 13 September. Afternoon till evening.

Flying fast and low Captain Jacob Hamilton piloted his singleseat P-38 down the west coast to Sicily, landing safely at Licata airfield, on the south of the island, at 1.30 p.m.

Tired from his urgent flight, he refused to answer Air Force officers pressing him to explain his sudden arrival. He told them only that he carried a message from General Clark for General Ridgway and insisted he must deliver it personally.

Colonel James Gavin, the Division's youthful, lean-featured Chief of Staff, was on the tarmac when Hamilton climbed out of the cockpit. 'General Ridgway is on his way to Salerno,' Gavin explained. 'He wants to check out the tactical situation there.'

Stubbornly, Hamilton refused to hand over Clark's letter. 'I must see General Ridgway,' he insisted.

Recognizing his reluctance to part with the letter, Gavin went with him up to the control tower to contact Ridgway's transport plane. Taking over the microphone, Hamilton convinced the pilot that he must turn back to Licata.

Gavin guessed that Clark wanted a drop made without delay. For two days his paratroopers had been camping in pup tents close to the airfield. After Sicily had fallen to the Allies the men of the 82nd Airborne had returned to 'a cactus patch' near the holy city of Kairouan, close to the airfields from which they had taken off five weeks earlier for the Sicily invasion. By now their strenuous training was over, the days of 'endless push-ups', as one paratrooper described them, 'to build up our arms and shoulders for snatching on those risers'. Now the task was to iron out serious problems encountered during the Sicilian drops. 'I'd never been on a drop that wasn't all screwed up,' complained one paratrooper. At Kairouan airborne planners worked on the problem of getting aircraft and paratroopers to the drop zones during hours of darkness. Two new pieces of equipment were developed. One was the Krypton lamp which produced a one-second flash sufficiently intense to illuminate a landscape from 10,000 feet; the other was a radar set with which aircraft could be accurately guided to the zones. A small unit was formed which would jump into the zones ahead of the main assault force to put these devices into operation. A third aid was also necessary, the division leaders agreed. Troops on the ground would fill cans with sand and gasoline, place them in the shape of a giant 'T' in the area of the drop, and set them alight on the approach of the aircraft.

When Ridgway arrived back at the airfield he strode aggressively into the HQ to read Clark's letter. The Fifth Army commander wanted the 504th Parachute Infantry Regiment dropped inside the beachhead south of the Sele at nightfall and a second battalion, the 509th, dropped the following night on the mountain village of Avellino behind German lines. Clark knew he was asking almost the impossible. And Ridgway agreed. 'A tall order,' he snapped. But he sent Clark a two-word reply: 'Can do.'

Calling the planners and staff officers together he hammered out a plan to reinforce the beachhead. To Ridgway 'the invaders had now practically become defenders'. Both he and Gavin knew they must convince their men of the plight of the Fifth Army.

Hamilton sat in on the conference. He produced a second message which Clark had given him. This was confirmation that the beachhead troops would use the system worked out at Kairouan. When the first flight of transports reached the drop zone they would light the letter 'T' with the prearranged tins of gasoline and then douse them with sand when the aircraft had passed overhead. Clark also asked for pathfinding equipment to be dropped with the first 'stick' of jumpers from the first aircraft; it would be used to assist subsequent aircraft in making accurate drops.

Yet Ridgway and Gavin believed that while the Krypton lamps could be used to illuminate the beachhead at Salerno, it would be unwise to attempt their use at Avellino. The paratroopers would be far behind enemy lines and in great danger.

At 2.40 p.m. the cruiser *Uganda*, shelling enemy positions behind the Montecorvino airstrip, was struck by a glider bomb. None of the crew saw the attacking plane. The bomb tore through the cruiser's seven decks, exploding below.

Gunner Roy Jensen was on board the tug *Favorite* which answered the call for assistance. He saw the damage to the cruiser's main control tower. As the *Favorite* drew alongside she secured the crippled cruiser and eased her into shallow water. Tons of water were pouring through the lower decks as the crew worked frantically to shore up the threatened bulkheads. When Jensen went on board they were washing down the bloodstained decks. Five of the crew were dead and fifteen injured.

Despite the loss of the *Uganda* the monitor ship HMS *Roberts*, assisted by cruisers and destroyers, continued pouring fire on enemy batteries and tanks on shore, directing the main fire on the Battipaglia area. Within an hour of the *Uganda* attack two destroyers, *Loyal* and *Nubian*, narrowly missed strikes by glider bombs. With two cruisers out of action and other craft running low on ammunition, calls for assistance were sent to Admiral of the Fleet Sir Andrew Cunningham at Palermo who ordered HMS *Aurora* and *Penelope* up from Malta. But they would not reach Salerno until the next morning.

The bombing of the armada and the loss of the *Uganda* could not be compared to the desperate battle for the Sele–Calore corridor, seventeen miles south of Salerno, reckoned as one of the most critical confrontations of Avalanche. It began in earnest at three p.m. By then the entire left flank of the 36th Division was perilously exposed to a crippling counter-attack by the superior German forces.

General Middleton's 45th Division had been unable to cover Lieut. Colonel Jones's left flank beyond the Sele River. Jones's 2nd Battalion of the 143rd Infantry, ordered to fill the gap left by the withdrawal of the 179th, had taken up positions earlier in the day and General Walker had accepted, 'without checking', reports that Middleton's 157th Infantry were covering positions in the vital corridor. Walker also failed to warn Jones that the Germans had driven the 179th out and that he was entering an area where the enemy had tasted victory.

The deceptive calm of the afternoon was broken by the rattle of approaching tanks and the spatter of machine gun fire. Then, near the banks of the river, the Germans' heavy mortars opened up. 'Before we knew what was happening,' recalled a GI, 'the place was absolute hell.'

Smoke from burning American vehicles formed drifting black clouds in the afternoon sky and stretcher bearers were unable to move into the bloody battle area to collect the wounded. In an effort to protect the left flank G Company of the 2nd Battalion 143 RCT was pulled from its outpost position, but it seemed to one observer that 'only God was protecting our left flank, and He was taking a ten-minute break'.

Enemy tanks and infantry intensified the attack on the battered company. Already reeling, the GIs were stunned by the sheer ferocity of the assault. The Germans had uncovered the crossing over the Sele and entered the vital corridor, striking the left rear of the battalion and catching it totally by surprise, while more enemy tanks and infantry entered the corridor near the Ponte Sele and cut around the battalion's right. Captain Theodore Andrews of the 2nd Battalion heard Jones tell the commander of G Company, 'You have my permission to withdraw.'

Jones directed Andrews to drive to the regimental HQ to report this savage onslaught by enemy tanks and infantry and the mounting casualties. Bluntly, the colonel told him, 'We're going to hold this ground at all costs. But we'll have to get some kind of support – especially artillery support.' To make the situation worse Jones had no radio communications.

Driving back along the narrow roads Andrews heard the noise of heavy firing behind him in the area of the bridge west of Persano, not far from the 2nd Battalion command post. Reporting Jones's plight to Lieut. Colonel Joseph McShane of the 36th Division, he emphasized that the battalion was short of anti-tank weapons to counter the attacks on its rear and front and that it desperately needed artillery fire. But at that moment urgent calls for help were also coming in from Altavilla. 'Tell Jones,' McShane urged him, 'to hold on at all costs.'

Knowing this message would be of scant help to a commander in distress, Andrews turned his jeep around and began the return journey. Immediately north of the Calore he came under heavy fire. Realizing with dismay that the corridor must now be cut off, he reversed the jeep, deciding to report back with the news to the regimental command post.

By the end of the battle only sixty men remained of Jones's shattered and bloody battalion.

Father Carucci, with Soffietti and Lieutenant Gatti, was preparing to leave the stifling atmosphere of the tunnels close to the sanatorium during the afternoon to negotiate a ceasefire with the Germans, when a young English soldier stumbled through the entrance, wounded and lost. So severe were his injuries that, though he was given medical attention, the sisters knew he would never walk again. Laying him in a corner, they covered him with a blanket to hide him from the curious stares of almost a thousand sick and hungry patients and civilians sheltering in the tunnel.

Carucci and the others were about to leave when two Germans arrived, one with an arm wound, asking for a doctor. Carucci stood facing them. The English soldier lay directly behind him, but he was so completely hidden by the blanket that the Germans did not catch even a glimpse of his uniform. The sisters dressed the man's wound and the soldiers went away.

It was time to go. Stepping into the daylight they were met with a barrage of fire. Their task seemed hopeless. 'It might be easier,' Soffietti suggested, 'if we went down to the English commander.' It was imperative that the people in the tunnel be evacuated to a safe place.

The others agreed and they doubled out of the tunnel, along the paths through the woods and across the grounds, sheltering behind trees or in ditches when the tracer fire became intense. Reaching the sanatorium they washed and shaved quickly before setting off for the city to present themselves to the British.

Hurrying down to the main road they were halted by an English officer who waved his revolver at them, shouting words they could not understand. Gatti tried to explain the purpose of their mission, but the officer simply pointed the revolver in their faces and ordered his soldiers to arrest them.

The three were marched to a field hospital where Gatti again began his explanation of their mission to an amiable officer. But the officer who had arrested them continued shouting. Ushering them out, he halted a 15-cwt truck, ordered them into the back and climbed in after them. The three Italians were driven down the Via del Carmine to the Diana, the city's principal hotel, on the Via Roma. From the hotel they were taken to the mayor's office and then to the Town Hall, faced at each stopover with uncomprehending American and British officers and officials. It seemed to Carucci that nobody was prepared to listen to their case.

All that afternoon the battle for Hill 424, overlooking Altavilla, continued unabated. At 4.30 p.m., as yet another attack by the 142nd was in preparation, Captain Parks Bowden of the 3rd Battalion decided to send four men to knock out a machine gun nest in a gulley on their left flank. While the little force, led by Lieutenant John Morrissey, worked their way down into the gulley, within sight of the nest, they were confronted by some 70 Panzers who at once split up to take them from two sides. At the same time the machine gun began its chatter.

With a burst from his BAR Private Charles Kelly wiped out the three-man MG crew and silenced the gun. Seeing the German patrol swarming down on him, Kelly swung his Browning at them, firing a full magazine. While he reloaded the other T-Patchers began shooting, Morrissey firing a .30 calibre MG from the hip. With a new magazine in his BAR Kelly pulled the trigger again, slaying more Panzers. Though hopelessly outnumbered the four men inflicted severe casualties before gradually giving ground. So close were the Germans in this open, hilly country that Captain Bowden ordered his men to fix bayonets. It could only be a short time before they were fighting the enemy hand to hand. By 5.15 p.m. the Panzers came within five yards of the American lines, killing and wounding the T-Patchers with grenades and MG fire.

Crippled by a grenade, Captain William Yates, a company commanding officer, passed his command to Lieutenant William Langston. In the growing darkness the Germans swarmed over the crest of Hill 424. One staff sergeant recalled, 'The men had only one hand grenade with them, and we had to send back for more.'

'The Germans have broken through,' the officer explained. 'I'm taking the staff back to HMS *Hilary*.'

It was late afternoon at the tobacco farm and for some hours telegraphist James Sharkey had sensed that something was wrong. He had seen a camouflaged Major Randolph Churchill, 'wearing a bush in his helmet', arriving on a motor-cycle and striding into a conference with the officers at the communications post. Only when the beachmaster's jeep drove into the yard did he realize the situation was critical.

The conference over, Sharkey was ordered to prepare demolition charges to blow up his truck and equipment at the approach of the enemy. 'We're giving you Major Churchill's motor-bike,' the officer told him. 'We'll have a launch waiting for you, if you can make it.'

'Very good, sir. But there are three of us, sir.'

'The bike will take you all,' the officer assured him. 'And remember the password is "Yankee" and the reply is "Bounders".'

'Yes, sir.'

'At the first sight of Jerry, you know what to do.'

'Yes, sir.'

'Good luck, Sharkey.'

Ratings were loading the jeep with confidential books and ciphers. Churchill was one of the last to leave.

Sharkey set the charges and positioned his signalman, with a machine gun, and his OD near the entrance to the farm to await the enemy. At dusk he peered into the shadows beyond the farm. 'Do you see something?' he whispered to the signalman.

(*above*) Commanders view the terrain at Salerno: General Mark Clark (wearing helmet), centre; General Sir Harold Alexander, right, and General Sir Richard McCreery (wearing beret)

(*below*) Reunion almost 40 years after the invasion . . . Former 'mutineers' (from left) Wally Innes, Hugh Fraser and John McFarlane meet again on the beach at Salerno

An Italian woman and her daughter salvage possessions from their shelled farmhouse near Salerno

An American Ranger hands out rations to Italians, mostly children, who helped carry vital supplies up the mountainsides

'Can't be sure. Thought I did . . .'

He was certain he saw a shadow sneaking around the corner of the farm building. 'They're coming in,' he warned. 'Open fire when I tell you.'

Hands gripping the plunger, ready to depress, he called to the shadow, 'Yankee!' Within seconds he would blow the signals truck to smithereens.

A voice answered softly, 'Bounders.'

Sweat poured down Sharkey's forehead and into his eyes. He lay on the ground, thinking, *I could have blown us all to Kingdom come.*

With growing apprehension at the swift turn of events, General Clark decided to exert his personal influence at the front. Leaving his HQ, he drove by jeep to the lines to view the critical situation for himself. Approaching the Calore River he met men of the 189th Field Artillery Battalion and the 158th Field Artillery Battalion who had placed their guns on the south bank, where a gentle slope runs down to the river, covering the bridge the Germans had destroyed at the start of the invasion. 'Burned Bridge', the Americans dubbed it.

The battalion commanders had stripped the gun crews on the batteries to a minimum and sent the men forward as infantry. As German tanks came rumbling down the narrow dust road leading to the bridge the Americans were rounding up every serviceman, from clerk to mechanic, who could fire a gun or throw a grenade, posting them to the slopes between the artillery and the river, indeed to any point where a break was threatened. Officers and NCOs halted trucks and jeeps, hauling out bewildered soldiers, handing them rifles and sending them into the line.

Clark noticed an unmanned hill on their flank which offered a vantage point to the enemy. Were there any troops left to take it over? Only a regimental band acting as stretcher bearers, he was told. 'Then get them here at once,' he ordered a senior staff officer.

By now the German tanks were advancing to the river's edge, followed by the massed infantry. Nothing, it seemed, could stop them from crossing the Calore and descending on the beaches. Opening with everything they had the two American battalions pulverized the road and the fields and woods. The German infantry valiantly fought their way across the ford until, yard by yard, the artillery fire drove them back.

As darkness fell Clark returned to his headquarters. It had been the narrowest of escapes. Studying reports at his tent HQ he learned that the enemy had infiltrated in the direction of Maiori and that the situation at Vietri remained critical. In the American sector the troops had suffered most severely. Reports of GIs abandoning their positions and of tank units 'bugging out' dismayed him. Men were jumping onto retreating Shermans, taking lifts back to the beaches like frightened rabbits going to ground. Enraged officers tried to drive the men back by waving their 45s at them.

Clark knew the situation was desperate. To an aide he confided, 'We're in a bad way. I don't know what the devil to do.' Only the paratroopers, it seemed, could save the situation and, more important, salvage his pride.

Still in the American sector, Captain Emmett Allamon, surgeon with the 2nd Battalion 143 RCT, sent an ambulance into Persano to pick up wounded troops. It never returned. Soon afterwards Allamon saw T-Patchers drifting through the aid post area, dirty and demoralized, from Persano. He could not tell whether they were stragglers or remnants of the mauled 2nd Battalion in retreat. Behind them he heard the characteristic rattle of tank tracks. Looking out from the doorway of the stable serving as his aid post he saw a line of Mark 4s. A German was standing in the turret of one of the tanks, shouting at him. Alarmed, the surgeon slammed the door as the German 'carved an 18-inch semi-circle out of the brick doorpost with a machine gun'. When the tanks passed Allamon thought he was safe. But within an hour the German infantry surrounded his aid post, taking him prisoner with his assistant, Staff Sergeant Frank Holland.

General Troy Middleton's 45th Division was even more precariously exposed in the Sele–Calore corridor. Yet when Middleton learned of the rout of the 2nd Battalion and the rumour, spreading fast, that preparations were under way for an evacuation from the beachhead, he issued a forthright statement: 'Put food and ammunition behind the 45th. We are going to stay.'

General von Vietinghoff had moved his headquarters further north to Sant' Angelo in the mountains, out of reach of the battle area. Yet so sure was he of victory that at 5.30 p.m. he impulsively ordered a telegram to be sent both to Kesselring and *OKW*: AFTER DEFENSIVE BATTLE LASTING FOUR DAYS ENEMY RESISTANCE COLLAPSING + TENTH ARMY PURSUING ENEMY ON WIDE FRONT + HEAVY FIGHTING STILL IN PROGRESS NEAR SALERNO AND ALTAVILLA + MANOEUVRE IN PROCESS TO CUT OFF PAESTUM FROM RETREATING ENEMY.

General Herr told him he regarded the telegram as 'premature', arguing that the enemy's collapse was certainly not as complete as he suggested. At that moment there were reports of stiffening Allied resistance near Persano.

But Vietinghoff was supremely confident. 'Isn't it obvious,' he asked Herr, 'that the enemy will guard his retreat with all possible forces? He may even execute a counter-attack. But the fact of the matter is that he is collapsing. How can you doubt it if he splits his forces in two halves?'

He issued instructions to both Corps to 'throw everything into the battle to secure the complete annihilation of the Fifth Army.' A message that evening from Kesselring added buoyancy to his hopes. The Field Marshal confirmed reports of radio intercepts that the Allies were 'evacuating'. Vietinghoff wrote in his war diary: 'The battle of Salerno appears to be over.'

But Herr, and General Balck, remained sceptical. They preferred to wait a while before hailing the German victory. However, shortly before 6.30 p.m. 15 German tanks reached the heavy underbrush north of the Calore River, just where it joined with the broader Sele to form the critical point of the beachhead corridor, four miles from the sea.

At his HQ Clark was shaken by this news. He realized at once that he was now at Kesselring's mercy. West Point offered no marks in its curriculum for what he decided he must do. Sending an urgent message to Admiral Hewitt on the *Ancon*, he asked for preparations to reembark his Fifth Army HQ and for all available craft to be made ready to evacuate the Sixth Corps from the beachhead and reland it in the British sector.

During the evening the war correspondents were shown the operations map in Clark's tent. A senior staff officer grimly indicated the German concentration area, 'shaped like a sledgehammer with its handle running along the highway from Battipaglia to Eboli and its blunt head shading the area between the Sele and the Calore rivers'. As darkness fell over the beachhead the sledgehammer struck its blow.

Colonel Gavin exuded confidence. On his desk at Licata airfield a large map lay before him with the drop zones boldly outlined. They straddled the Sele River and the town of Altavilla.

In his opinion airborne risks must be accepted, but on this occasion the planners were gambling on extreme speed. There was no opportunity for the airborne commanders to check out intelligence reports; at such short notice this was going to be an extremely difficult and dangerous mission. But he was determined nonetheless to land his men on their targets.

Customary briefings were impossible at this late hour; there was time only to give the paratroop company commanders basic information to pass on to their platoon leaders. Gavin recalled that by the time the briefing had reached the squads the message was reduced to simple terms: 'The Krauts are knocking the shit out of our boys at Salerno. We're going to jump into the beachhead tonight to rescue them.'

Repeatedly he checked the final plans for the jump. Lieut. Colonel Reuben Tucker's 504th Parachute Infantry Regiment would take off at 7.30 a.m. and drop on the beaches near Agropoli, two and a half miles south of Paestum. The regiment's mission was to seize the town of Altavilla and the strategic Hill 424. Trucks would be waiting near the drop zones to drive the paratroopers directly to their front line positions. Three aircraft carrying pathfinder teams, equipped with Krypton lamps and radar devices, would precede the main body of paras by fifteen minutes; these teams would reach the ground in time to mark out the drop zones. Gavin wanted none of the confusion his paratroopers had experienced in Sicily when Allied gunners had fired on them in error.

So eager was the enthusiastic, cigar-chewing Colonel Tucker for action that he drove around the bivouac area and the airstrip in his jeep, helmet almost covering his face, pistol in his holster, announcing to the paras, 'It's open season for Krauts, men. You know what to do.'

Gavin, however, was intensely worried about demoralizing rumours making the rounds. Had the men heard the alarming reports that the Fifth Army might evacuate the beachhead?

XVIII
The Blazing 'T'

Monday, 13 September. Evening till midnight.

Looking tense and tired on his return from the field, General Clark was shaken by the gravity of the situation. At 7.30 p.m. he summoned Generals Dawley, Walker and Middleton to his HQ, at precisely the time aircraft carrying paratroopers of the 82nd began taking off from scattered airfields on the west coast of Sicily, bound for Salerno.

The generals discussed the turn for the worse in the battle. Clark's tension eased as he talked about the 82nd Airborne which was to be dropped on the beachhead later in the night. Was the commander expecting too much of the paratroopers? To the generals, especially Walker, it seemed so. But, unknown to them, he had already set in motion plans for the evacuation of both Corps, one codenamed *Sealion*, which was for the evacuation of the Americans to the British sector, the other *Seatrain*, to move the British south to the American sector. He had directed General Gruenther, his chief of staff, to take up with the navy 'the task of evacuating the beachhead'. It was to be a cause of much resentment later that he failed at this conference to confide these plans to his front line generals.

Dawley was convinced he was receiving incorrect information from the front, and Walker would admit later that reports were 'not always up to date because of our fast-changing situation'. The night before the worried Sixth Corps general had gone without sleep, pulling out units from one sector and transferring them to another 'to plug the line'. It promised to be another gruelling night. An aide, Colonel Eddie O'Neill, wrote: 'Things not too hot on the home team today; the 36th too far out, the 45th on the left not far out enough. Enemy tanks assembling on the back roads to the east and infiltrating our perimeter line.' When Dawley advised Walker to keep a close watch on the gap between the 157th and the 36th Walker assured him he understood the situation and 'could handle it'. South of the Calore, he said, 'all was well'.

Dawley was understandably confused. At the close of Sunday he had written in his diary: 'Reorganized and prayed.' Tonight his only written comment was: 'Disaster'.

After the conference Walker drove over to Colonel Martin at his improvised CP. The Panzer infantry had crossed the Calore north of Altavilla and were on the left flank of the 3rd Battalion 143 RCT. With troops under attack on both flanks and about to be surrounded on the left Walker decided there was only one step to take. He directed Martin to pull his command back behind La Cosa Creek; otherwise he would find himself cut off.

It was now almost nine o'clock. When Walker went to Dawley to report what had happened the Sixth Corps commander decided that the 36th should defend a position between the Calore and Monte Soprano with La Cosa Creek as an eight-mile-long front line. It was to be 'a last ditch stand.'

Walker split his front into three sectors, placing a brigadier general in command of each sector. He had four infantry battalions and he could only hope they would be sufficient to meet an attack. General William Wilbur, who had come ashore with Major Edward Ball, was given a sector to defend with a task force which included cannon and anti-tank companies of the 143rd; General 'Mike' O'Daniel was given a task force from the 141st, 142nd, and 143rd, and General Otto Lange was given two companies and promised the 1st and 2nd Battalions of the 504th when they parachuted onto the beachhead before midnight. Lange at this moment was 'supervising affairs' at the beaches, so Walker placed Colonel John Forsythe temporarily in command. Next day the 'physically exhausted' Lange was relieved.

Just as Clark's meeting with the generals ended, the pilot Jacob Hamilton landed on the makeshift airstrip near Paestum and took a jeep to the Fifth Army commander's HQ. Enemy planes were strafing the road and Hamilton had to abandon the jeep to take cover in a ditch, dislocating his shoulder in the tumble.

At this moment Clark was contacting Admiral Hewitt, who had moved his headquarters from the *Ancon* to the *Biscayne*. Without the knowledge of his generals he requested Hewitt to make urgent plans to evacuate the Sixth Corps and attempt to reland it north of the Sele in the Tenth Corps sector. When Hamilton arrived at the HQ he told Clark that Ridgway was sending in his paratroopers as requested. Alexander had already informed the Fifth Army commander that the drop originally scheduled for Avellino would be carried out on Tuesday night to harass the enemy's rear. Hamilton delivered a message from Ridgway which emphasized: *It is vitally important that all ground and naval forces in your zone and in the Gulf of Salerno respectively be directed to hold fire tonight. Rigid control of anti-aircraft fire is absolutely essential for success.*

To make doubly certain these orders were understood, Clark despatched staff officers to every battery to ensure that all firing cease after eleven p.m. He knew of Ridgway's unnecessary casualties in the Sicily landings and wanted no repetition of that disaster.

Meanwhile, in some desperation, General Eisenhower in Algiers instructed Air Chief Marshal Tedder to 'put every plane that can fly' over Salerno. And he gave enthusiastic support to Admiral Cunningham's request to bring ships close to the shore to pound the Germans. Cunningham had waived rank to serve under Eisenhower.

At dusk the fiercely determined young commander of the 2nd Battalion, 15th Panzergrenadier Regiment, launched his attack on Altavilla.

Captain Helmut Meitzel's grenadiers had arrived from Rimini on the east coast, travelling in a convoy of Opel army trucks by way of Sala Consilina, in the valley near Polla. Meitzel had found General Fries uncharacteristically angry because the 3rd Battalion was bogged down for lack of fuel; Meitzel, however, had successfully commandeered fuel for his trucks from Italian troops after the surrender of Badoglio and reached the Altavilla area early on the morning of 12 September. That evening, with orders to take over from the 71st Panzergrenadier Regiment, Meitzel's Panzers began a march through rugged terrain, climbing slopes overgrown with thick scrub and thorn bushes, wading through mountain creeks, and scaling steep rock outposts. Shortly before midnight they relieved their comrades of the 71st and prepared to meet the expected counter-attack by the *Amis*.

Meitzel's men were developing a healthy respect for their fairhaired, 23-year-old captain, who had gone straight to cadet school from college near Kassel, the former Kurhesse and headquarters of the 'Kurhessian' Grenadiers, as the 15th Panzers were known. Reckoned by his superiors to have a highly promising army future, Meitzel had survived Stalingrad and the Russian winter and arrived in Italy to head the 2nd Battalion wearing a khaki Afrika Corps tropical uniform.

At dawn today the Americans had attacked, harassing the Grenadiers with artillery fire from all sides, inflicting some casualties and making vigorous advances. But at five p.m. Meitzel organized a counter-attack, lining up his 300 men to break through the enemy positions on both sides of Altavilla.

Shouting the battalions' fearsome '*Hur-ra!*' the grenadiers swarmed on the American lines. Within minutes of Meitzel's signal the companies broke through the American positions, reaching the cemetery south-west of the town. Only one company, the 7th, found the enemy too strongly entrenched; these Grenadiers decided to dig in halfway down the slopes of Hill 424. They needed help, and Meitzel decided to attack Hill 424 from west to east. But darkness closed in too quickly.

Meanwhile, some three miles away in the Sele–Calore corridor, Captain Jurgen Wöbbeking and his artillery battalion of the 29th Panzergrenadiers, transferred to the area of Persano to support an attack on the Americans by the 71st Panzergrenadiers. During the fighting the 71st battery was ordered to shell the Allied navy in the gulf. It was not an easy task. With only restricted observation the gunners found that the larger ships, anchored well clear of the beaches, were out of artillery range.

Yet, despite the difficulties, Wöbbeking was now convinced the Panzers would succeed in throwing the Allies back into the sea. He, too, had received reports that intercepted enemy radio messages indicated a planned evacuation of the American beaches.

Late in the evening a whistle blew at Fifth Army headquarters, summoning all officers in the area. Soon a greyhaired colonel addressed them laconically. 'German tanks have broken through our lines. They're coming down the Sele towards this camp. All officers will take a roll call of their men. All troops who have guns – and that means everybody – will be on alert for further instructions. That is all, gentlemen.'

Cooks, clerks, orderlies, mechanics, all were now front line infantrymen. They examined their rifles carefully, fitting cartridge clips into place. The last round of the battle was beginning.

Lionel Shapiro was warned that enemy tanks were only 2,500 yards away and that officers were forming patrols with every available HQ man and fanning out towards the Sele. He thought of the war despatches he had filed, of the 'open letters' addressed to Goebbels, Göring and Himmler, which no doubt were noted in Berlin, and he wondered about his fate.

That day newspapers in Britain and North America had reported the battle for the beachhead as 'the greatest since Gallipoli'. Army commentators made allowances for Montgomery's slow progress towards Salerno. 'Any student of Montgomery's campaigns,' wrote Drew Middleton in the *New York Times*, 'will recall that he has never committed his troops to battle after a lengthy advance without a considerable period in which they were regrouped and the artillery prepared for a further onslaught.' Although the Eighth Army's battalions were leapfrogging one another through the mountains, not even an advance party had reached the beachhead. Clark and Eisenhower both knew that Montgomery's arrival could bring about the occupation of vital airfields near the beachhead. Eisenhower 'would trade the thousands of square miles conquered in Africa and Sicily for one square mile of airfield around Salerno'. Readers were given the news that British forces planned to utilize the captured Montecorvino airfield 'as soon as possible'. But on the ground at Salerno it was obvious that the captured airfield would soon be of little use. The invasion had gone terribly wrong.

Shapiro suddenly thought of running away. But where could he run? Only to the beach. Instinct pounded words of panic in his mind, while reason argued differently. He sat with the other war correspondents, waiting for the Germans to arrive, assuming that the experienced officers of the Fifth Army would know what to do. Photographer Sammy Schulman produced a coveted bottle of scotch he had hoarded since leaving Africa. The correspondents shared it between themselves. Suddenly Shapiro felt a lot better.

Predictably, the Special Services Brigade was withdrawn to Salerno during the morning because of the heavy casualties on Dragonea. Brigade HQ was ordered to take over the area immediately to the north, including the historic Castello Longobardo high above the city, which troops had named 'the Castle', and the valleys east and west of it. For this task two companies of Yorks and Lancs and the 138th Field Company of the Royal Engineers, already positioned in the castle, were placed under Brigade control and the American 4.2 mortar company and the anti-tank gun troop were moved up in support. Marine Commandos and troops of 2 Commando were placed in reserve in billets at Vietri and Salerno.

For the first time since the landings the Commandos were able to get some real sleep. For days they had lived with death and the fear of death. Lieutenant Joe Nicholl and his depleted troop had made their way, exhausted, down the hill at Dragonea and marched into Vietri. From the town's square a lorry ferried them through Vietri to a row of houses nestling beneath the steep cliff on the coast road running down into Salerno. From the windows they could see German shells pitching into the harbour, preventing the navy from using the port. Nicholl and his men were now greedy for sleep. The young lieutenant had no watch – he had not seen Sergeant Hill again, but he found a clock with a luminous dial which he placed beside him. Stretching out on the stone floor he closed his eyes. Frequently during the night he awoke, instantly alert, at the sound of gunfire. Holding his breath he would reach for his Colt and listen expectantly for the slightest movement outside the house. It was eerily still and the bright moonlight pouring into the room made the darkness more intense. Commando sentries were posted in porches and at windows, in wait for the small patrols of Germans who still padded through the streets, firing at will.

Gunner Dettmer awoke in the field hospital. A surgeon was standing beside him. 'Move the fingers of your right hand,' he ordered.

Dettmer looked at him with surprise. 'What a ridiculous thing to ask,' he answered weakly. 'You know the damn arm's off.'

The surgeon repeated the question, and Dettmer said, 'You had better not meet my mother. She'll be damn annoyed.'

His mother had given him a Longines wrist watch when he went to war; he had been wearing it when the shell injured him. Emerging slowly from clinical shock, he tried to recall what had happened at Dragonea, remembering the day differently, perhaps, than his commander. Colonel Churchill was 'a warrior, a professional among amateurs'. A Commando knew no fear when Jack Churchill was around. 'With this amazing man you felt there was nothing to be afraid of. He created an atmosphere of confidence and command.' Yet whereas Churchill might consider Dragonea 'a good battle', Dettmer had not joined the Brigade for glory, but 'to prevent Hitler coming in to rule the roost'. He wondered who had planned this ill-conceived invasion against one of the world's finest armies. He thought of his officer turning on his back to die in the field ambulance. Brunswick's parents were German, living in the North of England, yet Brunswick had been 'an Empire man, and a brave soldier, far too brave'.

Captain Brian Lees had treated a long line of wounded in the small hut that was engulfed by the enemy during the battle. This evening he listed them: *Pte. Reilly – shoulder; Lt. Peters – face and lung; L/Cpl. Sanson – foot and back; Lt. Bowring – fractured leg, wounded foot; Lt. Keep – back and neck.* When a truck had transferred the last patient to a field ambulance, Lees reported back to Brigade HQ in Vietri. Since the landings 98 men from his own unit and 20 Marine Commandos had passed through his aid post, with another 20 men from neighbouring units, 30 German troops and an equal number of Italian civilians. This total did not include those killed or those who, like Gunner Dettmer, had gone straight to the field ambulance. His report completed, Lees pinned the pages together with a curved medical safety pin.

The surviving troop leaders also wrote their reports during the evening on odd pieces of paper. Wellington wrote his on the back of a map by candlelight as candle grease spilled over the words, listing his recommendations for decorations: *Sgt. O'Brien, recommended for DCM for complete disregard of his personal safety throughout the five days . . . Troop Sgt. Major Garland, wounded in the head, but continued in his duties, showing complete disregard for personal safety . . . Cpl. Webber for carrying out duties and attending to wounded constantly while under fire . . . Pte. Peachey for continuing to fire his LMG after being particularly disabled by blast . . .*

He signed the report, *Wellington, Capt.*

Colonel Churchill would write in his report of the 13th: *Dettmer, C.: wounded in action – same shell that caused Brunswick's death.*

On Dragonea Captain Gordon-Hemming crossed the hill again after the battle in search of his two wounded men. He found them, placed by the Germans in a small hut with a container of water beside them. With only field dressings, there was nothing more Hemming could do for the men, who were still conscious. Two Bren carriers from the 'Black Cats' came up the hill and the two Commandos were placed on stretchers, secured to the side of the carriers, and taken down to Vietri.

It was evening before Hemming discovered that he and his men were the only Commandos remaining on the hill. 'You're not supposed to be here,' an officer with the 138th told him.

'Where's the rest of my unit?' the Commando officer asked.

'They've gone. You've been relieved.'

Nobody had informed Hemming. He was the last to report back to Brigade HQ. 'Where the hell have you been?' Churchill barked at him.

During the evening companies of the 56th Division's Coldstream Guards were attacked from Battipaglia by Panzergrenadiers. Advancing with tanks and half-tracks the Germans assembled in wooded country directly opposite the Guards' line across the Fosso canal, close to a bridge. Alarmed, the battalion's commander, Lieut. Colonel Sir Terence Falkiner, realized that if the Panzers were to break through his lines the entire British front was in danger of collapsing.

Falkiner knew what to expect from his enemy lurking across the canal. During the afternoon a patrol, working its way through ditches to reconnoitre enemy positions, had been set upon by machine guns and snarling tracker dogs. Falkiner now ordered his men to prepare machine gun lines and plant mines. In the woods beyond the canal Corporal Mountford, manning a listening post, reported on the field telephone that half-tracks were passing within yards of his post. Falkiner gave instructions to prepare a barrage.

In the darkness, shortly after eight p.m., the first enemy tanks, with gunners crouched behind their low-slung 75 mm cannon, followed by half-tracks, emerged from the woods. Falkiner ordered, 'Open fire!' startling the Germans with the sudden eruption of smoke and flames crashing into the night sky. Royal Artillery mortars opened up, firing with deadly accuracy, as the gunners swept the advancing enemy with shells, destroying many of the tanks. Guardsmen took up the fire, striking at tanks which tried to back out from the assault. Some Mark 4s, reaching sheltered positions, pounded the Guards' positions with shell and MG fire. Panzer infantrymen, sleeves rolled up, protected only by their distinctive 'coal scuttle' helmets, ran crouching from the woods, weapons at the port, determined to destroy the British and drive them back to the beaches. In Sicily some of the younger Panzergrenadiers who had previously experienced battle conditions had fled from the beachhead 'crying hysterically'. The episode had brought a stern rebuke, threatening the 'severest measures', 'punishments on the spot', even 'death sentences'. It was a display of cowardice which would never be repeated by the Panzers.

Within minutes the fusillade of small arms swamped the infantrymen who fell dead or wounded or retreated to the shelter of the woods. The field between the woods and the canal was littered with bodies. Falkiner watched coldly until the terrible slaughter was over. Then he turned to a staff officer and said, 'What a ghastly business we're in.'

One half-track, its 75 mm gun threatening the Guards, broke through the British line and was pursued by anti-tank shells. Falkiner was shocked to discover that the vehicle was driven all the way to the beach before the shelling reduced it to a crumpled piece of smoking wreckage.

The Germans had actually reached the water's edge where his men had landed five long days ago.

At nine p.m., on Clark's orders, every gun on the beachhead fell silent.

At his headquarters in the woods Clark heard the sound of aircraft break the eerie silence soon after eleven p.m. Suddenly he realized that something was amiss. These planes were approaching from the wrong direction. It was the moment the *Luftwaffe* had chosen to make a raid. For five minutes the fighters swooped low, strafing the beaches. But not a single gun fired on them.

At 11.26 p.m., four minutes ahead of schedule, the first American transports droned over the beachhead. Guided by the blazing letter 'T' towards flat land five miles north of Agropoli, between the sea and the coast road, the pathfinder team jumped from the first aircraft squarely on the designated drop zone. Within minutes the men had set up their radar and radio sets and were directing the approach of the oncoming aircraft. Jumping from 35 C-47s at 800 feet Colonel Tucker's paratroopers of the 504th Parachute Regiment drifted out of the sky, their canopied chutes like floating dots of white in the moonlight. Landing within 200 yards of the drop zone they prepared to join the battered Fifth Army's defence lines.

Lieut. Colonel Tucker was pleased. Not a single aircraft had been fired on by those trigger-happy gunners of the 36th. Before midnight he had gathered his first paratroopers together. More were on the way. By daylight they would be in the front line.

XIX
Mission to Avellino

Tuesday, 14 September. Pre-dawn till afternoon.

In the inky darkness before dawn combat teams of the 504th Parachute Infantry, burdened with unusually heavy kit, piled into waiting trucks at the drop zone to be driven to an area west of Albanella. Soon after 1.30 a.m. a second drop had been made by fifty-five aircraft which flew from Sicily after several hours' delay because of technical problems. Some pilots were unable to find the designated zones or the blazing 'T' signal, and one company came down ten miles away.

At three a.m. the helmeted Colonel Tucker, pistol in his holster, knife strapped to his thigh, strode into the headquarters of the Sixth Corps. Despite the loss of 73 injured in the jump, Tucker had more than 1,200 men at his disposal. At daylight he would move them into the lines. Their principal mission would be to seize Altavilla and the two hills dominating the area. But first he sent a six-man scouting party towards Altavilla to discover the enemy strength. Before dawn the men reported back that the area was filled with enemy troops and tanks. Tucker decided to bide his time.

Dawn was the cue for the Allies' heaviest air and sea bombardment since the landings. Tons of explosives flayed the German positions. The *Philadelphia*, her targets designated by fire control parties on shore, fired salvo after salvo of six-inch shells on tanks, batteries and troops. Fighters and fighter-bombers roared through the sky, patrolling the beaches or sweeping inland to flatten targets behind enemy lines, dive-bombing roads, railways and bridges. The Strategic Air Force had orders to smash the enemy's internal lines of communication.

It was the ear-splitting thunder of these aircraft that woke correspondent Lionel Shapiro. He and the other correspondents had been moved from PR headquarters during the night and he was uncertain of his whereabouts. Overhead formations were flying 'propellor to tail'.

A GI handed him a mug of tea. 'Who's tent is that?' he asked, indicating a large canvas tent nearby.

'That's General House,' he was told. Brigadier General Edward House had come ashore during the night to direct his fighters from the beachhead. Shapiro, who had met House on the *Ancon*, crossed to the tent.

'The Germans are seeing something this morning they never expected,' House told him enthusiastically. 'We're going to blast 'em hard today. We're tossing everything at them except the kitchen sink.'

The reporter could not share the general's optimism. Driving back to the headquarters from which he had been trucked during the night he found the area transformed. Heavy guns were emplaced, munitions were piled high, troops were dug into slit trenches exchanging artillery fire. The chatter of their machine guns was diminished by the deep rumble of naval guns and the roar of the squadrons overhead. Mesmerized by this display of air and naval power, Shapiro gazed up at the passing aircraft. It seemed to him that every fighter and bomber from the airfields of Sicily and North Africa was over Salerno. It was a concentrated, last-minute attempt to smash the German forces before they swept the Allies from the beaches.

At seven a.m. Clark left his HQ to view the situation at the front. Accompanied by an aide, Captain Warren Thrasher, he rode by jeep along Highway 18 to a small road running parallel to the south bank of the Sele River. From here he followed the front line eastward to the critical point of yesterday's German breakthrough. Moving along the shortened line he stopped at points where small units had been posted. It was obvious that the officers and men he met had taken a 'severe drubbing'. He assured them that the situation had 'improved slightly', that reinforcements were arriving, and that 'this is where we stop giving ground.' Men crowded around his jeep to see at close quarters their gangling general, his shirt, worn under a khaki uniform jacket, tieless and open at the throat. He repeatedly emphasized, 'We don't give another inch. We don't yield. We're here to stay.'

Driving to where the most forward elements had dug in, he found most of the 36th grouped defensively behind the line of La Cosa Creek, more a shallow watercourse than a stream, which emptied into the Calore a mile and a half north-east of the junction of the Calore and Sele rivers. From this point La Cosa Creek twisted south between the town of Albanella and the heights of Monte Soprano. West of the creek the terrain was moderately hilly with Monte San Chirico, about 450 feet high, as its dominating feature. Clark climbed to the top of this hill, searching for a glimpse of his forces 'still hanging on'. Walker had divided this eight-mile stretch into three sectors under Generals Wilbur, O'Daniel and Lange; it was a line that Clark ordered must be held at all costs. Last night the enemy, thrusting against the bottom of the Sele–Calore corridor, had been halted, 'largely by artillery of the 45th Division'; if the Panzers had broken through, he knew his forces would have been completely at Kesselring's mercy. From his vantage point he could see eighteen enemy tanks heading towards the American lines; they had found a vulnerable gap in the defences. Hurrying down the hill he called in an anti-tank unit and an engineer unit he had seen nearby and ordered them to 'get into favourable positions as quickly as possible' to lay down fire against the advancing tanks. A regiment of the 45th would soon be landing on the beachhead and he promised the officers he would send in paratroopers of the 504th to help hold the line.

Driving back towards his HQ, worrying over the situation, he passed a convoy of trucks retreating from the front. The troops were wearing gas masks. As first he attributed this to the dusty roads. Then he saw that almost every single man was wearing a mask. Ordering his driver to stop the jeep he halted the convoy.

'Why the masks?' he called out to the driver of the first truck.

'Gas,' the man replied, declining to remove his mask, and motioning back towards the front.

'Where's the gas? Who said so?'

'Somewhere up front, sir.' The driver shrugged. 'I don't know who said so, sir.'

Angry, Clark ordered the men to remove the masks at once and the drivers to turn the trucks around and return to the lines. Such false alarms could only make a bad situation worse.

Despite the Allied bombardment the Germans renewed their attacks with probing tank and infantry thrusts. From his headquarters in Sant' Angelo di Lombardi General von Vietinghoff directed his commanders to concentrate their forces east of the Sele. A satisfactory tank route to the Sele River had been worked out; during the night all available Pioneers had worked on the road.

Lieutenant Günter Schmitz, returning to service with the Pioneer Battalion, 16th Panzer Division, after his injuries at Montecorvino airfield, was dismayed by the Allied destruction of roads and railroads. Yet he managed to free blocked roads, create diversions, and offset the lack of rail transport by the use of trucks taken from the Italians. By seven a.m. the first Panzer tanks were able to pass through to the Sele.

Remaining units of the 26th Panzers were arriving from the south and a regiment of the 3rd Panzer Division was entering the northern area from Rome. Reports reaching Vietinghoff during the morning indicated that enemy resistance had stiffened right across the front and his advancing troops were experiencing the heaviest air and naval bombardment since the invasion began. His reaction was to launch further assaults.

On Altavilla Captain Helmut Meitzel resumed his attack, sending in an assault party to check on the town, which he hoped was now free of the Americans. Grenadiers scoured the narrow streets and old buildings without encountering a single enemy soldier. Was it possible that all the *Amis* had withdrawn through the German lines during the night? The party leader was about to fire the agreed light signal that Altavilla was cleared of enemy forces when his group was suddenly sprayed by a hail of bullets. A group of 'T-Patchers' were holed up in the Castle. Private Charles Kelly, the young Pennsylvanian who had fought off seventy Panzers on the hill yesterday, was among the GIs determined to defend the building. As the assault party advanced Kelly fired a variety of weapons to protect the position, using his BAR, a bazooka and even a 1903 Springfield rifle. One officer fell mortally wounded, others were injured. Straddling the balcony of the building, some seventy feet above the ground, Kelly removed the pins from 60 mm mortar shells, tapped them on the base to arm them, and casually tossed them on the attackers below. Landing nose first, the shells exploded on contact, devastating the Panzers. It was an unequal contest and the Germans withdrew.

Meitzel was grateful at least for the information his depleted force brought back to him. He would have to reorganize his assault. Ground conditions were unfavourable; the bombardment from the navy guns in the gulf was transforming the hills into 'fire-spitting mountains'. Sweeping the bay with his high-powered glasses, he noted two ships in particular directing their gunfire from a distance of more than 25 kilometers. Their shells were falling in front of the town where his men were positioned, yet not 300 yards away the Americans were entrenched. He was astonished at the accuracy of the fire-power. This was not going to be what the Panzers called a '*ruhige Kugel*' – an easy job.

Before dawn the Royal Scots Greys had received reports from the 167th Brigade of an attack by enemy tanks along the east bank of the Tusciano River. Two squadrons of the Greys moved out to repulse the tanks, 'disproving the theory that tanks cannot fight in the dark'. But the Sherman commanders now realized with dismay how thinly the line was held.

Early on this same morning forward units of the Coldstream Guards, operating east of the Tusciano River, also in the Battipaglia area, were pursued by enemy half-tracks. On the right of the Guards the 167, the Ox and Bucks and remnants of the Fusiliers were threatened by more German tanks. During the retreat from Battipaglia Fusilier Albert Fitzgerald had been handed a box of 'sticky' bombs by a sergeant. 'What am I supposed to do with them?' Fitzgerald asked. 'Creep up to a Tiger and throw 'em,' was the sergeant's reply. But the Fusiliers had not been trained for such combat. Only 50 of them had survived Battipaglia, and five had emerged without weapons. Now Fitzgerald saw the Tigers advancing, infantrymen riding on the 72-ton monsters, in the daring, disconcerting manner they employed to create panic. As they neared the British lines they leaped off, doubling across the enemy as the tanks pounded the positions across the reclaimed marshland.

At this point the 56th Divisional Commander, General Graham, alarmed at the precarious nature of the line, decided to seek help. From his HQ close to the mouth of the Tusciano River he informed the commander of the Royal Artillery, 'I have only one squadron of tanks in my reserve. The enemy is nearly through on the front of two battalions. I have every rifleman in the line, even men from the beaches.' If help was not forthcoming Graham saw 'only the worst happening' to his forces. 'What can you do?' he pleaded.

The artillery responded swiftly. Reserve ammunition was brought up from the beaches and 36 heavy anti-aircraft guns were switched from their positions to fire in a ground role. Alongside Fitzgerald an OP officer raised a quaint telescope to his eye to scan the enemy lines. Spotting a group setting up an anti-tank gun about a quarter of a mile away he radioed back to the artillery. Within seconds 25-inch shells had knocked out the enemy position.

Soon after midday the immediate crisis was over. The artillery guns had saved the day. A relieved Fitzgerald watched the Tigers backing out, tracks spinning wildly. He knew that if the battle had lasted just another hour the British line might have broken. As the lumbering tanks pulled away he whispered, 'Thank God for it.'

But right through the British lines the rumours of evacuation that had first surfaced among the Americans were spreading fast. Bombardier Walter Harvey, still confined to his early position near the beach, in the 46th Division's sector, shifted ammunition and small arms to the infantry. Last night he had used his Thompson to fight off infiltrating Panzers. Now an officer told him, 'We may have to get out. The enemy is bringing in reinforcements all the time.' Private John Thomas, pressed into the role of infantryman as part of the desperate expedient of flinging every available man into the hastily improvised defence, carried food and ammunition to the artillery. His camouflaged truck remained parked in the wooded area to which he had driven from the landing craft on D-Day, the mines and explosives had not been unloaded, and now he heard talk of evacuation.

In the American sector, at Walker's forward HQ, Technical Sergeant Sam Kaiser and his men were told to assemble their gear ready for a possible withdrawal. Kaiser sensed that the 36th Division was threatened with imminent defeat and doubted whether the Fifth Army could get them off the beaches. The most sensible course, it seemed to him, was to retreat towards the toe of Italy where they would meet the Eighth Army troops advancing from the south.

During the night many troops in both Corps had heard the taunting radio voice of Germany's 'Axis Sally': 'They're bringing transports to take you off the beaches, boys. But this time you won't get away. Sorry, boys, it's the end of the line for you . . .'

In the city Arturo Carucci had gone without sleep. The priest, with his colleagues from the sanatorium, Lieutenant Gatti and Dr Soffietti, had been driven late last night from the city to Pontecagnano and the headquarters of the Tenth Corps commander. General McCreery had assured them he would speak in their defence, but he insisted that at least one of the group must be questioned. In the small hours Gatti was selected for interrogation by an intelligence officer who wanted detailed information about the staff at the sanatorium. On Gatti's release an Italian-speaking officer offered Carucci his bed for the night.

'Thank you,' the priest replied. 'But I would prefer to sleep on the cobblestones of Salerno.'

The three men were dropped at a city police station. When dawn broke they walked up to the Duomo to visit the Archbishop. The aged Monterisi looked haggard and talked despondently about the looting in parts of the city. But he welcomed his visitors who told him of conditions at the sanatorium and of their efforts to get help from the Allies. As they set out to return to the sanatorium shells were falling on the city. Treading between crumbling walls and the rubble of demolished buildings they reached the foothills and began the climb to 'Hospital Hill'. It was nine a.m. and the gunfire was intensifying. For a while they took shelter in the regional seminary where Antonetta Allevata, a woman orderly who had made her way down from the sanatorium, reported that conditions in the tunnels were now appalling.

Food had run out, the lack of hygiene was shameful, the fear of typhus very real. The hospital building, its roof top red cross obliterated, had been converted into a blockhouse by the Allies; it was surrounded by barricades, with mortars positioned at strategic points, two of them pointing from the balconies of the chapel.

The news only confirmed Carucci's worst fears. In the tabernacle of the chapel he had placed a pyx containing consecrated hosts. At all costs he must retrieve them.

At many points in the mountainous country between the opposing armies, other defenceless Italian civilians also found themselves trapped. At Coperchia, north of Fratte, in the valley west of the 'Hospital Hill', the village and house where Mario Marino was sheltering with his parents and members of his family was shelled during the morning's bombardment. Two German soldiers arrived at the house just as his older brother, Aurelio, 18, was shaving. All Italian men between the ages of 17 and 55, the Germans announced, would be armed to fight the advancing Allied troops. One soldier ordered the youth, 'Report to the local commandant.'

'Is this an order from the Germans,' Aurelio asked, 'or from Marshal Badoglio?'

Badoglio's name was unacceptable to the Panzers. One of the soldiers raised his rifle menacingly.

'*Certamente*,' the youth acquiesced. 'I'll finish shaving – then I'll go.'

Mario, a year younger than his brother, feared that he, too, would be conscripted. When the soldiers had gone he found an old pair of shoes two sizes too small, stretched them by soaking the insides with cream, and squeezed his feet into them. Now he hoped to pass for 16 when the Germans looked at his feet.

Germans from the nearby OP came to draw water from the well in the courtyard outside the house. One of the young soldiers had been a student in Berlin before conscription. Conversing with him in German Mario learned that his brother was to be deported by way of Naples to Germany.

'If the Germans take you,' the soldier promised, 'I will give you the address of my family in Berlin. They will help you.'

Clark arrived at Walker's command post at two p.m. in a foul temper. Walker had never seen him in such an unpleasant mood.

Bluntly Clark demanded, 'What the hell has gone wrong with the 36th?'

The veteran Walker, who had at least expected a preliminary discussion on the tactical situation and the morning's fighting, was taken aback. He assumed Clark was referring to the reverses suffered in the Sele–Calore corridor the previous evening and the setbacks on Altavilla.

'Nothing has gone wrong with the 36th,' he answered. He felt his attitude was justified. Though he did not say so, he resented Dawley's despatch of Jones's 2nd Battalion of the 143 into the corridor. The battalion had met with unexpectedly stiff resistance and he sensed the Fifth Army commander did not fully understand the implications of this move.

Clark did not delay. He informed Walker he had ordered the naval bombardment of Altavilla. Walker listened to him, wondering how the destruction of buildings and the killing of civilians could help the situation. The Panzers in Altavilla would take cover, and a few might become casualties, but most of their forces were on high ground outside the town and when the shelling was over they would simply resume their attacks.

Clark did not ask for his views. And Walker did not offer them.

During the afternoon the Scots Guards in the British sector mortared the tobacco factory and moved forward in a strong attack. To Guardsman John Weir the advance was a relief. For days they had battered remorselessly at the solid grey building with no result. Now, he thought, they might, with luck, throw the Germans out.

Approaching the factory he doubled past abandoned vehicles and equipment, sidestepping dead bodies bloated and festering on the dusty ground. As the Guards stormed the building the Germans suddenly opened up from concealed emplacements with intensive artillery fire. The air was torn with the sound of shells whistling overhead. Weir hit the earth at once, hardly daring to move, as shells exploded into the ground around him and wounded comrades cried out in pain.

Slowly, the disheartened Guardsmen withdrew. The factory had become an almost impenetrable objective. It would be many days, Weir knew, before they could hope to drive the enemy out of such entrenched positions.

Meanwhile, fifteen miles north-west of the factory, companies of the 4th US Ranger Battalion were trucked from the British Commando base at Vietri back to Maiori. Now, for the first time since the landings, the three Ranger battalions formed a common front stretching across the Chiunzi Pass from east to west, high above the plain which the enemy held so tenaciously. The pass, a giant fissure sliced through the granite hills, was a constant target for the German batteries.

At Ranger Force HQ in the cramped San Francesco hotel at Maiori Lieut. Colonel Darby was informed of the critical situation on the beachhead. What worried him now was the new threat to the Ranger positions. His men were in real danger of becoming isolated from the rest of the Fifth Army, separated by the gap driven by the Germans through the Tenth Corps. A section of the road from Maiori to Salerno and the viaduct carrying the road over the ravine into Vietri were under heavy artillery, mortar and machine gun fire.

At the command post of the 509th Parachute Infantry Regiment in an olive grove near Licata in Sicily a message was received at three p.m.: 'General Ridgway arriving in one hour. Battalion commander, staff, and all company commanders to be on hand to meet the general and receive a special briefing.'

Lieut. Colonel Doyle Yardley, commander of the 509th and a former Texas schoolteacher, immediately sent an aide to notify the officers and staff. 'Tell everybody to make sure to look damned sharp when they report here.' Ridgway had no patience with officers who were careless about their personal appearance.

On his arrival at the airfield from his Divisional Command Post on the north-west coast of Sicily at Trapani, the square-shouldered general ignored pleasantries. Striding determinedly into the HQ he informed the waiting officers, 'Gentlemen, the Fifth Army is in serious trouble over at Salerno. They need immediate assistance to enable them to hold on to what's left of their beachhead until reinforcements can be landed over the beach. You and your men will be jumping tonight well behind the lines – at a place called Avellino.'

Avellino was twenty-five miles north of Salerno. The stern-faced Ridgway outlined the mission. The 509th was to occupy before daylight a crossroads area at the south edge of the town and deny its use to enemy units moving through it down to Salerno. It would be a risky and dangerous mission. 'You can count on plenty of trouble from the Germans. But remember, it's absolutely necessary that you and your men do everything within your power to disrupt the German units flowing into Salerno.'

The paratroopers, Ridgway said, would carry with them five days' rations, enough to last until the Fifth Army arrived to link up with them; he seemed convinced the link-up would take place at the latest five days after the jump. Should the battalion find itself unable because of the strength of the opposing forces around Avellino to carry out its mission the general directed that the paratroopers should divide into small groups, fighting guerilla-style, to 'do as much damage as possible'. If after five days the Fifth Army troops had not made contact the men were to withdraw to Allied lines 'by infiltration'.

To the officers who had parachuted into North Africa last autumn this night's mission seemed 'impulsive and suicidal'. The mountains around Avellino would be crawling with German tanks and infantry. The operation was now marked with great haste. Commanders were given only a few hours in which to draw up plans and move the paratroopers to adjoining airfields where C-47s were lining up. Even this afternoon no intelligence of the area was available at battalion headquarters and only during the briefing were maps and aerial reconnaissance photographs produced. Each officer received one map on a scale too large for company and platoon leaders. The only orders given to the paratroopers at this moment was, 'Roll bundles!'

Private James Nunn climbed into a truck with other 509th paratroopers to be driven to an airfield at Comiso from where they would emplane at seven p.m. Nunn, a tall, strongly-built 23-year-old, had transferred to the paratroopers from the infantry in 1941, making his first jump in January of last year at Fort Benning, Georgia. 'From then on,' he recalled, 'it was a breeze.' Like most men in his battalion Nunn was an athlete, a middle-distance runner at school and welterweight in the regimental boxing team. His best friend in the battalion, Private Richard Fisco, was a marathon runner. Both men had fallen foul of Colonel Yardley during their time in North Africa. The battalion commander had sent them on punishment runs in the hot African sun 'wearing raincoats and carrying musette bags filled with rocks'.

Now Nunn saw Yardley clambering onto the hood of his jeep to outline the details of the mission. He asked the paratroopers to 'give of their utmost'. Then he added, 'For God's sake don't get captured tonight – and don't get shot in the ass!'

XX
'He Should Go Down with his Ship'

Tuesday, 14 September. Afternoon till midnight.

On board *Biscayne*, at the time Ridgway's arrival at Licata was announced to the 509th, Admiral Hewitt was signalling Admiral Cunningham to ask if heavier naval forces were available. His message began: 'Germans have created a salient dangerously near the beach. Military situation continuing unsatisfactory.' He added that an evacuation was planned and that all unloading in the southern sector was stopped. Cunningham promised what assistance he could muster. The battleships *Valiant* and *Warspite*, with six destroyers, were ordered from Malta; *Nelson* and *Rodney* were ordered to Augusta in Sicily and would be available when needed.

Later in the afternoon Hewitt asked Commodore Oliver, of the Northern Attack Force, to come to *Biscayne*. Oliver rode out in his launch and found an atmosphere of 'intense gloom' aboard the flagship. Navy staff were preoccupied with plans for the transfer of the Fifth Army headquarters to the communications ship HMS *Hilary*. Hewitt explained that Clark had asked him to prepare two sets of emergency plans, one for the evacuation of the Tenth Corps from the beachhead and its re-embarkation through the Sixth Corps beaches, the second and the most likely, for the transfer of the Sixth to the Tenth Corps sector.

Oliver was shocked. He protested that to re-embark heavily engaged troops from one shallow beachhead and then disembark them elsewhere was 'simply not on'. To shorten the front line now would be 'suicidal'. 'It would allow the enemy artillery to rake the beaches from end to end. We would lose the immense supply of stores and ammunition already ashore.'

Hewitt did not seem surprised at the commodore's vehemence.

'Has McCreery been informed?' Oliver asked.

'I don't think so,' Hewitt replied. 'I mean – I haven't expressly conveyed to him what I've said to you.'

The incredulous Oliver could not comprehend why no one had told the Sixth Corps commander of this vital decision which could have a devastating effect on Avalanche. Leaving *Biscayne*, the 'extremely angry' commodore rode back to the beaches and drove to McCreery's command post at Pontecagnano. When he told McCreery of his conversation with Hewitt the commander was 'furious'.

'I'll go at once to Fifth Army headquarters,' he announced, 'and discuss this matter with Clark.'

At that moment General Clark was studying the battle reports. The German attacks, it appeared to him, were losing momentum. The Allied air and naval bombardment was destroying, yard by yard, the enemy's concentration in the triangle formed by the towns of Battipaglia, Eboli and Altavilla. Sensing a slight upturn in his fortunes, Clark decided to order a British armoured division ashore with more American units. Though the battle map spread across his desk in his tent did not indicate any progress, he felt the crisis might be easing.

Philadelphia, relieved for a time by *Boise*, had returned for a two-hour bombardment of shore installations and enemy positions. And at 5.32 p.m. Cunningham, reacting to Hewitt's request for naval reinforcements, ordered Admiral Vian to speed up the loading of more troops at Philipville on board HMS *Euryalus*, *Scylla* and *Charybdis*.

At his headquarters in Oran General Alexander received an instructive message from Prime Minister Churchill: 'I hope you are watching above all the battle of Avalanche which dominates everything. None of the commanders engaged has fought a large-scale battle before. The Battle of Suvla Bay was lost because Ian Hamilton was advised by his CGS to remain at a remote central point where he would know everything. Had he been on the spot he could have saved the show. At this distance and with time-lags I cannot pretend to judge, but I feel it my duty to set before you this experience of mine from the past. Nothing should be denied which will nourish the decisive battle for Naples. Ask for anything you want, and I will make allocation of necessary supplies, with highest priority, irrespective of every other consideration.'

Even now, as the dapper Alexander read these words with a feeling of encouragement, events were overtaking the Prime Minister's aspirations. At his villa headquarters in Algiers General Eisenhower received a garbled version of Hewitt's despatch to Cunningham which suggested a total evacuation was under consideration, preceded by an evacuation of Clark's HQ. Eisenhower was alarmed. He told his aide,

Captain Harry Butcher, that headquarters should leave the beachhead last.

'Clark should show the spirit of a naval captain,' he said. 'If necessary, he should go down with his ship.'

He feared they had arrived at the most dangerous moment of the war for the Allied forces in Europe. An army of two corps, with four divisions, was on the verge of annihilation. Yet even now he refused to accept that the defeat staring his troops in the face was inevitable. He remained confident that his command structure, which he had geared to make fast decisions, could beat the crisis. Until now, Clark's handling of the battle had impressed him; he saw no reason to change his opinion despite Clark's alarming proposals; he was certain his friend would hold on.

When General Walker heard of Clark's plan to evacuate the beachhead he was both hurt and angry. Why had not the Fifth Army chief taken him fully into his confidence? Clark had never discussed his unease with him, nor the detailed dispositions of his troops. It seemed to Walker that the anxiety on Clark's part was unnecessary and due in great measure to his lack of knowledge of Walker's plans for countering the enemy attacks.

Meanwhile at Frascati Field Marshal Kesselring was cheered by the news that Panzer troops had broken through to the beaches in the American sector. Vietinghoff expressed his hope that the Allies would quickly be thrown into the sea.

Kesselring, who had been informed earlier of the concentrated Allied air and naval attacks, accepted his Tenth Army commander's views with caution. He did not altogether share Vietinghoff's extreme optimism. Reports clearly showed strong resistance by the enemy on all fronts. Moreover, he had hoped that before Montgomery's Eighth Army reached the Salerno beachhead German troops would have won the battle. Until now Montgomery's caution had been a godsend to him, but he was forced to admit that hopes of a victory before Montgomery's arrival were receding. Intelligence reports suggested that the Eighth Army would be in Salerno within two days at the most. There was not much time.

This night Berlin Radio told its listeners: 'Allied troops are evacuating the Salerno bridgehead under the cover of strong naval forces, having been pushed back from Eboli, sixteen miles south-east of Salerno, to their initial positions. The evacuation began at dawn when landing barges began to take out troops to the transports standing off the coast under the protection of two battleships and strong cruiser and destroyer forces.'

Carucci, with Gatti and Soffietti and the woman orderly, Antoinetta Allevato, set out from the seminary to reach the sanatorium. An exploding shell blew them off their feet, without injuring them. Covered with dirt, they decided to travel singly, but the incessant gunfire forced two of them to abandon the journey. For the first time since the invasion Carucci was close to despair. Halting on the hillside he was shaken with a spasm of uncontrollable weeping. After some moments he recovered and turned back to the seminary. The frustration of being unable to bring help to the patients and families in the tunnels and his failure to reach the sanatorium chapel had proved too much for the frail young priest.

After dark Antonetta Allevato arrived back. She had reached the sanatorium alone and entered the chapel to rescue the pyx with the consecrated hosts. Astonished that the woman had reached the objective alone, the priest took the sacred container from her and placed it in the tabernacle of the sisters' chapel.

Late at night Clark debated with himself his plans for evacuation. Both McCreery and Alexander had declared themselves fiercely opposed to it. Alexander argued that a reverse amphibious operation under hostile fire would be exceedingly difficult to carry out. Cunningham, too, saw no merit in a withdrawal. He agreed with Oliver that any further progress by the troops depended on keeping the beaches open and unloading more men, ammunition and stores. This in turn depended on the security of the Allied flank along the twenty-mile stretch of coast over which the landings were made. He was certain that evacuation, even partial evacuation, from one or other of the narrow beachheads would result only in 'a reverse of the first magnitude' and 'possibly an Allied defeat'.

At his headquarters in Algiers Eisenhower dictated a memorandum for his war diary, explaining that the decision in the first place to proceed with Avalanche was entirely his own; if the invasion went wrong there was no one to blame but himself. He was 'prepared to accept the consequences'. When word came that the combined Allied air and naval bombardment had halted the enemy breakthrough he dictated a message of encouragement to Clark: 'We know you are having a sticky time, but you may be sure that everybody is working at full speed to provide the reinforcements you need. You and your people have done a magnificent job. We are all proud of you, and since the success of the whole operation depends upon you and your forces, you need have no fear that anything will be neglected in providing you with all possible assistance.'

Heartened by these words from his friend, Clark sent a note to Dawley, 'We have arrived at our initial objectives. Our beachhead is secure. Additional troops are landing every day, and we are here to stay. Not one foot of ground will be given up.' He decided to defer his decision on evacuation for one day. But Dawley's nerve had gone. In his diary he again wrote: 'Reorganization and prayer'.

It was now nearly midnight. Men of the 509th Parachute Regiment would soon make their hazardous drop behind the lines at Avellino. Walker was totally opposed to the mission. He argued that his troops were now on the defensive and in no position to push forward to co-operate with the paratroopers. He could not understand how the 509th could influence the course of the battle at this stage, and he feared they were parachuting into a deadly trap.

Private James Nunn sat among his stick of jumpers in the fold-down bucket seats stretching along the walls of the C-47, one of 600 men of the 509th Parachute Regiment approaching Avellino from Comiso. Like the other jumpers Nunn wore a khaki jump suit, a helmet with camouflage netting, rubbersoled jump boots, and two parachutes. He carried a musette bag with a raincape, a Thompson sub-machine gun with 300 rounds of ammunition and thirty rounds of clips, a .45 automatic, three fragmentation grenades and ten rounds of plastic explosive. Like the others he had thrown away most of his K rations, retaining only chocolate and cigarettes and filling his pockets with tobacco and cigarette papers to roll his own. Strapped into the racketing Dakota, 'psyched up for the drop and scared', he reflected that he and the men in his stick had come through the war so far unscathed. Nobody walked around the aircraft; burdened with such equipment they could only waddle to the door when it was time to fall out.

The C-47s roared on, showing white position lights on their wings to hold the squadron in formation. Just before midnight the red light came on. Nunn, as jumpmaster, shouted, 'Stand up – and hook up!' Jumpers began scuffling up the metal floor of the aisle. Then the green light was on. Static lines made a 'chung-chung' noise as the paratroopers dropped into the darkness. Nunn was the last to go. He heard the scream of the wind as he came out of the door. Then, with his parachute blossoming above him, it became eerily quiet. Even the aircraft noise was lost. In the brilliant moonlight he looked down to discover he had been dropped above a mountain range and was floating into a valley. He could see a small town, with a church tower bathed in moonlight; he was not to know this was not Avellino, but Montella, more than sixteen miles to the west.

Then he heard a bell in the tower tolling midnight.

XXI
'The Last Attack'

Wednesday, 15 September. Pre-dawn till evening.

LIEUTENANT ROCHOLL WAS awakened abruptly. One of his men was shaking his shoulder violently. 'Lieutenant! Lieutenant! Paratroopers!' Drowsy with sleep, the officer forced his eyes open. The soldier posted on guard duty at the foot of a hill near Penta was pointing towards the moonlit sky. Looking up, Rocholl saw some sixty parachutists floating towards the ground 'like individual white flecks'. In the distance he heard the faint drone of departing aircraft.

Jumping to his feet, he shouted, 'Prepare to fire!' Gunners sprang to their turrets. Within seconds their 20 mm guns and machine guns were raking the descending paratroopers. His men continued their barrage until the angle of fire became so reduced that they were in danger. 'Cease fire!' Rocholl ordered. Paratroopers who had dropped through the curtain of fire were landing halfway down the slopes of the thickly wooded hill. Rocholl knew the enemy would have good cover from the trees and the advantage of the slope from which to attack his patrol and place stick grenades and 'similar toys' on his armoured cars. Ordering the cars to proceed to the main road to secure it from attack, he set off with a handful of men towards Penta to carry out a reconnaissance.

High above Montella paratrooper James Nunn was 'going up the suspension lines like crazy' when the tracer fire started. After some two minutes in the air he was trying to collapse his chute to reach the ground more quickly when a machine gun, firing straight up from a vehicle in the roadway, began 'making passes' at him. But the shots passed over his canopy.

Landing in a wheatfield, about 400 yards from where the gunner was firing, Nunn slipped deftly out of his T4 harness, whipped his Thompson from its Griswold carrier and assembled it. Then he saw Fisco land beside him. His stick and a second stick had landed about the same time; three more C-47's were dropping their sticks about the time they hit the ground. He reckoned there must be at least a hundred jumpers in the area. On the road he could hear voices shouting in German and the sound of trucks revving up. 'Let's move,' he advised. Doubling towards the high ground, the two men moved away from the road, prepared to lie low for the night. But where were the other jumpers?

Private Edward Kowlaski, who landed close to the town of Avellino, ran to a nearby forest to hide out for the night, fearing he would be mistaken for a German by his own men. But Major William Dudley, the battalion's executive officer, calculated that he had been dropped in the mountains some forty miles from the beachhead. He explained to the disheartened men who landed around him that it would be suicidal to try to fight their way back to Avellino; instead, he ordered them to hide out until British or American troops arrived.

Lieut. Colonel Yardley, commander of the 509s, however, was one of the jumpers who had come down closest to his drop zone. Rounding up his paras he first ordered them to cut telephone lines in the area. Then, on learning that a tank battalion had pulled into Avellino, he set out for the town. For two miles they encountered no enemy fire until a scout reported they were beside an enemy tank park. Caught in this impossible situation the jumpers began shooting their way out of the area, but the tank gunners simply sprayed them with machine gun fire, killing more than a score. Returning fire, the paratroopers found their bullets bouncing off the tanks' armoured plates. With their massive guns brought to bear on the helpless Americans, the Germans sent up flares to light the area, exposing every paratrooper who was not hidden in a ditch. Men died where they lay, others were grievously wounded. Yardley was wounded and rounded up as a prisoner with many of his men. Those who survived crawled away from the bloody battlefield.

At 1.30 a.m. Rocholl's men began searching the houses in Penta. They found no trace of parachutists until they reached the last house in the village. Kicking open the bolted door, they burst into the house to be met by a burst of fire from three Thompsons. Retreating swiftly, the Panzers escaped the Americans' bullets. Now, lobbing grenades at the front of the house, they stormed back, firing their Schmeissers. Inside, the house was pitch black. The enemy firing had ceased. Rocholl flashed his torch around the room, calling out, 'Hands up!' His light caught a group of paratroopers lying wounded in the hallway; blinking in its rays the men raised their arms hesitantly. The others in the group had escaped through the back door.

At the armoured cars Rocholl examined the booty his men had

collected: a sack of mines, two AT rifles, two light machine guns, two light mortars, and five days' rations for thirty men. Each of the captured paratroopers was equipped with a Thompson, a revolver, three hand grenades, fuses, knife, compass, first aid, even a knuckle duster.

Rocholl's ten prisoners were part of the 600 men dispersed through navigational errors, ineffective radar, and the high altitude at which the mission had flown. Only fifteen transports had dropped troops within five miles of the target, and two planeloads were still unaccounted for. Now, in deep woods and vineyards, even those paratroopers who had landed in the same valley could not find one another. Much of their equipment, including mortars and bazookas, was lost or had become entangled in treetops.

General Clark had a trailer brought ashore in which he arranged for a Sergeant Chaney to prepare his meals. It was in this trailer that he had breakfast served to General Alexander and Air Marshal Coningham when they arrived by destroyer from Oran soon after daylight. By now the *Boise* had ceased firing, having expended 893 rounds during the night; she was relieved by the *Philadelphia* which was pounding enemy tanks near Persano.

Over breakfast Alexander tactfully suggested to Clark that he ought to reconsider his plan to evacuate the beachhead. Even with the reinforcements Kesselring was pouring into the beachhead the German strength was still equivalent to only four divisions against the Fifth Army's seven divisions; the Germans were reckoned to have only 100 tanks against the Fifth's 200, although nothing the Allies could field could match the terrifying Tigers. Alexander wanted to see the front for himself. He had heard of the men's panic, and, unlike Clark, what he feared most at this stage was a crack in the army's morale.

At 8.15 a.m. Clark arrived at Walker's CP with Alexander and Coningham. The general was away 'checking the Cosa Creek's defences'. Alexander seemed surprised. A Colonel Kerr explained the strategic situation to the visitors who made no comment. He also thought it opportune to complain to Coningham that Walker had not received the early air support that had been promised.

At that moment Walker, en route to La Cosa Creek, was seeking out General Lange and his party at their bivouac. Walker had recalled Lange from the beaches, directing him to take over the southern sector and prepare his troops for an attack this morning. Colonel Forsythe had done well in Lange's place, but Walker felt he should have a

The town and beach at Maiori where U.S. Rangers landed before dawn on September 9. The road running through the centre of the town leads to the Chiunzi Pass

Altavilla, hilltop town near Salerno and scene of long and bitter battles between American and German troops. This photograph was taken in later years by a former German Panzer officer

General Montgomery finally arrives at Salerno from the south – and inspects troop positions with General Clark

General Sir Richard McCreery – commanding the British Tenth Corps at Salerno

brigadier general in charge. He was surprised to find Lange and his officers just getting out of bed. Lange admitted he had not yet complied with his orders.

'Why not?' Walker demanded.

'I'm worn out – I need a rest.'

'Everybody's worn out,' Walker snorted. 'We all need a rest. Wilbur and O'Daniel and Forsythe – they've had no sleep for two nights – and they've done excellent work.' Deciding he would prefer to have one of the three as assistant division commander, he told Lange, 'I intend to make such a recommendation to Dawley.'

When he arrived back at his CP Clark and Alexander had gone. Kerr told him of their promise of air support. Walker retorted, 'I don't think their orders will make any difference.'

By now he was ready to admit his impatience with Fifth Army HQ. All yesterday Clark and Dawley had sent him messages directing, 'There must be no retreat' and 'Not one foot of ground must be given up.' Did they imagine he was incapable of repelling a German attack? From what he so far had experienced during Avalanche it seemed 'typical of the Fifth'. He heard that HQ staff had abandoned the Palazzo Bellelli because of 'some wild rumour that they were about to be overrun by German tanks'. Why had they been so dangerously close to the front? Because the palace was the most spacious and comfortable building in the area? 'In their enthusiasm for comfort, they overlooked the tactical situation.' Some HQ staff, he knew, had already gone back to their ships.

From Walker's CP Alexander and Clark moved on to Dawley's headquarters. Alexander noticed the Sixth Corps commander's hands were trembling. As the two visitors drove down to the beaches to take a boat ride to the British sector Clark raised the question of Dawley's command. He had 'growing doubts', he told Alexander, about the calibre of Dawley's leadership. Alexander, less than impressed with the general, agreed that perhaps a change in the command of the Sixth Corps was necessary. But, to his surprise, Clark admitted he had 'already taken steps' to instal General Ridgway as Dawley's deputy.

From where they had hidden during the night at Montella paratroopers Nunn and Fisco emerged to see the heavy concentration of enemy tanks and armoured cars.

'Fisco,' said Nunn, 'I figure we had better head for the hills.'

Moving back towards the jump area, they spotted a German patrol working from the wheatfield towards the high ground. Although the two paratroopers had been trained to work behind enemy lines, they had no idea of where they were. Before the jump they had been told that if they needed maps they could get them from the battalion leader; that was when they had been ordered to assemble 'a whole damn battalion' and cut the crossroads below Avellino, a stopping point for German units and a road junction between Naples and the south. Nunn wondered how many men of the 509th had found their way to that crossroads.

On the edge of the wheatfield the stalks rustled, and a voice said, 'Ten cents.' The two paratroopers froze. Fisco called, 'California', the password to which the answer was 'Grapefruit'. The wheat moved, but no voice answered. Fisco stepped closer, calling again, 'California!' A burst of Schmeisser fire cut through the stalks. Fisco shot off a round of automatic fire in reply. Nunn, his Thompson on full automatic, squeezed the trigger, sweeping the immediate area of the field. The Schmeisser was silenced. Crawling from the field Nunn knew the German patrol would start tracking them. 'Fisco,' he said, 'we gotta move faster than this.'

The two men jumped to their feet and ran towards the high ground below which lay a dried-up creek. Dropping some seven feet into the creek they walked quickly from the drop area. They had not gone far when they saw in the distance two Germans in Afrika Corps uniforms, with coal-scuttle helmets and rifles slung over their shoulders, approaching them. They were about two hundred yards away, out of range of a Thompson. 'Krauts,' Fisco cautioned. 'Keep walking.' He waved nonchalantly at the distant enemy, and the Germans waved back. For another hundred yards the paratroopers continued walking until, on reaching a low bank, they climbed out of the creek. Half a mile further on they crawled under some bushes. 'Nunn,' Fisco confided to his partner, 'there were three Krauts in that field.' Hungry, they opened their only tin of rations: cheese, beef and carrot flakes. Nunn grimaced. 'Fisco,' he said, 'it all tastes the damn same.'

During the morning Field Marshal Kesselring flew down from Rome, landing his aircraft near Naples from where he was driven along Highway 7 to Vietinghoff's new headquarters at Sant' Angelo. He listened intently as the Tenth Army commander explained that, in spite of incessant enemy bombardment which had halted the Panzer attacks, he still hoped to destroy the Allied beachhead. He had evolved a new plan of campaign: the 26th Panzer Division would attack north west from Battipaglia to Salerno while the Hermann Göring Panzer Division attacked from the area of Vietri; the junction of these two divisions would be the point from which they would finally drive out the Fifth Army.

Kesselring nodded approvingly, but cautioned against reverting to 'positional warfare'. 'This must not happen,' he warned. If further attacks in the Salerno plain proved impractical because of enemy navy fire and air bombardment then the Panzers must attack from another direction, attempting perhaps to strike the flank of the Fifth Army by advancing from positions near Albanella or even further south.

Vietinghoff was embarrassed. He had to confess to Kesselring that his engineers had been sent to carry out extensive demolitions in the Albanella area which would make such an offensive impossible. Discouraged by this news, Kesselring insisted on discussing the future strategy of the Tenth Army should Salerno be lost.

When Kesselring had gone Vietinghoff asked General Herr if the parachute regiment en route from Apulia could be used in an attack in the Albanella area. Herr thought not. Troop and supply movements during daylight hours were becoming difficult because of concentrated Allied air and naval attacks, and he doubted if he could now reach the coast.

In no way disheartened by the continued enemy resistance, the optimistic Vietinghoff determined to fling all his resources into 'the last attack on the beachhead'. He asked General Schmalz of the Hermann Göring Division to prepare a new line of assault to include the defence of Cava and an attack on Salerno itself. One group was to storm the heights south of Sordina, north-east of Salerno, and push towards the sea; another group was to form at daylight and move towards the sea from San Mango Piemonte to join the first group of Panzers. Both groups would then reform to recapture Salerno.

The 16th Panzers, who were to be included in this final assault, had been hampered since dawn by the naval bombardment and by low-flying British Spitfires and American Lightnings which plastered the road between Battipaglia and Eboli with bombs, knocking out tanks, armoured cars and installations. Even those units which had dug themselves in were in trouble.

Since the landings General Clark had received regular messages from General Montgomery conveying 'greetings', 'best wishes' and 'good luck'. This afternoon, before leaving for the British sector with General Alexander, he received another, more detailed message: 'It looks as though you may be having not too good a time, and I do hope all will go well with you. We are on the way to lend a hand, and it will be a great day when we actually shake hands.' The commander of the Eighth Army hoped to have his 5th Division, now fifty miles south of Salerno, at the beachhead within two days, with the 1st Canadian Division echeloned behind. He had directed the 5th Division to send detachments beyond Sapri, and asked, 'Perhaps you could push out a reconnaissance along the road from Agropoli to meet my people, who have already started from Sapri?'

Clark replied, with possible irony: 'Please accept my deep appreciation for the assistance your Eighth Army has provided by your skilful and rapid advance. It will be a pleasure to meet you again at an early date. Situation here well in hand.' He did not offer to send out a reconnaissance patrol. Did not 'Monty' realize 'we had nearly been pushed into the sea'?

At the time Clark received Montgomery's message the American Daniel de Luce, of Associated Press, was among a party of nine war correspondents, the rest British, travelling towards Salerno from the south in a dust-covered convoy comprising one jeep, one truck and two staff cars. Impatient with the tardy progress of Montgomery's Eighth Army, the reporters had decided to push ahead independently to ascertain if the reports of German opposition were correct.

Although escorted by two armed British officers, no one had fired a shot throughout the journey. For almost a hundred miles they had driven along the shores of the Tyrrhenian Sea on the assumption that the retreating Germans would use only the inland roads to avoid American patrols below Paestum. They drove over mountains crowned with medieval villages and monasteries; they were welcomed by local people and guided by *carabinieri* who warned them of reported sightings of enemy units. They found detachments of the Italian Army guarding railway tunnels, bridges and stations against German sabotage, yet throughout the journey the only demolitions de Luce saw were an ammunition dump and a railway bridge that had been blown up. Nowhere did he see a single enemy soldier.

Using barefoot Italian boys as guides they weaved through side roads, taking cover when German tanks were reported rumbling towards a crossroads. They had spent last night in a monastery at Castelnuovo. Now, approaching Paestum on Highway 18, they were suddenly confronted with a 50 calibre machine gun pointed squarely at their small convoy from a green-painted half-track with a white American encircled star. The drivers braked to a halt, the officers stood up, waving their arms. A young tank corps soldier in a crash helmet stared down at them in amazement.

'Eighth Army!' shouted the British officers.

Private John Dowling could hardly believe his eyes. Then his face broke into a grin. 'Another inch,' said the American, 'and I would have given you one hell of a burst!'

At Coperchia, south of Lieutenant Rocholl's position at Penta, an Italian-speaking Panzer sergeant arrived at the Marinos' house to confront Mario. 'You have been talking to a German soldier about resistance,' he told the youth. 'I warn you to be careful. In Russia boys younger than you have been executed. I'm Austrian and Catholic, so I will not report you to my officer. But you are in danger. Don't speak to that young soldier again. You are suspected of being a resistance fighter.'

Alarmed, the youth could find no answer. The sergeant walked away, then suddenly turned back. 'If I were a Prussian,' he remarked, 'you would be a dead man.'

In every mountain village the *sfollati*, or evacuees, were sheltering. In the valley west of Salerno another youth, Lorenzo Fusco, with his mother and other members of his family, was sheltering with a farmer's family near Cava de' Tirreni. His father, a commander in the Italian Army at Taranto, had sent them to Cava for safety, not realizing that this was the area where the real battles would take place. Lorenzo's brother Paolo, an Italian Army lieutenant, was hiding in the nearby hills, with other Italian Army men who had abandoned their positions after the armistice. They were 'without orders and without a leader', convinced that if the Allies had delayed the armistice announcement for just a few days the Italian Army could have organized to join with the invasion forces. This afternoon they came down from their hiding place to eat in the farm kitchen. At the sound of German voices they quickly left the table and withdrew to the adjoining stable from which an outer door led into the farmyard.

A Panzer officer, flanked by an NCO and a private, burst through the kitchen door. Sweeping the room with their guns, the Germans saw mostly women and children. On the other side of the door Paolo cocked his .22 pistol, ready to shoot.

'Who knows the Ponte della Molina?' the officer asked. 'We want someone to show us the way.'

Lorenzo knew the way, but his uncle, the Marchese Andrea Genoini Fusco, who spoke German, offered to accompany them. In the stable Paolo and the others hesitated, uncertain if other Germans were waiting outside the farm. As the marchese was marched out one of the Italian soldiers whispered to Paolo, 'If he is shot, you are to blame.'

At the roadway the marchese was escorted to a group of Panzers in armoured cars and half tracks. A major in command was drinking from a bottle of red wine. The marchese, who reckoned there were some eighty soldiers in the convoy, gave precise directions as to how they should proceed to the bridge. The major turned to ask an officer, 'Shall we shoot him?'

Knowing the major was quite drunk, the officer suggested, 'Why not just send him back to his farm?'

Uncertain whether he had authority to shoot civilians, the major hesitated. Then he ordered the marchese, who could not believe he was to be spared, 'Go home, old chap.'

From the regional seminary near 'Hospital Hill' Father Carucci set out again, this time with Lieutenant Gatti, for the Allied headquarters in Salerno, from where a small army van took them to McCreery's HQ at Pontecagnano. On the way Carucci was shocked to see civilians lying in their own blood by the side of the roads. At the HQ they were told McCreery was 'at the front and could not possibly see them'. Bitterly frustrated, the priest decided they should go down to Salerno again. When they reached the Town Hall they were allowed to talk to Colonel Lane, the military governor, who promised to do what he could.

But Carucci knew that only the influential McCreery could help them now.

At this time McCreery was meeting with Clark and Alexander, who had crossed to the Tenth Corps sector by PT boat. He was relieved to learn from Clark that while general orders for evacuation were prepared they had not been issued. He was pleased to see Alexander at Pontecagnano. At just such a moment in North Africa, with the Germans threatening the Kaserine Pass, 'Alex' had arrived at the front. It had happened, too, in Burma. And at Dunkirk. To the British, Alexander was a perceptive leader in a crisis 'with the rare talent of seeing things clearly and wholly at a time when he himself was under fire and when from all around the most alarming and confusing information was pouring in'.

Before dusk Alexander and Clark rode back by boat to Fifth Army HQ. By now the battleships *Valiant* and *Warspite*, escorted by six destroyers, had arrived off the southern beaches from Malta, though it had taken the gunnery officers so long to get their forward observation parties ashore that only now could the ships open fire. *Warspite* began firing round after round of 15-inch shells at targets close to Altavilla; at the same time *Philadelphia* and the returned *Boise* plastered the town to Clark's orders. *Philadelphia* had expended almost all her ammunition, but the American naval commander at Palermo, Captain Leonard Doughty, anticipating a shortage of ammunition on the beachhead, had loaded 780 rounds of six-inch shells, his entire available stock, on *Ancon* which was leaving for Salerno to resume duty as Hewitt's flagship.

From Fifth Army HQ Alexander signalled Eisenhower: 'Although not actually happy about the situation, I am happier than yesterday.' To Prime Minister Churchill he signalled: 'Everything possible is being done to make Avalanche a success. Its fate will be decided in the next few days.' Eisenhower, who had decided only this morning to send another regiment of the 36th Division to Salerno, now changed his mind and cancelled the operation.

Expectantly, the war correspondents waited to meet the general who disliked publicity as much as Clark courted it. Whereas the Fifth Army commander enjoyed putting his feet up and chatting with the press corps, Alexander stood spruce and erect this evening, his clipped moustache giving him a handsome, slightly raffish appearance. In measured words he told the correspondents, 'Let me see – it was a highly successful landing, opposed strongly by the Germans in position with tanks and guns 200 yards from the sea. They were pushed back to the foot of the high mountains. It was a magnificent job – magnificent!'

All this the correspondents already knew. 'But now, sir?' Lionel Shapiro pressed him.

'Now? Why now, we are pouring our troops, tanks and guns into the bridgehead. That's about it.'

Shapiro wondered if Alexander had decided the battle was almost over; certainly he must believe the German offensive was fading. Yet at this very moment the enemy was mounting a fresh assault.

Preparing to return to the destroyer, Alexander was given what seemed astonishing news. A group of press correspondents had arrived from the Eighth Army. Although the Eighth was not expected for another couple of days, nine travel-stained correspondents were at the Press HQ asking to see him. Clark's officers were both surprised and pleased to see the reporters. The region between the two Allied armies through which the correspondents had crossed had been marked on their maps as occupied by two German divisions. Now it seemed that these divisions did not exist.

Alexander agreed to speak to two of the correspondents. Daniel de Luce of AP and Eric Lloyd Williams of Reuters were introduced to him.

'You chaps do get around extraordinarily well,' the general remarked. 'It must have been quite a trip.'

'Not really,' de Luce told him frankly. 'Not half as tough as getting out of Burma with you, sir.'

Shapiro tapped out a despatch on his typewriter: 'Fifth Army, Salerno area, 15 September – For the first time since the Allied landings in Salerno Bay the Germans today failed to mount a substantial counter-attack. They gave some indication that they are making a limited withdrawal from the salient they drove into the beachhead on Monday night and Tuesday morning . . .'

XXII
Assault on Piegolelle

Wednesday, 15 September. Evening till midnight.

COLONEL JACK CHURCHILL had no illusions about the task facing his Commandos. Undeniably, it was the toughest since the landings. In full battledress, he stood in a clearing near a farmhouse above Mercatello, a village two and a half miles south-east of Salerno along the main coast road, and spoke tersely to his order group. 'Last night the Huns attacked the battalion holding the head of this valley at the very moment they were being relieved,' he announced. 'The men coming in had no idea of their positions. They were simply the advance party. Result – the Huns have infiltrated right down into the valley. If we don't stop them they'll be into the plain tomorrow and the entire beachhead will be cut off.'

Late in the afternoon 41 RM Commando and 2 Commando were both ordered to leave their brigade commands and move swiftly to Mercatello, with the troops following in transport provided by the 46th Division. The commander of the 167th Brigade outlined the critical situation in the area north of Mercatello: the Germans had seized three prominent hills overlooking the beachhead defences and once again were threatening the beachhead.

From Mercatello a narrow lane wound up through the foothills for three miles to the small village of Piegolelle through which it twisted south-west to run along the hills and back into Salerno. On each side of that village the hills rose steeply. To the east a great crag, to become known as '41 Commando Hill', soared sharply almost from the roadside; to the west the road curved around a valley and, beyond the valley, a long ridge ran north-east to south-west joining the 'Pimple' on the north-east and 'White Cross Hill' on the south-west. The village and the hills had been seized by the Germans who had driven regiments of the 46th back to the foothills near the coast. 41 Commando were ordered to attack and capture 'Commando Hill', 2 Commando to search the valley as far east as the 'Pimple' and including the village of Piegolelle, which for ease of pronunciation became known as 'Pigoletti'. Churchill recalls his orders as, 'Do a raid. Strike at the bloody Hun.'

As the Commandos were trucked out of Vietri enemy mortars opened up on the trucks leaving the main square. To Lieutenant Nicholl, in charge of 6 Troop, it seemed that 'each time the three-tonners changed gear a fresh batch of bombs came down on us'. On the road out of Salerno dust clouds raised by the convoy brought down more fire from the hills.

From Mercatello second-in-command Captain Blissett led the convoy through the plain towards the hill country. At a farmhouse the stocky Churchill, Beretta at his left side, claymore hanging in a scabbard from his webbing belt on his right, explained his plan. While 41 RM Commando would advance immediately to attack the hill on the right 2 Commando would prepare to advance on Piegolelle.

'Somewhere up there,' Churchill told his troop leaders, 'there's a company of Ox and Bucks hanging on by their eyebrows. We'll have a squadron of tanks to support us. Harry Blissett will have the mortars. We'll advance up the valley in three parallel columns on each side: 1, 2 and 3 Troops on the left under Morny, 4, 5 and 6 Troops under me on the right. Understood? If you meet any opposition shoot 'em up. And, remember, it's a grouse shoot. We're the beaters. Old Harry has the guns. Keep in touch by yelling, "Commando!" Any questions? No? Very good. 1 Troop move off.'

Nicholl recalls that he smiled sceptically at Colonel Jack's directions. This was to be no textbook advance, rather the colonel's idiosyncratic scheme. Most of the troop commanders were by now too weary to care. 'We thought we might as well go this way as any other.'

Keeping in file to one side of the track leading up from the clearing the Commandos were overtaken by three Shermans, detailed to provide close support. The tanks curved in front of the troops towards a narrow stone bridge over a dry creek. Safely across, the first Sherman swung into the turn at the other end. Tracks ground against the parapet, sending the tank crashing into the wadi below. The second tank took the bridge gingerly, but in attempting to turn too short toppled sideways. Quickly, the crew jumped clear as the ponderous mass of armoured metal tumbled like a toy over the bridge, carrying huge blocks of masonry with it, to hit the wadi below with a hollow thud. Backing his Sherman away, the commander of the third tank decided to leaguer for the night. 'There,' remarked one Commando wryly, 'goes our close support.'

Troops of 41 RM Commando moved off to the right, some clinging precariously to the sides of the surviving Sherman, to start the climb to 'Commando Hill'. Advancing on their objective under covering artillery fire they secured the hill with the loss of only one man killed and two wounded. Immediately they consolidated their positions, preparing for a counter-attack. It was the first time since the landings they had been so lucky.

At 6.30 p.m., exactly one hour after the troops of 41 RM Commando had begun their attack, 2 Commando set out on their sweep up the valley to the left. The moon had not yet risen and the dark was intense. The terrain through which they climbed was broken and irregular, with rocky hillsides, dense woodlands and steep terraces covered with vines, a countryside through which silent movement was impossible. Realizing that the Marines' attack on the right was bound to alert the enemy in the valley and that surprise would be difficult, Churchill had asked the leaders of his six troops to call out to one another as they made the ascent; he hoped this would both scare the Germans into betraying their whereabouts and prevent the Commandos from losing their direction.

Sword in hand, the colonel attached himself to Nicholl's 6 Troop. Nicholl was luckier than the other troop leaders: he had discovered a dirt road leading up the valley to their objective. As they advanced a burst of Schmeisser fire came from a small house along the road. Churchill demanded to know where the scout was. 'RTU the blighter when this is over,' he snapped. A line of pylons stretched across the middle of the valley and he had ordered the troop commanders to report by wireless to him as soon as they were beneath the pylons. He and Nicholl waited until the other five had radioed them. 'Now,' said the colonel, 'we had better try to get up higher.'

Clear of the vineyards, they worked their way up a crumbling outcrop to the crest of the ridge where a company of Ox and Bucks were isolated. 'Well – where's the enemy?' Churchill demanded.

'We don't exactly know,' an officer admitted.

'Right, then – we'll soon find out.' Pointing towards the village of Piegolelle, the colonel ordered Nicholl, 'See those houses? Get your Brens up here and see if the Hun is there.'

Two Brens fired bursts at the houses in the village, but no answer came.

'Either the line is dead,' Churchill decided, 'or the Germans are. Push on.'

Meanwhile, Captain Gordon-Hemming, shouting, 'Larry! Morny! Joe!' to the other troop leaders to maintain a semblance of line in the steep terrain, led 4 Troop up the valley. The moon had now risen, intensifying the darkness of the trees, yet clearly outlining the 'Pimple' to his left.

Moving with his batman, Corporal Davidson, some twenty-five yards ahead of his men, Hemming was suddenly confronted by a German who stepped from a clump of trees five yards in front of him, followed quickly by a second and third German. Hemming shouted to the rest of his troop. Within seconds there was a mingling of Commandos and enemy. Commandos whipped the Germans' helmets from their heads as Hemming shouted, 'Hände hoch!' He counted forty soldiers, frightened and without officers, and wondered, *What the hell am I to do with this lot?* Hidden in the woods the Germans had seen the Commandos advancing. Hearing the shouts they had probably imagined a division was climbing the hill.

Not daring to advance further up the valley with so many prisoners in tow, he ordered two of his men to march them down to Bissett's HQ. Then he moved to take up a position close to the top of the 'Pimple'.

By now Churchill had led Nicholl's troop beyond the Ox and Bucks' position and down to the road. Moving silently in their rubber-soled boots, two forward scouts noticed that the hairpin road turned sharply to the right. Some thirty yards ahead Churchill could hear the unmistakable sound of digging, of metal scraping against hard earth. Probably Germans digging emplacements near the village.

The scouts reported a narrow footpath leading up from the dirt road between two old houses into the village street. Churchill turned to Nicholl, 'Look here. I'm going up to the village. Give me a reliable man to take with me.'

Nicholl chose a young corporal, Bill Ruffel.

'Got your tommy gun?' Churchill asked.

'Yes, sir.'

'Wait here,' he ordered Nicholl. 'Don't move until I, or the corporal, come back to you.' To Ruffel he explained, 'I'm going up with my sword and revolver. Stay fifteen yards behind me. If I'm surprised I'll yell – and when I yell start shooting. But, for God's sake, don't shoot *me*!'

The quarter moon lit the details of rooftops like a stage set. One side of the village street was in shadow, the other bathed in moonlight. Churchill and Ruffel paused in the shadows at the edge of the village. The colonel's eye caught the tiny glow of a cigarette. 'I think there's a sentry,' he whispered. 'Give me thirty yards.' The approach took them almost half an hour. First they pulled back 150 yards, then waited for the moment to cross the silent street. Backs flat against the wall, they inched along the houses towards the archway where

Churchill had seen the telltale glow. Two sentries were conversing with an Italian who appeared to be urging them to go for a drink. Sword gripped in his left hand, Beretta in his right, the colonel was creeping stealthily towards the trio when suddenly one German strolled away with the Italian. *Hell*, Churchill thought, *that's a nuisance.*

He waited, perhaps five minutes, noticing a large *VV* painted in white letters on the wall – *Viva il Duce, Viva il Re.* When the two men returned he sensed that the second sentry was about to leave. Instantly, he rushed into the archway, shouting the only German words he knew, 'Hände hoch!' With a clatter, the sentry who had gone for a drink dropped his rifle; the other, his rifle slung over his shoulder, shot his arms in the air, petrified at the sight of the fierce, moustached warrior who had materialized out of the night, brandishing a pistol and a fearsome sword. Running off into the darkness the Italian was swallowed by the doorway of a nearby house. Through the narrow archway was a lane with a courtyard to one side. With a shock Churchill found himself staring at an 88 mm mortar barrel, ammunition piled around it. Sitting around the courtyard, their heads resting on their arms, were a dozen sleeping Germans. 'Ruffel!' Churchill shouted. Following his colonel through the archway the astonished corporal stared at the enemy.

'Cover these buggers with your tommy gun,' Churchill ordered him. 'Can anybody speak English?'

One soldier admitted, 'I can speak a little.'

'Right,' declared Churchill. 'Wake everybody up.' Kicking some of the mortar crew who were still sleeping, he stood them hands against the wall. 'Tell them,' he instructed the soldier, 'this village has been captured by the English. Nobody's going to be hurt. But if one of them moves we'll shoot the lot.'

The soldier translated the colonel's words. 'Now,' directed Churchill, 'I want you to lead me to the other sentries in the village.' To Ruffel he said, 'Stay here and cover this lot. If one man moves, shoot them all.'

Removing from around his neck the thick lanyard on which he wore his revolver he slipped it over the neck of the terrified German soldier. 'The first sentries who challenge us – call out the password. Understand?' He tightened the lanyard and jabbed the tip of his sword into the man's back. 'Say anything else and you're dead.'

With his prisoner tugging like a dog on a lead they moved through the winding village street until a voice called, 'Halt!'

Churchill jerked the lanyard tight around the German's throat, hissing in his ear, 'Password!'

The prisoner spoke a password and moved forward, the point of the claymore in his back. As they reached the sentries the colonel shouted, 'Hände hoch!' 'Tell them,' he ordered his prisoner, 'the war for you is over.'

Between the archway and the end of the village they captured two groups of sentries. Returning to Ruffel, the colonel found the first prisoners still standing with their hands spread against the wall. Methodically he removed the bolt from each man's rifle. 'I never believed,' he recalled, 'in bringing in prisoners empty-handed.'

'Ask if there are any more bloody sentries in this village,' he ordered his interpreter. There were none, but he was led to an aid post from which he took four wounded men prisoners and had them placed on a farm cart for transportation. Two severely wounded Germans he left behind.

Ordering his prisoners to sling their empty rifles over their shoulders, he explained, 'We're going to walk down the hill. Nobody will be harmed. You are officially prisoners of war. When we reach our headquarters you will sit down with my regiment and we'll have a meal together.' But he warned, 'If any one of you tries to run away as you go down my corporal will shoot the man in front of him. You will therefore be responsible for your comrade's death. Is that absolutely understood?'

'Jawohl.'

Lieut. Colonel J. M. T. F. Churchill had taken Piegolelle almost single-handed. By now other Commando troops were swarming over the 'Pimple'. Germans tumbled 'out of nooks and crannies'. In a farm shed one patrol heard the sound of snoring. 'Pigs?' someone suggested. But a sleepy, guttural voice asked, '*Wer?*' Commando guns were trained on the occupants who stumbled into the night. Lieutenant Ray Keep saw a figure moving down the hill. Shouting, he fired a shot. The German ducked, calling to troops who were manning a trench below him; these were the Germans Churchill had heard digging as he climbed to Piegolelle. Now, advancing through the village, the Commandos had unexpectedly come down on top of them.

By midnight the Commandos had swept up the valley, through the village and onto the 'Pimple' and were now on their way back to their start line. They had taken 136 prisoners, most of them captured by Churchill and Hemming, greater than the numbers taken to date by the rest of the 46th Division.

Churchill contacted the brigadier of the 167th on his wireless.

'We've had a very successful raid. A lot of prisoners. The operation has gone extraordinarily well. We're on our way back to have a meal.'

'Good God!' the brigadier protested, 'I think you should stay up there. If you can hold on, we can save the entire Salerno bridgehead.'

Churchill looked at his watch. It was just after midnight, 16 September, his birthday. He was thirty-seven years old.

Now the night's success on Piegolelle demanded an immediate follow-up. Because no other troops were available, he and his Commandos would have to return up the valley to the village where the Panzers were reassembling in force.

XXIII
'Put Wellington on the Line'

Thursday, 16 September. Pre-dawn till midnight.

The order to retake the village of Piegolelle and the 'Pimple' meant the exhausted Commandos would have no rest. At precisely 1.30 a.m. the entire 2 Commando moved up the ten-foot wide dirt road. Within reach of Piegolelle enemy gunners began raking them with machine gun fire and from the heights of the 'Pimple' and 'White Cross Hill' mortars pounded their path with shells. By the time the troops encircled the village the Germans were close enough for bloody street fighting.

Contact was made with 41 Commando on the right and, with a line established covering the village and 'Commando Hill', two troops of 2 Commando under Captain the Duke of Wellington went forward to attack the 'Pimple', 300 yards from the village.

For seven days and nights Churchill had known the situation was desperate; he had learned of the preparations to evacuate. 'It seemed we just could not get off that bridgehead.' A wireless message came through to his post close to the village from one of Wellington's troops. His signaller called to the colonel, 'Message from 2 Troop, sir. I think you had better talk to them.'

At the other end the signaller sounded agitated. 'Put Captain Wellington on the line,' snapped Churchill.

'Captain Wellington can't get to the telephone, sir.'

'Why not? Where is he?'

'Not far away, sir. But we're completely pinned down. We can't move an inch.'

'Is there another officer there?'

'No, sir.'

'An NCO?'

'No, sir. Nobody can get here.' The signaller blurted out, 'We're caught!'

Churchill thought quickly. 'Can you shout to Captain Wellington?'

'No, sir.'

'Then put the bloody telephone down and crawl to him. Say that if the situation is absolutely desperate to try to come in.'

Churchill waited and worried. Within twenty minutes Wellington had brought his troops down from the 'Pimple'. 'I'm sorry,' Churchill commiserated. 'Have you had very bad losses?'

'Two or three people wounded.'

'But I understood you were in desperate straits?'

'Not in the least. We were under attack, but we were all right.'

'Then you had better talk to the bloody man who telephoned me. He suggested you were being murdered, that you couldn't get to the wireless set.'

'Of course I could get to the wireless,' protested Wellington.

Churchill realized he should not have ordered Wellington and his men to return.

'Would you like us to go back to recapture the "Pimple"?' the Duke asked him. 'I don't know if the Germans have occupied it. When you gave your order I assumed there was an alteration in the position.'

Churchill thought for a moment. 'Right,' he said. 'Better go back.' Then he suggested, 'But while you're here give your men a good meal.'

It was nearly dawn when Wellington's men returned to the 'Pimple' to be met with a withering hail of machine gun fire and grenades. On the slopes of the hill, before daylight, the great-great-grandson of the Iron Duke fell, killed by a grenade. With Wellington died Troop Sergeant Major Garland. Courage alone could not take the 'Pimple', and slowly the remnants of the Commandos were forced to withdraw. By now the Commandos were fighting hand-to-hand battles with the enemy in the narrow village street, and in the steep alleyways, hacking desperately with bayonets and knives, fighting even with their bare hands. The Commando reports described it laconically as 'close-quarter fighting'.

German half-tracks had overrun the infantry during the night in the 56th Division's sector south of the bridge at Fosso, below Battipaglia. At this same time B Squadron of the Royal Scots Greys, in position near Santa Lucia, was taking over the sector from C Squadron. Moving into position the tanks quickly restored calm; but it was to be shortlived.

Undaunted by the stiffening Allied opposition from Vietri to Paestum, General von Vietinghoff had ordered a renewed offensive at dawn: he wanted an 'all-out assault' on the enemy bridgehead at the northern and southern ends. Units of the 26th Panzer Tank Division had moved into the area north of Paestum, and in the area around Battipaglia the 16th Panzers were reinforced by parachute battalions. South of the town the 9th Panzergrenadiers, supported by batteries of 88s in the hills and their own heavy mortar companies, were to attack the 56th Division. Vietinghoff wanted this attack to start at five a.m. But during the night units lost their way and Panzers and artillery were stuck for hours in a traffic jam between Eboli and Battipaglia, only reaching their assembly points at five a.m. 'Once again,' a Panzer was to write, 'into the gulf of hell.' It was not until 7.30 a.m. that the tanks and infantry of the Panzers began their first counter-attack, driving out a squadron of the 44th Reconnaissance Regiment from the area north of Santa Lucia. By now A Squadron of the Greys was approaching from the south and C Squadron was ordered to carry out a sweep from the crossroads south of Fosso to the crossroads north of Santa Lucia to cut the enemy's flank.

Led by Lieutenant Fitzgeorge Parker's troop, the Shermans began their charge. Sighting a Mark 4, Sergeant Munro knocked out the tank at 800 yards; further on, Parker's gunner, Trooper McKenzie, knocked out a second Mark 4 at 1,000 yards. Suddenly the Greys were surrounded by milling infantrymen. Parker ordered his troop to use their machine guns freely to cut through the opposition to reach the enemy's armoured vehicles. His men fired their machine guns incessantly; only later were they to find almost 200 enemy dead in the area. While his Sherman was under assault by 88s Munro destroyed, at point blank range, a half-track which was towing an anti-tank gun. Under Lieutenant Michael Howard a troop was ordered to go to Parker's help, but drove almost to Battipaglia in error. Two of Howard's three Shermans were destroyed by fire from the 88s; Howard and the crews of both tanks died. Capturing an abandoned mortar, a patrol of Panzergrenadiers turned it on the British, devastating them with their shelling until a platoon of 2/5 Queen's moved in, killing the crew and turning the mortar again on the Germans.

Two survivors from Howard's Shermans, Corporal Scott and Trooper Slade, were captured. A Panzergrenadier officer, who appeared to have detailed information about the regiment, interrogated them. One matter puzzled him. 'Your commanding officer, Sir Ranulph Twistleton-Wykeham-Fiennes,' he asked. 'How does he pronounce his name?'

The sweep by C Squadron had overrun the forward platoons of the Panzers. After A Squadron had pushed the enemy back towards the main road and B Squadron had cleared the area south of Santa Lucia, the attempt to drive the 56th to the beaches was almost foiled.

The Germans were now prepared to admit that it was becoming almost impossible to throw the enemy back and link up with the Hermann Göring Division. All they could do was try to hold on to what they had. The officers found their troops dispersed, their fuel running low, their tanks and artillery inadequate in numbers. They faced an enemy whose supplies of ammunition were 'far superior' and who 'absolutely controlled the air space'. The enemy, they reported to Vietinghoff, was 'using artillery for every single man'. Even despatch riders were under attack by fighter aircraft.

In the mountains beyond Montella paratroopers James Nunn and Richard Fisco of the 509th had spent the night resting with their backs against a rock wall at a small hillside farm. At dawn the farmer warned them that '*Tedeschi*' were all around. Soon after daylight the two men set off into the hills. Fisco, who spoke some Italian, met two local girls who brought them bread and salami, but advised them to move lest their family betray them to the Germans whose trucks and armoured cars were moving up and down the mountain road. Further on, Fisco spoke to another Italian who reported seeing a small group of American paratroopers in the mountains. Fisco and Nunn decided to try to find them.

What they did not know was that the paratroopers of the 509th had been scattered over an area of 100 square miles. However unfortunate the failure of the C-47s to find the designated drop zones, the botched operation meant that the Germans were spending considerable time and many troops searching for the dispersed paratroopers.

Nunn and Fisco had eluded the determined Panzers of the 26th Tank Division who had arrived from the south on 14 September, relieving troops in Colonel Stempel's area between Salerno and the Sele. In the belief that the main force of paratroopers had landed at Montella two officers, Lieutenant Käpke and Lieutenant Krause, led patrols into the area where parachutists had come down. 'Group after enemy group' was wiped out. One officer and 35 men were captured, together with a large haul of explosives and what the Germans believed was a new type of bazooka.

It was General Walker who suggested to General Dawley that the Sixth Corps should 'go over to the offensive' with an attack during the hours of darkness with two battalions of the 504th Parachute Infantry, supported by a company of tank destroyers. Dawley agreed, and Colonel Reuben Tucker was directed to seize the hills around Altavilla, in particular the disputed Hill 424, with his paratroopers of the 504th.

Shortly after midday Walker asked for navy fire 'to soften up the enemy positions' and for a bombing attack by Air Support Command. The air request was turned down, 'as usual'; Air Support Command reported that one of their reconnaissance planes had flown over the area and seen no enemy tanks. Walker was angry; he had seen no reconnaissance aircraft and Division HQ had informed him at noon that forty enemy tanks were on the eastern slopes of the ridge, less than a mile south of Altavilla.

Across the Calore, towards Albanella, from where Tucker was about to launch his attack, correspondent Richard Tregaskis, who had come ashore that morning with *Life* photographer Robert Capa, went with Reynolds Packard in search of the paratrooper colonel. Tregaskis had already met Clark at Fifth Army HQ and been told by him, 'We have our chins up, and we're keeping them up.' But an aide confided that the general was 'putting out the good side' and that 'last night the Krauts almost drove us back into the sea'.

On the outskirts of Albanella Lieutenant Forrest Richter, adjutant of the 504th, explained the objectives of the mission. Then the short, stocky Tucker, with a disconcerting habit of removing his cigar to spit on the ground, pointed to the distant town of Altavilla, high on a ridge to the north-east. 'The Germans are in there,' he announced. 'First we'll soften them up with our artillery.' Indicating a wide circle with a sweep of his arm, he added, 'We're going to go way around – and come up on that ridge overlooking the town.'

As he talked a line of German ME-109s, glinting white in the sun, swept overhead, passing to the far right of the group before curving to dive in a bombing raid over the valley.

'Nasty little fellers, aren't they?' the grim-faced Tucker remarked.

Early in the afternoon General McCreery, under the impression that he was protected by a reconnaissance screen, drove in a convoy of armoured cars through the narrow winding lanes near Pontecagnano. Standing in the open turret of his car he noticed burned-out tanks and half-tracks along the roadside. Halting the convoy, he got out of his armoured car and climbed to the top of a rise to scan the countryside with his binoculars. At the sound of a loud explosion he turned to see the vehicles in his convoy ablaze and those crew men who had not been killed instantly running for cover. Enemy observers had been watching the small convoy from the heights of Montestella, waiting for the vehicles to halt.

As the convoy was shelled McCreery, with his personal staff, retreated on foot to the lines. Though shaken by the experience, the general insisted that this was perhaps the enemy's 'last desperate assault'. He knew that the cruisers *Euryalus*, *Scylla* and *Charybdis*, ordered by Alexander, had reached the gulf with reinforcements from Tripoli and since morning *Warspite* and *Valiant* had pounded the enemy's defences relentlessly.

But now the *Luftwaffe* was swooping over the gulf. While fighter-bombers dived to distract the AA guns' crews' attention heavy bombers, carrying the deadly glider missiles, swept unobserved into positions from which to direct their bombs on the targets.

At 2.27 p.m., just as *Warspite*'s gun crews had ceased firing on Altavilla and Hewitt was signing an authorization for the battleship's release, the bombers struck. A group of high-flying *FW-109*s launched four glider bombs. Two tore into the battleship, ripping through her steel decks with a tremendous explosion, killing two crew members; two burst close to her hull. Billowing clouds of black smoke poured from her funnels and gangways and cabins were filled with dust and débris.

For a time her commander, Captain H. A. Tucker, was able to keep his ship under way and point her seawards. But her engine rooms were awash and water was rising swiftly. When the last boiler flooded she lost power and lay wallowing in the gulf.

General McCreery bowed to Father Carucci's persistence. He directed during the afternoon that 85 patients and refugees be brought out of the tunnels and housed in a deserted city school provided by the Archbishop, who fretted because he had not enough room or food for all the refugees. To Carucci and the sanatorium staff Monterisi offered the hospitality of his home, but the chaplain refused, determined to remain with the patients. Soffietti suggested that the patients should be transferred as soon as possible from the school to another sanatorium, perhaps to Naples. The only possible route, he reckoned, was along the coast road and through the Chiunzi Pass.

Carucci was thankful that at least he had been able to make the transfer from the Giovanni da Procida sanatorium. Some patients had died, others were very ill. But he knew that if they had been left to rot any longer in the deplorable conditions in the tunnels many would have faced certain death.

With the Commandos withdrawn from Vietri the Rangers in the Chiunzi Pass could no longer maintain contact with their fellow storm troops by agreed red and blue flashlight signals. Stretched thin, the Rangers continued to deny the pass to the Germans.

Corporal Don Earwood recalled no hand-to-hand fighting. From 50 to 100 yards up on a knoll, his platoon fired their weapons on tanks and half-tracks, or threw stick grenades on the tracks. Captured half-tracks were requisitioned by the newly-formed Ranger Provisional Cannon Company. Moving to the crest of the pass, in full view of the enemy in the plain, these half-tracks, carrying self-propelled cannons, hurled hundreds of shells at direct range, then 'got the hell out' as the enemy retaliated.

On a forward slope Sergeant Arthur Schrader, searching enemy targets for which to call up the 4.2 chemical mortars, saw through his field glasses this afternoon a German walk to the edge of a field and drop his pants.

'We've got a Kraut taking a crap,' he called. 'Let's get him.'

Giving the coordinates to the 83rd Chemical Warfare Mortar Battalion section he watched the shells exploding; the German had emerged from a store of fuel and ammunition supplies hidden in the olive groves. Schrader saw the dump obliterated with a hail of phosphorus shells.

At the south end of the pass was a shell-dented, granite-walled house first used by Captain Emil Schuster, medical officer of the 3rd Ranger Battalion, as his aid station. Though pounded incessantly by German guns, Schuster, like the Commandos' 'Doc' Lees, refused to move, even though one shell came so close that it blew out his windows. Schuster continued with his operations, convinced the staunch walls would not collapse even under the heaviest shellfire. The house, nicknamed 'Schuster's Mansion' and sometimes 'Fort Schuster', also served as a forward headquarters for Colonel Darby, who lived with the continuous threat that 'overwhelming forces might sweep aside our thinly-held lines and knock out the Allied left flank'. At Maiori, Darby's main headquarters, wounded men were carried down the steep slopes to the monastery on the seafront where the baroque church was transformed into a makeshift hospital. By the light of a hissing Coleman lamp doctors worked day and night at a portable operating theatre with the help of Italian nuns and nurses. Nearby a local carpenter hammered simple pine coffins together.

For some of Darby's Rangers this monastery was the last stop.

'Darby', Clark radioed Eisenhower early in the afternoon, 'has done his usual good job.' He had promised to reinforce the Rangers' flank at Maiori. The situation, however, was changing swiftly and the full force of the German counter-attack had again struck the 36th Division. In one week at Salerno the British had suffered 531 dead, 1,915 wounded, 1,561 missing; the Americans, with little more than half as many men, had lost 225 dead, 853 wounded, 589 missing. Clark admitted, 'We have made mistakes, and we have learned the hard way, but we will improve every day, and I am sure we will not disappoint you.'

An hour ago, at two p.m., patrols of the Fifth Army probing the area south of the bridgehead had met the first patrols of the Eighth Army about fifteen miles south-east of Agropoli. The tide was turning, and, clearly, Kesselring's gamble of throwing the Fifth Army into the sea before the Eighth could reach them had failed. Now the two armies, fighting side by side under Eisenhower, would control some 200 miles of coastline from Reggio to Salerno. Yet this optimism was not noticeable at Dawley's HQ. 'The dead are getting awfully ripe,' wrote an aide. And once again Dawley wrote in his increasingly sketchy diary, 'Reorganization and prayer'.

Even the pragmatic General von Vietinghoff now wondered if complete success at Salerno could be achieved. The Eighth Army was so close he must soon switch to defensive strategy. Regretfully, during the afternoon, he asked Kesselring for permission 'to break off the battle'.

Admitting that the enemy air and navy superiority had in the main prevented his army from gaining complete control, he suggested the break-off should be in the southern sector not later than the night of 18–19 September, since it was essential that his troops occupy favourable defensive positions in advance.

But he asked to be allowed to attempt to clear the area north of Salerno of enemy troops to gain a 'pivotal point' for the Tenth Army.

Just before seven p.m. the American war correspondent Richard Tregaskis and a handful of his colleagues reached the 504th Parachute Regiment's CP on the hillside at Albanella. Major Julian Cook, temporarily in charge of the post, told them that Colonel Tucker and a couple of battalions had moved on; by now they should be in the valley ahead of them. But he wasn't certain because he had neither telephone nor radio contact with the colonel.

'How can we find him?' Tregaskis asked.

Cook shrugged, pointing towards the valley. 'That's the way, guys,' he said.

In the gathering darkness Tregaskis and the others stumbled down the hillside. For half an hour they crossed rough ground, finding no trace of the paratroopers. At a farmhouse they asked the usual questions, '*Dove Tedeschi?*' and '*Dove Americani?*' The Americans, a farmer told them, were a couple of hundred yards away; the Germans had passed through yesterday.

Descending into the valley the group were challenged by a soft American voice, 'Red River'.

Tregaskis answered, 'Valley'. Satisfied, the sentry allowed them to advance and brought them to a little group of paratroopers huddled under the lee of a bank at the corner of a dirt road.

'Get down!' a lieutenant shouted as shells came whining across the valley. Tregaskis ducked as the shells burst in a string of explosions less than 200 yards away. Undeterred by the barrage, he and the others decided to move on in search of the elusive colonel, halting each time they heard the shells coming. At the edge of the valley they found Tucker and his HQ company positioned in an irrigation ditch. Chewing on his cigar, Tucker pointed to two high hills with a saddle between. 'That hill on the left looks right down on Altavilla. That's our main objective. Once we get up there it's gonna be hard for the Krautheads to stay in town. The other hill on the right – that should be in our hands by now.'

From behind the hills came white flashes, followed by the boom of guns, the whistling of shells and then the impact of the explosions. In the moonlight that now lit the valley the Germans had spotted Tucker's company. Tregaskis lay as flat as he could, curling up his lanky frame, hoping to present a smaller target, as the batteries blasted them from different corners of the dark hills. A shell fragment bounced off his tin helmet with a clang like a loud bell. His head was ringing. Tentatively, he fingered the top of his helmet; the fragment had dented, but not broken through, the metal.

'They got our range!' Tucker yelled as a stick of shells smashed directly behind them. Dirt showers and heavy tree branches came crashing into the trench. 'Let's go!' the colonel shouted, pushing aside the branches that had fallen on top of them. Tregaskis followed, sprinting towards another ditch and reaching it just as more shells came down to explode between this ditch and the one they had just left. During a lull Lieutenant Leslie Freeman, the regimental executive, came running across the no man's land; he had stayed behind to care for Captain Tom Wight who had been hit by the last shell. But a fragment had caught Wight squarely in the back and he was beyond care.

Working their way forward, the HQ company moved into open

country, running, halting to look ahead, running again, stopping dead along the hedges, stumbling across the uneven furrows of ploughed fields. The contours of the surrounding hills appeared to be constantly changing. *Does Tucker know where we're heading?* Tregaskis wondered. Crossing through a grove Colonel Freeman suddenly stooped to pick up a black wire shining in the moonlight. A telephone line to an enemy forward artillery observer's position, perhaps to the man who had given their position away.

Matter of factly, Freeman said, 'We'll cut that.'

Marching down the far side of the ridge Tucker pointed across the valley to the steepest hill, the first of his two objectives. Moving cautiously, they reached the lower slopes as enemy artillery fired from behind them into the American lines. Slogging up the steep slope they were challenged again with 'Red River' as a group of American paratroopers, an advance party of the 504th, materialized from the shadows. Their NCO reported that no paratroopers had reached the hill.

Tucker remarked to Tregaskis, 'We are the point.' He meant that the troops of his company were apparently the only paratroopers in this sector of the front line. They had reached their objective with less than 150 men to hold the hills commanding Altavilla. Yet Tucker was determined, in the motto of the paratroopers, to 'seize and hold'.

Crossing a carpet of moonlight Tregaskis heard a voice behind him snap, 'Keep your hands up – high!' Spinning round he saw a paratrooper officer levelling his .45 at three Germans wearing square-visored infantrymen's khaki caps. The men dropped their guns. Tregaskis did not know where they had come from, but he obeyed the officer's order to frisk them. One German suddenly made a run for it jumping across a foxhole and disappearing into the thicket. He was a corporal from Major Wöbbeking's unit near Altavilla. Nobody fired a shot.

The paratroopers moved on, across the low saddle to the final objective. Tucker admitted that unless reinforcements came up they would have difficulty in holding their position. The Germans must surely strike back. Tucker then got back to a phone head which had been pushed up to him and told General Walker, 'We can hold – with assistance. But I can't wait here until somebody makes a decision.'

'Hold on,' Walker begged him. 'You'll get reinforcements – and food and ammunition.'

At eleven p.m. the Panzer artillery observer with the 11th Battalion on Hill 424 telephoned Captain Meitzel at his command post in a tiny chapel near the cemetery. He reported the sound of marching infantrymen advancing. 'Are they our troops, sir?' Before Meitzel could answer the line went dead.

The captain was puzzled. Deciding to investigate, he sent a sergeant and two privates down the hill to the observation post. Almost immediately a second call from another company reported that the *Amis* were already at the command post. Again the line went dead.

At that moment Meitzel heard shooting near his post. A Panzer dashed in shouting, 'Enemy reinforcements! They're already at the cemetery!'

Men grabbed their weapons. Within seconds a heavy machine gun which had been kept in reserve rattled a sheaf of tracer into the night. With no luck, Meitzel tried to raise the other companies. No line to the regiment either. This could only mean the Americans had cut all the lines.

At Frascati Field Marshal Kesselring had interviewed at length an officer who had flown up from Tenth Army HQ. Now he pondered Vietinghoffs request and studied the day's reports from the battlefront. He had spent the evening at his desk, leafing through the papers, unable to find a report that did not reveal frustration at the overwhelming barrage from enemy ships. At length he pushed the reports away and decided to contact Vietinghoff. He felt he could do nothing more to win the battle of Salerno.

Just before midnight he detailed an aide to signal the authorization for disengagement of the coastal front, with the express proviso that the Volturno Line, 20 miles north of Naples, to which the Tenth Army was to fall back, must not be abandoned before 15 October. And there must be no headlong retreat. That was not Kesselring's way. Every hill, every bridge, every crossroads was to be fought for until the Panzers found it timely to withdraw.

He looked out from the windows of his villa into the darkness. Below him lay Rome. How long would it be before he might have to abandon the city?

Vietinghoff had fought well, yet he had failed to drive the enemy to the beaches at the moment when he appeared to have them at his mercy. Now he could no longer exploit Montgomery's 'cautious advance'. To Kesselring it was a most bitter blow.

Part Four

MUTINY

Then fare weel, ye banks o'Sicily,
Fare ye weel, ye valley an' shaw,
There's no Jock will mourn the kyles o' ye.
Puir bliddy bastards are weary.

Hamish Henderson,
'*The Highland Division's Farewell to Sicily*'.

XXIV
The Angry Veterans

Friday, 17 September.

Despite the heavy Commando losses, General Hawkesworth finally decided that the 'Pimple' above Piegolelle should be attacked by 138 Brigade of the 46th Division under covering fire from Commandos and the 46th Divisional Artillery. Zero hour was fixed for two a.m. Before midnight, however, he had unexpectedly changed his mind. 41 RM Commando were now ordered to carry out the attack supported by the Divisional Artillery. This left inadequate time for planning. Inevitably, officers and men were weary after the distances covered and the bloody fighting during the previous twenty-four hours. Hastily it was agreed that the Divisional Artillery would lay down intense fire on the objective for eleven minutes; then the Commandos would advance.

Major John Edwards, second in command of 41 RM Commando, moved his unit forward from 'Commando Hill' through Piegolelle village, about 300 yards south of the 'Pimple'. As he reached the start line the artillery fire was brought down, not on the objective, but on Edwards and his men. The troops dashed for any cover they could find.

At that moment Captain John Parsons was leading his exhausted troop of Royal Marines towards Piegolelle. Within 100 yards of the village he found a 'shambles' as intense artillery fire was directed on the road and on the houses beyond. Among the Commandos 'strewn dead and wounded' in the roadway he recognized Major Edwards. A medical orderly was bending over him, but Edwards was mortally wounded.

The tragic mistake by the artillery had ruined any chances of success. Shaken, the Commandos were recalled to their former positions. But the order did not reach Parsons's rear troop and he continued leading his men forward in what he imagined was the general direction of the objective. Dropping into an olive grove he was met by the loathsome stench of dead bodies. The green and bloated corpses of Germans loomed grotesquely in the moonlight.

At the bottom of the valley two spurs ran at right angles. Branching left, he climbed for about a mile up a series of terraced slopes until, after two hours, he found himself close to the top of 'White Cross Hill'. As they advanced towards the summit a shattering burst of fire met the Commandos. Flattening themselves, they froze as tracer bullets whizzed over their heads into the valley below. Parsons could hear the enemy 'laughing and talking'. Creeping forward he organized his troop into a close assault position. Two scouts went ahead and reported back that the Germans were in two groups about fifty yards from them. Parsons whispered brief orders and his men swarmed on the machine gun nests. Commandos fell in the attack, but the nests were wiped out and the enemy survivors fled down a steep, densely wooded hill.

Reorganizing his troop, Parsons now set up a defensive position. It was not a moment too soon. German paratroopers, their faces painted green, their padded helmets and smocks heavily camouflaged, suddenly pounced on them. The Commandos repulsed attack after attack, yet each one took its inevitable toll. The *Fallschirmjäger* set the hedge in front of their position alight and as the Commandos sought desperately to get close to shoot at the enemy beyond the hedge one of them tumbled into the burning bushes. His comrades tried heroically to drag him clear, but were driven back by the heavy fire. One man was caught in a burst of tracer from the flank. Parsons saw the bullets 'ripping a deadly furrow in his back'.

All night the noise of shooting was heard at Altavilla. Small units of Colonel Tucker's paratroopers of the 504th temporarily lost touch with one another and the colonel was driven from his observation post on Hill 424.

The Panzergrenadier Captain Meitzel, without telephone contact, sent messages to the other companies through an ordnance officer. Meitzel's only outside contact was a wireless set. Crouching against the wall of the cemetery he sent his messages to the regiment.

Now, at dawn, the town and surrounding hill were enveloped in a milky fog. Meitzel decided that this was to his advantage. Under such natural cover a tireless breakdown gang repaired the telephone lines while at the same time Meitzel regrouped his men of the 11th Battalion Panzergrenadiers and transferred his HQ to the castle from which the Americans had been driven. When the sun broke through, dispelling the fog, he saw that the Americans had occupied the cemetery and his former command post in the chapel. 'Our artillery and two assault guns,' one of his sergeants, Kurt Finke, was to recall, 'gave them a warm welcome.'

At ten a.m. Meitzel received a report that the Americans were advancing towards the area of Padula. The reason was immediately clear to him. The Americans planned to cut off Altavilla, preparing the same fate for his Grenadiers that he had inflicted on them a few days before. He was determined to drive them back.

At the 36th HQ Walker found Tucker's messages from Altavilla alternating from favourable to pessimistic, according to the turn of events. He decided to discuss with General Ridgway, who had just been appointed deputy commander of the Sixth Corps by Clark, the increasing predicament of the paratroopers. To reinforce the paratroopers Ridgway suggested employing a battalion of the 18th Infantry, then decided instead to move the 3rd Battalion of the 504th to Albanella as a back-up force. Both artillery and navy guns would shell the area of Altavilla.

Of the German forces available, the rearguard regiment of the 26th Panzer, withdrawn from Calabria the night before, had arrived near Eboli. At the same time a regiment of the 1st Parachute Division from Apulia was near the beachhead. Vietinghoff might have used both of these reinforcements to help hold Altavilla. But Kesselring had given his reluctant consent to Vietinghoff to break off the battle, requesting only that he launch a last attack on the paratroopers.

At sunrise, in a field skirting the beach about a quarter of a mile from Salerno, below Montecorvino airfield, a group of 300 soldiers sat smoking and talking.

These men were part of Alexander's 1,500 reinforcements from Tripoli who had disembarked the night before. Among them were young draftees who were to see combat for the first time; the rest were veterans, battle-fatigued after arduous months in the desert campaign, with no stomach for further battle. They were badly needed by the exhausted battalions in Vietri, Piegolelle and Battipaglia, yet they had gathered on the beach, angry and bewildered, determined not to join with the 46th and 56th Divisions to which they had been assigned. The seeds of mutiny had been sown.

Prominent on their khaki uniforms were the insignia of their regiments: the Argyll and Southern Highlanders, the Durham Light Infantry and the Black Watch. Sergeant Joe Pettit was a Durham and immensely proud of it. Boarding *Charybdis* at Tripoli he believed he was going home to England on leave, and the prospect of seeing his family again made him forget the boring weeks of hospitalization at the port. Alamein was his bloody introduction to war, yet it was the sheer ferocity of the battle of the Mareth Line had stayed with him. The heroism of the troops of the 9th Durham Light Infantry gave him new pride as a 'DLI'. At the age of twenty he was promoted to sergeant, one of the youngest in the Eighth Army; he was one of the first men into Sicily with Montgomery, but on the seventh day he was wounded in the chest and thigh by fragments of an enemy grenade. A padre gave him the Last Rites as a medical officer tried to stop the bleeding. 'You'll be okay, son,' the medic whispered. 'It's not as bad as it looks.' In hospital he came to know scores of other front-line soldiers and found they were sustained by the same emotions of loyalty, comradeship and pride. Loyalty to their regiments was ingrained in each of them and sometimes carried with it even antagonism towards other regiments.

Six-foot Corporal Hugh Fraser had boarded the *Charybdis* with no thought of Italy in his mind. 'Once a Cameron, always a Cameron,' Fraser would boast; his brother William, also a Cameron, had been wounded in France. Regimental loyalty greatly appealed to Fraser, a single-minded young man; it was particularly strong among the Camerons and other Scots regiments comprising the 51st Division. The tall Cameron Highlander, Major General Douglas Wimberley, 'Big Tam' to his men, led the division. Fraser recalled Wimberley's advice, 'If wounded and separated from your own units, do not allow yourselves to get drafted to other battalions, but see that you come back to us.' Fraser had been hospitalized in Tripoli and on his recovery moved to 155 Transit Camp in the same area, joining some thousand veterans of the North African campaign who comforted themselves that they would soon be 'going home to Blighty'.

On the night before they sailed for Salerno the bugle had sounded in the camp. Some men were in bed, others getting ready for bed, and a few were returning from the town. NCOs and men turned out and fell in under the cool North African sky. It was then, Fraser recalled, that they were specifically told that they would be returning to their own units. Yet, a few hours later, on board the *Charybdis*, he was astonished to hear a voice announcing over the loudspeakers: 'You are going as reinforcements to Salerno.' Salerno? He had scarcely heard of the place.

At that moment Sergeant Pettit also heard the announcement. Around him men murmured angrily that they should have been told about Salerno before they sailed. 'It's a bloody trick!' one veteran shouted. 'We've been misled. We'll not fight in Salerno!' Simul-

(*above*) After the battle . . . one of the first British jeeps enters the ruined town of Battipaglia

(*below*) Smoking ruins of the tobacco factory near Battipaglia, an objective for which British troops fought fiercely, after the Germans had finally withdrawn

An American Ranger patrol moves out to make contact with the enemy above Maiori

taneously, the announcement was made on the three cruisers. The reaction among veterans of the 51st Division and the Tyne Tees 50th Division was the same – bitter disappointment and disillusionment. To Sergeant Wally Innes, on board *Scylla*, it was something else: a betrayal by his superior officers. Innes remembered the words of Montgomery: 'Always make sure you get back to your own units.' Montgomery had promised them that 'if they chased the Hun out of North Africa they could go back to England'. Innes had escaped death at Alamein. In Sicily the battle for the 400-foot-high Primo Sole bridge had been the grimmest of his experience. Soon afterwards he caught malaria and was flown to a field hospital in Tripoli. Separation from his battalion hurt him; to Innes, the DLI was a 'fighting family' that clung together with 'a fierce, unshakable pride'.

At 155 Transit Camp he had asked an officer, 'Are you sure we're going back to our unit, sir?'

'Quite sure,' the officer had reassured him.

'Then why are we being issued with rifles, sir? Our rifles are with our own units.'

Hearing the announcement over the ship's loudspeakers Private John McFarlane wasn't certain he had heard correctly. Turning to a Durham beside him, he asked, 'Are you sure he said Salerno?'

'I'm sure,' the man replied.

McFarlane, a fiery little Scot, was astonished. Since leaving the coal pits near Motherwell to make the army his career McFarlane had shown himself a good soldier. During the desperate fighting following the fall of Tobruk he worked himself to exhaustion as a stretcher bearer. The 50th Division made an heroic stand to hold the line, suffering over 8,000 casualties. During an enemy onslaught one of the gunners was trapped beneath his gun carriage. McFarlane heard calls for volunteers to help the injured man as the enemy continued their fire. The carriage had pinned the screaming gunner by the shoulder, pulping his arm; his chest and stomach were peppered with splinters. Unable to move him, McFarlane gave the soldier two morphine tablets. McFarlane returned to tell the padre, 'There's only one chance to save him. I'll have to take his arm off.' Borrowing a jack knife from a corporal he returned to the gun carriage and severed the remaining tendons of the trapped man's useless arm. Freeing him from the weight of the carriage he applied a shell dressing. It was not enough. He applied a second dressing and secured both in place with a towel. Then, grabbing the man by the heels, he pulled him slowly down the ridge out of range of the enemy guns. With the padre, he ministered to the dying man for an hour. But they could not save him, and they buried him in the desert.

McFarlane was recommended for decoration. He was told he would receive the Military Medal for gallantry from the King when he got back to Britain. Two days after landing in Sicily he was wounded in the left arm by a mortar bomb and evacuated to a hospital in Tripoli. Now, on this September morning on the beach at Salerno, even his Military Medal seemed unimportant. He sat brooding on how he had been deceived into believing he was sailing to Sicily to join the Durhams when all the time his officers knew he was bound for Salerno.

Missing from the large group on the beach was Private William White of the 51st. His suspicions had been aroused in the transit camp by reports of increasing numbers of casualties from the Italian mainland, suspicions which he voiced to his comrades. The Allies were 'obviously having a rough time at Salerno' and would need reinforcements. On the night before the three cruisers sailed White and another soldier left the camp to take a walk along the beach, determined not to board the ships. Returning to the almost-deserted camp the next morning they were confronted by an officer who asked where they had been all night.

White replied, 'Down on the beach – having a swim, sir.'

'You've missed the boat,' the officer retorted. 'Your men are on their way home.'

White did not believe him.

The dedicated Father Carucci felt the day of liberty had dawned for his patients. Kneeling in the square outside the Archbishop's house at the Duomo in Salerno the 87 men and women were blessed by the feeble Monterisi before setting out for Vietri, led by a young Salernitano bearing a large Red Cross flag. It was a curious, slow-moving procession that wended its way through the ruins of the city and up the steep coastal road to Vietri. Carucci, tall and conspicuous in his worn cassock, moved along the column, encouraging the patients, helping the nursing sisters.

At Vietri the column was met by the noise of a gun battle. Sadly, Carucci realized that his hopes of escaping with his patients from the war were illusory. Taking shelter in nearby houses, priest and sisters tried to calm the patients. When the firing died down they moved on. Beyond the town they rested and Carucci was offered a donkey and cart in which to transport his weaker patients and their belongings.

At ten a.m., his ammunition running low, Royal Marine Captain Parsons on 'White Cross Hill' sent a runner down towards the start line for supplies; and, if possible, reinforcements.

An hour later the troop's position was covered with a thick mortar smoke screen; Blissett had fired the screen to allow the depleted Marines to extricate themselves. By now Parsons had only seven men and his ammunition was almost expended. Under covering fire he led his survivors down the hill, carrying with them their wounded. On reaching the HQ of 2 Commando he reported to Colonel Jack Churchill. Churchill had worked all night at a blanket-covered table by the light of a guttering candle. Incredibly, he did not seem exhausted. He told Parsons that the fire that had caught his men at the start line and smashed the 41 RM Commando attack before it got under way had been mistakenly directed by British artillery.

This morning the Commandos were exchanging fire with the enemy in Piegolelle, but due to heavy casualties and dwindling ammunition on the German side the firing gradually decreased. The Commandos still occupied the same positions as the day before: 41 RM Commando on their hill, 2 Commando in and around Piegolelle. By this time, however, the Special Services Brigade HQ had been relieved of their responsibility for the sector of the line immediately north of Salerno and were now able to send a company of 4.2 mortars of the 83rd US Chemical Mortar Battalion, which was under their command, to reinforce 2 Commando. With their help, and using all their firepower, 2 Commando, urged on by Colonel Churchill, kept up a continuous mortar and machine gun fire on the enemy's positions.

Meanwhile at Pontecagnano an aide told General McCreery, 'Sir, your presence is urgently required at the beachhead.' He gave the general his first intimation of the mass disobedience by the troops from Tripoli.

This morning the spare Commander of the Tenth Corps had begun to feel easier about the 56th Division on the right, though he was still anxious about the 'very tired' battalions of the 46th around Salerno and Vietri where enemy opposition was strong. Now, expecting an enemy attack to cover the withdrawal and eager to keep the 7th Armoured Division fresh for the advance on Naples, he was relying heavily on Alexander's reinforcements from North Africa to assist his troops on the beachhead. He was puzzled by the news he had been given; he had never before encountered disobedience in any of his commands.

Accompanied by two HQ officers he was driven to a large field near the beach. As his jeep bumped across the field he saw groups of soldiers, sitting or standing about aimlessly. Rising to his full height in the jeep he spoke loudly so that all should hear him. 'I'm shocked to find you men here,' he told them. 'I had expected all of you to be with your new divisions by now. I can assure you that you are genuinely needed in these hard-pressed divisions.' He reminded them of their 'solemn duty' to the army and urged them to 'get up like men' and join the divisions to which they were now assigned.

From the body of the crowd came loud boos and catcalls. Raising his hand like a preacher, McCreery admitted a mistake had been made in not informing them they were bound for Salerno; it was a wrong decision and he promised to have it righted as early as possible. But the men only booed louder. One Durham shouted. 'Get us back to our units!' and another, 'We're not fighting for you, general!' Shocked at this outburst, McCreery became impassioned. 'I appeal to you all to change your minds before it's too late. You are aware of the consequences for mass disobedience like this. They are very serious indeed.'

Deliberately, he refrained from using the word 'mutiny' for fear of alienating these men further. As he stepped down from the jeep a small number of draftees responded to his appeal and moved away from the general body of the troops. But the majority was unmoved. To Sergeant Pettit it seemed that the general had said little except to admit that a mistake had been made. Corporal Fraser felt McCreery had not taken into account the essential factor of the men's regimental loyalty. Sergeant Innes was bitter that he had failed to recognize the men's feelings. Private McFarlane, angry at 'the betrayal of the men', vowed not to fire a shot at Salerno.

What was now clear was that the generals had a mutiny on their hands.

At noon Captain Meitzel gave his 6th Company the order to counterattack the enemy on Hill 424. It was, in his opinion, 'a very good attack' which the Americans were not expecting, providing him with an opportunity to withdraw his 5th and 7th companies to deploy them on the left wing of the 6th. Meitzel reckoned that the attack had been halted and that the town was now safe. At all times in the battle for Altavilla he had sought to be in front of the enemy and now, once again, he had achieved that position.

But at two o'clock he was surprised to receive orders from General Fries to withdraw his battalion and move north. He was unaware then that Vietinghoff's principal task was withdrawal and that, despite Kesselring's request, he had decided to commit no further reinforcements to the defence of Altavilla. Instead, Vietinghoff was preoccupied with Kesselring's cautionary advice to pay particular attention to his left flank around Salerno and Amalfi to ensure the success of the withdrawal. The defensive line must be held until the end of the month.

Just as Meitzel's troops began moving out the Allies launched a ruthless naval bombardment of the town. The Panzer withdrawal was the cue for the shelling to intensify. Meitzel would claim later that by this time 'there were no Germans in Altavilla'.

Only sporadic German fire was heard that morning as General Eisenhower came ashore on his first visit to the beachhead. The Supreme Commander arrived with Admiral Cunningham to view the front and discuss with Clark and the other commanders the progress of Avalanche.

Clark was in the operations room of his tent studying the maps in front of him, unaware of the trouble facing McCreery in the British sector of the beachhead. He was now convinced that the thirty-five-mile advance through rugged terrain towards Naples would be 'punishing'. Kesselring had clearly demonstrated in his Panzers' withdrawal from Calabria that he was master of the art of delaying tactics. At Salerno, though the German retreat seemed inevitable, Kesselring controlled the battle the way he wanted. Now, with staff officers in attendance, Clark accompanied Eisenhower and Cunningham to Dawley's Sixth Corps HQ at the tobacco warehouse, where they were joined by Walker and Ridgway. Walker found the atmosphere 'somewhat strained'.

Eisenhower greeted Dawley coolly and shook his hand without a smile. For a while he pored over the situation map. Then he turned to Dawley and asked, 'For God's sake, Mike, how did you ever get your troops into such a mess?'

Dawley's reaction was inconsistent. He made no effort to argue with Eisenhower, admitting that his men had 'run into trouble' in the Sele–Calore corridor. Walker was surprised. Why had Dawley made no attempt to explain that 'there was no mess'? He was about to interject that Dawley should not be held responsible for a 'mess that did not exist' when the Supreme Commander changed the subject. He could only assume that Eisenhower had decided to hold the Sixth Corps commander responsible for all that had gone wrong in the Sixth Corps sector. Running through his mind were incidents that might have prompted Eisenhower's affront to Dawley. He recalled his instructions from Dawley to move the 2nd Battalion of the 143rd to a position between the Sele and Calore Rivers. General Middleton had been present at that meeting and heard the instructions. Yet when Dawley indicated the front line of the area the battalion was to occupy, stating that the right flank of Middleton's 45th would be on the left of the battalion across the Sele, Middleton had made no comment. Walker had assumed the information he was given regarding the 45th Division was 'correct and reliable' and passed it on to his regimental and battalion commanders. In fact, the left flank of the 45th was two and half miles south-west of the point Dawley had indicated, and the result of that meeting and those instructions was the next day's disaster. Later, Walker admitted he should have been 'more cautious' and instructed his staff to ascertain the true location of the 45th. The professional ability of Dawley and Middleton was not in doubt. He felt, therefore, that all three of them were responsible for 'an unfortunate misunderstanding': Middleton and Dawley for passing on 'unverified information', himself for not having checked it out. Yet at the HQ meeting Eisenhower did not include him in the conversation.

After Eisenhower had left, Clark drove over to Albanella with Dawley, Walker and Ridgway to view the ground where an attack was planned by Ridgway's paratroopers. Walker rode in Ridgway's jeep, but on the return journey Clark asked him to join him and Dawley. En route to the tobacco warehouse Dawley began to argue with Clark about decisions he and Eisenhower had made. The argument became decidedly unfriendly. At one point Dawley shouted, 'You are just a pair of boy scouts!' Stung, Clark refused to speak to the Sixth Corps commander and sat in stony silence all the way back to the headquarters. After Dawley and Walker had got out of the jeep, Clark drove quickly away 'in a huff', according to Walker, who had received 'no instructions' and 'no criticism'.

This evening Dawley received a letter dated 16 September from the Fifth Army HQ:

> Dear General Dawley,
>
> As your Army Commander, I want to congratulate every officer and enlisted man in the Fifth Army on the accomplishment of their mission on landing on the western coast of Italy. All the more splendid is your achievement when it is realized that it was accomplished against determined German resistance at the beaches. Every foot of our advance has been contested.
>
> We have arrived at our critical objective; our beachhead is secure. Additional troops are landing every day, and we are here to stay. Not one foot of ground will be given up.
>
> General Montgomery's battle-proven Eighth English Army, our partner in the task of clearing the German forces out of Italy, is

advancing from the south and in a matter of hours its presence will be felt by the enemy. Side by side with this Eighth Army, the Fifth will advance to occupy Naples, Rome and the other cities to the north and to free Italy from German domination.

I am highly gratified by the efficient manner in which the US Sixth Corps and the British Tenth Corps have worked side by side in mutual support, each being proud to serve by the side of the other. Their performance has justified the confidence placed in them by the people of the United Nations. They know that we shall drive on relentlessly until our job is done.

I desire that the contents of this letter be communicated to all ranks of your command.

Sincerely yours,
Mark W. Clark,
Lieutenant General, USA,
Commanding.

The elated Dawley decided to send a copy of Clark's letter to the commanders of all units in his corps with the endorsement:

The receipt of this letter is a matter of intense satisfaction to me. To you who have made such a commendation possible belongs the credit.

F. J. Dawley,
Major General, US Army,
Commanding.

Eisenhower had not been told that soon after dawn General Ridgway had gone to Albanella and come close to death when American P-38s had bombed the forward positions. Colonel O'Neill, who had driven over with Ridgway, coded and transmitted a message to change the bomb release line. But the aircraft continued 'playing hell'. It took an hour for the message to be decoded. It had fallen into 'someone's hands who was not sure what it meant,' recalled O'Neill, 'and made no effort to find out'.

Other messages changed hands that evening. Prime Minister Churchill sent a personal message to Alexander: 'I am glad to feel you have taken a personal grip of the Avalanche position . . . I had, as you know, been worried about the rate of Avalanche build-up. It is great news that Montgomery expects to bring the Eighth Army into action today. It is right to use the battleships in the inshore squadron in view of favourable naval balance. Every good wish. Please continue to keep me informed. . . .'

In reply, Alexander assured the Prime Minister that, despite 'several strongish attacks' against the Tenth Corps in the north, the 'initiative is passing to us'. Fighting was still going on around Altavilla in the Sixth Corps sector, but the Fifth and Eighth Armies had joined hands. His immediate aim was to build up three strong fighting groups: the Fifth Army in the Salerno area, the Eighth Army in the centre, and the British Fifth Corps under the Eighth Army in the Taranto area. From these firm bases they could advance north, with the Fifth Army pivoting on the hills north-west of Salerno and securing the heights around Avellino. The Eighth Army would then take Potenza, the Fifth the port of Naples, and the Eighth the airfields at Foggia. Alexander did not wish to sound 'over-optimistic', but he told Churchill he was satisfied his troops would be able to carry out these operations according to plan. He referred to the arrival of 1,500 troops from the transit camp in Tripoli; these would reinforce the Tenth Corps. He had not heard of the mutiny on the beaches.

In his diary entry Dawley wrote: 'Eisenhower. To reinforce 504th at Altavilla.'

It was almost dark when Father Carucci and his bedraggled column reached Maiori. They had made slow progress along the ten miles of coast road from Vietri. Allied troops had offered them cigarettes and chocolate from their rations, but Carucci knew his patients must have a night's rest. At the bend in the road leading into the town a Ranger roadblock halted their progress. An officer raised his hand to stop them. They could go no further, he said, and must return to Salerno.

Carucci was desperate, scarcely knowing what to do next. He pleaded with the American to allow them to move into the town. The officer insisted they could not move further without the necessary permit from Colonel Lane. Reluctantly, he agreed to send a GI by jeep to Salerno to seek the necessary authorization; but it was now the time of curfew.

The chaplain explained to the patients that they must return the way they had come. One of the patients, however, knew of a large cave near the beach. If they could make their way down the cliff they would have some shelter for the night. Carucci shrugged in agreement. He was beyond argument.

Saturday, 18 September.

At nine a.m. the first convoy of General Lucian Truscott's 3rd Infantry Division began unloading on the beaches before moving to an assembly area north of the Sele River.

The handsome, peppery Truscott, who in 1941 had been so impressed by the British Commandos that he received approval from General Marshall to establish the Rangers under Darby, now arrived at Fifth Army headquarters to discuss plans for his division which had fought well in Sicily.

It was acknowledged that the Germans were withdrawing and the Allied positions had been greatly improved by the advance of Middleton's 45th Division north of the Sele. The army plan appeared simple. The Sixth Corps, with the 45th and the 3rd Divisions abreast, would advance north through the mountains while the Tenth Corps would attack northwards from Salerno, through the passes where the Rangers were keeping a foothold, to gain the Naples plain. An armoured division would then pass through the plain to capture Naples and drive the enemy north of the Volturno.

Truscott learned that while the Germans were already preparing defences along the line of the Volturno river, they were expected to hold the difficult mountain terrain around Salerno as long as possible. They needed time to destroy the port of Naples.

Vietinghoff's moods had swung during the past few days from euphoria to frustration. Today he received a fillip with a message from the Führer that he was to be promoted to *Generaloberst* and given command over the army in northern Italy while Rommel was hospitalized with appendicitis.

He issued his order of the day to the troops of the Tenth Army, praising them for their part in the battle of Salerno. He claimed 5,000 Allied prisoners. 'The success has been ours,' he announced with pride. 'Once again German soldiers have proven their superiority over the enemy.' He was particularly pleased with the *Luftwaffe*'s performance. With few aircraft and outdated equipment they had inflicted terrible damage on the Allies. Not since the German air attacks on Malta in 1942 were so many missions flown as during the first days of the Allied invasion. Without achieving victory they had denied the enemy a swift entry to Naples. The battle had been 'at least a partial success'.

At Rastenburg Hitler was satisfied that the 88s and the glider bombs had wrought havoc on the invasion forces. He believed the Americans had been 'thrashed'. Jodl told him that more than nine-tenths of the prisoners who had surrendered were Americans; only the paratroopers were 'usable', the 'rest surrender the moment the position is hopeless' and 'never attack as long as a single gun is left firing from German lines'. Jodl's boast prompted Hitler to write off the threat of an Allied invasion elsewhere. 'No more invasions for them! They are much too cowardly for that! They only managed the one at Salerno because the Italians gave their blessing.'

Kesselring, however, felt that Hitler's heart was not in the Italian campaign, a fact borne out by his refusal to give priority to the despatch of reinforcements to the Naples area. To Kesselring, the Führer was more committed to the Russian front than to the success of his troops at Salerno. In the circumstances, he shared Vietinghoff's view that the German forces had performed heroically at Salerno against superior air, sea and ground forces. Now Naples was threatened. Fighting was already taking place around Castellammare, not fifteen miles south of the city, and Berlin Radio was admitting 'line-shortening operations' and referring for the first time to 'an imminent battle for Naples'. The city was reported to be 'in ruins from enemy bombing'. But it remained a strategic port and Kesselring would not abandon it easily.

In the late afternoon Scots Guardsman John Weir saw flames shooting from the grey buildings of the tobacco factory followed by swirls of thick, black smoke rising skywards. It had taken 10,000 Allied bombs to finally destroy the factory and its defences.

Weir felt an intense relief. The factory held bitter memories for him; he had lost many of his comrades here. Now, as they moved forward, enemy resistance was faltering. By now the forward elements of the 7th Armoured Division had arrived on the beaches and were making their presence felt among the exhausted Germans. Only sporadic firing came from the factory as the enemy took up new positions well behind the blazing buildings.

At the same time a Bren section of the Coldstream Guards was ordered to protect their right flank as they moved forward with orders to shoot on sight any Panzers trying to escape in the smokescreen. After the din of battle it was uncannily quiet now as the troops pushed cautiously forward for fear of booby traps. At that moment the Coldstream commander, Lieutenant Christopher Bulteel, gallantly decided to hold back, leaving the Scots Guards to go forward to make the official capture of the factory. Coughing and choking from the dense smoke, Weir and the Guardsmen darted through the smaller buildings encircling the main factory, encountering no resistance. As dusk closed in the flames died down, leaving only a burned-out shell. The enemy guns were silent as they set up new positions a mile behind the factory.

Meanwhile the Coldstream Guards moved on towards Battipaglia, climbing over ridges to avoid the dead bodies of British and German troops. Dead buffalo lay bloated in the fields. Wrecked tanks still smouldered. Trees were stripped of their foliage and fallen fruit lay rotten on the ground. In the town the air was foul with the stench of death. Only a handful of Germans remained, and they offered little resistance.

The nine-day nightmare was ended.

Throughout the day 2 Commando had continued to pound the 'Pimple' with mortar and machine gun fire. By nightfall return fire had ceased. 41 RM Commando was withdrawn some four hundred yards from their hill positions and replaced by the Ox and Bucks. During the night both Commandos were relieved and withdrawn into reserve at Mercatello where they again came under the command of the Special Services Brigade HQ. Fresh troops would find the 'Pimple' deserted, but strewn with enemy dead.

As on other nights, Colonel Churchill asked his batman Stretton for his pipes with their silver chanter. For half an hour he marched up and down, infuriating some of his troops, enthralling others, with the melodies he loved, 'The Road to the Isles' and 'Will Ye Nae Come Back Again?'

'Mad Jack,' the troops muttered.

For the Commandos the battle was over. Salerno had been a costly operation. They had lost 17 officers and 54 other ranks killed; 15 officers and 225 other ranks were wounded, one officer and 59 other ranks were missing. The total of 367 represented almost half the force that had landed on 9 September on the beach at Vietri. Yet in those nine days their achievement was remarkable. They had inflicted considerable casualties on the enemy, defended the La Molina Pass against repeated attacks by superior forces, and saved a critical situation at Piegolelle, turning it to the advantage of the Allies.

To most Commandos the error made at Salerno was to deploy their élite troops, trained primarily as an attack force, to fight a defensive battle. It was a situation foreign to them, and the real victory was in holding their positions.

To one Commando in retrospect, 'It was a bungled operation and a bad operation. We should have been out before the 13th, making an attack elsewhere. It wasn't that they forgot to take us out – they *couldn't* take us out. It was a badly conceived operation signalled to the Germans all the way.'

Sunday, 19 September.

During the morning the Coldstream Guards were transported from the battered town of Battipaglia to Salerno. They passed through city streets littered with wrecked vehicles. Telephone lines lay entangled, electric cables festooned blitzed buildings. The silence was all-pervading. Marching through the deserted streets the Guards took over from the Durhams, the Foresters and the Leicesters.

By now most of the German front line units had withdrawn to new positions in the steep hills above the city. One Panzer officer recalled: 'One last look at the Gulf. Down there we could still see, on the right in the mist, the towers of Salerno, the gleaming grey strip of Montecorvino in the centre, the asphalt highway and the railway line with a loop near Battipaglia, Eboli down in the plain – and, in the distance, the sea. A warm wind blew up from the shore, taking no heed of the fresh graves lying in the shade of the olive groves.'

During the afternoon an American GI from the 45th Division came on the dead body of a German soldier near Eboli, still clasping a letter he was writing when a sniper's bullet killed him: 'You will be amazed, dear wife, to read about our bitter fighting in the Eboli sector. Casualties are ever increasing to add to the terror. The enemy air forces are bombing us relentlessly and atrociously. With all that, an uncanny and continual artillery fire is scoring hits. Our fight against the Anglo-Americans requires more strength from us than our fight against the Russians, and many of us are longing to get back to Russia – even longing for conditions as they were at Stalingrad.'

Since landing with the Reserve 505th Parachute Infantry Colonel James Gavin, responsible for the training and organization of the American first parachute platoon, had remained at Paestum. He reported to General Dawley, but it seemed to him the general had not anticipated the intensity of the early days' fighting and his disorganized command was unprepared when the fighting reached its bitterest point. Dawley appeared to be 'a man doing all a man could in the circumstances'. But he understood that Clark had now taken personal command and managed to stabilize the Sixth Corps' position.

Clark had meanwhile been trying to contact the 509th Parachute Regiment. It seemed to him that the Avellino drop to disrupt enemy communications behind the lines was proving 'suicidal'. He was not to know that individual units and troopers, like Nunn and Fisco, had been operating for five days behind enemy lines.

Only a few hundred paratroopers had returned to the Allied lines, and scores were wounded. Yet in some areas the mission was successful; paratroopers had blown up bridges and cut communications, causing the Germans to commit combat units against them. Lieutenant Rocholl had led three further patrols on foot. On each patrol he enlisted four men from his unit. Armed with automatic rifles, revolvers and hand grenades, with rags wrapped around their boots – they did not have rubber-soled boots like the Americans – they brought in six more prisoners, 'beating them at their own game'.

In his diary he wrote: 'Every time we were successful.' But success for Rocholl was over. During the day he was shot by a marauding group of the 509th. His diary, found later on his body, was to provide the Allies with one of the most revealing enemy reports of the Salerno campaign.

Meanwhile, Clark had been unable to contact the 509th since the night of its drop behind the lines. After several days of fruitless attempts to establish radio contact, he gave up the battalion as 'lost to enemy action'.

Late at night General Truscott was called to the Sixth Corps command post to confer with Dawley about plans for the Corps' advance. Driving his jeep through the countryside towards the tobacco warehouse with only blue sidelights showing, he was halted by a Corps MP. 'Put out that cigarette!' he was told forcefully.

Inside the command post he was amazed to find the rooms in total darkness. Through the gloom he could make out vague figures grouped in corners. An aide escorted him to a far corner where, sitting in the dark, surrounded by a handful of staff officers, he found Dawley. The Corps commander was facing what Truscott eventually identified as a map board leaning against the wall. Because there were many large windows in the warehouse which could not be adequately covered, Dawley had forbidden all lights, even cigarettes. Using a pencil flashlight the general illuminated the map to indicate the routes for the advance of the 45th and 3rd Infantry Divisions and the telephone lines with which they could maintain contact with each other and with the British.

To Truscott it was a strange encounter. Although the *Luftwaffe* had been active over the beachhead the danger from air attack at this stage of the operation hardly seemed sufficient to warrant such bizarre protective measures which precluded 'normal and efficient functioning of command and staff'.

When his eyes became accustomed to the darkness he saw that Dawley's face was drawn with strain. He had never seen a commander under such pressure.

XXV
'My Uncomfortable Task . . .'

Monday, 20 September

As Eisenhower had feared privately for some time, the pressures of command had gradually taken their toll of General Dawley. Overworked, exhausted, without sleep, he was intolerably edgy. The episode on the beaches when he had recoiled at the sight of the dead GIs had left its mark. He was a changed man from the eager general who had come ashore shortly after the landings. When Clark arrived at his HQ this morning the Sixth Corps commander greeted him as warmly as he could; the previous day's congratulatory letter had raised his spirits perhaps too highly.

In spite of Eisenhower's impatience, Clark had put off this moment as long as possible. Now he came quickly to the point. 'It's my uncomfortable task to inform you personally that I am relieving you of your command of the Sixth Corps.'

The words drained the colour from Dawley's face. He was stunned. What Clark was saying was as unexpected as it was incomprehensible. Had something gone terribly wrong? He accepted that Clark could be arrogant and vain, but no one could accuse him of hypocrisy or betrayal. Since the landings he believed their relationship had been good; if in recent days strain had shown he attributed this to the rigours of the battle. Searching desperately to find a reason he hardly heard Clark say that he was to be replaced by General John Lucas. During the training for Avalanche Dawley had come to the attention of Generals Marshall and McNair, and Clark at that stage had regarded him as 'vigorous and aggressive'. Yet Dawley had not expected to assume command of operations ashore until after the beachhead was securely established. Before the landings Clark had directed him explicitly to stay aboard ship until D-Day plus 2; he reckoned that the 36th Division was already 'overloaded with commanders'. When on D-Day he was instructed to take command Dawley was unprepared. His staff was scattered, his headquarters and communications scheduled for later unloading. He should perhaps have guessed the turn events were to take when Clark began to devote his personal attention to the affairs of the Sixth Corps. It was Clark who had instructed Dawley to lighten his forces on the right to strengthen those on the left; it was Clark who had told him his troop dispositions resembled 'a hotch-potch of units', and it was Clark who was to note that under the stress of battle Dawley had become 'increasingly nervous and shaky'. On his first visit to the Sixth Corps sector Alexander had remarked that Dawley compared unfavourably with McCreery. 'His briefings of the situation disappoint me,' he told Clark. 'He seems to me to be losing his grip on affairs'. Earlier, Eisenhower had predicted that 'the pressure at the beachhead may be too much for him'.

By now Dawley had already lost his Chief of Staff, Colonel Gibson, who had been invalided to the United States suffering from what was reported to be 'a stroke resulting from the strain of the battle'. Dawley had described Gibson's physical condition as 'rapidly deteriorating, necessitating hospitalization'.

Before driving away in his jeep Clark, somewhat awkwardly, handed Dawley the official letter from Fifth Army HQ:

20 September 1943.

AG 2 10.3-A.
Subject: Orders.
TO: Major General Ernest J. Dawley, 02843, USA.

You are relieved effective this date from duty as Commanding General of VI Corps, and will report to the Commander in Chief, Allied Force Headquarters, for further instructions. Travel by m/a is auth.

By command of Lieutenant General Clark.

M.F. Grant,
Colonel, H.G.D.,
Adjutant General.

General Truscott's advance was timed for eleven a.m. During the previous evening a reconnaissance patrol had been sent to make contact with the enemy on the road leading north from Battipaglia towards Acerno in the craggy mountains some four miles from Montecorvino. Captain Richard Savaresy moved out at midnight with two platoons, and a few hours later, near a fork in the road, one platoon attacked and killed a German detachment. Savaresy's men were the first of the 3rd US Infantry Division to 'draw blood' in the campaign.

Truscott was about to take his men on the road when a driver pulled into his CP with a note from General Dawley. The scribbled handwriting read: 'Dear Truscott – Sorry I will not be with you. I am leaving Corps. Sincerely, Dawley.' This was Truscott's first intimation that something was amiss. But his orders were to advance at 1100 hours and he could not delay. He believed his 3rd Division, fresh from Sicily, were ready for the task ahead. They were acquainted with German delaying tactics and the technique of moving and fighting in the mountains, and were prepared for the worst. Truscott provided them with a pack train to supply the infantry operating in difficult terrain, even a pack battery to provide artillery support, and a troop of mounted infantrymen to expedite the reconnaissance of difficult mountain areas. It was an unusual spectacle in the Sixth Corps sector.

Taking the one road forward they entered the high craggy country of the Apennines on the right of Battipaglia, following the course of the Tusciano, at this point a mountain stream, north to Acerno and Montella. About twenty miles north of the town the road joined Highway 7, near Montemarano, which was to be their route northwest for a dozen miles to Avellino. From Avellino one road led west over a divide to the Naples plain and along the mountains to the Volturno river at Caserta, another north to the junction of the Calore and Volturno rivers, also close to Caserta. This would be the zone of operations for the Division. Truscott saw how 'enormously difficult' was the terrain with narrow valleys and mountains rising to more than 5,000 feet. There would be many places where even pack mules could not climb, where supplies would have to be carried on men's backs. But first he must move artillery and supplies forward by the only road leading north through Acerno, a road that offered the enemy all too many opportunities for demolitions to delay his advance.

Meanwhile, in the vital Chiunzi Pass, Darby's Rangers were still, in the words of their commander, 'fighting without rest or relief and always short of food and water'. Stretched thin, despite British and American reinforcements, the Rangers worked in squads and platoons, bunking down in blitzed farm houses and hillside caves or digging shallow foxholes with knives and bayonets and tin cans.

For almost ten days Sergeant Schrader's platoon had been stalking a *Nebelwerfer* mortar firing at intervals of half an hour to an hour. This morning they spotted the elusive mortar in a haystack, the nozzle pointed upwards so that it looked like a pole. The Rangers called in 'half a dozen WPs' and burned off the gun and its crew with white phosphorus. The barrage had been called up from 'Fort Schuster' where Lieut. Colonel Darby and his executive officer Herman Dammer had been joined by a battalion of the 143rd Infantry under Walker's son, Lieut. Colonel Fred Walker, Jr. The previous night US war correspondent Richard Tregaskis had made his way up to the shell-torn command post from which Darby was 'roughing up the Heinies'. After the hills around Altavilla, Tregaskis was surprised by these pinnacles of dark rock above the Chiunzi Pass. This was, as photographer Robert Capa remarked, 'a place for fighting'. During the night the three-foot wall of the command post had rocked with the force of shelling in the pass and along the surrounding heights from the German 88s.

Away from the Chiunzi, Rangers continued to probe the Sorrento peninsula, sending patrols down to the coast. One group, ordered down by Major Roy Murray, entered Castellammare and strolled through its large squares and leafy gardens in their stained Ranger uniforms. Defiantly they boarded a tramcar and rode a few blocks before stepping off to buy themselves ice-cream. Although the Germans were in the town, nobody seemed surprised to see these Americans. They returned to Murray to report the position of anti-aircraft guns and that 'the ice cream was good'.

At his 46th Division regimental aid post on the British beaches medical officer Captain Rankin was approached by Sergeant Lauderdale. 'There's a rumour, sir, of trouble at the beaches with the troops from Tripoli. What do you think we should do?' DLIs, he reported, were among those disobeying orders. 'That's different,' Rankin said. 'We must do something to help them.'

With Lauderdale and a Corporal Jones, Rankin walked the mile to the beach. From the hills came the sound of German 88s.

In a field skirting the beach he saw a 'milling crowd of men' and instructed his sergeant and corporal to seek out the DLIs to ascertain their problems. Moving through the crowd he stopped beside a group of Durhams, and quickly concluded that they did not wish to join either the 46th or 56th Divisions; they just wanted to get back to their own regiments. A man with a white bandage around his forehead grumbled, 'It's a conspiracy, sir.' Some of the men were clearly unfit for combat, others were bewildered and were relying on their NCOs for directions. He tried to persuade the disgruntled Durhams to change their minds and disassociate themselves from the rebels.

Eventually about a dozen men agreed to go with him. The others would not be moved.

Rankin found it difficult to sympathize with them in the light of his own experience. He had been attached to the 6th Durham Light Infantry, but had been drafted into the 18th, which comprised remnants of the 6th and 9th Battalions. He did, however, feel that the men should have been informed by their officers that they were sailing for Salerno. This would have ruled out any confusion, even if it did not entirely excuse their subsequent behaviour. Excessive loyalty was understandable, deliberate refusal to fight when ordered amounted to mutiny. Under military law the men in this field were guilty of disobedience, a disobedience he did not expect from the Durhams, who to him were 'the finest fighting men in the British Army'.

The officers and men of 2 Commando had spent the night on the beach, having been relieved at Piegolelle and brought down to Mercatello. This morning Captain Gordon-Hemming was surprised to meet a padre who had been at school with him, Father Nicholas Holman, a Benedictine monk. 'What about a Mass?' he asked him.

Holman put up a portable table near the beach and Hemming asked Colonel Churchill to spread the word among the men that 'anybody who wants can come to Mass'. Many of the Commandos gathered round the makeshift altar in an almond grove. 'Most of the men were not Roman Catholics,' Hemming recalled. 'But they were saying, "Thank God I'm still alive".'

In the Sixth Corps sector north of Paestum Major Edmund Ball had gone again to the chapel in the quadrangle at the tobacco warehouse, where, at the rear, a large open field had been turned into a graveyard for the bodies of men killed in combat. Leaving the service Ball and the other members of the congregation avoided looking in the direction of this cemetery with its multiplying rows of corpses. The field was hidden from sight by a fence and canvas covering, but it was so close that it was 'impossible to avoid or forget it'. A major of the Engineers remarked sarcastically to Ball, 'With the Army's usual efficiency they've placed the graveyard, the latrines and the kitchen all in the same area – for the convenience of the flies.' Ball found it shocking to watch the trucks coming back from the front lines carrying bodies 'stacked like cordwood'. A bulldozer would scoop out a long trench about four feet deep, then prisoners or civilians would dig individual graves about two feet deep and a few feet apart in the bottom of the trench. The bodies, identified as carefully as possible, were wrapped in bedrolls or blankets and placed in the graves, with a white cross at the head, with an identification tag tacked to it if it could be found. Then the long trench was covered over. Before the landings each officer and other rank had been assigned a bed roll. When Ball saw how the rolls were used, to pull over a body like a sack and then tie with a piece of cord at the opening, he threw his away.

During the afternoon orders were received to move forward. Ball quickly packed his equipment and moved out with a convoy of vehicles through the hills towards Eboli. Riding into the foothills he looked back towards the beach, the scene of the landings, and wondered: *How did we survive?* From the vantage point of these hills the Germans had both 'dominating positions and perfect observation posts' for all the Allied actions.

A second burial site was required by Chaplain McCombie near Altavilla. Tucker and his men had regained the town at some cost. But to correspondent Richard Tregaskis the 'traditional verbiage which is supposed to tell all about a battle conveys nothing'; it certainly conveyed little of the blood and courage and the will to win on the nameless hills around Altavilla. A pitiful group of paratroopers, without food or water, had returned to Paestum from the Altavilla battle area, and Tregaskis had seen one of Colonel Tucker's officers, who had gone to seek help for his men, riddled to death by the Panzers.

'What a spot Jerry had from up here,' a Sixth Corps officer remarked. 'He could see the fillings in our teeth.'

Relentlessly pounded for days by navy guns, air force bombs, artillery and small arms fire, Altavilla was now occupied, for the third time, by the Americans. Slowly the townspeople were emerging from cellars and shelters. Although the Americans had taken the town the previous day the Italians had not dared to show themselves until now. For nine days they had listened to the crossfire and the sound of Allied and German patrols battling over their heads. Almost a hundred civilians were dead, some from hunger. Not daring to venture out in search of food they had remained hidden. A few had chickens or pigs and had killed them when food ran out; many had survived on cactus pears. Now they poked among the rubble for bodies, some weeping, some shellshocked. Looking down on the battered main square was the granite statue of an Italian soldier, a monument to the town's dead in World War One.

McCombie selected the second burial site near the town. Many bodies had to be buried without delay; he noted that 'the stench was nauseating'. The 141st searched the Altavilla area, the 142nd and 143rd Persano and the area between the Sele and Calore rivers.

The threat of a full-scale mutiny had not receded. For the first time since the invasion grey clouds rolled across the sky, matching the bleak mood of the three hundred men in the field close to the beaches. During the afternoon they formed up on parade as an officer made a roll call. Captain A. G. Lee of the 1st York and Lancaster Regiment was known to the men from his days at the transit camp in Tripoli; he had been wounded in the North African campaign and was still having daily dressings applied to his wound. He was as unfit for combat as many of the men drawn up on parade before him. At Tripoli Lee had been ordered not to convey the truth about their destination to the men, an order made for security reasons. He knew they were going to Salerno and not to their units. Privately he sympathized with the draftees, but as an officer he had a duty to perform.

The men were divided into two groups, one from the Durham Light Infantry, the other mainly from the Scottish Regiments. Surrounding them were armed guards spaced ten yards apart. As Lee climbed onto a jeep to address the Durhams a sullen silence fell on the crowd. Raising his voice, the officer read them Section 7 of the Army Act: 'Every person subject to military law who joins in, or does not use his utmost endeavours, to suppress any mutiny or sedition shall, on conviction by court-martial, be liable to suffer death . . .' He reinforced his sombre warning with an extract from the Manual of Military Law explaining what was meant by mutiny. Then he gave the order, 'Pick up your kits. Fall in on the road – and march off to the 46th Divisional area'.

A number of men separated themselves from the main body and moved towards the road adjacent to the field. But most stood firm. Lee again ordered, 'Pick up your kits. Fall in on the road – and march off to the 46th and 56th Divisional area.'

This time about two dozen men obeyed his order. Sergeant Pettit, standing close to the jeep, thought that Lee deliberately addressed his words to the NCOs, but neither he nor Sergeant Innes nor the third Durham, Sergeant Middleton, obeyed. Lee raised his voice to a higher pitch and gave the order for the third and final time. Slowly, more than twenty-five men moved towards the road. There remained now from the Durhams three sergeants, four corporals, seven lance-corporals and sixty-one private soldiers, including two who had won the Military Medal. Lee ordered the men to be disarmed and placed under arrest. He repeated the same procedure with the men from other regiments, with one difference; an officer of the Cameron Highlanders urged the Scots in the group to obey the order.

Standing in the centre of the crowd Corporal Fraser had listened intently to the words of the order, noting the words 'mutiny' and 'death'. Such words should have disturbed the young Cameron, but this afternoon he was indifferent to their implications. Although aware of the gravity of his actions, he was more determined than before to see them through. To fall out with his Camerons now would make 'a mockery of his principles'. He made no attempt to sway the opinions of those who stood beside him, looking calmly on as soldiers from his regiment obeyed. This time, after the order had been given, 118 soldiers stood fast. They included a lance-corporal and 22 privates of the Queen's Own Cameron Highlanders, 23 privates of the Seaforth Highlanders, 2 lance-corporals and 14 privates of the Gordon Highlanders, 2 privates of the Black Watch and the Cameronians, 23 privates of the East Yorkshire Regiment, a private of the Dorset Regiment, and a sapper of the Royal Engineers.

In all, 193 men were marched from the parade under arrest.

Suddenly, on the road, a loud explosion rocked the tail of the column. As the men made to scatter an officer pulled the revolver from his holster, an action resented by the prisoners. Further along they were herded into a PoW cage measuring 30 by 40 yards and surrounded by barbed wire, with slit trenches inadequate for the numbers. Guarding the cage were Italian servicemen. Close by was a German PoW cage. Sergeant Pettit felt humiliated. A blond German shouted across, 'Cowards! Deserters!' It was a bitter blow to British pride. Corporal Fraser decided to ignore the taunts. He considered himself neither coward nor deserter; he was simply sticking to his principles and placing regimental loyalty above all else.

Private McFarlane had been knocked unconscious by the blast. When he came to he was lying in a first aid tent. Beside him on another bed lay one of the guards. He looked to be dead.

When General Walker returned from his inspection of the battle area he found a note on his desk from Dawley: 'Goodbye to you and your fine Division. Mike'.

Puzzled, Walker read the note again. He could only assume that Dawley had been relieved of his command, and this distressed him. In his view Eisenhower and Clark would find it difficult to justify this sacking. It seemed to Walker a controversial decision, 'perhaps the most provocative of the Avalanche campaign'. He wondered if the Allies were deliberately trying to make a scapegoat of Dawley. Although aware that relations between Clark and Dawley had been strained in recent days, this surely did not justify the dismissal of a commander of Dawley's stature? He had come to admire 'Mike' Dawley, whose style was different to Clark's. Whereas Clark tended to place a distance between himself and his subordinates and rarely, if ever, asked their advice, Dawley, on the other hand, relied on the people around him and had welcomed suggestions from Walker and Middleton. There had been tactical errors of a 'minor nature' by the troops under Dawley's command, yet Fred Walker felt himself partly responsible for these errors. He could only assume that the defeat in the Sele–Calore corridor had motivated Eisenhower and Clark to act as they did. It was later suggested that Walker was upset by Clark's replacement of Dawley by General Lucas, accusing Clark of reneging on a promise made to him that if the command fell vacant he would get it. Clark, who referred to Dawley as 'my friend', was to say, 'So far as Lucas taking the Sixth Corps is concerned, Walker was never under consideration for the job'.

This afternoon Dawley called his staff to his HQ to break the news of his sacking. Almost in a whisper he introduced Lucas as 'my successor and best friend'. An aide wrote in his diary: 'God, I hope the truth comes out about this show. A blow to all of us. I can't say enough against Fifth Army, "the greatest show on earth", nor can I say enough for General Dawley who won this battle of the beachhead. Everyone had been talking about his second star, too.'

Dawley's entry in his diary read simply: 'Monday 20th: Relieved'.

Tuesday, 21 September.

At his headquarters during this morning Clark received the first of the 'censorship guidance' instructions which would in future arrive daily from 15th Army HQ. These instructions laid down broad outlines for daily communiques, specifying which towns and villages might be mentioned and indicating the general line to be followed 'for security reasons'. They reflected political factors, particularly relating to the units of varying nationalities which Clark had collected into his army group. Clark was unhappy about these instructions. His annoyance erupted into anger when the Fifth Army public relations officer, Lieut. Colonel Kenneth Clark, showed him a cable from AFHQ: FIRST, PLAY UP EIGHTH ARMY PROGRESS HENCEFORTH + SECOND, FIFTH ARMY IS PUSHING ENEMY BACK ON HIS RIGHT FLANK + 'AMERICAN' MAY BE MENTIONED + THERE SHOULD BE NO SUGGESTION ENEMY HAS MADE HIS GETAWAY.

The idea that the role of the Fifth Army should be played down and priority given to the exploits of the Eighth Army infuriated Clark. Had not his Fifth weathered the crisis without any help from the

Eighth? Had not his men endured a most bruising battle and emerged victorious? He considered it ridiculous at this point to differentiate between the two armies, particularly now that both were to combine for the assault on Naples.

At his Moorish villa outside Algiers General Eisenhower was heartened to learn that the drive for Naples and the airfields at Foggia was under way. At last the British Tenth Corps was nearing the high ground surrounding the beachhead which the German artillery had used to such devastating advantage. At the same time the Sixth Corps had made a firm link-up both with the Tenth Corps and Eighth Army, which, in turn, had joined with the British Fifth Corps from Taranto. The Allies were now forming a continuous line across Italy, though the losses had been unevenly distributed – Clark had suffered some 14,000 casualties to Montgomery's 600. Even now the Supreme Commander was receiving reports at his headquarters that detachments of motorized German infantry were dug in on important hillsides forcing his army to make wide, time-consuming envelopments every mile of the way, harassed by enemy artillery and machine gun nests.

At this time General Truscott's 30th Infantry was meeting the first of the big German demolitions some twelve miles north of Battipaglia. Two miles south of Acerno the Germans had blown a stone arch bridge, leaving a yawning gap of more than sixty feet. From emplacements in the hills to the east their riflemen, machine guns and mortars, supported by artillery fire in the town, were covering the approach to the bridge. The heavy firing made it clear to Truscott that the enemy would not give up Acerno without a fight.

It would be nightfall before other battalions could make their way over the mountains to the east to cut the road from Acerno and take up positions from which to attack the town from the south. Truscott had also sent a battalion of the 7th Infantry with mule transport into the mountains above Montemarano; they were to follow the paths across the ridges to cut the road north of Acerno in the hope of blocking the Germans' retreat.

Wednesday, 22 September.

In a mood compounded of 'nostalgia and hope' correspondent Lionel Shapiro made his final tour of the beachhead. Enemy pillboxes strewn with lacerated gun barrels in the battered town of Paestum looked like ruins from another war. He stopped his jeep to view the American graveyard with its hundreds of makeshift crosses, then drove on, past the forest by the Sele where he had spent the tortured night of the corridor crisis. A few miles further north, Battipaglia was a grey, deserted ruin, 'no longer a town'. He moved on to Eboli where he saw the evidence of a terrible bombardment. The navy guns had levelled every tree in sight. He began to understand why the Germans had failed to exploit their counter-attack: behind them was only death and destruction.

Allied troops were now trudging along roads filled with rolling armoured cars and trucks. Before leaving Shapiro had filed his last report from Salerno, referring to 'the combined American–British Fifth Army moving forward in a vast co-ordinated offensive all along the bridgehead front'. His report continued: 'Thrusting from Salerno town and the newly gained points of Battipaglia and Altavilla, the Allies, heavily reinforced by powerful new units, smashed forward against opposition of varying strength. The toughest fighting is in the hills north of Salerno, where the Germans are making a desperate stand for the Naples plain. Allied formations advancing from Battipaglia and Altavilla have met less opposition, and have regained contact with enemy outposts north-east of the bridgehead'.

He wondered when they would reach Naples.

Kesselring's strategy was becoming clear. He was endeavouring to stretch five or six divisions across a mountain defence of some 110 miles along a line drawn from Naples through Benevento to Foggia. It was a withdrawal that suggested he planned to defend the Potenza area only with rearguards. Clark recognized the merit in this plan. In the mountains the Panzers could be used economically and would retain all the advantages. But there were dangers, too. The Allies would be able to bring weight to bear on either flank, or both, and the Eighth Army, operating inland, might drive a wedge through the centre of the line and turn it. However, Clark accepted that Kesselring was in a position to conduct a lengthy delaying action.

By dusk this evening the Allied line ran from the Sorrento peninsula through Potenza to Bari on the Adriatic coast. On the peninsula the Allies now had a commanding position in the heights four miles from Amalfi and their artillery could command the shore of the Gulf of Naples around Castellammare and Torre Annunziata. However, the terrain around Salerno was as difficult as anything they had encountered in Sicily or Tunisia and the greatest problem was to expel the Germans from their lofty and easily defended positions.

Clark was receiving wild rumours from Naples, some clearly exaggerated, such as a report that the Germans were 'killing thousands of citizens'. It was known, however, from the numbers of refugees fleeing the city that many buildings were destroyed and the population of almost a million was without water. If further destruction and an outbreak of typhus was to be averted it was imperative that the Allies take the city by the end of the month. This evening the Eighth captured Potenza and its vital road junction, and Allied planes resumed their attacks on the airfields ringing Naples.

At last the 36th Division was withdrawn from action and would spend the next few weeks guarding the beachhead. Walker issued a memo to his troops: 'Our Division has completed its first baptism of fire. It has the unique honour of being the first American division to land on the mainland of Europe during this war. It likewise is the first American division to make a landing against German opposition. We all can be proud of the results obtained, for the Division accomplished its mission'. So far as Walker was concerned his Texas Army had given their best and 'that is all any commander has a right to expect from his troops', although later it would be suggested that the inexperienced Division was badly mauled and that many GIs lost their lives unnecessarily.

Over his HQ that day Walker had proudly flown the Texas flag and his general's flag. His men were now encamped in an assembly area seven miles from Altavilla, not far from the Calore. This evening Walker drove through Altavilla again. The streets were still blocked with debris, the smell of death was everywhere. Townspeople were moving among the wreckage with a 'haunted terror in their faces along with an expression of utter helplessness'.

He would always maintain that the Allied bombardment of the town was 'brutal and to no purpose'.

By now the mutiny had taken a dramatic turn. The 193 rebels in the PoW camp near the beaches, patently humiliated, were ordered to prepare for evacuation. Still stubbornly refusing to join the 46th or 56th Divisions, they were marched under escort to an LST for transportation to Constantine to await trial for mutiny.

Corporal Fraser was determined he would not lose hope. 'I saw myself as a victim of false promises. All any of us wanted was to be posted to our own regiment. That was not too much to ask. Never at any time had we refused to fight for our King and country'. Sergeant Pettit was prepared for whatever indignity lay ahead.

A few hours out of Salerno the prisoners realized that they were the butt of malicious gossip by the crew. Fraser overheard a crew member speak of them as 'soldiers who refused to fight'. Another crew man called, 'Cowards'. Furious, Fraser went to Sergeant Innes who, as senior NCO, was in charge of the men. 'The sailors are refusing to speak to us,' one Durham reported. 'They say we're cowards'. Another of the Durhams threatened to 'sling someone overboard'. Innes calmed them. 'Keep your heads,' he advised. 'If someone kicks you, let him. Up to now, it's not mutiny. It's just collective disobedience of an order. So don't worry about the bleeding crew.'

Later he confronted one of the sailors to ask why the crew refused to speak to the soldiers. 'We were told by an officer in charge not to speak to any of you,' the sailor retorted. 'You're mutineers, aren't you?'

'Listen,' snapped Innes. 'We're not mutineers until we stand trial and the court decides.'

Alone in his caravan shortly before midnight Clark took out his writing pad and wrote to his wife. It was a gentle ending to another day of battle.

He told Maurine he was writing from his 'house and office on wheels'. He had been to the hospital to see the wounded troops. 'I stood in an operation room so thick with ether you could cut it with a knife. I talked with many of the wounded. They never complain. All they want is to get back into the fighting. In my opinion, the Germans will never to able to stop the Fifth Army.'

He signed his letter, 'Lovingly, Wayne'.

XXVI
MONTGOMERY ARRIVES

Thursday, 23 September

GENERAL BERNARD MONTGOMERY arrived at Salerno like a conqueror.

Behind him were the decisive victories of Alamein and the Mareth Line, and the Sicilian landings. 'As a builder of morale alone,' one correspondent observed, 'Monty was a potent instrument of war.' The skilful strategist and administrator was also 'vain, egotistical, difficult, and a show-off'. Alan Moorehead, who reported the North African and Sicilian campaigns, noted his habit of 'high-handedly pushing people aside whenever it suited his purpose, of making jeering cruel remarks about other officers, and making little effort to understand Americans'.

Faced with such accusations the gifted general would invariably register surprise. To him victory was all. Provided he gained that victory, did petty misunderstandings matter? Now, as his Eighth Army, spread across the southern mountains, moved towards the vital airfields at Foggia his troops were a club again, 'a private expedition wandering off into the mountains, always with Montgomery leading them to one more conquest'.

This morning the commander of the Eighth was on his way to Clark's headquarters. If Montgomery was considered dictatorial and eccentric, though a born leader of men, Clark was, as one of his officers recalled, 'a man who was conscious of himself every waking moment, always acting a part'. Clark's weakness was his conceit, which drove him to seek publicity. To one combat infantryman, his commander's habit of haunting the front line had one interpretation: 'Yeah, he'd be up there all right, peering through his binoculars at the Krauts, while his photographers snapped away. But just about the time the Germans had him zeroed in, he'd take off in his jeep – and we'd catch the shellfire.' There may perhaps have been a modicum of truth in such an observation, but it was a simple view of a man who commanded loyalty from his troops.

Clark's self-assurance had won Eisenhower's admiration, and he was certainly not in awe of Montgomery, or his reputation. He towered over the desert hero, who was wearing an open-necked shirt and a black beret set at a jaunty angle, and shook his hand warmly.

The commander of the Eighth Army told Clark bluntly that his forces were greatly extended; the build-up of supplies was insufficient to enable him to provide any direct support for the Fifth as it swung west towards Naples. He planned to establish a supply base near Bari on the east coast, south of Foggia, but he did not expect to take the airfields before the end of the month.

From Montgomery's formality, Clark surmised he could be 'a potentially difficult ally'. He told him frankly, 'Monty, you're a battle-proven commander. I'd like to lean on you – ask your advice from time to time.' The hint of flattery in this remark broke the ice. Montgomery beamed as Clark added, 'The Fifth is just a young outfit trying to get along while your Eighth is a battle-hardened veteran. You've got to teach us a few tricks.'

Correspondents and photographers had gathered outside Clark's caravan. When the conference ended the generals posed for photographs. Lieutenant Alfred Miller, one of Clark's HQ staff, always ensured that Clark stood higher than any other person and was photographed from his left side so that the stars on his overseas cap showed. Today there was no need to worry about Clark's height. Montgomery was diminutive by comparison. He told the correspondents, 'We're going up Italy side by side. Where we shall spend Christmas I don't know. A correspondent bet me five shillings the war would be over by Christmas. I have taken the bet. But he didn't say what year.'

The pressmen laughed as the two commanders walked to Montgomery's jeep. Climbing into his seat the Eighth Army commander turned to Clark. 'Do you know Alexander well?'

'Not that well.'

Monty smiled sardonically. 'I do. From time to time you'll get instructions from Alex that you won't understand. When you do, just tell him to go to hell!'

Watching the jeep bump its way out of the HQ area Clark decided he knew the eccentric Montgomery a little better. Now that their armies were driving together towards Naples, it was important that he and Montgomery should establish a good working relationship.

Clearly the help offered by the Eighth was mainly psychological. Even Montgomery's chief of staff, General Francis de Guingand, was to admit as much: 'It must be remembered that the situation at Salerno was well in hand before we established any pressure in the area. However, some people are inclined to pat themselves on the back and take some of the glory for driving the Germans back from the beachhead. I now realize how very irritating this attitude must have been to the Americans and General Clark.' Montgomery himself was to recall: 'I have never thought we had much real influence on the Salerno problem: I reckon General Clark had got it well in hand before we arrived . . . In my view the Fifth Army did their own trick without our help – willing as we were.' Quentin Reynolds had sailed down to Sicily to meet Montgomery at his headquarters. 'The spectacle of Salerno fresh in my mind,' he wrote, 'I felt like telling the general not to waste any time.'

Clark admired Montgomery's fanatical zeal in pursuit of victory, even though he questioned his lack of modesty as a soldier. This fanaticism was needed if a swift advance to take Naples were to succeed.

It was noon when General Truscott reached Acerno, 'the scene of the action' in which his battalions were engaged. During the night Colonel Doleman's 3rd Battalion had made its way over the mountains to the west and across the Isca della Serra to clear the Germans from the eastern bank. With the 2nd Battalion, Colonel Rogers had cut the road leading north from Acerno and a company went through the mountains to positions from which to attack from the south. Supported by three battalions of the Division artillery, the regiment cleared the town. Only Doleman's battalion met determined resistance. Led by the colonel, the men fought desperately with bayonets and grenades in a grove west of the town before they were able to link up with other troops.

With his aide, Lieutenant Bartash, Truscott got out of his jeep at the bridge and watched the engineers working to span the demolished arches. What Truscott did not know at this time was that the German discovery of a threat to their rear had prompted them to hasten their withdrawal north of Acerno where he expected them to stand and fight. North of the town, he was soon to learn, they had destroyed five more bridges and blasted a hundred feet of cliffside into a gorge below. The coming days would be a nightmare of building bridges, constructing by-passes, sweeping roads clear of mines, laying landing strips for artillery observation aircraft, and providing engineer supplies while the engineers were using their weapons to fight as infantry. Acerno was in their hands today, but progress would now be limited to the speed with which the engineers could build and repair.

To the west, on Highway 18, in the British sector, above the pass of La Molina, the Germans were sending in more tanks to try to stem the Allied advance towards Cava de' Tirreni, four miles above Vietri. Casualties mounted on both sides as troops fought with bayonets and bare hands. Observers described the battle that was to last during the night as 'terrific and terrible'. Allied guns thundered and flares lit up the sky.

For some German units the withdrawal was effected with few casualties. Almost twenty-five miles to the east Captain Meitzel had taken his 11th Battalion Panzergrenadiers across the Calore River to Highway 19, where trucks were waiting to move them north towards Contursi. This morning at Valva, north of Oliveto, one of his officers was killed by enemy artillery. It was to be the last fatality in his battalion as they withdrew through Sant' Angelo to Benevento, even though his front extended at times as far as nine miles.

At the same time, Vietinghoff's Pioneers were pursuing Kesselring's policies of demolishing roads at critical points, destroying bridges and laying mines. Wherever possible they covered these points with artillery and machine gun fire. By now some German units were withdrawing so rapidly that their haste was evidenced by the simplicity of their graves. Instead of the conventional black cross embossed with an Iron Cross, graves found by advancing Fifth Army troops that day were marked only by two crossed pieces of wood on which the name of the dead man had been hastily painted. Kesselring had ordered the XIV Panzer Corps to fall back in front of the Fifth Army in a vast pivotal movement based on the Sorrento peninsula. His forces on this flank were expected to hold the mountain passes for as long as possible 'to allow the thorough destruction of the port of Naples and to safeguard the evacuation of the plain.' It was through this determined rearguard that the Fifth Army would have to force a passage.

On the previous night the 56th Division had begun thrusting up the San Severino road beyond Fratte, while on either side of the Cava road 139 Brigade of the 46th began probing northwards through the steep, terraced hills and scattered villages. The plan was to establish a base from Corpo di Cava on the left flank through La Molina to San Croce and 'Telegraph Hill' for a main attack by the 138. But the battle did not develop as planned. On the right, the Foresters lost their way before finally occupying most of San Croce early in the evening. The KOYLIs, who were to put in the main attack, were unable to get started because of heavy mortar and shell fire, and they suffered heavy losses. On the left, the Lincolns got a footing on the eastern end of the

Costa Piano spur and the Leicesters captured the hilltop of Alessia without attempting to take the village, which was crowded with refugee families. One of those refugees, Anna Digillo, a lawyer's daughter, remembered, 'We were hiding in a cellar. We could hear the Germans and the English coming and going, and we never knew who was who.'

But it was along the main road out of Vietri itself that the strongest headway was made. Early in the morning the Yorks and Lancasters pushed into La Molina, where they established a company north of the viaduct, cutting off a Tiger tank and infantry in the defile. Under a smokescreen sappers began clearing the mines along the road and soon the first tank edged towards the village. The British were in position at one end, the Germans at the other.

General McCreery issued an Order of the Day to the troops of the 46th and 56th: 'After ten days of heavy fighting Tenth Corps has forced the enemy onto the defensive and on our right he is carrying out a big withdrawal. His object was to drive us back onto our beaches and for this purpose he concentrated against us the 16th Panzer Division and elements of four other German divisions. He has failed – thanks to the courage, endurance, and splendid fighting spirit of you all. You have inflicted very heavy losses on the enemy, and he has lost much equipment. We will now turn to the offensive in conjunction with the US Rangers on our left, who have harassed the enemy continually in very hilly and mountainous country. Once we have the enemy on the run we will keep him moving.'

For Staff Captain Arthur Fuller, a young South African with McCreery's headquarters, the tension of previous days at Pontecagnano had eased considerably. Yet his commander continued to work 'painfully long hours, even by wartime standards'. Fuller found McCreery aloof, a 'loner', deeply religious and conscientious. During the afternoon the general addressed his staff in a nearby fruit orchard on the coming Naples offensive. As he made an impassioned speech one of the geese adopted by the troops as pets waddled towards him to peck furiously at an insect climbing up one bare knee. McCreery broke off his address, in which he was about to invoke divine assistance in battle, to take a swipe at the goose, swopping pious words for what Fuller called 'the worst that angry flat race or jump jockeys could utter'.

(*above*) A Ranger patrol climbs a hillside near the Chiunzi Pass under cover of a smokescreen

(*below*) Rangers mortar a hill held by the Germans in the Chiunzi Pass area

(*above*) A Ranger gunner sprays advancing enemy forces in the hills above Maiori

(*below*) After the battle for Battipaglia . . . wrecked rolling stock and twisted rails at the town's railway junction

By now LST 309, carrying the 193 Salerno rebels, had reached the Tunisian port of Bizerta. With an escort of three captains, three lieutenants, three NCOs and twenty private soldiers they boarded a train for Constantine in Algeria.

From the station at Constantine they were marched to a large barbed-wire enclosure on the outskirts of the town to be guarded by troops of the Bedfordshire and Hertfordshire Regiments. One prisoner had become ill on the train, another was ill on arrival at the camp. That left 191, and for reasons of security the affair was now given the code name 'Case 191' by the Army's legal branch.

Sergeant Innes was determined that none of the men should prejudice the case by his behaviour in the camp. He ordered them to set about smartening up their quarters, whitewashing fixtures, and reproducing their regimental badges in shells on the side of their tents. When Captain Lionel Daiches arrived from the Judge Advocate's Department he was greeted by a guard of honour made up of a dozen prisoners. In collecting evidence for a summary of the case, he was promised 'full co-operation' by Innes. He found the men had organized themselves into units under their NCOs, laying out their own unit areas. It seemed to him an example of 'self-contained discipline'.

Daiches' visit was followed by the arrival of fifteen defending officers, who took statements from the prisoners, lending an air of urgency to the impending court-martial proceedings. The officers showed sympathy, expressing the view that the men would not be found guilty of mutiny. One prisoner told his comrades jubilantly, 'We've got two KCs for our defence. It must be costing thousands to bring that crowd here!'

Before leaving the camp one of the defending officers remarked to Lieutenant Ted Everett, the camp commandant: 'These men are fighting soldiers. They weren't trained to appreciate the niceties of the law. What they did was a technical offence. It boils down to this – they had a grouse, and somewhere along the line there has been mismanagement'.

Everett didn't think this was the view the court martial would take.

Friday, 24 September.

At Fratte, in the valley beyond the sanatorium, the German commander had opened his supply stores to the hungry refugees in the town and from the tunnel near the sanatorium. But during the night Allied artillery bombarded the district so heavily that it seemed to observers 'like a frightening earthquake'. The shelling continued until six a.m.

That morning the refugees, huddled in the tunnel, saw a German officer stagger towards the entrance. Some called to him, but he did not seem to hear. As the shelling resumed a woman refugee ran to him, seeking to pull him to safety, but he refused. He sat on the slope of the hill, placed his elbows on his knees and buried his face in his hands. From the tunnel they shouted to him again as the firing from the surrounding hills continued, but he crouched motionless until a shell blew him into the air.

At the sanatorium the battle raged for days. Forced out of the buildings and grounds, the British had retreated to the neighbouring hills. Then, with reinforcements, they returned to the attack. Under Lieutenant Michael Howard a platoon of Coldstream Guards climbed the hill to the hospital with bayonets drawn. His men fell under the Spandau hail as thirty Panzers fought them off. But the Germans' ammunition was dwindling and they had lost contact with their headquarters; retreating yard by yard through the grounds, they pulled back towards Fratte, carrying their wounded on their shoulders. Only sixteen escaped from Giovanni da Procida. The bodies of the dead lay among the flowerbeds and gravelled walks. One German died on his knees, still clutching a Spandau which he had emptied of bullets.

By early afternoon the Germans were pulling out of Fratte. At four p.m. the British entered the town.

During the night, after thirteen days of the bitterest fighting in their history, the Rangers had made their way down the winding road in the Chiunzi pass for the push to Naples.

Husbanding their resources, they had hung on, trusting that eventually the American and British forces below Salerno must break out of their beachhead. Only the tip of the Sorrento peninsula, as Darby was to recall, was left 'to the mountain goats and any Germans who wanted to act like them'.

In their retreat from Cava the Germans blew up the San Francesco bridge at the entrance to the town. Engineers worked feverishly to try to span the river. The British were to surprise the American engineers by their use of the Bailey bridge, built on rocking rollers, and pushed out across the span, counter-balanced by its own weight. To Colonel Truscott it was like a 'boy's erector set'.

By now Matera and Altamura had fallen to the Allies, both important objectives on high ground. Matera, built on the side of a ravine, commanded an excellent view of the countryside north and west. Altamura, an old walled town, as its name implied, was even higher than Matera and gave the Allies superb observation posts.

Returning from Maiori to the Fifth Army HQ at Paestum, correspondent Richard Tregaskis met Colonel Lazar, who was worried about the difficulties of the advance against the Germans in the mountains. 'Jerry has pockets of resistance in the hill mass. Wherever there's a gorge, it's easy to put a machine gun or a mortar or a little artillery on it. That can hold us up for a while.' But the main objectives now were 'Foggia for the airfields and Naples for the port.' The Northwest African Tactical Air Force was sending up medium and fighter-bombers over the Naples area. Wellingtons had dropped bombs on the aerodrome near Leghorn, setting hangers and administration buildings on fire and reducing parked aircraft to 'incandescent skeletons' in one gunner's description. Another Wellington formation had hit the railway yards at Pisa. This afternoon aircraft flying over Naples reported that the Germans had sunk a score of ships in the harbour, and that the city was 'ringed with fire and palled with smoke' from demolitions. 'Practically every usable berth along the docks has been blocked.'

The destruction was designed to reduce Naples to a completely useless objective for the Allies. Colonel Lazar remarked that Clark had a further worry. The roads were deep in dust. 'If we get caught by the rains without a port, we're going to be in a bad way.'

Saturday, 25 September.

Early in the morning Clark called on Walker to lay down a plan of action for the 141st Infantry Combat Team to 'make an envelopment by sea', landing in the Gulf of Naples around Pompeii. General 'Mike' O'Daniel would command the force. The operation required careful planning; Clark knew the Germans would be waiting on the beach and the landing must be timed to coordinate with the forces advancing towards Naples. Walker insisted, 'I don't want any more of my men isolated and defeated'.

Walker was worried about the morale of his men. Some were not responding to his instructions based on the lessons learned in the landings. They were taking training lightly and 'would suffer needless casualties because of their indifferent attitude'. He told an aide, 'These men imagine the war is over. They think they should be allowed to rest.'

Fifth Army HQ reports described combat efficiency as 'lessened due to casualties and fatigue'. But Clark was beset with other problems. Air Vice Marshal Sir Arthur Coningham, in command of the Northwest African Tactical Air Force, was impatient with the Army's slow progress in reaching Naples; he wanted to establish units on the fields in the Naples area. Sharing his impatience, Clark ordered the Sixth Corps to outflank the city as soon as possible to loosen the German grip on the port area. He directed General Lucas to put pressure on Middleton and Truscott. 'It is absolutely essential that they continue at full speed ahead in order to influence decisively the Allied attack on Naples.'

But there was not much the commanders could do to increase progress. Pitting themselves against superb German withdrawal tactics and the impossible nature of the terrain, they found their progress infuriatingly slow. Narrow roads hampered the movement of trucks and artillery. Bridging materials were scarce. And shortage of supplies at the front proved the worst problem of all.

Clark decided that more mules were needed to ensure the movement of supplies. He reckoned he needed 1,300 mules for his divisions, but few were available. The Germans had slaughtered most of those they did not take with them. He had no other option but to import them and at this late stage he decided to request shipments from the United States.

General Dawley had gone by LST to Termini in Sicily, still showing the effects of his sacking on the beachhead. His aide, Colonel O'Neill, had asked the ship's medical officer for sleeping pills for him the previous night. This morning they flew to Algiers where Dawley was to report to the Allied Forces HQ. But Eisenhower was not available and the general was received by General Hughes, deputy commander of the North African Theatre of Operations. Hughes handed him a brief letter:

23 September, 1943

AG 210 DTC Dawley, Ernest J. (Off).
Subject: Termination of Appointment (temporary) AUS.
TO: Major General Ernest J. Dawley, 02843, AUS.

By direction of the President your temporary appointment to the grade of Major General in the Army of the United States is, effective 23 September 1943, terminated. You will therefore revert, effective 24 September 1943, to your permanent grade of Colonel, Field Artillery, Regular Army.

By command of General Eisenhower.

H. V. Roberts,
COLONEL, A.G.D.,
Adjutant General.

'I was dumbfounded for the first time in my life,' recalled O'Neill. 'General Dawley went in his office a Major General and came out a Colonel of FA with orders transferring from ETO. I wanted to go home, but certainly not under these conditions. Couldn't have felt worse had it happened to me.'

That evening the pair stayed with General Wilson at his villa at Oran. Dawley drank more than he was accustomed to and 'let off some necessary steam'. According to O'Neill, 'It's really hitting him now.'

Few officers realized that General Eisenhower invariably took criticism from General Marshall, America's Army Chief of Staff, to heart. Towards Marshall the Supreme Commander was vulnerable. A letter received from Marshall during the day suggested that if Avalanche had been launched before the invasion at the toe of Italy the Germans would have been caught unawares and have 'fallen back beyond Naples'. Marshall asked the Supreme Commander if he was about to make the same mistake twice. If he took too long to develop a secure position around Naples, the Germans would have time to prepare their defences and would make the road to Rome for the Fifth Army 'long and difficult'. Shouldn't 'Ike' halt the efforts of the Fifth and Eighth Armies in Naples once it was 'under the guns' and invade Rome without delay, perhaps through a landing by sea?

Eisenhower went through 'a great deal of mental anguish' preparing his reply. At his villa outside Algiers he paced the ornate room, cluttered with map tables, dictating rapidly to his secretary, and then absent-mindedly wandered out of the room and into the hallway while his secretary hurried after him, scribbling notes as they walked up and down. After the strain of Avalanche, he was upset at the accusation of over-caution. Dictating two pages defending his actions, he insisted that he could not agree – 'repeat, not agree' – that the Salerno landings could have logically preceded the landing on the toe of Italy. Marshall may have been disappointed that Eisenhower had failed to take Rome at the time of the landings, but Eisenhower replied that he had given much study to the possibility of a Rome operation, and had rejected it because the port was inadequate and beyond the range of fighter cover at the time. Even now, he reminded Marshall, the Germans had a Panzer division in the Gulf of Gaeta and another in Rome; a small landing force would be quickly overrun, and a large force could not be mounted 'for a very considerable period'. Defending his command, he assured Marshall, 'I do not see how any individual could possibly be devoting more thought and energy to speeding up operations or to attack boldly and with admitted risk than I do. My staff is imbued with the same attitude, and I should like to assure you that nothing that offers us a chance for a successful stroke will be ignored.'

While Eisenhower was dictating his letter a note arrived from Churchill, congratulating him on the success of Salerno. The Prime Minister wrote, 'As the Duke of Wellington said of the battle of Waterloo, "It was a damned close run thing"'. What Wellington had actually said was, 'It has been a damned nice thing – the nearest run thing you ever saw in your life . . . By God! I don't think it would have been done if I had not been there!'

Eisenhower decided to pass Churchill's message to Marshall with the comment, 'I feel certain some of his correspondents in this area look upon me as a gambler'.

Before noon Clark called to the headquarters of General Lucas. The round-faced commander with old-fashioned steel-rimmed glasses and greying moustache was proving a decisive leader, making no secret of the fact that he was a firm believer in making the maximum use of artillery to speed the advance of his troops. He realized, however, that the delaying tactics of the enemy were succeeding in mountain country with poor roads and narrow bridges difficult to by-pass. By now the Germans had demolished more than twenty-five bridges between Paestum and Oliveto. In such conditions artillery, tank destroyers and tanks were proving a liability rather than an asset, so Lucas decided that progress could best be made by a small advance foot patrol accompanied by a few vehicles transporting weapons, ammunition and communications.

Clark urged him to take Avellino as quickly as possible. Its capture, he advised, would mean that the German defenders of Naples could be outflanked. Lucas saw one problem: the 3rd Division would have to advance across mountains without roads. If he could deploy the 133rd Infantry to move within striking distance of the enemy he perhaps could take the pressure off the British, who were attacking through the Sorrento ridge and 'making slow progress'. Fortunately, without strong air cover or the advantage of the rugged heights around Salerno, the *Luftwaffe* was forced during the day to withdraw its aircraft from the multiple air base at Foggia. It was doubtful now whether the Germans could make a stand below Foggia except by the use of mines and demolitions.

Lucas lunched with General Ryder and together they worked out plans to move the 133rd Infantry forward. Using only blackout lights, the regiment would travel over a narrow mountain road in the dark. But in the late afternoon rain began to fall. By night it had become a torrential downpour which was to last all night, washing away the road repairs which had been laboriously constructed through the mountains, making the movement of vehicles almost impossible, and reducing the movement of troops to a difficult and painfully slow pace.

'Everything has gone to hell,' declared Lucas.

By now the bridge into Cava was ready and the 128 Brigade passed through. But the Hampshires were heavily shelled when they arrived in the main piazza in close formation. Beyond the town, 2 Hampshires were held up at the cemetery and 1/4 Hampshires were slowed down by snipers. Resistance had hardened and there were to be considerable battles before the troops pushed further north to Santa Lucia.

On the road east out of Salerno the Germans had been driven beyond Fratte by the 56th. The 201 Guards Brigade were clearing the heights overlooking the valley north to Baronissi while the 169th were moving round the right flank towards San Mango. The 8th Fusiliers had waited so long for reinforcements that they were prepared with seventy-two hours' rations for a trek across the mountains, a plan that was cancelled when the badly needed reinforcements arrived.

At Coperchia in the same valley Mario Marino's father had been taken by the Germans. His brother Aurelio had not returned and three older brothers were missing at other war fronts. Mario had decided the previous night to cut the telephone wires into the Germans' tunnels behind his house. But now, when he looked out of the window, the Germans had gone. At Baronissi they held out briefly, destroying two Shermans. And when they withdrew, patrols reported that further on, towards San Severino, a bridge where the road crossed a deep railway cutting had been blown. While the Fifth and Eighth Armies moved north Berlin Radio claimed 'the city and harbour of Naples have lost their importance'. According to the bulletin, Allied bombings had made it impossible to consider Naples 'worthwhile from a military standpoint'. The city, said the broadcast, was cut off from the outside world. 'It no longer has any railway connections, and all factories are in ruins. The sirens are still screeching day and night, but the people, who were once seized with terror whenever the alarm sounded, are now apathetic.'

It seemed as though the Germans wished to play down the importance of the city in the event of its capture. Intelligence from ULTRA revealed much of the port unserviceable, with no railway activity, a dozen industrial works destroyed, no electricity or gas, only well water available and not for drinking, and the sewage works out of service. 'No epidemic, but conditions indicate probability of impending spread'. One observer who had flown over the city pronounced it 'as dead as Pompeii itself'.

Reaching Amalfi, with the co-operation of the Rangers, Father Carucci and his patients decided, now that the battle was easing, to return to Salerno and the sanatorium. Willing Americans commissioned a couple of trucks and sent priest and patients back along the route by which they had come. As the trucks climbed the hill to Giovanni da Procida Carucci saw a tall column of smoke rising from the sanatorium. At the entrance gates a burned out tank lay overturned; near its tracks was the body of a dead English officer. In the gardens pillars had been demolished, trees uprooted, and the dead lay everywhere. The building was shell-pocked, some quarters were a mass of rubble, and his beloved chapel lay in ruins. Spent cartridges and empty shell cases were strewn everywhere. The smell of rotting bodies and excrement was nauseous.

From the tunnel hundreds of refugees who had lived in its fetid shelter for almost two weeks emerged on the arrival of the chaplain and the patients. The dark still held terror for them, and their fears were well founded. At nine p.m. shelling began which was to last, without interruption, all night.

XXVII
THE FALL OF FOGGIA

Monday, 27 September.

SWIFT MOBILE UNITS captured the key air bases at Foggia against weak opposition from the depleted German 1st Parachute Division. The units consisted of men from the 78th Division who had landed at Bari a few days before with the 8th Indian Division. Even Montgomery was surprised at their achievement. He had not expected his troops to enter Foggia for at least a few more days. Foggia was some two hundred miles from the heel of Italy on a line about forty miles east of Naples. The Germans now faced the prospect not only of Allied aircraft operating out of the main air base at Foggia, and its twelve satellite fields, but also the risk of pressure on their left flank.

Eighth Army troops found the city deserted and half in ruins. Overnight, it seemed, the population had vanished. In fact, they had fled weeks before from the Allied mass bombing, leaving behind most of their possessions. The Germans had looted, but so had the civilian mob who followed the German withdrawal. Correspondent Alan Moorehead thought he had witnessed the extremes of looting during his three years on the road with Montgomery's Eighth, but at Foggia it touched 'the peak of wild, senseless abandon' . At the principal stores people had clawed down steel shutters with pickaxes and run past the counters snatching all they could 'without caring what they got'. It was the same in shop after shop. At an exclusive jeweller's the looters had smashed through the plateglass windows, snatching rings and necklaces in handfuls. From the cellars large wooden cases from Switzerland had been hacked open and they had burrowed through the straw to reach the watches and trinkets. 'I must have seen,' Moorehead recalled, 'a hundred empty silk lined boxes which yesterday were full of diamond brooches and rings and pendants.' The looters had then raced upstairs, ripping open the owner's cupboards, trailing forlorn dinner suits and dresses on the floor, smashing wine glasses to get at the valuable silver plate that lay beyond. Perched on top of the debris was a forlorn top hat that nobody wanted.

Militarily, it was a hard decision for Kesselring to abandon Foggia. The airfields were vitally important, he knew, both for the Allies' campaign in Italy and for their air attacks on southern Germany. Yet his hand was forced by the numerical inferiority of his forces and the ceaseless enemy bombing of his communications.

The morning's achievement by the Eighth Army drew praise from Roosevelt: 'The fall of Foggia is one of the most important strategic successes yet by the Allies.'

Meanwhile, on a broader front, the concerted drive towards Naples continued with a powerful momentum. The passes that were to be freed from the Germans were steep and narrow with hillsides rising sharply from the valleys. It was difficult to imagine a more ideal position for enemy defence. Yet McCreery's plan for the British forces to force a way through the Sorrento ridge pass to reach the plain of Naples was working. He calculated that the 46th Division would advance through the Cava valley while the 56th, advancing through San Mango, would clear the valley running north from Salerno, swinging west at San Severino. A small flank guard was to be mounted just north of San Severino until the Sixth Corps had secured Avellino. The 7th Armoured Division was to follow through the 46th Division from Camerele, while the Rangers, with the 23rd Armoured Brigade, were to help the 46th's advance.

McCreery's plan involved much regrouping of forces within the Sixth Corps. He had appealed to Darby to extend his already stretched Rangers further east from Monte Sant' Angelo to bring the road between Cava and Camerele under machine gun fire, and, if necessary, concentrate all available artillery fire on this sector. He wrote to the Rangers' commander, 'I again wish to emphasize the decisive sector is the axis Nocera–Vietri, and you must thin out still further in the hilly country east of Castellammare if necessary.' However, the nature of the slopes on the western side of Cava prevented the Rangers from giving the assistance to the 46th that at first sight had seemed possible to McCreery.

By evening Santa Lucia (the village north of Cava, not the village near the beaches) was taken by the 128th Brigade and forty tanks rolled into Camerele. McCreery could now put into effect his plan for passing the 7th Armoured Division through the 46th Division and at the same time secure the Sala defile with the help of the Rangers to permit the 23rd Armoured Brigade to emerge into the Naples plain.

During the night Colonel Gavin's 82nd Airborne Division jumped off to reach the Naples plain by morning while the 505th Parachute

Infantry moved up the mountain road from Amalfi to the top of the Sorrento Peninsula. Near Agerola, where the road from Amalfi to Castellammare runs through a tunnel, Gavin set up his command post. The Americans were at one end of the tunnel, the Germans at the other.

Tuesday, 28 September

At daylight Gavin climbed to the top of the peninsula for his first view of Naples. He found that billowing black clouds of smoke covered the waterfront, and buildings were burning throughout the city. McCreery had directed him to attack and take Gragnano, some five miles away at the foot of the mountain, the next morning, and he had prepared a plan involving three separate columns moving down the spurs of the mountains to make a combined attack on the hill overlooking the town. He had never fought in such terrain and the prospect worried him.

Yet the progress of his paratroopers had enabled the 46th Division to move three more miles. McCreery directed the York and Lancasters and the Leicesters to advance, allowing him to launch the 7th Armoured Division into the Nocera defile during the morning, although he knew there were still 'numerous pockets to be cleared'. With British tanks approaching Nocera and American infantry threatening Avellino, the Germans began falling back from San Severino, allowing the 56th Division to advance north of Salerno.

Truscott's progress was impressive, his 45th and 3rd Divisions moving forward over difficult ground to get into position for a concerted attack on Avellino. Hardly had his engineers effected essential repairs after the rains of the previous days than another torrential downpour washed them out again. Fearing the rains would wash away more bridges, Truscott moved his supply dumps forward, closer to the front than was the custom. This morning, although the Sixth Corps had re-established contact with the Germans at the approaches to the town, the entrance to Avellino was blocked and the roads were impassable.

Lucas wrote in his diary: 'Am running this thing on a shoestring, and a tiny shoestring at that.' Panic in war, he knew, is caused by rumours, and reports were spreading through the Division that the Germans were using gas. A wire-laying party had sustained severe burns from contact with wet bushes along the road. Containers found nearby led them to believe the enemy was using mustard gas.

Truscott had no protective clothing for his troops, and without such clothing he could not send men into an area drenched with gas. He could not believe the Germans would dare employ such gas in the circumstances, yet it needed little imagination to picture the consequences of such a swiftly spreading rumour; the resulting panic could seriously threaten the Corps' entire operations. Issuing strict orders to isolate the casualties, he ordered an end to all talk of the incident while the report was investigated.

At the place where the men had been burned several empty containers which had contained gas were found, and some full containers. Truscott sent them at once for analysis which showed the contents to be a relatively harmless form of tear gas. The casualties recovered quickly and were sent back to their assigned tasks.

Ironically, troops who should have been helping the Fifth Army to take Naples were at Constantine, marching to their court martial.

One of their number, a private of the Argyll and Sutherland Highlanders, who had been ill with malaria, had died in hospital. Now with heads held high, uniforms neatly pressed, and the toecaps of their boots gleaming, the 191 prisoners halted, still under heavy guard, outside the entrance to a big stone building. An RSM of the Welsh Guards remarked to the escort party, 'These men are a good deal smarter than you are – but you'll be smarter tomorrow!'

Each prisoner was issued with a numbered card which he was ordered to wear on his chest, hung from a cord around his neck. On the right of the courtroom sat the president, a major general, and on either side of him two officers of the court. Beyond them was the Judge Advocate. To their left, at a long table, sat the defending officers, and directly facing them the officer of the legal team who was to present the prosecution.

The charge, framed under Section 7, paragraph 3, of the Army Act, was:

> when on active service joining in a mutiny in His Majesty's forces that they, in the field, on September 20, 1943, when ordered by Captain A. G. Lee, 1st Battalion, the York and Lancaster Regiment, to pick up their kits, fall in on the road, and march off to 46th Division area, joined in mutiny and disobeyed the said order.

'No. 1. Do you plead guilty or not guilty?'
'Not guilty, sir.'
'No. 2. Do you plead guilty or not guilty?'
'Not guilty, sir.'

All the defendants pleaded 'Not guilty.' In vain, the defence tried to change the charge to one of lesser degree, such as 'disobedience to superior officer'.

When the summary of evidence was taken the prosecution cross-examined the prisoners. Then the prisoners were permitted to ask questions of Captain Lee. Corporal Hugh Fraser asked him if he recalled a promise to the men by the deputy assistant general of the Tenth Corps that they would go back to their original divisions. Lee answered, 'Yes, in his speech he reminded the men of a promise which he had already been given that, as circumstances permitted, the men would be returned to their original units.'

Private McFarlane asked, 'When at Transit Camp you knew we were going to Salerno, did you ask why this fact had not been communicated to the troops?'

Lee: 'No, I did not. I had received an order from the officer commanding 155 Transit Camp, who gave me the information that the troops were not to be informed.'

McFarlane: 'Are you aware that members of certain regiments at 133 Transit Camp had previously been informed that they were definitely going to their own units in Sicily?'

Lee: 'I did not know then, when I was at the camp, but I heard about it at Tenth Corps Transit Camp at Salerno.'

The court-martial was to continue for six days, and after each day's hearing the accused were escorted back to the camp.

Corporal Fraser was impressed by the defending officers and the manner in which they put their case, even though few of them were legally trained. Halfway through the proceedings his own defending officer, Captain James Mitchel, a Cameron Highlander, confided to him that he thought the men would be acquitted. Sergeant Pettit noticed that some of the defending officers had become emotionally involved, so strongly did they feel about the case. He found this understandable since these were regimental officers who had fought their way across the Western Desert alongside the accused men, facing death with them under the banner of the Eighth Army. Innes was pleased that the court had noted the defendants' battle history and the fact that two members of the group had been awarded Military Medals. He was confident the charge would be thrown out. In fact, the men became so certain they would be acquitted that they prepared for their departure from the PoW camp at Constantine. Around a Gordon Highlander's belt they fixed the cap badges of all the units they had risked so much to join, with the badge of the Argyll and Sutherland Highlanders in the centre, since it was the biggest badge. Then they presented the belt to the camp commandant 'for the good work you have done and the kindness you have shown'.

On the sixth day the court martial ended. One man was acquitted, a sapper from the Royal Engineers who had become involved in the mutiny by accident. The remainder were told: 'The findings of this court, being subject to confirmation, will not be announced now, but will be promulgated later.'

Wednesday, 29 September

General Alexander at last removed the restrictions that had held back the advance of the Fifth Army's right flank to await the link up with the Eighth Army. He discussed with Clark the Fifth's next objective and decided it should be Benevento. 'You should get Benevento early,' he urged Clark. This meant that Lucas would have to send the 3rd Division alone into Avellino while the 133rd Infantry cut the highway between Avellino and Benevento and the 46th Division moved directly against Benevento itself.

Meanwhile McCreery directed the 7th Armoured Division to drive west to secure the bridgehead across the Sarno River. Once across, the main body of the armoured division was to skirt Mount Vesuvius on the east and north and drive to the Volturno at Capua while elements of the 23rd Armoured Brigade took the road to Naples. If the Germans had left Naples the smaller force was to skirt the city on the east, then drive north along the coast to the Volturno, leaving the 82nd Airborne Division to occupy the city. By now San Severino was occupied and by evening Rangers would be patrolling Torre Annunziata.

Leading troops of the 7th Armoured Division surprised even McCreery by their rapid advance, and more so the Germans. They seized the bridge across the Sarno at Scafati intact, although the Germans had prepared charges for its demolition, thus speeding the approach to Naples; all the other bridges across the river had been blown.

When Gavin learned to his surprise that the Germans had withdrawn from Gragnano at the other end of the tunnel he moved at once down into the town, and then on to Castellammare.

Along the road to Naples Fifth Army troops were encountering members of the lost 509th Parachute Battalion. Their numbers were few. Avellino had, as many feared, proved a 'suicide mission'. Of the 641 paratroopers who had jumped only 532, many of them wounded, were to make it back to the Allied lines. In strict military terms, the mission had probably been worthwhile for, apart from deflecting

German units to search the mountains, the paratroopers had inflicted casualties on the enemy.

Paratroopers Nunn and Fisco had hidden in the mountains, making night raids into villages where Germans were billeted. In their rubber-soled shoes they moved silently; in his boyhood days in Jacksonville Nunn had learned to hunt without making a noise by even breaking a twig. The pair met up with other paratroopers and an RAF pilot whose Spitfire had crashlanded in a bowl in the mountains. They took no Germans prisoner. Nine days after their landing they arrived back at the beachhead, led by a teacher who guided them over the mountains in a direct line, avoiding roads busy with German transport, towards the advancing Fifth Army troops. The pilot made the forty-mile journey wearing shorts and a pair of English boots. Unaccustomed to walking in such rough country he took his boots off at the end of the journey to reveal feet which were 'like raw meat'.

Clark was to send a letter of commendation to the survivors of the 509th: 'I wish to commend the officers and men of the 2nd Battalion 509th Parachute Infantry on the superior manner in which they performed their recent mission of dropping behind the enemy lines to disrupt his supply and communications facilities. Such an operation demands courage, resourcefulness, initiative and a high sense of duty not only of the unit as a whole, but of each individual in the unit.'

While flattered by this letter, the Avellino survivors derived wry amusement from the last line: 'Our wish is that you will continue to have equally happy and successful landings.'

During the day Father Carucci went down into the city to visit Archbishop Monterisi, who welcomed him with the affection of a father. 'All my priests remained at their posts,' he said. 'I am happy you have done your duty.'

Carucci saw that the war and the invasion had taken their toll of the aged prelate, and he was not to live much longer. Kneeling to kiss his ring, he was drawn by the archbishop's arm into a sudden embrace.

Monterisi was shocked by the looting and thieving in the city. Salernitani were to blame, but the behaviour of the Allied soldiers, often drunk, was inexcusable. *Scugnizzi*, homeless boys, had taken to the streets with women prostitutes. The *scugnizzi* would exploit the soldiers by telling the women, 'This soldier is mine. You want him? Then pay me money.' Some soldiers found the prostitutes ready to accept food instead of money.

Monterisi had asked Colonel Lane to respect the treasures and antiquities of the old city. Not only had many historic buildings been damaged, but troops began cutting the famous curtain in the opera house, painted by Domenico Morelli, into small sections as souvenirs. The theatre watchman's family alerted the mayor, who ordered the troops to stop this desecration.

Monterisi told Lane heatedly, 'I am the custodian of the church, yes. But I am also the custodian of the honour of all my children.'

Expressing his admiration for the prelate's courage, Lane decided to ask him to nominate a committee to collaborate with the Allied administration. Such a committee could work for the restoration of the city services and ensure that necessary measures were taken to end the looting and prostitution. A black market was to continue in the city, mainly in flour, sugar, coffee and blankets. The population were issued with ration cards but they improvised by cutting up parachute silk to make shirts and stealing rubber tyres to make shoes. Girls who became involved in prostitution found their names written on street walls. And in the areas now marked out of bounds for the troops notices appeared, 'A Soldier's Pleasure Ends in Hospital'.

Many of the *sfollati*, or refugees, were now returning to the city. Mario Papa, whose officer father had been taken prisoner by the British in North Africa, came down from the village of Acquamela to the city district of Carmine with his mother to their apartment which had been occupied by Allied troops.

They had lost all their furniture and valuables and a bomb had demolished the wall between their apartment and the apartment next door. Mario Marino returned during the day with his father, who had been freed by the Germans, while the rest of the family remained at Coperchia; the men were traditionally the first to return. Climbing the stairs, they met groups of British soldiers. On the third floor their apartment door was open. Their furniture and belongings had been pushed into a corner and servicemen were using the rooms as a centre in which to read or write.

'You can't come in here,' a sergeant said to Mario's father, barring the way. The elder Marino snatched up a photograph that had been placed on top of the furniture. 'See?' he asked. 'This is my family, and this is my house!'

Convinced, the sergeant let them enter. Father and son had no mattresses, so that night they slept on the floor.

Half the buildings in the city were uninhabitable and some 450 inhabitants were dead. More than 70,000 rooms had been destroyed and the returning families were to live three or four to every apartment, with one bedroom for each family.

Towards midnight a group of patients had arrived at Giovanni da Procida from the sanatorium at San Severino with 'fear on their faces'.

They told Carucci that their sanatorium had been destroyed in the fighting and their chaplain, Father Daelli, killed.

On his return from the city Carucci was confronted by a British officer who had arrived with a patrol to requisition 200 beds. Carucci protested that he now had a further 20 patients from San Severino, but the officer refused to listen. The chaplain then complained to the American officer for public health. Captain Szigereff could only promise him supplies of flour, but offered to report any further abuse of authority by British officers.

Colonel Jack Churchill was determined to find Wellington's body. On leave from Sicily, he returned to Salerno and drove up to the 'Pimple' with soldiers from the Body Recovery Unit. Equipped with shovels, spades and paper sandbags they went searching for telltale mounds of earth on the scorched and blackened hill. If the body were there, Churchill knew it would probably be so badly burned as to be unrecognizable, so he had jotted down, as he customarily did when Commandos went missing and were presumed dead, items by which he might be identified. He learned that Wellington had worn a plaited belt with a metal clip, metal stars on his shoulder, and had an upper dental plate. He had smoked a pipe and carried a plain tobacco tin. Six clues. He also wanted to find the body of Wellington's Troop Sergeant-Major Garland. If all else failed he could probably identify the bodies from their distinctive Commando boots. 'Skeletons or not, just bones and boots, you couldn't mistake them for Germans.'

On the hilltop, under six inches of earth, close to the body of a German officer, they found Wellington. The body had been burned, probably by British mortar bombs, but the colonel identified the belt buckle, the pipe bowl and part of the aluminium tube that ran through the pipe, the tobacco tin, and the boots. He watched the 'body snatchers' place the body in one of the paper sandbags and write the name and rank on the outside. When Garland's body was also found, recognizable by the size of his boots, the unit drove down to Salerno to bury the bodies temporarily in a grass square near the town. Churchill was now certain that Wellington and the German officer had confronted each other on the 'Pimple'. 'I think they both pulled the triggers of their pistols at the same time.'

Thursday, 30 September.

At three a.m. Sergeants Pettit, Innes and Middleton were awakened abruptly in the PoW camp at Constantine.

'What's the matter?' a sleepy Innes asked the NCO.

'Get dressed. Bring all your kit.'

'Are we going away?'

'Yes, you and the other two sergeants.'

Outside the camp a truck waited, rear doors open. The three climbed in. Their guards carried tommy guns. 'This isn't our idea,' one of them said to Pettit. 'It's orders.'

The truck drove off in the darkness. When it stopped they were outside a long hut, divided into three rooms. Innes was the first to be taken to one of the rooms and told to remove all his clothing. He was searched, then directed to dress again. All that was returned of his personal possessions was a pocket handkerchief. He was escorted to a second room where an officer, seated at a table, looked at him, his face expressionless.

'I've got a job to do that I don't like doing,' he began. He gestured to a chair. 'Sit down.' The officer leaned across and handed Innes a sealed envelope. The sergeant made to put it in his pocket, but the officer interjected. 'No. Don't do that. Read it.'

Innes opened the envelope and drew out a single typewritten sheet. Glancing quickly at it, he saw the words, *The court have found you guilty. . . .* The lines became blurred and he could not read on. 'I'm sorry, sir,' he said, his voice trembling. 'I can't read any more, sir.'

The officer asked bluntly, 'What? Can't you read?'

'Of course I can read, sir.'

'All right, then. Put the letter in your pocket. Read it when you get to your destination.'

As Innes walked into the third room his place in the middle room was taken by Sergeant Pettit; Sergeant Middleton had entered the first room to be strip-searched. Pettit read the typewritten sheet as the officer directed and was stunned when he came to the words, *The court has passed sentence of death on you. . . .* He was still dazed when he joined the other two sergeants in the truck. The court, he thought, had made no recommendation to mercy.

At a prison on a hillside at Bône, each man was placed in a separate cell. Innes's cell was No. 1 Death Row. He heard a rumour that the Durham Light Infantry were to supply the firing party. If they're going to shoot us, he reflected, they're going to shoot us. I've seen my mates die on the battlefield. It doesn't matter now if I'm going to get it. He asked a prison guard, 'Will they tell my wife that I've been executed?' The guard answered, 'No. They'll probably say you've been killed in action.'

Corporal Fraser and the other NCOs were held in solitary confinement in the same prison. Fraser hated the confinement of four walls and spent his time futilely polishing his mess tin. He was informed that he had been found guilty of the charge of mutiny and, with the other corporals, was reduced in rank and sentenced to ten years' penal servitude. Private John McFarlane was paraded with the other private soldiers to hear sentence. He could scarcely believe the words of the young officer who announced the sentence of seven years' penal servitude. However, before he could feel too aggrieved the officer added that these sentences were to be suspended. Such suspension did not mean complete release; one minor act of indiscipline would bring the sentence into effect. Meanwhile, the privates were to return to the front where they would have an opportunity to win back their lost honour. When they boarded a transport ship at Philippeville for Italy McFarlane found that the other troops on board shunned them. This was as shameful to him as the jeering from the German prisoners at Salerno.

After serving a short sentence in the prison camp Corporal Fraser and his fellow corporals were released on suspended sentences with the proviso that any future indiscipline would mean an automatic prison sentence of ten years. Fraser was told he was to be sent to Italy to another unit; he was now prepared to serve anywhere if only to get away from a prison where his fellow prisoners were murderers and rapists. Assigned to the Yorks and Lancs regiment, he determined to soldier on.

Sergeants Innes, Pettit and Middleton, waiting for the death sentence to be carried out, were surprised by a visit to their respective cells by armed guards. The three were escorted to a room where an officer told them that their sentences were to be commuted to twelve years' penal servitude. Then, next day, they were brought before the prison commandant and further informed that these sentences were suspended.

The commandant ordered, 'Get yourselves ready to leave tomorrow.'

'Do I go to the Durham Light Infantry, sir?' asked Innes.

'You go,' said the commandant, 'where you are sent.'

Innes went back to Italy, but not to the Durham Light Infantry. General Montgomery would say later, 'While the men's mutiny was inexcusable, it was to some extent caused by bad decisions.' Sergeant Pettit summed up for his fellow sergeants: 'We were wronged, it's as simple as that. How can regimental loyalty be classed as a crime?' And the 'father' of the 51st Highland Division, Major General Wimberley, who had told the Scotsmen, 'If separated from your units do not allow yourselves to be drafted to other battalions,' later wrote to the War Office, seeking to get the men's convictions waived. He was not successful.

Near Avellino Colonel Truscott travelled with Bartash along Highway 7 to a point on the eastern slope of the valley where Colonel Sherman and his command group were waiting for the engineers to construct a bypass around the first of several blown bridges. Westward across the valley in which Avellino lies hung a sea of fog, and above the fog the sun shone brightly. From the area came the sounds of gunfire, of scattered actions with machine guns and mortars, and the occasional salvoes of artillery. Truscott's infantry battalions had by-passed the enemy in the fog and infiltrated the German defences. Now, fighting desperately in small pockets, the Germans were trying to escape. Truscott watched as Sherman and his group set off on foot down the highway towards the town. He waited until the sounds of firing were more widely spaced. Finally, there was no sound at all. 'I knew then,' Truscott recalled, 'that Avellino was in our hands.'

During the afternoon he went into the town to be confronted by a sight that was to become increasingly familiar to him in Italy: all around him were bomb craters, shell holes and demolished buildings. During the darkest days of the invasion the Allies had bombarded the town to prevent German reinforcements from reaching the beachhead, and in recent days the Germans had set about their own demolitions. Avellino reeked of putrefying bodies buried in the debris. 'It seemed strangely sad to me,' recalled Truscott, 'that the townsfolk who had suffered so much should greet us with cheers and flowers, fruit and wine.'

His task now was to turn his 3rd Division northwards towards the Tenth Corps. They had come through sixty miles of rugged mountains in appalling weather and the men were exhausted. But their colonel told them, 'There can be no stopping now. The Germans are on their knees.' Before they could dig in on new defences they had to reach the Volturno River.

By now the Fifth Army had occupied Nocera and were moving towards Naples. The battle for Nocera had reached its final, bitter peak around the tiny village of Scala, on a zigzag road west of Maiori. Several times the village changed hands in renewed bursts of savage fighting. Only after heavy casualties were suffered on both sides did the Germans give way. By noon the capture of Nocera facilitated the drive to push the enemy out of his final ring of rocky defences west and north-west of Salerno. Faced with this accelerating Allied offensive and the loss of their natural barriers, the Germans sped their withdrawal throughout the Salerno front. All the evidence now indicated to the Allied commanders that they planned no further stand before the wrecked city of Naples. Clark expected its capture within twenty-four hours.

It was not Naples, however, but the loss of Foggia that had proved the cruellest blow for Kesselring. The decision by Hitler and *OKW* not to release a single division from Northern Italy for the defence of the air bases had resulted, he was certain, in their loss. He admitted, 'It was a terrible blow.' Nevertheless, by contesting every inch of the ground, Vietinghoff's Tenth Army had established a weak front for the enemy 'from the Tyrrhenian to the Adriatic'. And Kesselring had kept his finger on the pulse of the situation by frequent flights over the front and inspections of the progress made in fortifying the rear defences. 'I must,' he wrote, 'have been a thorough nuisance to the senior engineer officer, General Bessel.'

This evening, after four days' fighting, the Fifth burst from the narrow pass at Camerele and fanned out into the plain of Naples with only occasional German rearguards and demolitions to overcome. Around the slopes of Vesuvius and from Torre Annunziata, just eleven miles from their goal, the Allies were beginning their final thrust. No challenge came from the *Luftwaffe*, although the retreating army had laid large minefields and used mobile three inch guns to slow up the Allied advance, swinging them from one natural strongpoint to another.

By nightfall heavy tanks of the Fifth were rumbling round both sides of Vesuvius and were only a few miles from the city centre. At the same time, standing offshore in the Gulf of Naples, battleships poured 16-inch shells into the last pockets of German resistance.

Already most of the German troops had left the city for new positions along the Volturno River. Vietinghoff's withdrawal plan had been circulated yesterday morning to unit commanders and was now in full operation. Clark would find 'an unusable port'. The city, Vietinghoff decided, would not be defended by his Panzers.

In his finest hour it mattered little now to Clark that it had taken three weeks instead of three days – his original estimation – to reach Naples, at a cost of 13,614 casualties. B. H. Liddell Hart argued that it was 'the penalty paid for choosing a too obvious line of attack and place of landing, at the sacrifice of surprise, on the ground that the Salerno sector was just within the limit of air cover'. Kesselring and his Chief of staff, General Westphal, felt the Allies had paid 'a heavy strategic forfeit for their desire to ensure tactical security against air attack.' And Alexander, Deputy Supreme Commander, admitted that he had misjudged the situation. 'When we landed at Salerno, the idea was to drive straight across the Italian leg and trap those German divisions contained in southern Italy. We had expected a few Germans in the Salerno area, certainly not more than one division. We no sooner landed, however, than we found ourselves with a four division front.'

The outcome of Avalanche was crucial to Clark's reputation. It was his first test at this level as commander. A disaster at Salerno would have destroyed him; instead, he was now emerging with an impressive record. War cartoonist Bill Mauldin wrote, 'The Italian campaign was a nasty job to begin with, and I think Clark got saddled with it, but he ended up doing it as well as anyone could.' Although some of Clark's decisions were questionable, especially his obstinacy in preventing a preliminary naval bombardment of the American landing sector near Paestum, he remained rocklike in face of crisis. Admittedly, most of the time he enjoyed the support of Eisenhower, whose faith in the command structure of Avalanche never wavered, and in spite of differences with Dawley, Walker and McCreery he never allowed these moments to influence the mainstream of the battle. He emerged with a strong hand, even if he had entirely misjudged the time his Fifth Army would take to reach his initial objective.

On the German side, Kesselring continued to have faith in Vietinghoff's strategy, agreeing with his axiom, 'One cannot fight and build defences at the same time.' Neither commander lost face in defeat.

It was left to General Westphal, attached to Field Marshal Kesselring's HQ at Frascati, to emphasize the real reasons for the German failure at Salerno. The *Luftwaffe* was weakened, he argued, and unable to provide the expected assistance. The number of U-boats, evacuation vessels and other craft available was comparatively insignificant. The main burden of the invasion had to be borne by the land forces. Furthermore, supplies of ammunition fell short, while all the time the German coastal defences were subject to 'appalling bombardment' from naval gunfire. Westphal felt that the leadership in the Italian war theatre was frequently inhibited. Hitler was suspicious, believing that something was being hidden from him. With Göring, who continually tried to blacken Kesselring's reputation, he accused the Field Marshal of 'Italophile' tendencies. Gradually, however, Hitler was to change his mind about Kesselring and hold him in higher esteem than either Göring or Rommel.

As Clark and Montgomery pushed on with their advance,

Eisenhower received a message from Churchill. 'I rejoice with you at the brilliant turn our affairs in the Mediterranean have taken.' For Clark's sake particularly Eisenhower was pleased. Everything they had set out to achieve had been achieved, and at the end of the day he was to agree with Churchill that September had been indeed a fruitful month. Anglo-American inter-Service co-operation by land, sea, and air had reached a new record. Had not Vietinghoff stated that 'the harmonious co-operation between our Army, Air, and Naval forces under one supreme command was regarded by Germany with envy'?

Montgomery was more cautious. In a message to Churchill he pointed out, 'We have advanced a long way and very quickly. It had to be done in order to come to the help of the Fifth Army, but it has been a very great strain on my administration, which had to be switched from the toe to the heel during the operations and which is now stretched to the limit.'

When the battle was concluded the official figures showed that British casualties were 7,398, American 6,216. US Navy casualties were 296 dead, 551 missing and 422 wounded; Royal Navy casualties 83 dead and 43 wounded. Among British troops 982 were dead, 2,230 missing and 4,060 wounded; of the American troops 788 were dead, 1,318 missing and 2,814 wounded.

In General McCreery's view the high casualty rate might have been avoided by a more judicious choice of invasion beach in the first place. Numerically, German losses were fewer, which was to be expected because of the geographical and strategical advantage they held over the invading task force. Yet this combined American and British operation had succeeded, however painful the progress, in gaining a vital foothold for the Fifth Army and opening the way for an eventual advance on Rome. At the same time, Avalanche exposed the unexpected vulnerability of the German forces to incessant air, sea and ground attacks.

As General Clark was to admit, the invasion had been a 'near disaster'. He confessed, 'I thought for a while they were going to drive us into the sea.' What had saved him from this ultimate indignity was Vietinghoff's inexplicable hesitancy in driving home his undeniable advantage in the German assault on the Sele–Calore corridor. Clark knew he had been extremely fortunate to hold on.

While Eisenhower, the Supreme Commander, never lost faith in his commanders, especially in Clark, his own choice to lead Avalanche, he was to declare that superior air power had proved the decisive factor in the operation's eventual success; Alexander, Clark and McCreery maintained that the unremitting naval bombardment had done most to crack the German morale and drive the enemy from the Salerno beachhead. When Montgomery's forces arrived the crisis was over; the Eighth Army had no material effect on the fighting at Salerno.

For the Germans, the Fifth Army's stand had shaken Hitler's confidence in his forces, even though the Führer was prepared to favour Kesselring's strategy in defending Italy 'line by line'. Kesselring would soon be entrusted with the unified German command in Italy. As the Panzers withdrew in characteristically organized fashion, Clark's confidence grew, and he was eager to put behind him the tense, precarious days on the beachhead when his reputation was in danger of being destroyed.

All that concerned Clark now was the capture of his objective – the port of Naples.

XXVIII
Piazza Garibaldi

Friday, 1 October.

Sleeping soundly on the floor of a farmhouse near Torre Annunziata, Colonel Gavin was wakened by an officer from the British 23rd Mechanized Brigade. In the shafts of morning sunlight filtering through the narrow window he noticed the officer was so impeccably turned out that he looked as though ready to march out on parade.

Today the 82nd and 23rd were together to make an early jump-off for Naples. By now the Germans were out of sight and resistance in the area had petered out. Along the main road into Naples and in village streets excited Italians greeted them, tossing flowers and fruit and shouting, '*Viva Inghilterra! Viva America!*' What, Gavin wondered, if the Germans decided now to make a counter-attack?

Riding in the turret of his Sherman, Lieutenant Ted Robinson of the Scots Greys found the welcoming Italians 'unusually friendly', so friendly that among the fruit and flowers thrown at the troops was an apple that caught him smack in the centre of his forehead, knocking him back in the turret.

At Torre del Greco a jeep carrying a small group of war correspondents, including Richard Tregaskis and Reynolds Packard, dashed past a slow-moving column of British vehicles until it was slowed by the throngs of shouting, handclapping Italians. At Portici, the entrance to Naples, people pelted them with purple and yellow flowers, crying, '*Viva, Viva!*' They swarmed over the jeep, fighting to kiss their cheeks, or clasp them in their arms, clawing at their shirts, some weeping hysterically, '*Grazie, grazie!*' Driver Private Delmar Richardson pushed the stick into bottom gear and accelerated to throw them off as they clung to the moving vehicle. As they drove past shattered factories and tenements, skirting fallen electric wires and deep pits which had been blasted in the streets, the crowds thinned. Beyond them stretched the harbour, a tangle of broken cranes and twisted girders etched against the sky 'like awkward elbows'. Here the city was ominously empty and Richardson drove carefully through cobblestoned streets, not knowing if they were mined with buried Tellers.

At 8.50 a.m. Colonel Gavin reached the city limits with his paratroopers. He was ordered to halt while a unit of the 23rd Armoured Division made a reconnaissance. Allied bombers had sketched a broad pattern of destruction in the harbour; the enemy had filled in the rest of the picture, sinking ships scientifically to create the greatest problems for the Allies, even chaining them together to make the obstruction difficult to clear. In the city's bombed buildings they had skilfully placed charges which had blasted out floors, leaving only the walls precariously standing, making the buildings useless. The city was alive with booby traps. Even intact buildings were suspect, and every doorknob, chair and floorboard would have to be tested. The armoured column drove through, searching for mines and snipers.

Near Portici General Walker met Lieut. General Fred, Jnr, with a British armoured brigade. Walker was surprised that his son had been detached from the 82nd. He was to write in his diary: 'I do not like to have any of my units attached to a British command because my people are more aggressive and will expect close, prompt support by artillery and tanks which they will not get.'

Shortly afterwards he met General Clark on his way to the city and asked him to allow his son's battalion to enter Naples with the 82nd Airborne Division. Clark refused. 'They must go with the British,' he said. Walker felt disenchanted. Just three days earlier Clark had told him he was sending an artillery colonel to the 3rd Division to command the 142nd Infantry, replacing Colonel Forsythe who would go to Army HQ. 'Forsythe is too old for his job,' was Clark's comment. Walker saw no valid reason why Forsythe should be relieved; he had done excellent work with the 142nd, and he had found no fault with him. 'It's quite irregular,' he wrote, 'for an Army commander to prescribe, arbitrarily, who shall command regiments in a division.' Clark's real reason for removing Forsythe, he decided, was 'to give one of his friends a regiment'. By now the 36th had received so many replacements of officers and enlisted men that only about half the personnel were Texans.

Clark had driven in a jeep towards Naples with General Juin, who had joined with the Allies a year previously and fought against Rommel in Africa. On his way to the city, hoping, as he said, 'to see something of the action near the outskirts', they met General Ridgway and the 23rd Armoured Brigade. Ridgway admitted to Clark that leading elements of the Brigade had already entered the city during the morning. The Fifth Army commander was embarrassed: he had wanted to lead the cavalcade. Even now he did not think it would be politic to enter Naples with Juin at his side since the French had not yet taken any part in the battle. Excusing himself, he left Juin and climbed into the half-track with Ridgway.

Gavin was standing with the advance guard discussing the situation when Major John Norton approached him to explain 'We must wait until a triumphal entry is organized.'

'A triumphal entry!' the tough paratrooper colonel echoed. 'How the hell can we organize such a thing? That takes participation by the natives.' He thought of Napoleon's entries into Europe's capitals, of Allenby's arrival in Jerusalem, of brass bands playing and beautiful women leaning over balconies tossing flowers on the conquerors. Was this really what General Clark wanted?

Norton explained that the general would come to the head of the column to lead the march into the Piazza Garibaldi. Gavin looked up his map and found the square in the southern section of the city, close to the central railway station. What if, instead of locals tossing flowers, there were Germans tossing grenades from the rooftops? The masses of people filling the square would have to be carefully scrutinized. Wild-haired youths were waving and shooting carbines into the air and he had reports of fighting between Fascists and Allied sympathizers. He decided he should lead the way in his jeep with the half-track following in which Clark would be standing, with Ridgway beside him. Behind the two vehicles would follow the trucks of the 3rd Battalion and the 505th Parachute Infantry. When the procession moved into the piazza the 3rd would make a complete sweep of the perimeter, sealing it off. Troopers would jump from the trucks to move the people back. Then Clark, if he wished, could make his conqueror's speech from one of the trucks, or from another suitable vantage point. At all costs Gavin wanted to avoid trouble.

At one p.m. the paratrooper colonel led the convoy along Corso Garibaldi into the city, negotiating his way by map. The streets looked ominously empty.

Standing his full six foot four in the half-track Clark was seized with 'an intense feeling of pride'. For weeks he had looked forward to this momentous moment. He viewed the 'terrible wreckage' as they drove along. The great port was a scene of 'utter destruction' which not even Pompeii, through which he had passed earlier in the morning, had witnessed. And there was something else. He was riding through a city of ghosts. He saw only wrecked vehicles, piled debris, bombed-out buildings. Where were the people? Where were the flowers? Where was the cheering, the applause? It was not until later than he discovered that thousands of Neapolitans were at this moment crowding into the Piazza del Plebiscito at the other end of the city, a splendid piazza, enclosed on one side by the Royal Palace and on the other by the great church of San Francesco di Paola and the equestrian statues of Bourbon kings, where conquerors had traditionally been received. No conqueror had ever entered Naples from the south, and so it was in the Plebiscito that the Neapolitans awaited the Allies.

Nobody had told Mark Clark. His half-track drove through a silent and empty Piazza Garibaldi. The Fifth Army commander was conscious of closed shutters on every house and building. Were curious eyes peering at him from behind these shutters? His cavalcade continued on its way through the city without glimpsing any person except a handful of carabinieri. He saw no civilians, yet he had an odd sensation that thousands were watching him.

It was no welcome for a conquering hero.

After Naples . . .

One of the ironies of the subsequent advance on Rome was that Generals Alexander and Clark both figured in the dismissal of General Lucas, commander of the Sixth Corps.

At Salerno it was Alexander who had noticed the decline of General Dawley and recommended that he be replaced. One month after the Fifth Army had landed on the Anzio beaches he decided Lucas was 'defeated'. Convinced that Lucas could no longer stand the pressures, Clark removed him 'without prejudice'. Lucas was to remark, 'I thought I was winning something of a victory.'

After a successful crossing of the Volturno the Allied forces found their progress frustrated. Rains churned the terrain into rivers of mud. Roads were hub-deep in mire, bivouacs were flooded. One GI recalled, 'You walked in it, ate in it, often slept in it.' In four months the Allied forces had advanced only seventy miles.

The landings at Anzio in January 1944 gave Clark hopes of a swift advance, but a powerful build-up of German forces in the area dashed these hopes. However, with General Truscott, in place of Lucas, in charge of the beachhead, Clark felt the situation would improve. By March Churchill announced that Kesselring was accepting failure. 'He had frustrated the Anzio expedition. He could not destroy it.'

Alexander had no illusions about the tenacity of Kesselring's forces. Their stubborn resistance had slowed the Allied advance, but he was determined to drive them back to Rome. For Clark, Rome remained the 'all consuming interest'. He became angry when told that Alexander had talked to Truscott 'behind my own back' six days before the Allied attack on Anzio. His suspicions were aroused. Was Alexander planning to bring the Eighth Army up the Liri Valley and into Rome ahead of his Fifth Army? Drawing up his four sets of plans for Truscott, he directed him to be ready at forty-eight hours' notice 'to take whichever becomes appropriate'.

On 11 May Alexander launched the Great Spring Offensive. More than 1,000 guns emplaced between Monte Cassino and the sea boomed out a cannonade, the signal for Polish troops to storm the hill. Their initial attacks were repulsed, and it was the French who were to break the Cassino line.

With four divisions, Clark made his final push for Rome, ensuring that his troops would be the first to enter the Eternal City, thus winning the race against the Eighth Army, whose armoured divisions were making difficult progress up the Liri valley. On 25 May, two weeks after the attack on the Cassino line, and 125 days after the landings at Anzio, the two separate Allied fronts in southern Italy became one powerful unit. Clark's mother in the States wrote her son, 'Please take Rome soon. I can't stand the wait much longer. I'm all frazzled out.' For Clark, who felt his army had taken the brunt of the battle in Italy, Rome was his special prize.

Kesselring by now had withdrawn the bulk of his Tenth Army from the Liri valley. Truscott soon broke through the great strategist's last defences south of Rome and on 2 June the Germans began to withdraw, leaving only rearguards to obstruct the Americans. On 4 June the Americans entered Rome through lines of cheering crowds. At last the coveted prize of the Italian campaign was Clark's. This was not like the day of his entry into Naples. Now there were jubilant Romans to greet him and photographers and newsreel cameramen to record the occasion as he drove in a jeep with his generals into St Peter's Square.

Kesselring was to write: 'The conclusion is that the battle for Italy was not only justified, but even imperative, and the problem one of simply doing whatever seemed best for one's own theatre irrespective of the general strategic plan. Of course, if the objective was to bring the war to an early end, regardless of what chances remained of snatching a semi-political victory, then the Mediterranean war must be considered unnecessary, but this is a view I cannot share.'

On 6 June 1944, two days after Rome was taken, Allied forces under General Eisenhower assaulted the Normandy beaches in Operation Overlord, the last momentous sweep to liberate Europe.

Authors' Acknowledgments

Our story of the Allied landings at Salerno in September 1943 is based mainly on accounts by survivors and eye-witnesses, military and civilian, and on contemporary reports and historical documentation.

From among the many persons who generously helped us during our researches we are particularly grateful to the following:

UNITED STATES: Former US Ranger officers Herman W. Dammer and James T. Altieri, who provided us with reminiscences and material; John W. Taylor and Wilbert B. Mahoney and the staffs of the National Archives in Washington who went to immense trouble to furnish us with all available material relating to the invasion;

BRITAIN: Henry Brown, MBE, Secretary of the Commando Association, for his introductions; Lieut. Colonel J. M. T. F. Churchill, DSO, MC, for his patience during our lengthy interviews and for providing valuable material relating to the Commandos; Rev. J. H. Nicholl, who furnished us with his unpublished account of his experiences with 2 Commando; Lieut. Colonel D. N. Stewart, DSO, MC, and Major E. R. W. Robinson, MC for material relating to the Royal Scots Greys; Hugh Fraser, who supplied special material relating to the 'Salerno Mutiny'; Walter Harvey, chairman of the Merseyside and Wirral branch of the *Fédération des Combattants Alliés en Europe*, for much information, and James Sharkey for his written description of the landings.

GERMANY: Former Panzer Captain Helmut Meitzel, former Major Jürgen Wöbbeking, former Lieutenant (now Dr. jur.) Reimar Spitzbarth, and former Lieutenant Hasso von Benda, all of whom made available personal material relating to Panzer operations at Salerno;

ITALY: Bishop Arturo Carucci for his co-operation and for material provided; Dr Fernando Dentoni-Litta, Salerno survivor and local historian, for his account of the invasion and his detailed tours of the battlefields; Prof. Dott. Lorenzo Fusco, Prof. Adolfo Volpe, and Dr Mario Papa for their reminiscences and valuable introductions.

SOUTH AFRICA: Arthur J. Fuller and Kathleen M. Klev for their introductions to other South African participants.

Our thanks are also due to W. Roger Smith at Heinemann for his patient work on the manuscript, to Derek Priestley who preserved two lay historians from military pitfalls, and to John St John who gave us the initial encouragement.

Individuals
Stephen Alldridge
Melvin L. Allison
James T. Altieri
Walter T. Amphlett
Jack Baldwin
Hans von Benda
Henry Brown
Ronald M. Bulatoff
Robert W. Burch
E. J. Buttigieg
E. L. Carr
Patrizia Carta
Arturo Carucci
Victor Cassoni
George Chalou
J. M. T. F. Churchill
Antonia Cinefra
Eric W. Clapham
Brian Clark
Charles J. Coffey
Erwin Cohrs
Edd Cook
Frank Counihan
Desmond Cox
Herman W. Dammer
James W. Daniel
D. N. Davies
R. K. Delaney
K. Dean
Charles Dettmer
Anna and Fernando Dentoni-Litta
James Docherty
Don A. Earwood
Oswald Edwards
S. J. Edwards
Robert Ehalt
J. Neville Evans
Priscilla Farron
Raymonde Farron
Kurt Finke
A. J. Fitzgerald
Hugh Fraser
Arthur J. Fuller
Lorenzo Fusco
Pasquale Fusco
E. J. Gilvear
Silvio di Giuliomaria
Tom Gordon-Hemming
Wilbur Gallup
Terry Hammond
Terence Harrel
Walter D. Harvey
Bill Haynes
W. A. E. Hickman
G. Hodgson
Niall Hogan
Kieran Horgan
Tom Hoyle
David Hughes
Aubrey W. St J. Human
Wally Innes
K. J. Jamieson
Roy Jensen
Sam J. Kaiser
Arthur Kidson
Betty Kimmins
Kathleen M. Klev
Herman L. Koznatz
L. A. Lambe
Joachim Lemelsen
Bill Lewis
Donald E. Lilly
D. M. Loveland
Pail Low
John McFarlane
A. J. McKenna
Wilbert B. Mahoney
G. E. Marriott
Jim Martin
G. D. D. Maxwell
Helmut Meitzel
Robert C. Middleton
Alfred N. Miller

B. G. Morris
J. Mortimer
G. Muhm
Roy Murray
J. E. Nicholl
John Nichols
J. W. H. Nicholls
M. Novack
James W. Nunn Jr
Michael O'Brien
Gus O'Keeffe
Harry Palmer
Joe Pettit
Peter H. Powell
Diana Powell
Alfred E. Purcell
Fred Purnell
William Ramsay
William Rankin
P. D. Riall
John Roe
F. R. W. Robinson
Vincent and Stella Ruocco
F. A. Schatz
Arthur Schrader
Dr Karl Sedelmaier
Frances M. Seeber
James Sharkey
Samuel J. Stein
Reimar Spitzbarth
D. N. Stewart
Delilah Sutherland
John W. Taylor
John Thomas
F. J. Tochel
William S. Trask Jr
S. H. Troke
Adolfo Volpe
George Wagner
W. B. Warner
R. Stuart Watson
John Weir
Jürgen Wöbbeking
T. S. Worthington
Jane Yates
C. K. Zenwirt

Institutions, Libraries, Organizations
Bibliothek für Zeitgeschichte, Stuttgart.
Bray Public Library, Co. Wicklow.
British Broadcasting Corporation.
British Museum Newspaper Library, Colindale.
Bundesarchiv, Koblenz.
Bundesarchiv (Abteilung Militärarchiv), Freiburg.
The Citadel, Military College of South Carolina.
Department of State Library, Washington.
Hoover Institution, Stanford, California.
Ministry of Defence, London.
National Archives and Records Service (Modern Military History Branch), Washington.
National Archives and Records Service, Suitland.
Naval History Library, Ministry of Defence, London.
Public Record Office, Kew.
Franklin D. Roosevelt Library, Hyde Park, New York.
Royal Canadian Military Institute, Toronto.
Royal Dublin Society Library.
Sappers' Association, Johannesburg.
Staatsbibliothek Preussischer Kulturbesitz, Marburg.
US Army Military History Institute, Carlisle.
United States Embassy, Dublin.

Bibliography

Books

Adleman, Robert H., and Colonel George Walton. *Rome Fell Today*, Little, Brown, 1968.
Alexander, Field Marshal The Earl. *The Alexander Memoirs 1940–45*, Cassell, 1962.
Allen, William Luck. *Anzio: Edge of Disaster*, Elsevier-Dutton, 1978.
Altieri, James J. *Darby's Rangers*, Darby Memorial Foundation, Arkansas.
Altieri, James J. *The Spearheaders*, Bobbs-Merrill, 1960.
Ambrose, Stephen E. *The Supreme Commander: The War Years of General Dwight D. Eisenhower*, Cassell, 1968.
Badoglio, Marshal Pietro. *Italy in the Second World War, Memoirs and Documents*, New York: Oxford University Press, 1948.
Baldwin, Hanson W. *Great Mistakes of the War*, Harpur, 1950.
Ball, Edmund F. *Staff Officer with the Fifth Army*, Exposition Press, 1958.
Barker, A. J. *Panzers at War*, Ian Allen, 1948.
Barker, A. J. *British and American Infantry Weapons of World War Two*, ARCO Publishing Co., 1969.
Bender, Roger James/Petersen, George. *From Regiment to Fallschirm-Panzer-Corps*, Roger James Bender, San Jose, 1975.
Blumenson, Martin. *Anzio: the Gamble That Failed*, Weidenfeld & Nicolson, 1963.
Blumenson, Martin. *The U.S. Army in World War II: Salerno to Cassino*, Office of the Chief of Military History, Washington DC, 1965.
Bourke-White, Margaret. *Purple Heart Valley*, Simon and Schuster, 1944.
Brown, Anthony Cave. *Bodyguard of Lies*, New York: Harper & Row, 1975.
Butcher, Captain Harry C. *My Three Years with Eisenhower*, Simon & Schuster, 1946.
Caputo, Philip. *Rumour of War*, Macmillan, 1977.
Carucci, Arturo. *Salerno: Settembre 1945*, Graffica Jannone, 1953.
Chamberlain, Peter/Gander, Terry. *Mortars and Rockets*, ARCO Publishing Co., 1975.

Churchill, Winston S. *Great Contemporaries*, Odhams Press, 1937.
Clark, Mark W. *Calculated Risk*, Harpur, 1950.
Clark, Maurine. *Captain's Bride, General's Lady*, McGraw-Hill, 1956.
Clayton, Aileen. *The Enemy is Listening*, Hutchinson, 1980.
Clement, Mepham. *With the Eighth Army in Italy*, Stockwell, 1951.
Cohen, Elliott A. *Commandos and Politicians*, Center for International Affairs, Harvard University, 1948.
Cruickshank, Charles. *The Fourth Arm: Psychological Warfare 1938–1945*, Oxford University Press, 1981.
Darby, William O./Baumer, William H. *We Led the Way*, Presidio Press, 1980.
Delany, John P. *The Blue Devils in Italy*, Infantry Journal Press, 1947.
Devlin, Gerard M. *Paratrooper!*, St Martin's Press, 1979.
East, Gordon, *Mediterranean Problems*, Thomas Nelson & Sons, 1940.
Eisenhower, Dwight D. *Crusade in Europe*, Doubleday, 1949.
Ellis, John. *The Sharp End of War: The Fighting Man in World War Two*, David & Charles, 1980.
Farago, Ladislas. *Patton: Ordeal & Triumph*, Granada Publishing, 1969.
Fielding, W. L. *With the 6th Division*, Shuter & Shooter, 1946.
Firbank, Thomas. *I Bought A Star*, White Line Publishers, 1951.
Foley, Charles. *Commando Extraordinary* (Foreword by Maj. Gen. Sir Robert Laycock), Longmans, Green & Co., 1956.
Foss, Christopher T. *World War II Tanks*, Salamander Books, 1981.
Galland, Adolf. *The First and the Last*, Methuen & Co., 1955.
Gallegos, Adrian. *From Capri Into Oblivion*, Hodder & Stoughton, 1959.
Gavin, James M. *On to Berlin: Battles of an Airborne Commander 1943*, Viking Press, 1978.
Gavin, James M. *Airborne Warfare*, Infantry Journal Press, 1947.
Gilchrist, Donald. *Castle Commando*, Oliver & Boyd, 1960.
Gorman, Major J. T. *The Army of Today*, Blackie & Son, 1939.
Grant, R. *The 51st Highland Division At War*, Ian Allen, 1977.
Hamilton, Nigel. *The Making of a General 1887–1942*, Hamish Hamilton, 1981.
Hammerton, Sir John (ed.). *The Second Great War* (Vol. 6), Amalgamated Press, 1946.
Harpur, Brian. *The Impossible Victory*, William Kimber, 1980.
Hart, Sir Basil Liddell. *History of the Second World War*, Cassell, 1970.
Hart, Sir Basil Liddell (ed.-in-chief). *History of the Second World War*, Phoebus Publishing, 1978.
Hastings, Max. *Bomber Command*, Michael Joseph, 1979.
Hay, Ian. *Arms and the Men*, HMSO, 1950.
Hibbert, Christopher. *Mussolini*, Gramol Publication, 1945. Pan/Ballantine, 1972.
Higgins, Trumbull. *Soft Underbelly*, The Macmillan Company, 1968.
Hutchinson, Lt. Col. Graham S. *The British Army*, Gramol Publication, 1945.
Irving, David. *Hitler's War*, Hodder & Stoughton, 1977.

Jackson, W. G. E. *The Battle for Italy*, B. T. Batsford, 1967.
Johnson, Curt. *Artillery*, Octopus Books, 1975.
Jones, Jack. *WWII*, Futura Books, 1977.
Kesselring, Field Marshal Albert, *Memoirs*, William Kimber, 1953.
Kesselring, Albert. *A Soldier's Record*, Greenwood Press, 1954.
Ladd, J. D. *Commandos and Rangers of World War II*, Macdonald and Jane's, 1978.
Ladd, J. D. *Assault From the Sea 1939–45*, David & Charles, 1976.
Laffin, John. *Surgeons in the Field*, J. M. Dent, 1970.
Lewin, Ronald. *Ultra Goes to War*, Hutchinson, 1978.
Linklater, Eric. *The Campaign in Italy*, HMSO, 1950.
Lockhart, R. H. Bruce. *Comes the Reckoning*, Putnam, 1947.
Lockhart, R. H. Bruce. *The Marines Were There*, Putnam, 1950.
Macksey, Kenneth. *Kesselring: The Making of the Luftwaffe*, B. T. Batsford, 1978.
Majdalany, Fred. *The Battle of Cassino*, Longmans Green, 1957.
Martel, Lt. General Sir Giffard. *Our Armoured Tanks*, Faber & Faber, 1974.
Montgomery, Viscount of Alamein, *Memoirs*, Collins, 1958.
Montgomery of Alamein. *El Alamein to the River Sangro*, Hutchinson, 1945.
Moorehead, Alan. *Eclipse*, Hamish Hamilton, 1945.
Moorehead, Alan. *Montgomery: A Biography*, Hamish Hamilton, 1945.
Moorehead, Alan. *The Desert War*, Hamish Hamilton, 1965.
Morrison, Samuel Eliot. *History of the United States Naval Operations in World War II (Vol. IX) Sicily–Salerno–Anzio*, Little, Brown & Co., 1954.
Orpen, Neil. *Victory in Italy (Vol. 5)*, Purnell, 1975.
Parkinson, Roger. *Encyclopaedia of Modern War*, Routledge & Kegan Paul, 1977.
Pennino, Prof. Lucian. *Paestum and Vella*, Editor Matonti, 1972.
Pond, Hugh. *Salerno!*, William Kimber, 1961.
Pond, Hugh. *Sicily*, William Kimber, 1962.
Portway, Donald. *Science and Mechanisation in Land Warfare*, W. Heffer and Sons, 1938.
Quarrie, Bruce. *German Paratroopers in the Mediterranean*, Patrick Stephens, 1979.
Reynolds, Quentin. *By Quentin Reynolds*, William Heinemann, 1964.
Reynolds, Quentin. *The Curtain Rises*, Cassell & Co., 1944.
Ridgway, Matthew B. *Soldier: The Memoirs of Matthew B. Ridgway*, Harper & Bros, 1956.
Roskill, Stephen. *Churchill and the Admirals*, Collins, 1977.
Roskill, Stephen. *The War at Sea 1939–1945*, HMSO, 1960.
Ryan, Cornelius. *A Bridge Too Far*, Hamish Hamilton, 1974.
Saunders, Hilary St. George. *The Green Beret*, Michael Joseph, 1949.
Shapiro, Lionel S. B. *They Left the Back Door Open*, Harrolds, 1944.
Shirer, William L. *The Rise and Fall of the Third Reich*, Secker & Warburg, 1960.
Snyder, Louis L. *War Correspondents*, Messnor, 1962.
Steinbeck, John. *Once There Was a War*, William Heinemann, 1959.

Starr, Chester (ed.). *From the Sangro to the Alps*, Infantry Journal Press, 1948.

Taylor, A. J. P. *The War Lords*, Hamish Hamilton, 1977.

Tedder, Air Marshal of the Royal Air Force Lord. *With Prejudice*, Cassell, 1966.

Tregaskis, Richard. *Invasion Diary*, Random House, 1944.

Trevelyan, Raleigh. *Rome '44 – The Battle for the Eternal City*, Secker & Warburg, 1981.

Truscott, Lucian Jr. *Command Missions*, G. P. Dutton, 1954.

Vaughan-Thomas, Wynford. *Trust to Talk*, Hutchinson, 1980.

Vian, Sir Philip. *Action This Day*, Frederick Muller, 1960.

Walker, Maj. Gen. Fred. *From Texas to Rome: A General's Journal*, Taylor Publishing Co., 1969.

Wagner, Robert L. *The Texas Army: History of the 36th Division in the Italian Campaign*, Austin, Texas/Wagner, 1972.

Wallace, Robert. *The Italian Campaign*, Time-Life Books, 1978.

Werstein, Irving. *The Battle of Salerno*, Thomas Y. Crowell Co., 1965.

Westphal, General Siegfried. *The German Army in the West*, Cassell, 1951.

Whipple, A. B. C. *The Mediterranean*, Time-Life Books, 1973.

Wilmot, Chester. *The Struggle for Europe*, Collins, 1952.

Winterbotham, F. W. *The Ultra Secret*, Harper & Row, 1974.

Wynn, Neil A. *The Afro-American and the Second World War*, Elek Books, 1976.

Wyss, M. de. *Rome under the Terror*, Robert Hale, 1945.

Young, Brigadier Peter (ed.). *The World Almanac Book of World War II*, World Almanac Publishing/Bison Books, 1981.

Yarborough, William. *Bail Out Over North Africa*, Phillips Publications, 1979.

Booklets, Pamphlets, Articles in Periodicals and Newspapers

American Journal of Sociology: 'Aggressive and Erotic Tendencies in Army Life' (Henry Elkin), March 1946, Vol. 51;

'The Soldier's Language' (Frederick Elkin), March 1946, Vol. 51;

'The Making of an Infantryman' (Anon.), March 1946, Vol. 51;

'Characteristics of Military Society' (Brotz and Wilson), March 1946, Vol. 51;

'Sentiments of American Soldiers Abroad Towards Europeans' (Daniel Glaser), March 1946, Vol. 51.

Army Magazines: *Crusaders*, *Eighth Army News*, *Stars and Stripes*, *Union Jack*.

Infantry Journal: 'Action at Salerno' (Col. Norman Hussa), December 1943.

Geschichte der 29 Panzergrenadier-Division, Podzun-Pallas Verlag, 1960.

Die Weissen Spiegel (3rd Year): Tribute to Oberleutnant K. D. Fitz; author: A. Otte, 1977.

Das War Altavilla: Report: *Kurhessische Grenadier Gegen Texas-Amerikaner* (Kurt Finke) from *Geschichte der 29 Panzergrenadier-Division*, 1960; author: Joachim Lemelsen. Podzun-Pallas Verlag, 1960.

Die 71er Südlich Salerno: Kark Sedelmaier, from *Der Geschichte der 29. Panzergrenadier-Division*. Podzun-Pallas Verlag, 1960.
Weekend Magazine: 'Mad Jack' by David Lampe, Dec. 9–15, 1964.
The Black Cats at War: Story of the 56th Division (unpublished) by David Williams.
The Story of the 46th Division, 1939–45 (printed in Graz, Austria, 1945).
Military Review ('Salerno': Major General W. H. Morris, Jr) Vol. 23, No. 12, March 1944.
The Rise and Fall of the German Air Force, HMSO, 1948.
The Signal Corps: The Outcome '45. (Report of the Battle of Altavilla, 143rd Infantry Regiment).
Bloody Salerno by Quentin Reynolds (*New York Times Magazine*, October 16 and 23, 1943).
What Makes the American Soldier? (*New York Times Magazine*, September 12, 1943).
Mutiny at Salerno, *The Listener*.

Private and/or Unpublished Material

Allied Fifth Army
Road to Rome: 9 September 1943–4 June 1944. (Fifth Army)
We Were All New Once (Fifth Army), 1944.
Daily Casualties Report, 34th Inf. Division.
Overlays: Salerno.
Ops. Memos: Salerno.
War Diary: Ordnance CO Aviation-Airborne.
HQ Special Troops.
G3 Operation Memos, 5th Army, August–September 1943.
G3 Operations Instructions, 4–29 September 1943.
GI Casualty Reports: Salerno.
G3 Periodic Reports: 10–30 September 1943.
Interrogation Reports: September–October 1943.
Operations of British Troops: Invasion of Italian Mainland: Fifth Army, 9 September–20 December 1943.
Fifth Army History, 5 January–6 October 1943.
Fifth Army Ops: Discipline/Infantry/Traffic Control/Dawley Report, 4 October 1943, HQ Army Ground Forces, Army War College, Washington.
History of the Commandos in the Mediterranean, September 1943–May 1945.
American Forces in Action ('Salerno: American Operations from the Beaches to the Volturno'), Washington, 1944.
Mark Clark Collection (The Citadel).
Italian Campaign: Salerno–Venafro (John T. Hoyne, Major GSC, attached to Chemical Section).
Supporting Documents: *Cassino to the Alps*, by Ernest Fisher.
Admiral Oliver Notes.
C-in-C Meetings; Salerno.

Operations in Sicily and Italy, July 1943–December 1944, New York/West Point, 1945.
Regimental History of the 36th Division (Texas).
Fifth Army History (unclassified September 6, 1961).
Second to None: History of the Royal Scots Greys 1919–45 by Lt Col. R. M. P. Carver, C.B.E., D.F.O., M.C.
Salerno Diary: Captain H. H. Blissett (Army Bureau of Current Affairs).
History of the 8th (1st City of London) Battalion, the Royal Fusiliers, during the 1939–45 War, 1948.
Diary of General Dawley's Aide in 1943.
Diary Account of the Salerno Landings in 1943: Major General E. J. Dawley.
46th Division Communications Report on Operation Avalanche (Most Secret).
'Allied Navies at Salerno' (US Naval Institute Proceedings), September 1953.
The Gallant 36th: A Pictorial History of the 36th 'Texas' Division (ed. Richard A. Huff), NP.

German Tenth Army

List of Commanders and Staff Officers: German Tenth Army.
Observers' Notes on Italian Campaign, 25 August–7 October 1943.
Notes on Operation Avalanche.
World War II German Military Studies (Vol. I); editor: Donald S. Detweiler.
Operations of 26th Panzer Division in Italy, September 7, 1943–January 23, 1944: Oberleutnant Douglas von Bernsdorff, 1947.
War Diary, Italian Campaign.
16th Panzer Division at Salerno by Magna Bauer.
The Italian Campaign: General der Kavallerie Siegfried Westphal/General Oberst Heinrich von Vietinghoff.
Tenth Army Field Fortifications in Italy, September 1943–October 1944.
Coast Artillery in Italy: 1943–44.
German Operations in Italy: List of Commanders (Ralph S. Mavrogordato, 1955).
Deutsche Heereskarten: Salerno.
The Battle of Salerno by Ralph S. Mavrogordato (A Study undertaken to support the volume *Salerno to Cassino* by Martin Blumenson), Histories Branch 111. Office of the Chief of Military History, Washington DC, 1957.

Newspapers and Periodicals

Collier's Weekly, *Daily Express*, *Daily Mail*, *Daily Mirror*, *The Listener*, *New York Times*, *New York Herald Tribune*, *News Chronicle*, *The Observer*, *Radio Times*, *Reynolds News*, *Sunday Express*, *Sunday Times*, *The Times (London)*.

Radio and Television

The Secret Mutiny, BBC Radio, February 19, 1981.
Mutiny, BBC 2 Television, February 24, 1982.
Newsnight, BBC 2 Television, February 24, 1982.

Chapter Notes

PART ONE

I Invasion Fleet

Ancon was a former Caribbean cruise ship. Three war correspondents, Reynolds Packard of AP, Lionel Shapiro of the *Montreal Gazette*, and Quentin Reynolds of *Collier's Weekly*, and photographer Sammy Schulman, were on board Clark's command ship for the amphibious operation. The rest of the correspondents were on other vessels. Much of the material concerning events on the command ship is drawn from books, magazine articles and reports by these correspondents.

The conversations between Clark and Hewitt are recorded in Clark's own autobiography, which describes his early career. We have also drawn on Eisenhower's autobiography and on Adleman's and Walton's detailed account of the period in *Rome Fell Today*, and in articles in the *New York Times Magazine*.

Kesselring's accounts of Salerno at this period can be found in his two autobiographical books and in Macksey's *The Making of the Luftwaffe*. Major Herbert Duppenbecker wrote in a diary of his time at Salerno with the 79th Panzers, and Lieutenant Rocholl's account of Salerno is given in detail in his diary which was captured by the Allies.

We list here only the books we have consulted; other sources are listed in the Bibliography.

BOOKS: *The Curtain Rises* (Reynolds), *They Left The Back Door Open* (Shapiro), *Calculated Risk* (Clark), *Crusade in Europe* (Eisenhower), *Supreme Commander* (Ambrose), *Captain's Lady* (Clark), *Otto Millioni Baionetti* (Roatta), *Hitler's Generals* (Irving), *The Battle of Salerno* (Werstein), *Eclipse* (Moorehead), *The Making of the Luftwaffe* (Macksey), *Salerno to Cassino* (Blumenson), *Rome Fell Today* (Adleman/Walton).

II The Betrayal

Commander Anthony Kimmins's widow provided background material relating to her husband's service during the invasion. Kimmins recorded his experiences in BBC broadcasts, in his autobiography, *Half-Time*, and further accounts written by him are included in *The Second Great War*. His passport at the time of the Salerno landings described him as 'Dramatic Author and Film Director'.

In *Hitler's Generals* David Irving describes Hitler's reactions to the news of the advancing armada. Ralph Mavrogordato's special notes for Martin Blumenson have provided us with accurate timings of the exchanges between Kesselring, his generals and *OKW*.

Reaction among invading troops is based on authors' interviews. The accounts of the bombings of Salerno are drawn mainly from authors' interviews with Salernitani who were eye-witnesses, particularly Mario Papa, Fernando and Anna Dentoni-Litta, Professor Adolfo Volpe, and Bishop Arturo Carucci, who provided material from the period, much of which he has incorporated in his book, *Salerno: Settembre 1943*. He and Dr Dentoni-Litta provided details of the shooting of General Gonzaga, an event also described in Werstein's *The Battle of Salerno*.

Quentin Reynolds' unusual briefing of troops over the *Ancon*'s loudspeakers is described by him in two of his books, *The Curtain Rises* and *By Quentin Reynolds*. In the latter book he writes: 'At the invitation of the *Ancon*'s commander, Admiral Hewitt, I opened the ship's microphone, introduced myself, and made the announcement of our destination.' John Mason Brown provided a similar service which he describes in *To All Hands*.

BOOKS: *Supreme Commander* (Ambrose), *They Left The Back Door Open* (Shapiro), *Half-Time* (Kimmins), *The Second Great War* (ed. Hammerton), *Hitler's Generals* (Irving), *Otto Millioni Baionetti* (Roatta), *Salerno: Settembre 1943* (Carucci), *Memoirs* (Montgomery).

III Walker's Men

For the account of General Walker's arrival in the Gulf of Salerno we have drawn mainly on his published diary of the period, *From Texas to Rome*, the *History of the 36th Division*, and Robert L. Wagner's *The Texas Army*.

The enthusiasm of Winston Churchill for the ULTRA system is described by F. W. Winterbotham in *The Ultra Secret*. It is now known that Clark and Eisenhower had little confidence in this intelligence system.

The code sequence for the Tenth Army in event of an Allied invasion is detailed in Kesselring's memoirs, in Mavrogordato's notes, and in Rocholl's diary.

For the reactions of individual combatants we have drawn on authors' interviews.

BOOKS: *The Curtain Rises* (Reynolds), *They Left the Back Door Open* (Shapiro), *Calculated Risk* (Clark), *From Texas to Rome* (Walker), *Eclipse* (Moorehead), *A Soldier's Record* (Kesselring).

IV The Earth Shook

Accounts of the landings are drawn mainly from authors' interviews with individual combatants or eye-witnesses. For the background of General McCreery we have drawn partly on Clark's conversation with Eisenhower as recorded in *Supreme Commander*.

BOOKS: *Salerno: Settembre 1943* (Carucci), *Eclipse* (Moorehead), *Half-Time* (Kimmins), *A Soldier's Record* (Kesselring), *Calculated Risk* (Clark), *Supreme Commander* (Ambrose).

V Trained to Kill

The account of the approach of the *Blackmore* towards the beaches comes from authors' interviews with Captain Harrel. The account of the Churchills' arrival in the Gulf of Salerno is from authors' interviews with Lieut. Colonel J. M. T. F. Churchill. The background to the formation of the Commandos is drawn from authors' interviews, chiefly with Colonel Churchill and the Rev. J. E. Nicholl.

The history of development of the Rangers is drawn from a number of sources, but mainly from authors' interviews with Ranger officers and NCOs, including Herman A. Dammer, Roy Murray, James Altieri, Arthur Schrader, Don Earwood and Wilbur Gallup.

BOOKS: *Commandos and Politicians* (Cohen), *Commandos and Rangers* (Ladd), *Darby's Rangers* (Altieri), *The Spearheaders* (Altieri).

VI 'Afraid of Being Afraid'

In *By Quentin Reynolds* the war correspondent describes the troops of the 36th Division approaching Salerno as 'boys rather than men . . . pathetically young. The carbines they carried, the grenades hanging at their belts, even their heavier automatic rifles, looked like toys. It is not clear how much the generals expected of these "children" against the battle-hardened veterans of the Afrika Korps.' Other descriptions of troops' reactions in this chapter are drawn from authors' interviews with former combatants. In describing the particular details of the assault, such as the timing of the boat waves, we have relied on the accounts by Martin Blumenson and Samuel Morison, and contemporary Fifth Army reports.

BOOKS: *The Curtain Rises* (Reynolds), *Sicily–Salerno–Anzio* (Morison), *Eclipse* (Moorehead), *From Texas to Rome* (Walker), *Darby's Rangers* (Altieri), *The Battle of Salerno* (Werstein), *Salerno to Cassino* (Blumenson).

PART TWO

VII Not Glory, but Survival

Many of the reports on the actions of the 36th Division can be found in Wagner's *The Texas Army*. The confusion during the landings and on the beaches is detailed in Blumenson's *Salerno to Cassino*. Much of the material on the Rangers' landings at Maiori has been drawn from authors' interviews with individual Rangers. The Commandos' landings were also described in authors' interviews with a number of individual former Commandos, particularly Colonel J. M. T. F. Churchill, the Rev. J. E. Nicholl, Tom Gordon-Hemming, and Charles Dettmer. Other material on the Commando landings at Vietri has been drawn from the Commandos' privately distributed history and the late Captain Blissett's Salerno diary.

Dr Fernando Dentoni-Litta provided us not only with his personal account of his experiences during the invasion, but also with material relating to life in Salerno and Vietri during this period. Other relevant individual accounts have come from authors' interviews with David Hughes, James Sharkey, John Thomas, Walter Harvey and James Docherty.

BOOKS: *From Texas to Rome* (Walker), *Once There was a War* (Steinbeck), *The Texas Army* (Wagner), *The Battle of Salerno* (Werstein), *Salerno to Cassino* (Blumenson), *Darby's Rangers* (Altieri), *Commandos and Rangers* (Ladd).

VIII 'Plain, Unadulterated Hell'

General Walker's misgivings, which appear to have dated from this period, are contained in his published diary, *From Texas to Rome*. Again, details of the landing schedules have come from Fifth Army papers, Blumenson's *Salerno to Cassino* and Wagner's *The Texas Army*. Correspondents Quentin Reynolds and Lionel Shapiro described the events on board the *Ancon* at this time.

Tom Gordon-Hemming, former Commando Captain, recalled that at Vietri after the early morning Mass he snatched some sleep in the open with his steel helmet over his face and was taken by the locals for dead.

Arturo Carucci's experiences during the invasion are recalled in authors' interviews, his diaries, and his published book, *Salerno: Settembre 1943*. Hugh Pond has also described Carucci's experiences in his book, *Salerno!* in which he also includes accounts of the period by other members of the Carucci family.

The account of the Scots Greys in the landings comes mainly from the regimental history and from two authors' interviews in particular, with Major E. R. W. Robinson and Lieut. Colonel D. M. Stewart.

Walter Harvey, who provided much material on the landings in the 46th sector, is a keen historian of the period and chairman of the Merseyside and Wirral branch of the *Federation Des Combattants Allies En Europe*.

BOOKS: *From Texas to Rome* (Walker), *They Left The Back Door Open* (Shapiro), *The Curtain Rises* (Reynolds), *The Texas Army* (Wagner), *Salerno!* (Pond), *Calculated Risk* (Clark).

IX 'Shall I Live, Sir?'

Admiral Vian, along with Blumenson and Morison, has described in some detail the air operations of the beachhead. Admiral Cunningham at this period was described as 'a dyed-in-the-wool sea-dog who resented deeply the introduction of aircraft into naval warfare'. For descriptions of life aboard *Samuel Chase* at the time of the landings we have drawn on authors' interviews with former Technical Sergeant Sam Kaiser. The 56th Division's fighting on the beaches is described in the official papers of the Division and in Hugh Pond's *Salerno!* For individual accounts we have drawn on our interviews with Oswald Edwards, James Sharkey and David Hughes. Much of the Ranger material in this chapter is based on authors' interviews with former Sergeant Robert Ehalt. The account of the medical events on the beaches is drawn mainly from authors' interviews with Captain William Rankin. For accounts of events at Coperchia we have drawn on authors' interviews with Mario Marino and his family.

Among the documents relating to Kesselring's actions at this time we have found Mavrogordato's notes invaluable, especially in terms of chronology.

BOOKS: *Action This Day* (Vian), *From Texas to Rome* (Walker), *The Battle of Salerno* (Werstein), *Salerno to Cassino* (Blumenson), *Sicily–Salerno–Anzio* (Morison), *Salerno!* (Pond), *The Sharp End of War* (Ellis), *Surgeons in the Field* (Laffin), *A Soldier's Record* (Kesselring), *Hitler's Generals* (Irving).

X Dawley Goes Ashore

Dawley's personal diary has proved invaluable, and it is complemented by other accounts of the Sixth Army commander's actions during the invasion, especially by Walker's published diary. Both generals indicate a serious breakdown in communications between Fifth Army HQ and the commanders on the beaches.

Apart from authors' interviews with individual Commando survivors, the descriptions of the early hours at Vietri have come from field reports by troop commanders written on September 13/14 and made available to the authors by Lieut. Colonel Churchill.

Accounts of the 46th Division's impeded progress have come from authors' interviews with survivors and from Division documents. In the Scots Greys' episode we have drawn on authors' interviews with Major E. W. Robinson.

Rocholl's account of his meeting with Carucci differs only marginally from

Carucci's more detailed account. Much of the material concerning Lieutenant Schmitz is from the official history of the 16th Panzer Pioneers.

For the sequence concerning the wounded we have relied on authors' interviews with the former Captain Rankin and with Charles J. Coffey.

BOOKS: *From Texas to Rome* (Walker), *They Left The Back Door Open* (Shapiro), *Action This Day* (Vian), *Calculated Risk* (Clark), *Salerno: Settembre 1943* (Carucci), *Supreme Commander* (Ambrose).

XI 'The Feel of Battle'

The sequence concerning Clark's dog has been drawn in the main from *Rome Fell Today*. The Hillersden episode at Battipaglia is based chiefly on authors' interviews with former Fusilier Albert Fitzgerald. For the Scots Guards sequence we have drawn on authors' interviews with former Guardsman John Weir.

Details of the meeting between Sieckenius and Schmitz are based chiefly on 16th Panzer Pioneer papers and reports.

The struggle between Commandos and Germans on 'White Cross Hill' is reconstructed from accounts by Colonel Churchill, from Captain Blissett's Salerno diary, and from the Commandos' own privately circulated history.

The reports of the incidents at Salerno harbour are based on authors' interviews with Fernando Dentoni-Litta and Roy Jensen. Adrian Gallegos describes his arrival on the beaches in *From Capri Into Oblivion*.

BOOKS: *They Left The Back Door Open* (Shapiro), *From Texas to Rome* (Walker), *The Battle of Salerno* (Werstein), *Salerno!* (Pond), *Commandos and Rangers* (Ladd), *Salerno: Settembre 1943* (Carucci), *Calculated Risk* (Clark).

XII 'A Bloody Toll'

The account of McCreery at Salerno is based on authors' interviews with former combatants and on Brian Harpur's interviews in *The Impossible Victory*.

For the Commando episode the Rev. J. E. Nicholl made available his unpublished and highly detailed account of his experiences at Salerno.

Again, Ralph Mavrogordato's notes have helped us recreate the chronology of the Tenth Army's movements and describe the chain of messages that passed between Kesselring and Vietinghoff.

Major Edmund Ball provides an account of his first days on the beachhead in *Staff Officer with the Fifth Army*.

David Irving's book, *Hitler's Generals* has a detailed account of Hitler's broadcast from *OKW* which was reported at length in many newspapers the next day. In his book, *Rome under the Terror*, M. de Wyss describes the effect of that broadcast on the Romans and the results of the Nazi appointments to the new Axis Government in Italy.

BOOKS: *The Impossible Victory* (Harpur), *Calculated Risk* (Clark), *The Spearheaders* (Altieri), *Darby's Rangers* (Altieri), *A Soldier's Record* (Kesselring), *Memoirs* (Kesselring), *Salerno: Settembre 1943* (Carucci), *The Curtain Rises* (Reynolds), *Sicily–Salerno –Anzio* (Morison), *Salerno to Cassino* (Blumenson), *Staff Officer with the Fifth Army* (Ball), *Hitler's Generals* (Irving), *Rome under the Terror* (de Wyss), *From Capri into Oblivion* (Gallegos).

XIII 'This Reminds Me of Gallipoli'

The broadcast by Marshal Badoglio was reported in a number of newspapers the following day; only the American papers reported on the Toscanini concert.

Arturo Carucci provides the background detail to the arrival in Salerno of Colonel Lane as city governor. Colonel Wilbur, who came ashore with Major Ball, was to play an important role in the 36th Division's battles during the ensuing days. Sergeant Stein's Captain Peterson was to be killed by German troops towards the end of the campaign in the village of Giovanni di Napoli. Irving Werstein provides a description of the British RSM who confronted the American troops in *The Battle of Salerno*. Other material in this chapter is drawn from original accounts and from Hugh Pond's *Salerno!*

There are a number of conflicting accounts of why General Clark's HQ staff chose the Palazzo Bellelli as a headquarters and then decided against it; we have drawn on accounts by Clark, Blumenson and Walker and interviews with Fifth Army staff to reconstruct a satisfactory picture of the event.

Charles Dettmer provided the detailed account of his experiences on Dragonea in authors' interviews.

The account of the action at Altavilla comes from both Tenth Army and 36th Division reports. Robert L. Wagner's *The Texas Army* and the personal account of Jürgen Wöbbeking, specially written for the authors, have been particularly useful.

In the Dawley episode in this chapter the war diary of Colonel E. J. O'Neill has proved illuminating. In the Ranger episodes James Altieri and Herman A. Dammer were helpful to the authors, who are also grateful for interviews given by Wilbur Gallup.

BOOKS: *The Curtain Rises* (Reynolds), *They Left The Back Door Open* (Shapiro), *Sicily–Salerno–Cassino* (Morison), *Sicily to Salerno* (Blumenson), *Action This Day* (Vian), *Salerno: Settembre 1943* (Carucci), *From Texas to Rome* (Walker), *Salerno!* (Pond), *The Battle of Salerno* (Werstein), *Calculated Risk* (Clark), *The Texas Army* (Wagner), *A Soldier's Record* (Kesselring).

XIV 'Fight to the Last Breath'

Material relating to Clark's HQ situation ashore has come from Fifth Army aides and from the accounts by Blumenson in *Salerno to Cassino*. Again, Robert Wagner's *The Texas Rangers* has proved helpful in its detailed accounts of the 36th's attack on Altavilla, for which former Panzer Captain Helmut Meitzel has also provided information. Equally, the former Captain Jürgen Wöbbeking provided us with his personal account of his attack on the tanks.

The account of the continuing confusion in communications, and the apparent misunderstanding between Generals Walker, Dawley and Middleton, is drawn from a number of sources. Clark's Fifth Army aides have referred to Dawley's 'cracking up' on the beaches; Dawley's aides prefer not to discuss this incident which was to have far-reaching consequences.

The Ranger sequence is drawn from authors' interviews with individual Rangers and from accounts by Altieri and Darby. The Mavrogordato notes have helped place the talks between Kesselring, Vietinghoff and Herr in sequence.

BOOKS: *Calculated Risk* (Clark), *Salerno to Cassino* (Blumenson), *Salerno: Settembre 1943* (Carucci), *The Texas Army* (Wagner), *From Texas to Rome* (Walker), *The Spearheaders* (Altieri), *Darby's Rangers* (Altieri), *A Soldier's Record* (Kesselring).

XV The 'Fitz Battalion'

Background to Major Fitz was provided for the authors by his widow. Other material relating to Fitz and his battalion comes from the tribute published after his death in 1977 in *Die Weissen Spiegel*.

BOOKS: *Officer with the Fifth Army* (Ball), *The Texas Army* (Wagner), *Salerno: Settembre 1943* (Carucci), *Calculated Risk* (Clark), *From Texas to Rome* (Walker), *Darby's Rangers* (Altieri), *The Spearheaders* (Altieri).

PART THREE

XVI BATTLE FOR DRAGONEA

In the episodes dealing with the Commandos' battle for Dragonea hill we have drawn on interviews with former combatants, particularly Lieut. Colonel J. M. T. F. Churchill, Rev. J. E. Nicholl, Charles Dettmer, Tom Gordon-Hemming, on the privately circulated *History of the Commandos in the Mediterranean 1943–45*, on troop commanders' reports, on Blissett's *Salerno Diary*, Nicholl's unpublished account, and on books relating to 2 Commando and 41 RM Commando. Captain Brian Lees wrote an additional report of his experiences at the medical aid post behind enemy lines.

The account of the 23rd Armoured Division is based on authors' interviews with Edd Cook and Edward Martin. Alexander's intervention is described in *Rome Fell Today*. Hamilton's dramatic flight to Sicily is described in a number of sources; those we have drawn on include Major General Gavin's and Gerard M. Devlin's.

BOOKS: *The Green Beret* (Saunders), *Commandos and Rangers* (Ladd), *The Marines Were There* (Lockhart), *Darby's Rangers* (Altieri), *The Spearheaders* (Altieri), *The Texas Rangers* (Wagner), *The Alexander Memoirs* (Alexander), *Eclipse* (Moorehead), *Calculated Risk* (Clark), *On to Berlin* (Gavin), *Paratrooper!* (Devlin), *Salerno!* (Pond), *The Battle of Salerno* (Werstein).

XVII A MESSAGE FOR RIDGWAY

The Hamilton flight is described in the sources outlined for Chapter 16. Other paratrooper material is drawn from authors' interviews. The sinking of the *Uganda* was described to the authors by Roy Jensen, there are also descriptions in Blumenson's and Morison's books on Salerno.

Individual exploits by members of the 36th Division are described in interviews in Wagner's book, *The Texas Army* and in *Salerno: American Forces in Action Series, 38*. Corporal Charles E. Kelly was later awarded the Congressional Medal of Honour.

Colonel Reuben Tucker, who makes his first appearance in this chapter, is referred to by Gavin in *On to Berlin*, by Yarborough in *Bail Out*, and by Tregaskis in *Invasion Diary*.

BOOKS: *Paratrooper!* (Devlin), *On to Berlin* (Gavin), *Salerno to Cassino* (Blumenson), *Sicily–Salerno–Anzio* (Morison), *Salerno: Settembre 1943* (Carucci), *A Soldier's Record* (Kesselring), *Memoirs* (Kesselring), *Calculated Risk* (Clark), *They Left The Back Door Open* (Shapiro), *Bail Out Over North Africa* (Yarborough), *Invasion Diary* (Tregaskis).

XVIII THE BLAZING 'T'

Dawley's state of mind at this period is not mentioned by his aide, Colonel O'Neill, in his diary, but it is indicated by Dawley's own diary entries at the time.

The exploits of the Panzers are described in the 16th Panzer Division histories; in the main, details in this chapter have come from authors' interviews with the then Captain Meitzel who was most helpful when faced with our barrage of questions.

Lionel Shapiro's description of the impending crisis on the beachhead is well documented in *They Left The Back Door Open*. Although American commentators wrote of Montgomery's slow progress, some British newspapers at this date reported 'Monty racing his two armies' at 'a spectacular rate.'

In the Dragonea episode we have drawn on troop commanders' reports, most of them written on September 13/14. Captain Lees' medical reports were also useful. The report of the Coldstream Guards incident comes from the Guards' own history and from Hugh Pond's account in *Salerno!* and from Tenth Army reports.

BOOKS: *Calculated Risk* (Clark), *Salerno to Cassino* (Blumenson), *Sicily–Salerno –Anzio* (Morison), *From Texas to Rome* (Walker), *The Texas Army* (Wagner), *On to Berlin* (Gavin), *Supreme Commander* (Ambrose), *They Left The Back Door Open* (Shapiro).

XIX Mission to Avellino

Detailed accounts of the Avellino mission are to be found in Gavin's book *On To Berlin* and in Devlin's *Paratrooper!*

The return of Lieutenant Schmitz to operations with the Pioneers is described in the History of the 16th Panzer Division and in Tenth Army reports. The Altavilla episodes are from Tenth Army and 36th Division histories, from interviews in Wagner's *The Texas Army*, and from authors' interviews with Helmut Meitzel.

BOOKS: *On to Berlin* (Gavin), *Paratrooper!* (Devlin), *Calculated Risk* (Clark), *They Left The Back Door Open* (Shapiro), *Salerno: Settembre 1943* (Carucci), *From Texas to Rome* (Walker), *Darby's Rangers* (Altieri).

XX 'He Should Go Down with his Ship'

Admiral Oliver's reactions to events on the *Biscayne* are described in a report he wrote after his meeting with Hewitt. Alexander's reactions to the evacuation plans are described in his *Memoirs*.

The mismanaged Avellino drop is described in both Gavin's and Devlin's books. Further details have come from authors' interviews.

BOOKS: *Sicily–Salerno–Anzio* (Morison), *Salerno to Cassino* (Blumenson), *The Alexander Memoirs* (Alexander), *A Soldier's Record* (Kesselring), *Salerno: Settembre 1943* (Carucci), *Calculated Risk* (Clark), *Supreme Commander* (Ambrose).

XXI 'The Last Attack'

The hit-and-miss movements of the Fifth Army commanders as described in this chapter have been pieced together from accounts by Clark, Walker, Alexander and Dawley. The exploits of paratroopers Nunn and Fisco are drawn from authors' interviews.

For descriptions of the progress of Montgomery's Eighth Army we have drawn on reports by newspaper correspondents, particularly Alan Moorehead, who also wrote of this period in further detail in his books *Eclipse* and *Montgomery*, and on agency reports by Daniel de Luce.

The descriptions of the *sfollati* at Coperchia and Cava de' Tirreni have come from authors' interviews with Mario Marino and Professor Lorenzo Fusco.

BOOKS: *Montgomery* (Moorehead), *Eclipse* (Moorehead), *Calculated Risk* (Clark), *A Soldier's Record* (Kesselring), *Memoirs* (Kesselring), *Salerno: Settembre 1943* (Carucci), *The Alexander Memoirs* (Alexander), *They Left The Back Door Open* (Shapiro).

XXII Assault on Piegolelle

Almost all the accounts, including the Special Services Brigade account, of the Piegolelle battle refer to 'Pigoletti'; this version was current at the time, probably for ease of pronunciation. Churchill's attack on the village was described in a *Weekend Magazine* report by David Lampe, but we have drawn mainly from authors' interviews to produce this final and, hopefully, fully authentic account of the episode; we have also drawn on interviews with the Rev. J. E. Nicholl and Tom Gordon-Hemming.

BOOKS: *Commandos and Rangers* (Ladd), *The Green Beret* (Saunders).

XXIII 'Put Wellington on the Line'

The account of Lieutenant Parker's troop attack is contained in the history of the Scots Greys. The most complete account of Tucker's attack on Altavilla is in Tregaskis' *Invasion Diary* on which we have drawn for this chapter. General McCreery's near escape from death at Pontecagnano is described in Hugh Pond's *Salerno!* and in the 46th Division's history. In the British newspapers of 16 September, headlines included *Will Fifth Hold Out?* and *Still Touch and Go*. Henry Stinson, US Secretary of War, announced, 'In a short time Montgomery's Army may be in a position to influence the battle of Salerno.'

BOOKS: *The Marines Were There* (Lockhart), *The Green Beret* (Saunders), *Salerno!* (Pond), *From Texas to Rome* (Walker), *Invasion Diary* (Tregaskis), *Sicily–Salerno–Anzio* (Morison), *Salerno: Settembre 1943* (Carucci), *Darby's Rangers* (Altieri), *The Mediterranean* (Whipple), *Memoirs* (Kesselring), *A Soldier's Record* (Kesselring).

PART FOUR

XXIV The Angry Veterans

Details of the final battle for the 'Pimple' have come from authors' interviews with individual Commandos, from the Commandos' own history, and from the account by the then Captain John Parsons. The account of the German withdrawal from Altavilla comes mainly from authors' interviews with Helmut Meitzel and from the account by the former Panzer Sergeant Kurt Finke.

Details of the 'mutiny' on the beachhead in this and succeeding chapters come from interviews with former 'mutineers', including Hugh Fraser, Wally Innes, John McFarlane and Joe Pettit, from a post-war series in *Reynolds News*, from BBC material, and from private papers and contemporary accounts.

Most commentators agree on the details of the eventual meeting between Eisenhower and Dawley. The letters to Dawley are in the archives of the Hoover Institution, Stanford, Calif.

The Panzer officer's account of the leaving of Salerno comes from the official history of the 16th Panzer Division.

BOOKS: *Salerno!* (Pond), *The Battle of Salerno* (Werstein), *Salerno: Settembre 1943* (Carucci), *Supreme Commander* (Ambrose), *Calculated Risk* (Clark), *From Texas to Rome* (Walker), *Command Mission* (Truscott), *Hitler's Generals* (Irving), *A Soldier's Record* (Kesselring), *Memoirs* (Kesselring), *On to Berlin* (Gavin).

XXV 'My Uncomfortable Task'

Richard Tregaskis and Robert Capa recorded the details of their visit to the CP known as 'Fort Schuster'. Other material in the Rangers' episode is drawn from authors' interviews with individual Rangers. Before the end of the Salerno campaign Major Herman Dammer became ill with hepatitis and was shipped to Tripoli. One commentator reported a large number of Rangers weakened by illness. 'Many were felled by a recurrence of malaria contracted in Sicily.'

Material for the account of the American re-entry into Altavilla comes from Ball's book *Officer with the Fifth Army* and from the diary of Lt. Colonel E. J. O'Neill; O'Neill's diary also describes Dawley's farewell to his officers: 'He was badly hurt, but of course he hid it well.' In 1947 Dawley called to see O'Neill at Arlington, Virginia. After this meeting O'Neill wrote to his former commander: 'I know the grievous disappointment that has been yours ever since the event happened of your relief and demotion at Salerno – even though that disappointment must always have been assuaged right from the start, and in increasing intensity as time has gone by and actions been revealed, by your knowledge and those of others familiar with the situation of how completely and utterly unjustified both actions were.' In this letter O'Neill recalled Dawley's encouragement during 'the darkest days at Salerno' and Dawley's remark to General Lucas, his successor after the sacking, 'Johnnie, I am turning over to you the best staff that anyone ever had.' O'Neill wrote, 'You shook hands with each of us, thanked each one personally, and walked away like the soldier you were, and are – with your shoulders squared, your head up, and with never a sign to indicate how unjust you knew the deal that you were getting was.' Early in October 1943, O'Neill, back in Washington, put Dawley's case before Congressman May, House Military Affairs Committee.

BOOKS: *Calculated Risk* (Clark), *Supreme Commander* (Ambrose), *Crusade in Europe* (Eisenhower), *Command Mission* (Truscott), *Invasion Diary* (Tregaskis), *From Texas to Rome* (Walker), *The Italian Campaign* (Wallace), *Officer of the Fifth Army* (Ball), *They Left The Back Door Open* (Shapiro), *Memoirs* (Kesselring), *A Soldier's Record* (Kesselring).

XXVI Montgomery Arrives

Details of the progress of the 46th and 56th Divisions are taken from Divisions' histories and from authors' interviews. Descriptions of McCreery at this time are from authors' interviews with Arthur J. Fuller.

At Minori, close to Maiori, where the Rangers' vigilance after the landings prevented damage to the town by the Germans who had mined the cliffs, the inhabitants erected a shrine beneath the cliffs in honour of the town's patron saint: 'To Saint Trofimena, the people of Minori give thanks for her singular protection. Minori 8.9.43.'

As in Chapter XXV, much of the material relating to Dawley is from the Hoover Institution archives. For material relating to Lucas at this period we have drawn on Truscott's *Command Missions*.

BOOKS: *Eclipse* (Moorehead), *Montgomery* (Moorehead), *El Alamein to the Sangro* (Montgomery), *Memoirs* (Montgomery), *The Curtain Rises* (Reynolds), *Command Missions* (Truscott), *Memoirs* (Kesselring), *A Soldier's Record* (Kesselring), *Salerno: Settembre 1943* (Carucci), *Invasion Diary* (Tregaskis), *From Texas to Rome* (Walker), *Calculated Risk* (Clark), *Supreme Commander* (Ambrose), *Purple Heart Valley* (Bourke-White).

XXVII The Fall of Foggia

For the description of Foggia after the arrival of the Eighth Army we have drawn on the newspaper despatches of Alan Moorehead and from his later published accounts. McCreery's advice to Dawley is from Fifth Army papers. Gavin describes the last days of the Salerno campaign in relation to the 82nd Airborne in *On to Berlin*. The 'mutiny' court martial material is drawn from the sources listed in Chapter XXIV.

Salerno inhabitants who described the return of the *sfollati* to the city in authors' interviews included Anna Dentoni-Litta, Mario Marino, Mario Papa and Prof.

Adolfo Volpe. Lorenzo Fusco's father was provided with a special letter by General Alexander to allow him to drive from Taranto to bring his family to safety.

German casualties at Salerno were listed as 1,558 dead, 984 wounded, 112 POWs (36th Infantry Division Report 1943). Official historians of the Allied armies, however, have written in reference to the enemy disengagement from the beachhead that the Allied air and naval attacks had caused such heavy enemy losses that 'the Germans had no choice but to call off the attack'.

Melvin Allison, then a Staff Sergeant with the US 34th Division, recalled in an authors' interview making daily Strength Reports of casualties. He rode around the clearing stations close to the front line in a company jeep, checking on the numbers in his regiment dead (KIA) or wounded. 'The clearing stations,' he remembered, 'were mostly in army tents, well marked with a red cross. I saw some pretty badly shot-up people. Some of them didn't make it – even with the blood transfusions they were given.'

BOOKS: *On to Berlin* (Gavin), *Command Missions* (Truscott), *Memoirs* (Kesselring), *A Soldier's Record* (Kesselring), *Paratrooper!* (Devlin), *Salerno: Settembre 1943* (Carucci), *Calculated Risk* (Clark), *History of the Second World War* (Liddell Hart).

XXVIII Piazza Garibaldi

Much of the material for this chapter has come from Colonel Gavin's account of the entry into Naples and from General Walker's account in his published diary. Other material has been drawn on, including authors' interviews with Fifth Army combatants, and Fifth Army HQ reports.

Although the main Allied armies pushed on through Naples and Foggia, minor battles and skirmishes continued in the Salerno area. In an authors' interview former Guardsman J. Baldwin recalled the two-week battle for Calabritto and Monte Camino as the October weather deteriorated.

Of Baldwin's platoon of 30 only 17 remained alive or uninjured to relieve the badly-mauled Grenadiers on Monte Camino. After a first night battle at Calabritto the platoon was minus officer and sergeant. Casualties in this area were high. Rains impeded the transport of supplies and the Germans used 88s and *Nebelwerfers* against the British.

When the Guards reached the top of Camino Baldwin recalled acting Major Davidson saying, 'You've been as near to hell as you'll ever be.'

BOOKS: *Calculated Risk* (Clark), *From Texas to Rome* (Walker), *Invasion Diary* (Tregaskis), *Purple Heart Valley* (Bourke-White).

Index